Thomas Fuller's

THE HOLY STATE AND THE PROFANE STATE

IN TWO VOLUMES

Thomas Fuller's

THE HOLY STATE AND THE PROFANE STATE

EDITED BY

MAXIMILIAN GRAFF WALTEN

VOLUME II

A FACSIMILE OF THE FIRST EDITION, 1642

REDUCED IN SIZE

AMS Press, Inc.
New York
1966

Reprinted 1966
with Permission of Columbia University Press

AMS Press, Inc.
New York, N.Y. 10003

Manufactured in The United States of America

Contents of Volume II

TRUTH
JUSTICE
THE CHURCH
THE STATE
THE
HOLY
STATE
By
Thomas Fuller
Bachelour of Divinitie, &
Prebendary of Sarum.
late of Sidney Colledge in Cambridge.
CAMBRIDGE,
Printed by R: D:
for John Williams
at the Signe of the
Crowne in St. Paules
Church-yard
1642
W: Marshall sculpt.

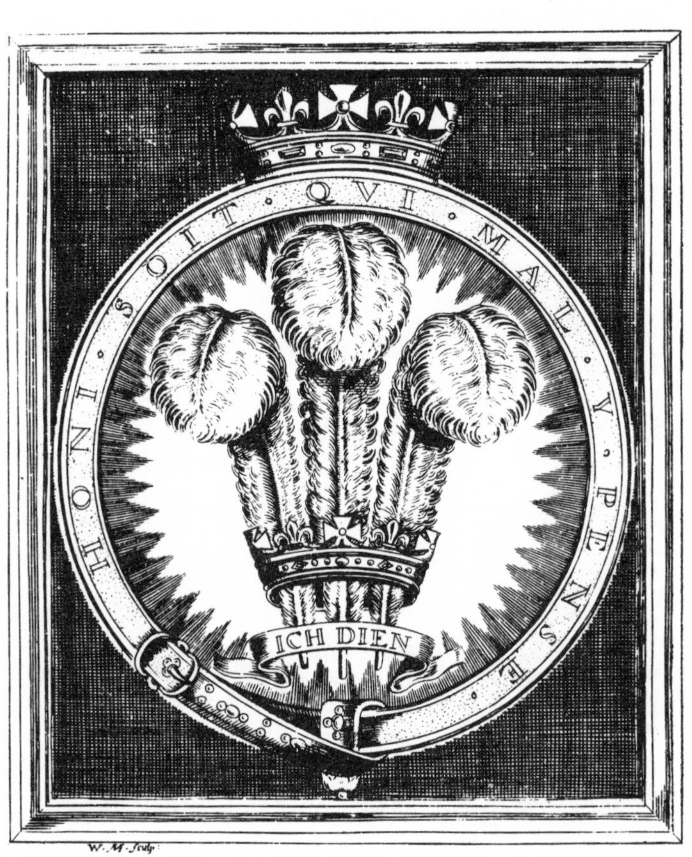
HONI SOIT QVI MAL Y PENSE
ICH DIEN
W. M. sculp.

THE HOLY STATE.

BY
THOMAS FULLER, B. D.
and Prebendarie of
Sarum.

ZECHARIAH 14. 20.

In that day shall there be upon the bells of the horses,
HOLINESSE UNTO THE LORD.

CAMBRIDGE:
¶ Printed by ROGER DANIEL for
John Williams, and are to be sold at the signe
of the Crown in S. Pauls
Churchyard. 1642.

To the Reader.

WHo is not ſenſible with ſorrow of the diſtractions of this age? To write books therefore may ſeem unſeaſonable, eſpecially in a time wherein the *Preſſe*, like an unruly horſe, hath caſt off his bridle of being *Licenſed*, and ſome ſerious books, which dare flie abroad, are hooted at by a flock of Pamphlets.

But be pleaſed to know that when I left my home, it was fair weather, and my journey was half paſt, before I diſcovered the tempeſt, and had gone ſo farre in this VVork, that I could neither go backward with credit, nor forward with comfort.

As for the matter of this Book, therein I am reſident on my Profeſsion; Holineſſe in the latitude thereof falling under the cognizanſe of a Divine. For curious method, expect none, Eſſays for the moſt part not being placed as at a *Feaſt*, but placing themſelves as at an *Ordinary*.

The characters I have conformed to the then

ſtanding Laws of the Realm, (a twelvemoneth agoe were they ſent to the preſſe) ſince which time the wiſdome of the King and State hath thought fitting to alter many things, and I expect the diſcretion of the Reader ſhould make his alterations accordingly. And I conjure thee by all Chriſtian ingenuity, that if lighting here on ſome paſſages, rather harſh-ſounding then ill-intended, to conſtrue the ſame by the generall drift and main ſcope which is aimed at.

Nor let it render the modeſtie of this Book ſuſpected, becauſe it preſumes to appear in company unmann'd by any Patron: If right, it will defen d it ſelf; if wrong, none can defend it: Truth needs not, falſhood deſerves not a Supporter. And indeed the matter of this Work is too high for a ſubjects, the workmanſhip thereof too low for a Princes patronage.

And now I will turn my pen into prayer, That God would be pleaſed to diſcloud theſe gloomy dayes with the beams of his mercie: which if I may be ſo happy as to ſee, it will then encourage me to count it freedome to ſerve two apprentiſhips (God ſpinning out the thick thred of my life ſo long) in writing the Eccleſiaſticall Hiſtory from Chriſts time to our dayes, if I ſhall from remoter parts be ſo planted, as to enjoy the benefit of walking, and ſtanding Libraries, without which advantages

tages the beſt vigilancie doth but vainly dream to undertake ſuch a task.

Mean time I will ſtop the leakage of my ſoul, and what heretofore hath run out in writing, ſhall hereafter (God willing) be improved in conſtant preaching, in what place ſoever Gods providence, and friends good will ſhall fix

Thine in all Chriſtian offices

THOMAS FULLER.

An Index of the ſeverall Chapters contained in this Book; the firſt figure ſhewing the book, the ſecond the chapter, the third the page.

The

ERRATA.

Page 70 *line* 29 *after* superstition *adde*, How the Fathers. 121. 9. *r.* wear. 152. 8. *r.* (Yea Mercury was a greater speaker then Jupiter himself) 202. 5. *r.* affectation.

The Holy State.

THE FIRST BOOK.

Chap. I.

The good Wife

St. Paul to the Coloſsians chap. 3. verſ. 18. firſt adviſeth women to ſubmit themſelves to their husbands, and then counſelleth men to love their wives. And ſure it was fitting that women ſhould firſt have their leſſon given them, becauſe it is hardeſt to be learned, and therefore they need have the more time to conne it. For the ſame reaſon we firſt begin with the character of a good Wife.

She commandeth her husband in any equall matter, by conſtant obeying him. It was alwayes obſerved, that what the Engliſh gained of the French in battel by valour, the French regained of the Engliſh by cunning in *Treaties: So if the husband ſhould chance by his power in his paſsion to prejudice his wives right, ſhe wiſely knoweth by compounding and complying to recover and rectifie it again. Maxime 1

* *Comineus lib. 4. cap. 8. & Bodinus De Repub. lib. 5. p. 782.*

2 *She never croſſeth her husband in the ſpring-tide of his anger, but ſtayes till it be ebbing-water.* And then mildly ſhe argues the matter, not ſo much to condemn him, as to acquit her ſelf. Surely men, contrary to iron, are worſt

to be wrought upon when they are hot; and are farre more tractable in cold bloud. It is an obſervation of Seamen, * That if a ſingle meteor or fireball falls on their maſt, it portends ill luck; but if two come together (which they count Caſtor and Pollux) they preſage good ſucceſſe: But ſure in a family it bodeth moſt bad, when two firebals (husbands and wives anger) come both together.

* *Eraſmus Dial. in naufragio.*

3. *She keeps home if ſhe hath not her husbands company, or leave for her patent to go abroad*: For the houſe is the womans centre. It is written, Pſalm 104. 2. *The ſunne ariſeth, ---man goeth forth unto his work, and to his labour untill the evening*: but it is ſaid of the good woman, Prov. 31. 15. *She riſeth whiles it is yet night*: For man in the race of his work ſtarts from the riſing of the ſunne, becauſe his buſineſſe is without doores, and not to be done without the light of heaven: but the woman hath her work within the houſe, and therefore can make the ſunne riſe by lighting of a candle.

4. *Her clothes are rather comely then coſtly, and ſhe makes plain cloth to be velvet by her handſome wearing it.* She is none of our dainty dames, who love to appear in variety of ſutes every day new, as if a good gown, like a ſtratageme in warre, were to be uſed but once: But our good wife ſets up a ſail according to the keel of her husbands eſtate; and if of high parentage, ſhe doth not ſo remember what ſhe was by birth, that ſhe forgets what ſhe is by match.

5. *Arcana imperii (her husbands ſecrets) ſhe will not divulge.* Eſpecially ſhe is carefull to conceal his infirmities. If he be none of the wiſeſt, ſhe ſo orders it that he appears on the publick ſtage but ſeldome; and then he hath conn'd his part ſo well, that he comes off with great applauſe. If his *Forma informans* be but bad, ſhe provides him better *formas aſſiſtentes*, gets him wiſe ſervants and ſecretaries.

6. *In her husbands abſence ſhe is wife and deputy husband,* which

which makes her double the files of her diligence. At his return he finds all things ſo well, that he wonders to ſee himſelf at home when he was abroad.

7. *Her carriage is ſo modeſt, that ſhe dis-heartens wantons not onely to take but even to beſiege her chaſtity.* I confeſſe ſome deſperate men will hope any thing; yea, their ſhameleſſe boldneſſe will faſten on impoſsibilities, meaſuring other folks badneſſe by their own: yet ſeldome ſuch Salamanders, which live in the fire of luſt, dare approch, without ſeeing the ſmoke of wantonneſſe in looks, words, apparell, or behaviour. And though charity commands me to beleeve, that ſome women which hang out ſignes, notwithſtanding will not lodge ſtrangers; yet theſe mock-gueſts are guilty in tempting others to tempt them.

8. *In her husbands ſickneſſe ſhe feels more grief then ſhe ſhews.* Partly that ſhe may not dis-hearten him; and partly becauſe ſhe is not at leiſure to ſeem ſo ſorrowfull, that ſhe may be the more ſerviceable.

9. *Her children, though many in number, are none in noyſe, ſteering them with a look whither ſhe liſteth.* When they grow up, ſhe teacheth them not pride but painfulneſſe, making their hands to clothe their backs, and them to wear the livery of their own induſtry. She makes not her daughters Gentlewomen before they be women, rather teaching them what they ſhould pay to others, then receive from them.

10. *The heavieſt work of her ſervants ſhe maketh light, by orderly and ſeaſonable enjoyning it:* Wherefore her ſervice is counted a preferment, and her teaching better then her wages. Her maids follow the preſident of their miſtreſſe, live modeſtly at home. One askt a grave Gentlewoman, How her maids came by ſo good husbands, and yet ſeldome went abroad; *Oh,* ſaid ſhe, *good husbands come home to them.* So much for this ſubject: and what is defective in this deſcription ſhall be ſupplied by the pattern enſuing.

MONICA WIFE *of* Patricivs, *and Mother to* S[t] Auguſtine. *She Died at* Oſtia *in* Italye. *A.º Do* *389. aged 56 yeares.* *W. Marſhall ſculp:*

Chap. 2.

The life of Monica.

Monica is better known by the branch of her iſſue, then root of her parentage, and was born in or nigh Tagaſta in Africk. * Her parents, whoſe names we find not, were Chriſtians, and carefull of her education, committing her to the breeding of an old maid in the houſe, who, though herſelf crooked with age, was excellent to ſtraighten the manners of youth. She inſtructed her with holy ſeverity, never allowing

* *Auguſt. conſeſſ. lib. 9. c. 8.*

allowing her to drink wine, or between meals. Having out-grown her tuition, ſhe began by degrees to ſip, and drink wine, leſſer draughts like wedges widening her throat for greater, till at laſt (ill cuſtomes being not knockt, but inſenſibly ſcru'd into our ſouls) ſhe could fetch off her whole ones. Now it happened that a young maid (formerly her partner in potting) fell at variance with her, and (as malice when ſhe ſhoots draws her arrow to the head) called her Toſ-pot, and drunkard; whereupon Monica reformed her ſelf, and turned temperate. Thus bitter taunts ſometime make wholeſome Phyſick, when God ſanctifies unto us the malice of our enemies to perform the office of good will.

After this was ſhe married to Patricius, one of more honour then wealth, and as yet a pagan; wherein ſhe brake S. Pauls precept, *To marry onely in the Lord.* Perchance then there was a dearth of husbands, or ſhe did it by her parents importunity, or out of promiſe of his converſion: and the hiſtory herein being but lamely delivered us, it is charity to ſupport it with the moſt favourable conſtruction. He was of a ſtern nature, none more lamb when pleaſed, or lion when angry; and which is worſe, his wild * affections did prey abroad, till ſhe lured them home by her loving behaviour. Not like thoſe wives who by their hideous outcries drive their wandring husbands farther out of the way.

* *Auguſt. confeſſ. lib.* 9, *c.* 9.

Her own houſe was to her a houſe of correction, wherein her husbands mother was bitter unto her, having a quarrell not ſo much to her perſon as relation, becauſe a daughter in law. Her ſervants, to climbe into the favour of their old miſtreſſe, trampled on their young, they bringing tales, and the old woman belief; though the teeth of their malice did but file her innocency the brighter. Yea at laſt her mother in law, turning her compurgatour, cauſed her ſonne to puniſh those maids which causelesly had wronged their mistresse.

When her neighbours, which had husbands of far milder dispositions, would shew her their husbands cruelty legible in their faces, all her pitying was reproving them: and whereas they expected to be praysed for their patience, she condemned them for deserving such punishment. She never had blow from, or jarre with her husband, she so suppled his hard nature with her obedience, and to her great comfort saw him converted to Christianity before his death. Also she saw Augustine her sonne, formerly vitious in life,and erroneous in doctrine (whose soul she bathd in her Tears) become a worthy Christian, who coming to have his eares tickled, had his heart touched, and got Religion in to boot with the eloquence of S. Ambrose. She survived not long after her sonnes conversion (God sends his servants to bed when they have done their work) and her candle was put out , as soon as the day did dawn in S. Augustine.

Take an instance or two of her signall piety. There was a custome in * Africk to bring pulse bread and wine to the monuments of dead Saints, wherein Monica was as forward as any. But being better instructed that this custome was of heathenish parentage, and that Religion was not so poore as to borrow rites from Pagans , she instantly left off that ceremony : and as for pietie's sake she had done it thus long, so for pietie's sake she would do it no longer. How many old folks now adayes , whose best argument is use, would have flown in their faces, who should stop them in the full career of an ancient custome.

* *August. confess. lib.6. c.2.*

There was one Licentius a novice-convert, who had got these words by the end, *Turn us again, O Lord God of hosts : show us the light of thy countenance and we shall be whole.* And (as it is the fashion of many mens tongues to echo forth the last sentence they learnt) he said it in all places he went to. But Monica, over-hearing him to sing it in the house of office, was * highly offended at him: because holy things are to be suted to holy places; and the harmonie could not be sweet where the song did jarre with the place. And although some may say, that a gracious heart consecrateth every place into a Chapell; yet sure though pious things are no where unfitting to be thought on, they may somewhere be improper to be uttered.

Augųst. lib. 1. De ordine, c. 8.

Drawing near her death, she sent most pious thoughts as harbingers to heaven, and her soul saw a glimpse of happinesse through the chincks of her sicknesse-broken body. She was so inflamed with zeal, that she turned all *objects* into fewell to feed it. One day standing with S. Augustine at an East-window, * she raised her self to consider the light of Gods presence, in respect whereof all corporall light is so farre from being match'd, it deserves not to be mentioned. Thus mounted on heavenly meditations, and from that high pitch surveying earthly things, the great distance made them appear unto her like a little point, scarce to be seen, and lesse to be respected.

August. confess. lib. 9. c. 10.

She died at Ostia in Italy in the fiftie sixth yeare of her age, Augustine closing her eyes, when through grief he had scarce any himself.

Chap. 3.

The good Husband.

HAving formerly deſcribed a good Wife, ſhe will make a good Husband, whoſe character we are now to preſent.

Maxime 1 *His love to his wife weakeneth not his ruling her, and his ruling leſſeneth not his loving her.* Wherefore he avoideth all fondneſſe, (a ſick love, to be praiſed in none, and pardoned onely in the newly married) whereby more have wilfully betrayed their command, then ever loſt it by their wives rebellion. Methinks the he-viper is right enough ſerved, which (as * Pliny reports) puts his head into the ſhe-vipers mouth, and ſhe bites it off. And what wonder is it if women take the rule to themſelves, which their uxorious husbands firſt ſurrender unto them?

* *Plin. Nat. hiſt. lib.* 10. *cap.* 62.

2 *He is conſtant to his wife, and confident of her.* And ſure where jealouſie is the Jailour, many break the priſon, it opening more wayes to wickedneſſe then it ſtoppeth; ſo that where it findeth one, it maketh ten diſhoneſt.

3 *He alloweth her meet maintenance, but meaſures it by his own eſtate:* nor will he give leſſe, nor can ſhe ask more. Which allowance, if ſhorter then her deſerts and his deſire, he lengtheneth it out with his courteous carriage unto her; chiefly in her ſickneſſe, then not ſo much word-pitying her, as providing neceſſaries for her.

4 *That ſhe may not intrench on his prerogative, he maintains her propriety in feminine affairs:* yea, therein he follows her advice: For the ſoul of a man is planted ſo high, that he overſhoots ſuch low matter as lie levell to a womans eye, and therefore her counſell therein may better hit the mark. Cauſes that are properly of feminine cognizance he ſuffers her finally to decide, not ſo much as per-

permitting an appeal to himſelf, that their juriſdictions may not interfere. He will not countenance a ſtubborn ſervant againſt her, but in her maintains his own Authority. Such husbands as bait the miſtris with her maids, and clap their hands at the ſport, will have cauſe to wring them afterwards.

Knowing ſhe is the weaker veſſell he bears with her infirmities. All hard uſing of her he deteſts, deſiring therein to do not what may be lawfull, but fitting. And grant her to be of a ſervile nature, ſuch as may be bettered by beating; yet he remembers he hath enfranchiſed her by marrying her. On her wedding-day ſhe was like S. Paul free born, and priviledged from any ſervile puniſhment. 5

He is carefull that the wounds betwixt them take not ayre, and be publickly known. Jarres conceald are half reconciled; which if generally known, 'tis a double task to ſtop the breach at home, and mens mouths abroad. To this end he never publickly reproves her. An open reproof puts her to do penance before all that are preſent, after which many rather ſtudy revenge then reformation. 6

He keeps her in the wholſome ignorance of unneceſſary ſecrets. They will not be ſtarved with the ignorance, who perchance may ſurfet with the knowledge of weighty Counſels, too heavy for the weaker ſex to bear. He knows little, who will tell his wife all he knows. 7

He beats not his wife after his death. One having a ſhrewd wife, yet loth to uſe her hardly in his life time, awed her with telling her that he would beat her when he was dead, meaning that he would leave her no maintenance. This humour is unworthy a worthy man, who will endeavour to provide her a competent eſtate: yet he that impoveriſheth his children to enrich his widow, deſtroyes a quick hedge to make a dead one. 8

Chap. 4.

The life of Abraham.

I Intend not to range over all his life as he ſtands threeſquare in relation, Husband, Father, Maſter. We will onely ſurvey and meaſure his conjugall ſide, which reſpecteth his wife.

We reade not that ever he upbraided her for her barrenneſſe, as knowing that naturall defects are not the creatures fault, but the Creatours pleaſure: all which time his love was loyall to her alone. As for his going in to Hagar, it was done not onely with the conſent but by the advice of Sarah, who was ſo ambitious of children ſhe would be made a mother by a proxie. He was not jealous of her (though a grand beauty) in what company ſoever he came. Indeed he feared the Egyptians, becauſe the Egyptians feared not God; ſuſpecting rather them of force, then her of falſeneſſe, and beleeving that ſooner they might kill him, then corrupt her.

Yet (as well as he loved her) he expected ſhe ſhould do work fit for her calling. *Make ready quickly three meaſures of meal and knead it.* Well may Sarah be cook, where Abraham was caterer, yea where God was gueſt. The print of her fingers ſtill remain in the meal, and of crumbling dow ſhe hath made a laſting monument of her good houſwifry.

Being falſely indited by his wife, he never travers'd the bill, but compounded with her on her own terms. The caſe this. Hagar being with child by Abraham, her pride ſweld with her belly, and deſpiſeth her miſtreſſe: Sarah, laying her action wrong, ſues Abraham for her maids fault, and appeals to God. I ſee the Plaintiff hath not alwayes the beſt cauſe; nor are they moſt guilty which are moſt blamed. However Abraham paſſes by her peeviſhneſſe, and remits his maid to ſtand or fall to her own miſtreſſe. Though he had a great part in Hagar, he would have none in Hagars rebellion. Maſters which protect their faulty ſervants hinder the proceeding of juſtice in a family.

He did denie himſelf to grant his wives will in a matter of great conſequence. Sarah deſired, *Caſt out this bondwoman and her ſonne.* Oh hard word! She might as well have ſaid, Caſt out of thy ſelf nature and naturall affection. See how Abraham ſtruggles with Abraham, the Father in him ſtriving with the Husband in him, till God moderated with his caſting-voyce, and Abraham was contented to hearken to the counſel of his wife.

Being to ſacrifice Iſaac, we find not that he made Sarah privie to his project. To tell her, had been to torture her, fearing her affections might be too ſtrong for her faith. Some ſecrets are to be kept from the weaker ſex; not alwayes out of a diſtruſt, leſt they hurt the counſel by telling it, but leſt the counſel hurt them by keeping it.

The deareſt Husband cannot bail his wife when death arreſts her. Sarah dies, and Abraham weeps. Tears are a tribute due to the dead. Tis fitting that the body when it's ſown in corruption ſhould be watered by thoſe that plant it in the earth. The Hittites make him a fair offer, *In the chiefeſt of our ſepulchres bury thy dead*: But he thinks the beſt of them too bad for his Sarah. Her chaſt aſhes did love to lie alone; he provides her a virgin tombe in the cave of Machpelah, where her corps ſweetly ſleep till he himſelf came to bed to her, and was buried in the ſame grave.

CHAP. 5.

The good Parent.

HE beginneth his care for his children not at their birth but conception, giving them to God to be,
* 1.Sam.1.11. if not (as * Hannah did) his Chaplains, at leaſt his Servants. This care he continueth till the day of his death, in their Infancy, Youth, and Mans eſtate. In all which,

Maxime 1 *He ſheweth them in his own practice what to follow and imitate; and in others, what to ſhun and avoid.* For though
*Eccles 12.11. *The words of the wiſe be as * nayles faſtened by the maſters of the Aſſemblies,* yet ſure their examples are the hammer to drive them in to take the deeper hold. A father that whipt his ſonne for ſwearing, and ſwore himſelf whileſt he whipt him, did more harm by his example then good by his correction.

2 *He doth not welcome and imbrace the firſt eſſayes of ſinne in his children.* Weeds are counted herbs in the beginning of the ſpring: nettles are put in pottage, and ſallads are made of eldern-buds. Thus fond fathers like the oathes and wanton talk of their little children, and pleaſe themſelves to heare them diſpleaſe God. But our wiſe Parent both inſtructs his children in Piety, and with correction blaſts the firſt buds of profaneneſſe in them. He that will not uſe the rod on his child, his child ſhall be uſed as a rod on him.

3 *He obſerveth * Gavel-kind in dividing his affections, though not his eſtate.* He loves them (though leaves them not) all alike. Indeed his main land he ſettles on the eldeſt: for where man takes away the birth-right, God commonly takes away the bleſsing from a family. But as for his love, therein, like a well-drawn picture, he eyes all his children alike (if there be a parity of deſerts) not parching one to drown another. Did not that mother ſhew little wit in her great partiality, to whom

* *Gives each child a part,* Verſteg. *Of decayed intell.* cap 3.

whom when her neglected ſonne complained that his brother (her darling) had hit and hurt him with a ſtone, whipt him onely for ſtanding in the way where the ſtone went which his brother caſt ? This partiality is tyrannie, when Parents deſpiſe thoſe that are deformed, enough to break them whom God had bowed before.

4 *He allows his children maintenance according to their quality:* Otherwiſe it will make them baſe, acquaint them with bad company and ſharking tricks; and it makes them ſurfet the ſooner when they come to their eſtates. It is obſerved of camels, that having travelled long without water through ſandy deſerts, * *Implentur cum bibendi eſt occaſio & in præteritum & in futurum*: and ſo theſe thirſty heirs ſoak it when they come to their means, who whileſt their fathers were living might not touch the top of his money, and think they ſhall never feel the bottom of it when they are dead.

* *Plin. Nat. Hiſt. lib. 8. c. 18.*

5 *In chooſing a profeſſion he is directed by his childs diſpoſition:* whoſe inclination is the ſtrongeſt indenture to bind him to a trade. But when they ſet Abel to till the ground, and ſend Cain to keep ſheep; Jacob to hunt, and Eſau to live in tents; drive ſome to ſchool, and others from it; they commit a rape on nature, and it will thrive accordingly. Yet he humours not his child when he makes an unworthy choice beneath himſelf, or rather for eaſe then uſe, pleaſure then profit.

6 *If his ſonne prove wild he doth not caſt him off ſo farre, but he marks the place where he lights.* With the mother of Moſes, he doth not ſuffer his ſonne ſo to ſink or ſwim, but he leaves one to * ſtand afarre off to watch what will become of him. He is carefull whileſt he quencheth his luxury, not withall to put out his life. The rather, becauſe their ſouls, who have broken and run out in their youth, have proved the more healthfull for it afterwards.

* Exod. 2. 4.

7 *He moves him to marriage rather by arguments drawn from his*

his good, then his own authority. It is a ſtyle too Princely for a Parent herein, To will and command, but ſure he may will and deſire. Affections like the conſcience are rather to be led then drawn; and 'tis to be feared, They that marry where they do not love, will love where they do not marry.

8 *He doth not give away his loaf to his children, and then come to them for a piece of bread.* He holds the reins (though looſely) in his own hands, and keeps to reward duty, and puniſh undutifulneſſe; yet on good occaſion for his childrens advancement he will depart from part of his means. Baſe is their nature who will not have their branches lopt, till their bodie be fell'd; and will let go none of their goods, as if it preſaged their ſpeedy death: whereas it doth not follow that he that puts off his cloke muſt preſently go to bed.

9 *On his death-bed he bequeaths his bleſsing to all his children:* Nor rejoyceth he ſo much to leave them great portions, as honeſtly obtained. Onely money well and lawfully gotten is good and lawfull money. And if he leaves his children young, he principally nominates God to be their Guardian, and next him is carefull to appoint provident overſeers.

CHAP. 6.

The good Child.

Maxime 1 HE *reverenceth the perſon of his Parent though old, poore, and froward.* As his Parent bare with him when a child, he bears with his Parent if twice a child: nor doth his dignity above him, cancell his duty unto him. When *S[r].Thomas More was Lord Chancellour of England, and S[r]. John his father one of the Judges of the Kings-Bench, he would in Weſtminſter-Hall beg his bleſsing of him on his knees.

* *Stapleton.in vita* Tho. Mori, *cap.* 1.

He

He observes his lawfull commands, and practiseth his precepts with all obedience. I cannot therefore excuse S. Barbara from undutifulnesse, and occasioning her own death. The matter this. Her father being a pagan commanded his workmen building his house, to make two windows in a room: Barbara, knowing her fathers pleasure, in his absence injoyned them to make*three, that seeing them she might the better contemplate the mystery of the holy Trinity. (Methinks two windows might as well have raised her meditations, and the light arising from both, would as properly have minded her of the Holy Spirit proceding from the Father and the Sonne.) Her father enraged at his return, thus came to the knowledge of her religion, and accused her to the magistrate, which cost her her life. 2

*Alphonf. Villeg. in the life of Barbara on the 4. of Decemb.

Having practised them himself, he entayls his Parents precepts on his posterity. Therefore such instructions are by Solomon, Proverbs 1.9. compared to frontlets and chains (not to a sute of clothes, which serves but one, and quickly weares out, or out of fashion) which have in them a reall lasting worth, and are bequeathed as legacies to another age. The same counsels observed are chains to grace, which neglected prove halters to strangle undutifull children. 3

He is patient under correction, and thankfull after it. When Mr West, formerly Tutour (such I count *in loco parentis*) to Dr. Whitaker, was by him, then *Regius Professor*, created Doctour, Whitaker solemnly gave him thanks before the University for giving him correction when his young scholar. 4

In marriage he first and last consults with his father: when propounded, when concluded. He best bowls at the mark of his own contentment, who besides the aim of his own eye, is directed by his father, who is to give him the ground. 5

He is a stork to his parent, and feeds him in his old age. Not onely if his father hath been a pelican, but though 6
he

he hath been an eſtridge unto him, and neglected him in his youth. He confines him not a long way off to a ſhort penſion, forfeited if he comes in his preſence; but ſhews piety at home, and learns (as S. Paul ſaith the 1. Timothy. 5. 4.) to requite his Parent. And yet the debt (I mean onely the principall, not counting the intereſt) cannot fully be paid, and therefore he compounds with his father to accept in good worth the utmoſt of his endeavour.

7 *Such a child God commonly rewards with long life in this world.* If he chance to die young, yet he lives long that lives well; and time miſpent is not lived but loſt. Beſides, God is better then his promiſe, if he takes from him a long leaſe, and gives him a free-hold of better value. As for diſobedient children,

8 *If preſerved from the gallows, they are reſerved for the rack, to be tortured by their own poſterity.* One complained, that never father had ſo undutifull a child as he had. Yes, ſaid his ſonne, with leſſe grace then truth, my grandfather had.

I conclude this ſubject with the example of a Pagans ſonne, which will ſhame moſt Chriſtians. Pomponius * Atticus, making the funerall oration at the death of his mother, did proteſt that living with her threeſcore and ſeven years, he was never reconciled unto her, *Se nunquam cum matre in gratiam rediiſſe*; becauſe (take the comment with the text) there never happened betwixt them the leaſt jarre which needed reconciliation.

* *In vita Attici in fine Epiſt. ad Attic.*

CHAP. 7.

Chap. 7.

The good Master.

HE is the heart in the midst of his houshold, *primum vivens et ultimum moriens*, first up and last abed, if not in his person yet in his providence. In his carriage he aimeth at his own and his servants good, and to advance both.

He oversees the works of his servants. One said *that the dust that fell from the masters shooes was the best compost to manure ground.* The lion * out of state will not run whilst any one looks upon him, but some servants out of slothfulnesse will not run except some do look upon them, spurr'd on with their Masters eye. Chiefly he is carefull exactly to take his servants reckonings. If their Master takes no account of them, they will make small account of him, and care not what they spend who are never brought to an audit. Maxime 1

* Plin. nat. Hist. lib. 8. cap 16.

He provides them victualls, wholsome, sufficient and seasonable. He doth not so allay his servants bread to debase it so much as to make that servants meat which is not mans meat. He alloweth them also convenient rest and recreation, whereas some Masters, like a bad conscience, will not suffer them to sleep that have them. He remembers the old law of the Saxon King Ina, * *If a villain work on Sunday by his lords command, he shall be free.* 2

* S. H. Spilman in concilis, An. ch. 692. pag. 188.

The wages he contracts for he duly and truly payes to his servants. The same word in the Greek ἰὸς signifies *rust* and *poyson*: and some strong poyson is made of the rust of mettalls, but none more venemous then the rust of money in the rich mans purse unjustly detained from the labourer, which will poyson and infect his whole estate. 3

*He never threatens * his servant but rather presently corrects him.* Indeed conditionall threatnings with promise of pardon on amendment are good and usefull. Absolute 4

* Ephes. 6. 9.

threatnings torment more, reform lesse, making servants keep their faults, and forsake their Masters: wherefore herein he never passeth his word, but makes present paiment, lest the creditour runne away from the debtour.

5 *In correcting his servant, he becomes not a slave to his own passion.* Not cruelly making new indentures of the flesh of his apprentice. To this end he never beats him in the height of his passion. Moses being to fetch water out of the rock, and commanded by God onely to speak to it with his rod in his hand, being transported with anger smote it thrice. Thus some Masters, which might fetch penitent tears from their servants with a chiding word (onely shaking the rod withall for terrour) in their fury strike many blows which might better be spared. If he perceives his servant incorrigible, so that he cannot wash the black-moore, he washeth his hands of him, and fairly puts him away.

6 *He is tender of his servant in his sicknesse and age.* If crippled in his service, his house is his hospitall: yet how many throw away those dry bones out of the which themselves have suckt the marrow? It is as usuall to see a young serving-man an old beggar, as to see a light-horse first frō the great saddle of a Nobleman to come to the hackney-coach, and at last die in drawing a carre. But the good Master is not like the cruell hunter in the fable, who beat his old dogge because his toothlesse mouth let go the game; he rather imitates the noble nature of our Prince Henrie, who took order for the keeping of an * old English mastiffe which had made a Lion runne away. Good reason good service in age should be rewarded. Who can without pity and pleasure behold that trusty vessell which carried S^r^. Francis Drake about the world.

** Hows continuat. of Stows Chron. pag. 836.*

Hitherto our discourse hath proceeded of the carriage of Masters towards free covenant servants, not intermedling with their behaviour towards slaves & vassals, whereof

whereof we onely report this paſſage: When Charles the fifth Emperour returning with his fleet from Algier was extremely beaten with a tempeſt, and their ſhips overloaden, he cauſed them to caſt their beſt horſes into the ſea to ſave the life of many *ſlaves, which according to the market price was not ſo much worth. Are there not many that in ſuch a caſe had rather ſave Jack the horſe then Jocky the keeper. And yet thoſe who firſt called England *the Purgatory of ſervants*, ſure did us much wrong: Purgatory it ſelf being as falſe in the application to us, as in the doctrine thereof; ſervants with us living generally on as good conditions as in any other countrey. And well may maſters conſider how eaſie a tranſpoſition it had been for God, to have made him to mount into the ſaddle that holds the ſtirrop; and him to ſit down at the table, who ſtands by with a trencher.

* *Pantaleon part. 3. De illuſt. Germ. & alii autores.*

Chap. 8.

The good Servant.

HE is one that out of conſcience ſerves God in his Maſter, and ſo hath the principle of obedience in himſelf. As for thoſe ſervants who found their obedience on ſome externall thing, with engines, they will go no longer then they are wound, or weighed up.

He doth not diſpute his Maſters lawfull will, but doeth it. *Maxime* 1 Hence it is that ſimple ſervants (underſtand ſuch whoſe capacity is bare meaſure, without ſurpluſage equall to the buſines he is uſed in) are more uſefull, becauſe more manageable, then abler men, eſpecially in matters wherein not their brains but hands are required. Yet if his Maſter out of want of experience injoyns him to do what is hurtfull, and prejudiciall to his own eſtate, duty herein makes him undutifull (if not to deny, to demurre in his performance) and chuſing rather to diſpleaſe then hurt his maſter, he humbly repreſents his reaſons to the contrary.

2 *He loves to go about his buſines with cheerfulneſſe.* One ſaid, *He loved to heare his carter though not his cart to ſing. God loveth a cheerfull giver*; and Chriſt reproved the Phariſees for disfiguring their faces with a ſad countenance. Fools! who to perſwade men that Angels lodged in their hearts, hung out a devil for a ſigne in their faces. Sure cheerfulneſſe in doing renders a deed more acceptable. Not like thoſe ſervants, who doing their work unwillingly, their looks do enter a proteſtation againſt what their hands are doing.

3 *He diſpatcheth his buſines with quicknes and expedition.* Hence the ſame Engliſh word *Speed* ſignifies celerity, and ſucceſſe; the former in buſineſſe of execution cauſing the latter. Indeed haſte and raſhneſſe are ſtorms and tempeſts, breaking and wrecking buſineſſe; but nimbleneſſe is a fair full wind, blowing it with ſpeed to the haven. As he is good at hand, ſo is he good at length, continually and conſtantly carefull in his ſervice. Many ſervants, as if they had learnd the nature of the beſoms they uſe, are good for a few dayes, and afterwards grow unſerviceable.

4 *He diſpoſeth not of his maſters goods without his privity or conſent*: no not in the ſmalleſt matters. Open this wicket, and it will be in vain for maſters to ſhut the doore. If ſervants preſume to diſpoſe ſmall things without their maſters allowance (beſides that many little leaks may ſink a ſhip) this will widen their conſciences to give away greater. But though he hath not alwayes a particular leave, he hath a generall grant, and a warrant dormant from his maſter to give an almes to the poore in his abſence, if in abſolute neceſſity.

5 *His anſwers to his maſter are true, direct, and dutifull.* If a dumbe devil poſſeſſeth a ſervant, a winding cane is the

fitteſt

fitteſt circle, and the maſter the exorciſt to drive it out. Some ſervants are ſo talkative, one may as well command the echo as them not to ſpeak laſt; and then they count themſelves conquerours, becauſe laſt they leave the field. Others, though they ſeem to yield and go away, yet with the flying Parthians ſhoot backward over their ſhoulders, and dart bitter taunts at their maſters; yea, though with the clock they have given the laſt ſtroke, yet they keep a jarring, muttering to themſelves a good while after.

Juſt correction he bears patiently, and unjuſt he takes cheerfully; knowing that ſtripes unjuſtly given more hurt the maſter then the man: and the Logick maxime is verified, *Agens agendo repatitur*, the ſmart moſt lights on the ſtriker. Chiefly he diſdains the baſeneſſe of running away. 6

Becauſe charity is ſo cold, his induſtry is the hotter to provide ſomething for himſelf, whereby he may be maintained in his old age. If under his maſter he trades for himſelf (as an apprentice may do if he hath*covenanted ſo before-hand) he provides good bounds and ſufficient fences betwixt his own and his maſters eſtate (*Jacob* Gen. 30. 36. *ſet his flock three dayes journey from Labans*) that no quarrell may ariſe about their proprietie, nor ſuſpicion that his remnant hath eaten up his maſters whole cloth. 7

* *Bracton. lib. 5. tract. 2. cap. 3. num. 7.*

Chap. 9.

The life of Eliezer.

Eliezer was Steward of Abrahams houſhold, Lieutenant generall over the army of his ſervants, ruler over all his Maſter had: the confidence in his loyalty, cauſing the largeneſſe of his commisſion.

But as for thoſe who make him the founder of Damaſcus, on no other evidence but becauſe he is called *Eliezer of Damaſcus*, they build a great city on too narrow a foundation. It argues his goodneſſe that Abraham, if dying without a ſonne, intended him his heir (a kinſman in grace is neareſt by the ſureſt ſide) till Iſaac ſtepping in ſtopt out Eliezer, and reverſt thoſe reſolutions.

The Scripture preſents us with a remarkable preſident of * his piety, in a matter of great moment: Abraham, being to ſend him into Meſopotamia, cauſed him to ſwear that he would faithfully fetch Iſaac a wife from his own kinred. Eliezer demurr'd awhile before he would ſwear, carefully ſurveying the latitude of the oath, leſt ſome unſeen ambuſhes therein ſhould ſurpriſe his conſcience. The moſt ſcrupulous to take an oath will be the moſt carefull to perform it, whereas thoſe that ſwear it blindly will do it lamely. He objects, *Peradventure the woman will not be willing to follow me.* At laſt being ſatisfied in this quære, he takes the oath: as no honeſt man which means to pay, will refuſe to give his bond if lawfully required.

* *That the nameleſſe ſervant, Gen. 24. was this Eliezer Abrahams ſteward, is the opinion of Luther in his comment on that chapter, Rivet on the ſame,* Exercit. 111. *with many others.*

He takes ten camells (then the coaches of the Eaſt-countrey) with ſervants and all things in good equipage, to ſhew a ſample of his Maſters greatneſſe; and being a ſtranger in the countrey asked direction of him who beſt knew the way, God himſelf. If any object that his craving of a ſigne was a ſigne of infidelity, and unmannerly boldneſſe to confine God to particulars; yet

yet perchance Gods ſpirit prompted him to make the requeſt, who ſometimes moves men to ask what he is minded to give, and his petition ſeemeth juſt becauſe granted.

Rebecca meets him at the well. The lines drawn from every part of the ſigne required centre themſelves in her. *Drink my Lord*, ſaid ſhe, *and I will draw water for thy camells*. Her words Propheſie that ſhe will be a good houſewife, and a good houſekeeper. Eliezers eyes are dazeled with the beams of Gods providence: Her drawing of water drew more wonder from him; and the more he drinks of her pitcher, the more he is athirſt to know the iſſue of the matter. He queſtions her of her parentage, and finds all his myſticall expectation hiſtorically expounded in her. Then he bowed down his head, and did homage to Gods providence, blesſing him for his protection. Many favours which God giveth us ravell out for want of hemming, through our own unthankfulneſſe: for though prayer purchaſeth blesſings, giving praiſe doth keep the quiet poſſesſion of them.

Being come into the houſe, his firſt care is for his cattell, whoſe dumbeneſſe is oratory to a conſcientious man; and he that will not be mercifull to his beaſt, is a beaſt himſelf. Then preferring his meſſage before his meat, he empties his mind before he fills his body. No dainties could be digeſted, whilſt his errand like a crudity lay on his ſtomach.

In delivering his meſſage, firſt he reads his commisſion, I am Abrahams ſervant; then he reports the fulneſſe of his Maſters wealth without any hyperboles. How many, employed in ſuch a matter, would have made mountains of gold of molehills of ſilver? not ſo Eliezer, reporting the bare truth; and a good eſtate if told, commends it ſelf. As plain alſo is his narration of the paſſages of Gods providence, the artificialneſſe whereof beſt appeard in his naturall relation. Then

concludes

concludes he, with desiring a direct answer to his motion.

The matter was soon transacted betwixt them; for seeing that heaven did ask the banes, why should earth forbid them? onely her friends desire Rebecca should stay ten dayes with them, which Eliezer would not yield to. He would speedily finish that bargain whereof God had given the happy earnest; and because blest hitherto, make more haste hereafter. If in a dark businesse we perceive God to guide us by the lantern of his providence, it is good to follow the light close, lest we lose it by our lagging behind. He will not truant it now in the afternoon, but with convenient speed returns to Abraham, who onely was worthy of such a Servant, who onely was worthy of such a Master.

Chap. 10.

The good Widow.

SHe is a woman whose head hath been quite cut off, and yet she liveth, and hath the second part of virginity. Conceive her to have buried her Husband decently according to his quality and condition, and let us see how she behaves her self afterwards.

Maxime 1 *Her grief for her Husband though reall, is moderate.* Excessive was the sorrow of King Richard the second beseeming him neither as king, man, or Christian, who so fervently loved Anna of Bohemia his Queen, that when she dyed at Shean in Surrey, he both cursed the place, and also out of madnesse * overthrew the whole house.

* *weaver fun. monum. p. 473. out of Stows Annals.*

2 *But our widows sorrow is no storm but a still rain.* Indeed some foolishly discharge the surplusage of their passions on themselves, tearing their hair, so that their friends

friends coming to the funerall, know not which most to bemoan the dead husband, or the dying widow. Yet commonly it comes to passe, that such widows grief is quickly emptyed, which streameth out at so large a vent; whilest their tears that but drop, will hold running a long time.

She continues a competent time in her widows estate. Anciently they were, at least, to live out their *annum luctus*, their yeare of sorrow. But as some * erroneously compute the long lives of the Patriarks before the flood not by solary, but lunary years, making a moneth a yeare: so many overhasty widows cut their yeare of mourning very short, and within few weeks make post speed to a second marriage. 3

* *vid. August. de Civitat Dei lib. 15. cap. 12.*

She doth not onely live sole and single, but chaste and honest. We know pesthouses alwayes stand alone, and yet are full of infectious diseases. Solitarinesse is not an infallible argument of sanctity: and it is not enough to be unmarried, but to be undefiled. 4

Though going abroad sometimes about her businesse, she never makes it her businesse to go abroad. Indeed *man goeth forth to his labour*, and a widow in civill affairs is often forced to act a double part of man and woman, and must go abroad to solicite her businesse in person, what she cannot do by the proxie of her friends. Yet even then she is most carefull of her credit, and tender of her modesty, not impudently thrusting into the society of men. Oh 'tis improper for tinder to strike fire, and for their sexe which are to be sued to, first to intrude, and offer their companie. 5

She loves to look on her husbands picture, in the children he hath left her: not foolishly fond over them for their fathers sake (this were to kill them in honour of the dead) but giveth them carefull education. Her husbands friends are ever her welcomest guests, whom she entertaineth with her best cheer, and with honourable mention of their friends, and her husbands memorie. 6

7 *If ſhe can ſpeak little good of him, ſhe ſpeaks but little of him.* So handſomely folding up her diſcourſe, that his virtues are ſhown outwards, and his vices wrapped up in ſilence, as counting it Barbariſme to throw dirt on his memorie who hath moulds caſt on his body. She is a champion for his credit if any ſpeak againſt him. Fooliſh is their project who by raking up bad ſavour againſt their former husbands think thereby to perfume their bed for a ſecond marriage.

8 *She putteth her eſpeciall confidence in Gods providence.* Surely if he be *a father to the fatherleſſe*, it muſt needs follow that he is an husband to the widow. And therefore ſhe ſeeks to gain and keep his love unto her, by her conſtant prayer and religious life.

9 *She will not morgage her firſt husbands pawns, thereby to purchaſe the good will of a ſecond.* If ſhe marrieth (for which ſhe hath the Apoſtles licence, not to ſay mandate, *I will that the younger widows marry*) ſhe will not abridge her children of that which juſtly belongs unto them. Surely a broken faith to the former is but a weak foundation to build thereon a loyall affection to a latter love. Yet if ſhe becomes a mother in law, there is no difference betwixt her carriage to her own and her ſecond husbands children, ſave that ſhe is ſevereſt to her own, over whom ſhe hath the ſole juriſdiction. And if her ſecond husbands children by a former wife commit a fault, ſhe had rather bind them over to anſwer for it before their own father, then to correct them her ſelf, to avoid all ſuſpicion of hard uſing of them.

CHAP. 11.

PAVLA *Widdow of* Toxotius, *and Mother to* Evstochium. *She Died at* Bethlehem, *An^o doni* 404 *Aged* 56 *yeares* 8 *moneths* 21 *dayes* *W.M. sculp.*

Chap. II.

The life of the Lady Paula.

WHat? (will some say) having a wood of widows of upright conversation, must you needs gather one crooked with superstition to be pattern to all the rest? must Paula be their president? whose life was a very masse-book, so that if every point of popery were lost, they might be found in her practice.

Nothing lesse. Indeed Paula lived in an age which was, as I may say, in the knuckle and bending betwixt the

the primitive times and ſuperſtition,popery being then a hatching,but farre from being fledg'd. Yea no Papiſt (though picking out here and there ſome paſſages which make to his purpoſe) will make her practice in groſſe the ſquare of his own : for where ſhe embraces ſome ſuperſtitions with her left hand, ſhe thruſts away more with her right. I have therefore principally made choice to write her life,that I may acquaint both my ſelf and the reader with the garb of that age in Church-matters, wherein were many remarkable paſſages, otherwiſe I might and would have taken a farre fitter example.

I know two trades together are too much for one man to thrive upon, and too much it is for me to be an Hiſtorian and a Critick, to relate and to judge : yet ſince Paula, though a gratious woman, was guilty of ſome great errours, give me leave to hold a pencil in one hand,and a ſpunge in the other, both to draw her life and daſh it where it is faultie. And let us that live in purer times be thankfull to God for our light, and uſe our quicker ſight to guide our feet in Gods paths, leſt we reel from one extremitie to another.

To come to the Lady Paula's birth : the Nobleſt blood in the world by a confluence ran in her veins. I muſt confeſſe the moſt Ancient Nobilitie is junior to no Nobilitie, when all men were equall. Yet give others leave to ſee Moſes his face to ſhine, when he knew it not himſelf ; and ſeeing Paula was pleaſed not to know, but to neglect and trample on her high birth, we are bound to take notice thereof. She was deſcended from * Agamemnon , Scipio , and the Gracchi's, and her husband Toxotius from * Æneas, and the Julian familie ; ſo that in their marriage the warres of the Grecians and Trojanes were reconciled.

** Hieron. Epiſt. ad Euſtoch. pag. 185.*

** Idem in eadem epiſt. p. 172.*

Some years they lived together in the Citie of Rome, in holy and happy wedlock, and to her husband ſhe bare foure daughters, Bleſilla,Paulina,Euſtochium,and Ruffina.

Ruffina. Yet ſtill her husband long'd for poſteritie, like thoſe who are ſo covetous of a male heir, they count none children but ſonnes : and at laſt God, who keeps the beſt for the cloſe, beſtowed Toxotius, a young ſonne upon her.

But commonly after a great bleſſing comes a great croſſe: ſcarce was ſhe made a mother to a ſonne, when ſhe was made a widow, which to her was a great and grievous affliction. But as a rubbe to an overthrown bowl proves an help by hindering it; ſo afflictions bring the ſouls of Gods Saints to the mark, which otherwiſe would be gone and tranſported with too much earthly happineſſe. However Paula grieved little leſſe then exceſſively hereat, ſhe being a woman that in all her actions (to be ſure to do enough) made alwayes meaſure with advantage.

Yet in time ſhe overcame her ſorrow, herein being aſſiſted by the counſel and comfort of S. Hierome, whoſe conſtant frequenting of her, commented upon by his enemies malice (which will pry narrowly and talk broadly) gave occaſion to the report, that he accompanied with her for diſhoneſt intents. Surely if the accuſations of ſlanderous tongues be proofs, the primitive times had no Churches but ſtews. It is to be ſuſpected that * Ruffin his ſworn enemie raiſed the report; and if the Lady Paula's memorie wanted a compurgatour, I would be one my ſelf, it being improbable that thoſe her eyes would burn with luſt which were conſtantly drownd with tears. But the reader may find S. Hierome purging * himſelf; and he who had his tongue and an innocent heart needed no body elſe to ſpeak for him.

** Eraſmus in ſcholia in epitaphium Paulæ p. 193.*

** In epiſtola quæ incipit,* Si tibi putem, *tom. 2. fol.* 368.

It happened that the Biſhops of the Eaſt and Weſt were ſummoned by the * Emperours letters to appear at Rome for the according of ſome differences in the Church. (It ſeemes by this that the Pope did not ſo command in chief at Rome, but that the power of

** Hieronym. Epiſt. prædict. pag.* 172.

congregating Synods ſtill reſided in the Emperour.) Hither came Paulinus Biſhop of Antioch, and Epiphanius Biſhop of Salamine in Cyprus, who lodged at the Lady Paula's, and his virtues ſo wrought upon her, that ſhe determined to leave her native countrey, and to travel into the Eaſt, and in Judea to ſpend the remainder of her life. The reaſons that moved her to remove, was becauſe Rome was a place of riot and luxury, her ſoul being almoſt ſtifled with the frequencie of Ladyes viſits; and ſhe feared courteſie in her would juſtle out piety, ſhe being fain to crowd up her devotions to make room for civill entertainments. Beſides, of her own nature ſhe ever loved privacie and a ſequeſtred life, being of the Pelicans nature, which uſe not to flie in flocks. Laſtly, ſhe conceived that the ſight of thoſe holy places would be the beſt comment on the Hiſtory of the Bible, and faſten the paſſages thereof in her mind. Wherefore ſhe intended to ſurvey all Paleſtine, and at laſt to go to Bethlehem, making Chriſts inne her home, and to die there where he was born, leaving three of her daughters, and her poore infant Toxotius behind her.

For mine own part, I think ſhe had done as acceptable a deed to God, in ſtaying behind to rock her child in the cradle, as to viſit Chriſts manger, ſeeing Grace doth not cut of the affections of nature but ripen them: the rather, becauſe Chriſtianity is not naild to Chriſts croſſe and mount Calvary, nor Piety faſtned (as we may ſay) to the freehold of the land of Paleſtine. But if any Papiſt make her a pattern for pilgrimages, let them remember that ſhe went from Rome: and was it not an unnaturall motion in her to move from that centre of Sanctitie?

She with her daughter Euſtochium began her journie, and taking Cyprus in her way, where ſhe viſited Epiphanius, ſhe came at laſt to Judea. She meaſured that

that countrey with her travelling, and drew the trueſt mappe thereof with her own feet, ſo accurately that ſhe left out no particular place of importance. At laſt ſhe was fixed at Bethlehem, where ſhe built one monaſterie for men, and three for women. It will be worth our pains to take notice of ſome principall of the orders ſhe made in thoſe feminine Academies; becauſe Paula's practice herein was a leading caſe, though thoſe that came after her went beyond her. For in the rules of monaſticall life, Paula ſtood at the head game, and the Papiſts in after ages, deſirous to better her hand, drew themſelves quite out.

Each monaſterie had a chief matrone, whilſt Paula was Principall over all. Theſe ſocieties were ſeverd at their meat and work, but met together at their prayers: they were carefully kept apart from men, not like thoſe Epicœne monaſteries not long ſince invented by Joan Queen of Sweden, wherein men and women lived under one roof, not to ſpeak of worſe libertines. Well were Nunnes called *Recluſes*, which according to the true meaning of the word ſignifie thoſe which are ſet wide open, or left at libertie, though that Barbarous age miſtook the ſenſe of the word, for ſuch as were ſhut up, and might not ſtirre out of their * Cloyſter.

* *Littleton fol.* 92.

They uſed to ſing Halelujah, which ſerv'd them both for a pſalm, and a bell to call them all together. In the * morning, at nine a clock, at noon, at three a clock in the afternoon, and at night they had prayers, and ſang the pſalmes in order. This I believe gave originall to canonicall houres. The Apoſtles precept is the plain ſong, *Pray continually*; and thus mens inventions ran their deſcants upon it, and confin'd it to certain houres. A practice in it ſelf not ſo bad for thoſe who have leiſure to obſerve it, ſave that when devotion is thus artificially plaited into houres it may take up mens minds in formalities to neglect the ſubſtance.

* Mane, horâ tertiâ, ſextâ, nonâ, veſperi. *Hieron. in præfat. Epiſt. p.* 180. *ſurely living in Paleſtine he meaneth the Jewiſh computation of houres.*

They

They roſe alſo at midnight to ſing pſalmes. A cuſtome begun before in the time of perſecution, when the Chriſtians were forced to be Antipodes to other men, ſo that when it was night with others, it was day with them, and they then began their devotions. Theſe night-prayers, begun in neceſſitie, were continued in Paula's time in gratefull remembrance, and ſince corrupted with ſuperſtition: the beſt is, their riſing at midnight breaks none of our ſleep.

Theſe virgins did every day learn ſome part of the holy Scriptures; whereas thoſe Nunnes which pretend to ſucceed them learn onely with poſt-horſes to run over the ſtage of their beads (ſo many Ave Maries, and Pater noſters) and are ignorant in all the Scripture beſides. Such as were faultie, ſhe cauſed to take their meat apart from others at the entrance of the dining-room; with which mild ſeveritie ſhe reclaimed many: ſhame in ingenuous natures making a deeper impreſſion then pain. Mean time I find amongſt them no vow of virginitie, no tyrannicall Penance, no whipping themſelves; as if not content to interre their ſinnes in Chriſts grave, they had rather bury them in furrows digg'd in their own backs. They wrought hard to get their living, and on the Lords day alone went out of their monaſterie to hear Gods word.

Yet was ſhe more rigid and ſevere towards her ſelf, then to any of them, macerating her body with faſting, and refuſing to drink any wine, when adviſed thereto by Phyſicians for her health. So that (as an * holy man complained of himſelf, whileſt he went about to ſubdue an enemie he kild a ſubject) ſhe overturned the ſtate of her bodie, and whileſt ſhe thought to ſnuff the candle put it quite out. Yea S. Hierome himſelf, what his Eloquence herein doth commend in her, his Charity doth excuſe, and his Judgement doth * condemne. But we muſt Charitably believe that theſe her faſtings proceeded out of true humiliation and ſorrow for

* *Bernard. devot. devotis*

* Hæc refero, non quòd inconſideranter & ultra vires ſumta onera probem, *p.* 181.

for her ſinnes ; otherwiſe where opinion of merit is annexed to them, they are good onely to fill the body with wind, and the ſoul with pride. Certainly prodigious Popiſh ſelf-penance is will-worſhip, and the pureſt Epicuriſme, wherein pain is pleaſant : for as long as people impoſe it on themſelves, they do not deny their own will, but fulfill it;and whilſt they beat down the body they may puff up the fleſh.

Nor can her immoderate bounty be excuſed, who gave all and more then all away, taking up money at intereſt to give to the poore, and leaving Euſtochium her daughter deep in debt, a great charge, and nothing to maintain it. Sure none need be more bountifull in giving then the Sunne is in ſhining, which though freely beſtowing his beams on the world keeps notwithſtanding the body of light to himſelf. Yea it is neceſſary that Liberality ſhould as well have banks as a ſtream.

She was an excellent text-woman, yea could ſay the holy Scriptures by heart, and attained to underſtand and ſpeak the Hebrew tongue, a language which Hierome himſelf got with great difficultie, and kept with conſtant uſe (skill in Hebrew will quickly go out, and burn no longer then 'tis blown) yet ſhe in her old age did ſpeedily learn it. She diligently heard Hierome expounding the old and new Teſtament, asking him many doubts, and Quæres in difficult places (ſuch conſtant ſcouring makes our knowledge brighter) and would not ſuffer his judgement to ſtand neuter in hard points, but made him expreſſe the probable opinion.

Moſt naturally flie from death ; Gods Saints ſtand ſtill till death comes to them;Paula went out to meet it, not to ſay, call'd death unto her by conſuming her ſelf in faſting : ſhe died in the fiftie ſixth yeare of her age, and was ſolemnly buried in Bethlehem. People of all countreys flockt to her funerall : Biſhops carried her

 corps

corps to the grave: others carried torches and lamps before it, which though ſome may condemne to be but burning of day was no more then needed, ſhe being buried in a cave or grot as an * eyewitneſſe doth teſtifie. Pſalmes were ſung at her buriall in the Hebrew, Greek, Latine, and Syriack tongue, it being fit there ſhould be a key for every lock, and languages to be underſtood by all the miſcelany company there preſent.

* *G. Sandys Travells, pag.* 179.

Euſtochium her daughter had little comfort to be Executrix or Adminiſtratrix unto her, leaving her not a pennie of monie, great debts, and many brothers and ſiſters to provide for, *quos ſuſtentare arduum, abjicere impium.* I like not this charitie reverſed, when it begins farre off & neglects thoſe at home.

To conclude, I can do her memorie no better right, then to confeſſe ſhe was wrong in ſomethings. Yet ſurely Gods Glory was the mark ſhe ſhot at, though herein the hand of her practice did ſometimes ſhake, and oftener the eye of her judgement did take wrong aim.

Chap. 12.

The conſtant Virgin

IS one who hath made a reſolution with herſelf to live chaſte, and unmarryed. Now there is a grand difference betwixt a Reſolution and a Vow. The former is a covenant drawn up betwixt the party and herſelf; and commonly runs with this clauſe, *durante noſtro beneplacito,* as long as we ſhall think fitting; and therefore on juſt occaſion ſhe may give a releaſe to herſelf. But in a vow God is intereſted as the Creditour, ſo that except he be pleaſed to give up the band, none can give an acquittance to themſelves. Being now to deſcribe the Virgin, let the reader know that virginity belongs to both ſexes; and though in Courtesie we make our Maid a female, let not my pen be chalenged of improprietie, if casually sometimes it light on the Masculine Gender.

Maxime 1 *She chooseth not a single life solely for its self, but in reference to the better serving of God.* I know none but beggars that desire the Church-Porch to lye in, which others onely use as a passage into the Church. Virginity is none of those things to be desired in and for it self, but because it leads a more convenient way to the worshipping of God, especially in time of persecution. For then if Christians be forced to run races for their lives, the unmarryed have the advantage, lighter by many ounces, and freed from much encumbrance, which the married are subject to; who, though private Persons, herein are like Princes, they must have their train follow them.

2 *She improveth her single life therewith to serve God the more constantly.* Housekeepers cannot so exactly mark all their family-affairs, but that sometimes their ranks will be broken; which disorder by necessary consequence will disturb their duties of pietie, to make them contracted, omitted; or unseasonably performed. The Apostle saith, *Such shall have troubles in the flesh*; and grant them sanctified troubles, yet even Holy-thistle and Sweet-brier have their prickles. But the Virgin is freed from these encumbrances. No lording Husband shall at the same time command her presence and distance, to be alwayes near in constant attendance, and alwayes to stand aloof off in an awfull observance; so that providing his break-fast hazards her soul to fast a meal of morning prayer: No crying Children shall drown her singing of psalmes, and put her devotion out of tune: No unfaithfull Servants shall force her to divide her eyes betwixt lifting them up to God and casting them down to oversee their work; but making her Closet her Chappell, she freely enjoyeth God and good thoughts at what time she pleaseth.

3 *Yet in all her discourse she maketh an honourable mention of marriage.* And good reason that virginity should pay a chief rent of honour unto it, as acknowledging her selfe to be a *colonia deducta* from it. Unworthy is the practice of those who in their discourse plant all their arguments point-blank to batter down the married estate, bitterly inveighing against it; yea base is the behaviour of some young men, who can speak nothing but Satyres against Gods ordinance of Matrimony, and the whole sex of women. This they do either out of deep dissimulation, to divert supicion, that they may prey the farthest from their holes; or else they do it out of revenge: having themselves formerly lighted on bad women (yet no worse then they deserved) they curse all adventures because of their own shipwrack; or lastly they do it out of mere spight to nature and God himself: and pity it is but that their fathers had been of the same opinion. Yet it may be tolerable if onely in harmlesse mirth they chance to bestow a jest upon the follyes of married people. Thus when a Gentlewoman told an ancient Batchelour who lookd very young, that she thought he had eaten a snake; *No mistris* (said he) *it is because I never meddled with any snakes which maketh me look so young.*

4 *She counts her self better lost in a modest silence then found in a bold discourse.* Divinity permits not women to speak in the Church; morality forbids maids to talk in the House, where their betters are present. She is farre from the humours of those, who (more bridling in their chinnes then their tongues) love in their constant prating to make sweet musick to their own ears, and harsh jarring to all the rest of the company: yea as some report of sheep, that when they runne they are afraid of the noise of their own feet; so our Virgin is afraid to heare her own tongue runne in the presence of graver persons. She conceives the bold maintaining of any argument concludes against her own civil behaviour;

behaviour ; and yet ſhe will give a good account of any thing whereof ſhe is queſtioned, ſufficient to ſhew her ſilence is her choice, not her refuge. In ſpeaking ſhe ſtudiouſly avoids all ſuſpicious expreſſions, which wanton apprehenſions may colourably comment into obſcenity.

She bluſheth at the wanton diſcourſe of others in her company. 5
As fearing that being in the preſence where treaſon againſt modeſty is ſpoken, all in the place will be arraigned for principalls : yea if ſilent, ſhe is afraid to be taken to conſent ; if offering to confute it, ſhe fears leſt by ſtirring a dunghill, the ſavour may be more noyſome. Wherefore that ſhe may not ſuffer in her title to modeſty, to preſerve her right ſhe enters a ſilent caveat by a bluſh in her cheeks, and embraceth the next opportunity to get a gaole-delivery out of that company where ſhe was detained in durance. Now becauſe we have mentioned Bluſhing, which is ſo frequent with virgins that it is called *a maidens bluſh*, (as if they alone had a patent to die this colour) give us leave a little to enlarge our ſelves on this ſubject.

1 *Bluſhing oftentimes proceeds from guiltines* ; when the offender being purſued after ſeeks as it were to hide himſelf under the viſard of a new face.

2 *Bluſhing is othertimes rather a compurgatour then an accuſer*; not ariſing from guiltineſſe in our Virgin, but from one of theſe reaſons : Firſt becauſe ſhe is ſurpriſed with a ſudden accuſation, and though armed with innocency, that ſhe cannot be pierced, yet may ſhe be amazed with ſo unexpected a charge. Secondly from ſenſibleneſſe of diſgrace, aſhamed, though innocent, to be within the ſuſpicion of ſuch faults, and that ſhe hath carried her ſelf ſo that any tongue durſt be ſo impudent as to lay it to her charge. Thirdly from a diſability to acquit her ſelf at the inſtant (her integrity wanting rather clearing then clearneſſe) and per-

chance ſhe wants boldneſſe to traverſe the action, and ſo non-ſuiting her ſelf, ſhe fears her cauſe will ſuffer in the judgements of all that be preſent: and although accuſed but in jeſt, ſhe is jealous the accuſation will be believed in earneſt; and edg'd tools thrown in merriment may wound reputations. Fourthly out of mere anger: for as in fear the blood makes not an orderly retreat but a confuſed flight to the heart; ſo in bluſhing the blood ſallies out into our Virgins cheeks, and ſeems as a champion to challenge the accuſer for wronging her.

3 *Where ſmall faults are committed bluſhing obtaines a pardon of courſe with ingenuous beholders.* As if ſhe be guilty of caſuall incivilities, or ſolœciſmes in manners occaſioned by invincible ignorance, and unavoidable miſtakes, in ſuch a caſe bluſhing is a ſufficient penance to reſtore her to her ſtate of innocencie.

6 *She impriſons not her ſelf with a ſolemn vow never to marry.* For firſt, none know their own ſtrength herein. Who hath ſailed about the world of his own heart, ſounded each creek, ſurveied each corner, but that ſtill there remains therein much *terra incognita* to himſelf? Junius, at the firſt little better then a * Miſogyniſt, was afterwards ſo altered from himſelf, that he ſucceſſively married foure wives. Secondly, fleſhly corruption being pent will ſwell the more, and Shemei being confin'd to Jeruſalem will have the greater mind to gad to Gath. Thirdly, the devil will have a fairer ſet mark to ſhoot at, and will be moſt buſie to make people break their vow. Fourthly, God may juſtly deſert people for ſnatching that to themſelves, which is moſt proper for him to give, I mean, Continency. Object not, that thou wilt pray to him to take from thee all deſire of marriage, it being madneſſe to vow that one will not eat, and then pray to God that he may not

* *Junius in his life writ by himſelf.*

not be hungry. Neither say that now thou may'st presume on thy self, because thou art well stricken in years, for there may happen an autume-spring in thy soul; and lust is an unmannerly guest, we know not how late in the evening of our lives it may intrude into us for a lodging.

She counts it virginitie to be unspotted, not unmarried. Or else even in old age, when nature hath given an inhibition, they may be strong in desiring who are weak in acting of wickednesse; yea they may keep stews in their hearts, and be so pregnant and ingravidated with lustfull thoughts, that they may as it were die in travail because they cannot be delivered. And though there be no fire seen outwardly, as in the English chymnies, it may be hotter within, as in the Dutch stoves; and as well the devils as the Angels in heaven, *neither marry nor are given in marriage.* 7

As she lives with lesse care, so she dies with more cheerfulnesse. Indeed she was rather a sojourner, then an inhabitant in this world, and therefore forsakes it with the lesse grief. In a word, the way to heaven is alike narrow to all estates, but farre smoother to the Virgin then to the married. Now the great advantage Virgins have to serve God above others, & high favours he hath bestowed on some of them, shall appear in this Virgin prophetesse, whose life we come to present. 8

HILDEGARDIS *a Virgin Prophetess*, Abbess *of* St Ruperts *Nunnerye. She died at Bingen* Ao *Do: 1180. Aged 82 yeares.* *W. Marshall sculpsit.*

Chap. 13.

The life of Hildegardis.

Hildegardis was born in Germany, in the County of Spanheim, in the yeare 1098. So that she lived in an age which we may call the first cock-crowing after the midnight of Ignorance and Superstition.

Her parents (Hidebert, and Mechtilda) dedicated her to God from her infancie: And surely those whose Childhood, with Hildegardis, hath had the advantage of pious education may be said to have been

been good time out of mind, as not able to remember the beginning of their own goodnesse. At eight years of age she became a Nunne under S. Jutta sister to Megenhard, Earl of Spanheim, and afterwards she was made Abbesse of S. Ruperts Nunnery in Bingen on Rhene in the Palatinate.

Men commonly do beat and bruise their links before they light them, to make them burn the brighter: God first humbles and afflicts whom he intends to illuminate with more then ordinary grace. Poore Hildegardis was constantly and continually sick, and so * weak that she very seldome was strong enough to go. But God who denied her legs, gave her wings, and raised her high-mounted soul in Visions and Revelations.

* Fuerunt ei ab ipsa penè infantia crebri ac ferè continui languorum dolores, ità ut pedum incessu perraro uteretur, *Theod. Abbas in vita Hildegardis, lib.* 1. *cap.* 2.

I know a generall scandall is cast on Revelations in this ignorant age: first, because many therein intitled the Meteors of their own brain to be Starres at least, and afterwards their Revelations have been revealed to be forgeries: secondly, because that night-raven did change his black feathers into the silver wings of a dove, and transforming himself into an Angel of light deluded many with strange raptures and visions, though in their nature farre different from those in the Bible. For S. Paul in his Revelations was caught up into the third heaven; whereas most Monks with a contrary motion were carried into hell and purgatorie, and there saw apparitions of strange torments. Also S. Johns Revelation forbids all additions to the Bible, under heavie penalties; their visions are commonly on purpose to piece out the Scripture, and to establish such superstitions as have no footing in Gods word.

However all held Hildegardis for a Prophet, being induced thereunto by the piety of her life: no breck was ever found in her veil, so spotlesse was her conversation; by the sanctity of her writings, and by the generall approbation the Church gave unto her. For Pope Eugenius the third, after exact examination of the matter, did in the Councell of Trevers (wherein S. Bernard was present) allow and priviledge her Revelations for authenticall. She was of the Popes Conclave, and Emperours Counsel, to whom they had recourse in difficulties : yea the greatest torches of the Church lighted themselves at her candle. The Patriarch of Jerusalem, the Bishops of Mentz, Colen, Breme, Trevers sent such knots as posed their own fingers to our Hildegardis to untie.

*Tritbemius de Scriptor. Eccles. fol. 92.

She never learn'd word of Latine ; and yet * therein would she fluently expresse her Revelations to those notaries that took them from her mouth ; so that throwing words at randome she never brake Priscian's head : as if the Latine had learn'd to make it self true without the speakers care. And no doubt, he that brought the single parties to her married them also in her mouth, so that the same Spirit which furnished her with Latine words, made also the true Syntaxis. Let none object that her very writing of fifty eight Homilies on the Gospel is false construction, where the feminine Gender assumes an employment proper to men : for though S. Paul silenceth women for speaking in the Church, I know no Scripture forbids them from writing on Scripture.

Such infused skill she had also of Musick, whereof she was naturally ignorant, and wrote a whole book of verses very good according to those times. Indeed in that age the trumpet of the warlike Heroick, and the sweet harp of the Lyrick verse, were all turned into the gingling of Cymballs, tinckling with rhythmes, and like-sounding cadencies.

But let us heare a few lines of her Prophecies, and thence guesse the rest. *In those dayes there shall rise up a people without understanding, proud, covetous, and deceitfull, the which shall eat the sins of the people, holding a certain order of foolish de-*

votion

votion under the feigned cloke of beggery. Also they shall instantly preach without devotion or example of the holy Martyrs, and shall detract from the secular Princes, taking away the Sacraments of the Church from the true pastours, receiving almes of the poore, having familiarity with women, instructing them how they shall deceive their husbands, and rob their husbands to give it unto them, * &c. What could be said more plain to draw out to the life those Mendicant friers (rogues by Gods statutes) which afterwards swarm'd in the world.

* *See much more to this purpose in Catalog. Testium veritatis in Hildegarde: Also in Foxes Acts and monuments, p. 461.*

Heare also how she foretold the low water of Tiber, whilest as yet it was full tide there. *The Kings and other Rulers of the world, being stirred up by the just judgement of God, shall set themselves against them, and run upon them, saying, We will not have these men to reigne over us with their rich houses, and great possessions, and other worldly riches, over the which we are ordained to be Lords and Rulers: and how is it meet or comely that those shavelings with their stoles and chesils should have more souldiers or richer armour and artillery then we? wherefore let us take away from them what they do not justly but wrongfully possesse.*

It is well the Index expurgatorius was not up in those dayes, nor the Inquisition on foot, otherwise dame Hildegardis must have been call'd to an after account. I will onely ask a Romanist this question, This Prophesie of Hildegardis, was it from heaven or from men? If from heaven, why did ye not believe it? If from men, why did the Pope allow it, & canonize her?

As for miracles, which she wrought in her life time, their number is as admirable as their nature. I must confesse at my first reading * of them, my belief digested some but surfeted on the rest: for she made no more to cast out a devil, then a barber to draw a tooth, and with lesse pain to the patient. I never heard of a great feast made all of Cordialls: and it seems improbable that miracles (which in Scripture are used sparingly, and chiefly for conversion of unbelievers) should

* *In Lipoman. in vitis Sanct. Tom. 5 fol. 91. & sequen.*

ſhould be heaped ſo many together, made every dayes work, and by her commonly, conſtantly, and ordinarily, wrought. And I pray why is the Popiſh Church ſo barren of true works nowadayes here wrought at home amongſt us? For as for thoſe reported to be done farre of, it were ill for ſome if the gold from the Indies would abide the touch no better then the miracles.

However Hildegardis was a gratious Virgin, and God might perform ſome great wonders by her hand; but theſe *piæ fraudes* with their painting have ſpoyled the naturall complexion of many a good face, and have made Truth it ſelf ſuſpected. She dyed in the 82. yeare of her age, was afterwards Sainted by the Pope, and the 17 day of September aſsign'd to her memory.

I cannot forget how Udalrick Abbat of Kempten in Germany made a moſt * courteous law for the weaker ſexe, That no woman, guilty of what crime ſoever, ſhould ever be put to death in his dominions, becauſe two women condemn d to die were miraculouſly delivered out of the priſon by praying to S. Hildegardis.

* *Bruſchius Demonaſter. & Centuriatores, Centur.* 11. *Col.* 350.

Chap. 14.

The Elder Brother

IS one who made haſt to come into the world to bring his Parents the firſt news of male-poſterity, and is well rewarded for his tidings. His compoſition is then accounted moſt pretious when made of the loſſe of a double Virginitie.

Maxime 1

He is thankfull for the advantage God gave him at the ſtarting in the race into this world. When twinnes have been even match'd, one hath gained the gole but by his length. S. * Auguſtine ſaith, *That it is every mans bounden*

* *Queſtionibus ex utroque mixtim Tom.* 40 *Col.* 874.

bounden duty solemnly to celebrate his birth-day. If so, Elder Brothers may best afford good cheer on the festivall.

2 *He counts not his inheritance a Writ of ease to free him from industry*: As if onely the Younger Brothers came into the world to work, the Elder to complement. These are the Toppes of their houses indeed, like cotlofts, highest and emptiest. Rather he laboureth to furnish himself with all gentile accomplishment, being best able to go to the cost of learning. He need not fear to be served as Ulrick Fugger was (chief of the noble family of the Fuggers in Auspurg) who was disinherited of a great patrimony onely for his * studiousnesse, and expensivenesse in buying costly Manuscripts.

* *Thuan. de obit. vir. doct. in Ann.* 1584.

3 *He doth not so remember he is an Heire, that he forgets he is a Sonne*. Wherefore his carriage to his Parents is alwayes respectfull. It may chance that his father may be kept in a charitable Prison, whereof his Sonne hath the keyes; the old man being onely Tenant for life, and the lands entaild on our young Gentleman. In such a case when it is in his power, if necessity requires, he enlargeth his father to such a reasonable proportion of liberty as may not be injurious to himself.

4 *He rather desires his fathers Life then his Living*. This was one of the principall reasons (but God knows how true) why Philip the second, King of Spain, caused in the yeare 1568. Charles his Eldest Sonne to be executed for plotting his fathers death, as was pretended. And a * Wit in such difficult toyes accommodated the numerall letters in Ovids verse to the yeare wherein the Prince suffered.

* *Opmerus was the Authour thereof: Famianus Strada de bello Belgico lib. 7. pag.* 432.

FILIVs ante DIeM patrIos InqVIrIt In annos.
1568.

Before the-tIMe, the oVer-hasty sonne
Seeks forth hoVV near the fathers LIfe Is Done.
1568.

 But

But if they had no better evidence againſt him but this poeticall Synchroniſme, we might well count him a martyr.

5 *His fathers deeds and grants he ratifies and confirms.* If a ſtitch be fallen in a leaſe, he will not widen it into an hole by cavilling, till the whole ſtrength of the grant run out thereat; or take advantage of the default of the Clark in writing where the deed appears really done, and on a valuable conſideration: He counts himſelf bound in honour to perform what by marks and ſignes he plainly underſtands his father meant, though he ſpake it not out.

6 *He reflecteth his luſtre to grace and credit his younger brethren.* Thus Scipio Africanus, after his great victories againſt the Carthaginians and conquering of Hannibal, was content to ſerve as a * Lieutenant in the warres of Aſia, under Lucius Scipio his younger Brother.

* *Plutar. in the life of Scipio.*

7 *He relieveth his diſtreſſed kinred, yet ſo as he continues them in their calling.* Otherwiſe they would all make his houſe their hoſpitall, his kinred their calling. When one being an Husbandman challenged kinred of Robert Groſthead Biſhop of Lincoln, and thereupon requeſted favour of him to beſtow an office on him, *Couſen* (quoth the Biſhop) *if your cart be broken, I'le mend it; if your plough old, I'le give you a new one, and ſeed to ſow your land: but an Husbandman I found you, and an Husbandman I'le leave you.* It is better to eaſe poore kinred in their Profeſſion, then to eaſe them from their Profeſſion.

8 *He is carefull to ſupport the credit and dignity of his family:* neither waſting his paternall eſtate by his unthriftineſſe, nor marring it by parcelling his ancient mannours and demeſnes amongſt his younger children, whom he provides for by annuities, penſions, moneys, leaſes, and purchaſed lands. He remembers how when our King Alfred divided the river of Lee (which parts Hartfordſhire and Eſſex) into three ſtreams,

ſtreams, it became ſo ſhallow that boats could not row, where formerly ſhips did ride. Thus the ancient family of the Woodfords (which had long continued in Leiceſterſhire and elſewhere in England in great account, eſtate and livelihood) is at this day quite extinct. For when S^r^. Thomas Woodford in the reigne of King Henrie the ſixth made almoſt an even partition of his means betwixt his five Grandchildren, the Houſe in ſhort ſpace utterly decay'd; not any part of his lands now in the * tenure or name of any of his male line, ſome whereof lived to be brought to a low ebbe of fortune. Yet on the other ſide to leave all to the eldeſt, and make no proviſion for the reſt of their children, is againſt all rules of religion, forgetting their Chriſtian-name to remember their Sir-name.

* *Burton in his deſcrip. of Leiceſterſhire, p.264.*

Chap. 15.

The Younger Brother.

SOme account him the better Gentleman of the two, becauſe ſonne to the more ancient Gentleman. Wherein his Elder Brother can give him the hearing, and a ſmile into the bargain. He ſhares equally with his Elder Brother in the education, but differs from him in his portion, and though he giveth allſo his Fathers Armes, yet to uſe the Herauld's language, he may ſay,

> *This to my Elder Brother I muſt yield,*
> *I have the* Charge *but he hath all the* Field.

Like herein to a young nephew of Tarquines in Rome, who was called * *Egereus*, from wanting of maintenance, becauſe his Grandfather left him nothing. It was therefore a mannerly anſwer which a young Gentleman gave to King James, when he asked him what kinne he was to ſuch a Lord of his name: *Pleaſe your Majeſtie* (ſaid he) *my Elder Brother is his Couſen german.*

* *Livi. lib. 1.*

He

Maxime 1 *He repines not at the Providence of God in ordering his birth.* Heirs are made, even where matches are, both in heaven. Even in twinnes God will have one next the doore to come firſt into the world.

2 *He labours by his endeavours to date himſelf an Elder Brother.* Nature makes but one; Induſtry doth make all the ſonnes of the ſame man Heirs. The fourth Brother gives a Martilet for the difference of his Armes: a bird * obſerved to build either in Caſtles, Steeples, or Ships; ſhewing that the bearer hereof, being debarr'd from all hopes of his fathers inheritance, muſt ſeek by warre, learning, or merchandize to advance his eſtate.

* *Gerard Leigh in his 9. differences of Brothers Armes.*

3 *In warre he cuts out his fortunes with his own ſword.* William the Conquerour, when he firſt landed his forces in England, burnt all his ſhips; that deſpair to return might make his men the more valiant. Younger Brothers, being cut off at home frō all hopes, are more zealous to purchaſe an honourable ſupport abroad. Their ſmall Arteries with great Spirits have wrought miracles, & their reſolution hath driven ſucceſſe before it. Many of them have adventured to cheapen dear enterpriſes, & were onely able to pay the earneſt, yet fortune hath accepted them for chapmen, and hath freely forgiven thē the reſt of the payment for their boldnes.

4 *Nor are they leſſe happy if applying themſelves to their book.* Nature generally giving them good wits, which becauſe they want room to burniſh may the better afford to ſoar high.

5 *But he gaineth more wealth if betaking himſelf to merchandize.* Whence often he riſeth to the greateſt annuall honour in the kingdome. Many families in England though not firſt raiſed frō the City, yet thence have been ſo reſtored and enriched that it may ſeem to amount to an originall raiſing. Neither doth an apprentiſhip extinguiſh native, nor diſinable to acquiſitive Gentry; and they are much miſtaken who hold it to be in the nature of bondage. For firſt, his indenture is a civill

contract,

contract, whereof a bondman is uncapable: ſecondly, no work can be baſe preſcribed in reference to a noble end, as theirs is that learn an honeſt myſtery to inable them for the ſervice of God and the Countrey: thirdly, they give round ſummes of money to be bound. Now if apprentiſhip be a ſervitude, it is either a pleaſing bondage, or ſtrange madneſſe to purchaſe it at ſo dear a rate. Gentry therefore may be ſuſpended perchance, & aſleep during the apprentiſhip, but it awakens afterwards.

Sometimes he raiſeth his eſtate by applying himſelf to the 6
Court. A paſture wherein Elder Brothers are obſerved to grow lean, and Younger Brothers fat. The reaſons whereof may be theſe.

1 Younger Brothers, being but ſlender in eſtate, are eaſier bowed to a Court-complyance then Elder Brothers, who ſtand more ſtiff on their means, and think ſcorn to crave what may be a Princes pleaſure to grant, and their profit to receive.

2 They make the Court their calling, and ſtudie the myſterie thereof, whileſt Elder Brothers, divided betwixt the Court and the Countrey, can have their endeavours deep in neither, which run in a double channell.

3 Elder Brothers ſpend highly in proportion to their eſtates, expecting afterwards a return with increaſe, which notwithſtanding never payes the principall: and whileſt they thus build ſo ſtately a ſtair-caſe to their preferment, the Younger Brothers get up by the back ſtairs in a private ſilent way, little expence being expected from them that have little.

Sometimes he lighteth on a wealthy match to advance him. If 7
meeting with one that is Pilot of her own affections, to ſteer them without guidance of her friends, and ſuch as diſdaineth her marriage ſhould be contracted in an exchange, where joynture muſt weigh every grain even to the portion. Rather ſhe counts it an act both of love and charity to affect one rich in deſerts,

who commonly hath the advantage of birth, as ſhe hath of means, and ſo it's made levell betwixt them. And thus many a young Gentleman hath gotten honourable maintenance by an Heireſſe, eſpecially when the crying of the child hath cauſed the laughing of the father.

8 *His means the more hardly gotten are the more carefully kept.* Heat gotten by degrees, with motion and exerciſe, is more naturall and ſtayes longer by one, then what is gotten all at once by coming to the fire. Goods acquired by induſtry prove commonly more laſting then lands by deſcent.

9 *He ever owneth his Elder Brother with dutifull reſpect:* yea though God ſhould ſo bleſſe his endeavours as to go beyond him in wealth and honour. The pride of the Jeſuites is generally taxed, who being the youngeſt of all other Orders, and therefore by canon to go laſt, will never go in * Proceſsion with other Orders, becauſe they will not come behind them.

* *Vid. Preface to the Jeſuites Catechiſm.*

10 *Sometimes the Paternall inheritance falls to them who never hoped to riſe to it.* Thus John, ſirnamed Sans-terre, or, Without land, having five Elder Brothers came to the kingdome of England, death levelling thoſe which ſtood betwixt him and the Crown. It is obſerv'd of the * Coringtons, an ancient familie in Cornwall, that for eight lineall deſcents never any one that was born heir had the land, but it ever fell to Younger Brothers.

* *Carew Survey of Cornwall, fol. 117.*

To conclude, there is a hill in Voitland (a ſmall countrey in Germany) called *Feitchtelberg*, out of which ariſe foure rivers running foure ſeverall wayes, viz. 1. Eger, Eaſt, 2. Menus, Weſt, 3. *Sala*, North, & 4. Nabus, *South*: ſo that he that ſees their fountains ſo near together would admire at their falls ſo farre aſunder. Thus the younger ſons iſſuing out of the ſame mothers wombe and fathers loyns, and afterwards embracing different courſes to trie their fortunes abroad in the world, chance often to die farre off, at great diſtance, which were all born in the ſame place.

The Holy State.

THE SECOND BOOK.

CHAP. I.

*The good * Advocate.* * we take it promiscuously for Civil or Common Lawyer.

HE is one that will not plead that cause, wherein his tongue must be confuted by his conscience. It is the praise of the Spanish souldier, that(whilest all other Nations are mercenary, and for money will serve on any side) he will never fight against his own King : nor will our Advocate against the Sovereigne Truth, plainly appearing to his conscience.

He not onely hears but examines his Client, and pincheth the Maxime 1 *cause, where he fears it is foundred.* For many Clients in telling their case rather plead then relate it, so that the Advocate hears not the true state of it, till opened by the adverse party. Surely the Lawyer that fills himself with instructions will travell longest in the cause without tiring. Others that are so quick in searching, seldome search to the quick ; and those miraculous apprehensions who understand more then all, before the Client hath told half, runne without their errand, and will return without their answer.

If the matter be doubtfull, he will onely warrant his own di- 2 *ligence.* Yet some keep an Assurance-office in their chamber, and will warrant any cauſe brought unto them, as knowing that if they fail they loſe nothing but what long ſince was loſt, their credit.

3 *He makes not a Trojan-ſiege of a ſuit, but ſeeks to bring it to a ſet battel in a ſpeedy triall.* Yet ſometimes ſuits are continued by their difficulty, the potencie and ſtomach of the parties, without any default in the Lawyer. Thus have there depended ſuits in * Glocester-ſhire, betwixt the Heirs of the Lord Barkley, and S[r]. Thomas Talbot Viſcount Liſle, ever ſince the reigne of King Edward the fourth untill now lately they were finally compounded.

* *Cambdens Brit. in Glocest.*

4 *He is faithfull to the ſide that firſt retains him.* Not like * Demoſthenes, who ſecretly wrote one oration for Phormio, and another in the ſame matter for Apolidorus his adverſary.

* *Plutarch. in vita Demoſth.*

5 *In pleading he ſhoots fairly at the head of the cauſe, and having faſtened, no frowns nor favours ſhall make him let go his hold.* Not ſnatching aſide here and there, to no purpoſe, ſpeaking little in much, as it was ſaid of Anaximenes, *That he had a flood of words, and a drop of reaſon.* His boldneſſe riſeth or falleth as he apprehends the goodneſſe or badneſſe of his cauſe.

6 *He joyes not to be retain'd in ſuch a ſuit, where all the right in queſtion, is but a drop blown up with malice to be a bubble.* Wherefore in ſuch triviall matters he perſwades his Client to ſound a retreat, and make a compoſition.

7 *When his name is up, his induſtry is not down, thinking to plead not by his ſtudy but his credit.* Commonly Phyſicians like beer are beſt when they are old, & Lawyers like bread when they are young and new. But our Advocate grows not lazie. And if a leading caſe be out of the road of his practice, he will take pains to trace it thorow his books, and prick the footſteps thereof whereſoever he finds it.

8 *He is more carefull to deſerve, then greedy to take fees.* He accounts the very pleading of a poore widows honeſt

cauſe

cause sufficient fees, as conceiving himself then the King of Heavens Advocate, bound *ex officio* to prosecute it. And although some may say that such a Lawyer may even go live in Cornwall, where it is * observed that few of that profession hitherto have grown to any great livelihood, yet shall he (besides those two felicities of * common Lawyers, that they seldome die either without heirs or making a will) find Gods blessing on his provisions and posterity.

* *Carew Sur. of Cornwall, fol.* 60.

* *Coke in his Preface to Littletons Tenures.*

We will respit him a while till he comes to be a Judge, and then we will give an example of both together.

CHAP. 2.
The good Physician.

Maxime 1 HE *trusteth not the single witnesse of the water if better testimony may be had.* For reasons drawn from the urine alone are as brittle as the urinall. Sometimes the water runneth in such post-hast through the sick mans body, it can give no account of any thing memorable in the passage, though the most judicious eye examine it. Yea the sick man may be in the state of death, and yet life appear in his state.

2 *Coming to his patient he perswades him to put his trust in God the fountain of health.* The neglect hereof hath caused the bad successe of the best Physicians : for God will manifest that though skill comes mediately from him to be gotten by mans pains, successe comes from him immediately to be disposed at his pleasure.

3 *He hansells not his new experiments on the bodies of his patients* ; letting loose mad receipts into the sick mans body, to try how well Nature in him will fight against them, whilest himself stands by and sees the battel, except it be in desperate cases when death must be expell'd by death.

4 *To poore people he prescribes cheap but wholesome medicines* : not

not removing the consumption out of their bodies into their purses; nor sending them to the East Indies for drugs, when they can reach better out of their gardens.

5 *Lest his Apothecary should oversee, he oversees his Apothecary.* For though many of that profession be both able and honest, yet some out of ignorance or haste may mistake: witnesse one of Bloys,* who being to serve a Doctours bill, in stead of *Optimi* (short written) read *Opii*, and had sent the patient asleep to his grave, if the Doctours watchfulnesse had not prevented him; worse are those who make wilfull errours, giving one thing for another. A prodigall who had spent his estate was pleased to jeer himself, boasting that he had cosened those who had bought his means; They gave me (said he) good new money, and I sold them my Great-great-grandfathers old land. But this cosenage is too too true in many Apothecaries, selling to sick folk for new money antiquated drugs, and making dying mens Physick of dead ingredients.

*Stephens Apology for Herodotus, lib. 1. cap. 16.

6 *He brings not news with a false spie that the coast is clear till death surprises the sick man.* I know Physicians love to make the best of their patients estate. First 'tis improper that *Adjutores vitæ* should be *Nuncii mortis*. Secondly, none, with their good will, will tell bad news. Thirdly, their fee may be the worse for't. Fourthly, 'tis a confessing that their art is conquer'd. Fifthly, it will poyson their patients heart with grief, and make it break before the time. However they may so order it, that the party may be inform'd of his dangerous condition, that he be not outed of this world before he be provided for another.

7 *When he can keep life no longer in, he makes a fair & easie passage for it to go out.* He giveth his attendance for the facilitating and asswaging of the pains and agonies of death. Yet generally 'tis death to a Physician to be with a dying man.

Vnworthy

Unworthy pretenders to Physick are rather foils then stains to the Profession. Such a one was that counterfeit, who called himself *The Baron of* Blackamore,* and feigned he was sent from the Emperour to our young King Henry the sixth, to be his principall Physician : but his forgery being discovered, he was apprehended, and executed in the Tower of London, *Anno* 1426. and such the world daily swarms with. Well did the Poets feigne Æsculapius and Circe, brother and sister, and both children of the Sunne : for in all times in the opinion of the multitude, witches, old women, and impostours have had a competition with Physicians. And commonly the most ignorant are the most confident in their undertakings, and will not stick to tell you what disease the gall of a dove is good to cure. He took himself to be no mean Doctour, who being guilty of no Greek, and being demanded why it was called an *Hectick fever* ; *because* (saith he) *of an hecking cough which ever attendeth that disease.* And here it will not be amisse to describe the life of the famous Quack-salver Paracelsus, both because it is not ordinarily to be met with, and that men may see what a monster many make a miracle of learning, and propound him their pattern in their practice. 8

* *Stowes Survey of London. pag.* 55.

CHAP. 3.

Physick Proffessor at Basil.
Philip Theophrastus PARACELSUS *He died at Saltzburge An^o. Dom: 1540. aged 47 yeares.*
W. Marshall sculpsit.

CHAP. 3.

The life of PARACELSUS.

PHilip Theophrastus Bombastus of Hoenhaim, or Paracelsus, born as he saith himself in the wildernesse of Helvetia, *Anno* 1493. of the noble and ancient family of the Hoenhaims. But Thomas Erastus making strict enquiry after his pedigree found none of his name or kinred in that place. Yet it is fit so great a Chymist should make himself to be of noble extraction: And let us believe him to be of high descent,

ſcent, as perchance born on ſome mountain in Switzerland.

As for his Education, he himſelf * boaſts that he lived in moſt Univerſities of Europe; ſurely rather as a traveller then a ſtudent, and a vagrant then a traveller. Yea ſome will not allow him ſo much, and * one who hath exactly meaſured the length of his life, though crowding his pretended travells very cloſe, finds not room enough for them. But 'tis too ridiculous what a * Scholar of his relates, that he lived ten years in Arabia to get learning, and converſed in Greece with the Athenian Philoſophers. Whereas in that age Arabia the Happy was accurſed with Barbariſme, and Athens grown a ſtranger to her ſelf; both which places being then ſubjected to the Turks, the very ruines of all learning were ruin'd there. Thus we ſee how he better knew to act his part, then to lay his Scene, and had not Chronologie enough to tell the clock of time, when and where to place his lies to make them like truth.

The firſt five & twenty years of his age he lived very civilly; being thirty years old he came to Baſill, juſt at the alteration of Religion, when many Papiſts were expell'd the Univerſity, and places rather wanted Profeſſours, then Profeſſours places. Here by the favour of Oecolampadius he was admitted to reade Phyſick, & for two years behaved himſelf fairly, till this accident cauſed his departure. A rich * Canon of Baſill being ſick promiſed Paracelſus an hundred florens to recover him, which being reſtored to his health he denied to pay. Paracelſus ſues him, is caſt in his ſuit, the Magiſtrate adjudging him onely an ordinary fee, becauſe the cure was done preſently with a few pills. The Phyſician enraged hereat talked treaſon againſt the State in all his diſcourſes, till the nimbleneſſe of his tongue forc'd the nimbleneſſe of his feet, and he was fain to fly into Alſatia. Here keeping company with

I the

* *In præfatione Chirurgia magnæ.*

* *Sennertus de Chymicorum conſenſu, cap. 4. pag. 35.*

* *Bickerus in Hermete redivivo.*

* *Bezoldus conſideratione vitæ & mort. p. 76, ex Andrea Jociſco.*

the Gentry of the countrey, he gave himſelf over to all licentiouſneſſe: His body was the ſea wherein the tide of drunkenneſſe was ever ebbing and flowing; for by putting his finger in his throat he uſed to ſpew out his drink and drunkenneſſe together, and from that inſtant date himſelf ſober to return to his cups again. Every moneth he had a new ſute, not for pride but neceſsity; his apparel ſerving both for wearing and bedding: and having given his clothes many vomits, he gave them to the poore. Being Codrus over night, he would be Crœſus in the morning, fluſh of money as if he carried the inviſible Indies in his pocket: ſome ſuſpected the devil was his purſebearer, and that he carried a ſpirit in the pomel of his ſword his conſtant companion, whileſt others mainta in that by the heat of the furnace he could ripen any metall into gold.

All the diet he preſcribed his patients was this, to eat what, and how often, they thought fitting themſelves, and yet he did moſt ſtrange cures. Like the quickſilver (he ſo much dealt with) he would never be fixt in one place, or live any where longer then a twelvemoneth: for ſome obſerve that by that time the maladies reverted again, which he formerly cured. He gave ſo ſtrong phyſick as ſummoned Nature with all her force to expell the preſent diſeaſe, but the remnant dregs thereof afterwards reinforcing themſelves did aſſault Nature tired out with the violence of her former task, and eaſily ſubdued it.

His Scholars brag that the fragments of his learning would feaſt all the Philoſophers in the world, boaſting that the gout, the diſgrace of Phyſick, was the honour of Paracelſus, who by curing it removed that ſcandall from his profeſsion: whereas others ſay he had little Learning, and leſſe Latine. When any asked him the name of an herb he knew not, he would tell them there was no * uſe thereof in Phyſick;

* *Beroldus ut prius, pag. 77.*

and

and yet this man would undertake not onely to cure men, but to cure the Art of curing men, and reform Physick it self.

As for his religion, it would as well pose himself as others to tell what it was. He boasted that shortly he would order Luther and the Pope, as well as he had done Galen and Hippocrates. He was never seen to pray, and seldome came to Church. He was not onely skilled in naturall Magick (the utmost bounds whereof border on the suburbs of hell) but is charged to converse constantly with familiars. Guilty hewas of all vices but wantonnesse; and I find an * honest man his Compurgatour, that he was not given to women; perchance he drank himself into wantonnesse and past it, quenching the fire of his lust by piling fuell too hard and fast upon it.

* *Oporinus in Epist. de Paracelso.*

Boasting that he could make a man immortall, he himself died at fourty seven years in the City of Saltzburg. His Scholars say he was poysoned through the envy (that dark shadow ever waiting on a shining merit) and malice of his adversaries. However his body should have been so fenced with antidotes, that the battery of no poyson might make a breach therein; except we impute it more to his neglect then want of skill, and that rather his own security then his enemies malice brought him to his grave. But it may be he was willing to die, counting a twelvemoneths time enough to stay in one place, and fourty seven years long enough to live in one world. We may more admire that so beastly a drunkard lived so long, then that so skilfull a man died so soon. In a word, He boasted of more then he could do, did more cures seemingly then really, more cures really then lawfully; of more parts then learning, of more fame then parts; a better Physician then a man, and a better Chirurgeon then Physician.

Chap. 4.

The Controversiall Divine.

HE is Truths Champion to defend her against all adversaries, Atheists, Hereticks, Schismaticks, and Erroneous persons whatsoever. His sufficiency appears in Opposing, Answering, Moderating, and Writing.

Maxime 1 *He engageth both his judgement, and affections in opposing of falsehood.* Not like countrey Fencers, who play onely to make sport, but like Duellers indeed, at it for life and limbe; chiefly if the question be of large prospect, and great concernings, he is zealous in the quarrell. Yet some, though their judgement weigh down on one side, the beam of their affections stands so even, they care not which part prevails.

2 *In opposing a truth, he dissembles himself her foe, to be her better friend.* Wherefore he counts himself the greatest conquerour when Truth hath taken him captive. With Joseph having sufficiently sifted the matter in a
* Gen. 45. 4. disguise, he discovereth himself, * *I am Joseph your brother,* and then throws away his visard. Dishonest they, who though the debt be satisfied will never give up the bond, but continue wrangling, when the objection is answered.

3 *He abstains from all foul and railing language.* What? make the Muses, yea the Graces scolds? Such purulent spittle argues exulcerated lungs. Why should there be so much railing about the body of Christ? when there was none about the body of Moses in the Act kept betwixt the devil and Michael the Archangel.

4 *He tyrannizeth not over a weak and undermatch'd Adversary;* but seeks rather to cover his weaknesse if he be a modest man. When a Professour pressed an Answerer

er (a better Chriſtian then a Clerk) with an hard argument, *Reverende Profeſſor* (ſaid he), *ingenue confiteor me non poſſe reſpondere huic argumento.* To whom the Profeſſour, *Recte reſpondes.*

In anſwering he ſtates the queſtion, and expoundeth the terms 5
thereof. Otherwiſe the diſputants ſhall end, where they ought to have begun, in differences about words, and be Barbarians each to other, ſpeaking in a Language neither underſtand. If the Queſtion alſo be of Hiſtoricall cognizanſe, he ſhews the pedigree thereof, who firſt brew'd it, who firſt broch'd it, and ſends the wandring Errour with a paſport home to the place of its birth.

In taking away an objection he not onely puts by the thruſt, 6
but breaks the weapon. Some rather eſcape then defeat an argument, and though by ſuch an evaſion they may ſhut the mouth of the Opponent, yet may they open the difficulty wider in the hearts of the hearers. But our Anſwerer either fairly reſolves the doubt ; or elſe ſhews the falſeneſſe of the argument, by beggering the Opponent to maintain ſuch a fruitfull generation of abſurdities, as his argument hath begotten ; or laſtly returns and retorts it back upon him again. The firſt way unties the knot ; the ſecond cuts it aſunder ; the third whips the Opponent with the knot himſelf tyed. Sure 'tis more honour to be a clear Anſwerer, then a cunning Oppoſer, becauſe the latter takes advantage of mans ignorance, which is ten times more then his knowledge.

What his anſwers want in ſuddenneſſe they have in ſolidity. 7
Indeed the ſpeedy anſwer addes luſtre to the diſputation, and honour to the diſputant ; yet he makes good payment, who though he cannot preſently throw the money out of his pocket, yet will pay it, if but going home to unlock his cheſt. Some that are not for ſpeedy may be for ſounder performance. When Melanchthon at the diſputation of Ratisbon was

preſſed with a ſhrewd argument by Ecchius, I will anſwer thee, ſaid he, to morrow. Nay, ſaid Ecchius, do it now or it's nothing worth. Yea, ſaid Melanchthon, I ſeek the Truth, and not mine own Credit, and therefore it will be as good if I anſwer thee to * morrow by Gods aſsiſtance.

* *Melchior Adam. in vitu Germ. Theolog. p.* 339.

8 *In moderating he ſides with the Anſwerer, if the Anſwerer ſides with the truth.* But if he be conceited, & opinioned of his own ſufficiency, he lets him ſwound before he gives him any hot water. If a Paradox-monger, loving to hold ſtrange yea dangerous Opinions, he counts it charity to ſuffer ſuch a one to be beaten without mercy, that he may be weaned from his wilfulneſſe. For the main, he is ſo a ſtaff to the Anſwerer, that he makes him ſtand on his own legs.

9 *In writing, his Latine is pure, ſo farre as the ſubject will allow.* For thoſe who are to climbe the Alpes are not to expect a ſmooth and even way. True it is that Schoolmen, perceiving that fallacy had too much covert under the nap of flouriſhing Language, uſed thredbare Latine on purpoſe, and cared not to treſpaſſe on Grammar, and tread down the fences thereof to avoid the circuit of words, and to go the neareſt way to expreſſe their conceits. But our Divine though he uſeth barbarous School-terms, which like ſtanders are fixt to the controverſie, yet in his moveable Latine, paſſages, and digreſsions his ſtyle is pure and elegant.

10 *He affects clearneſſe and plainneſſe in all his writings.* Some mens heads are like the world before God ſaid unto it, *Fiat lux.* Theſe dark-lanterns may ſhine to themſelves, and underſtand their own conceits, but no body elſe can have light from them. Thus Matthias Farinator Profeſſour at Vienna, aſsiſted with ſome other learned men, as the Times then went, was thirty years making a book of applying Plato's, Ariſtotle's, and Galen's rules in Philoſophy, to Chriſt and his Prophets, and 'tis call'd * *Lumen animæ ; quo tamen nihil eſt caliginoſius,*

* *Mercator Atlas in the deſcrip. of Auſtria.*

caliginosius, labore magno, sed ridiculo, & inani. But this obscurity is worst when affected, when they do as Persius, of whom * one saith, *Legi voluit quæ scripsit, intelligi noluit quæ legerentur.* Some affect this darknesse, that they may be accounted profound, whereas one is not bound to believe that all the water is deep that is muddy.

* *Scalig. de Arte poet. lib. 6. c. 6.*

11 *He is not curious in searching matters of no moment.* Captain Martin * Forbisher fetcht from the farthest northern Countries a ships lading of minerall stones (as he thought) which afterwards were cast out to mend the high wayes. Thus are they served, and misse their hopes, who long seeking to extract hidden mysteries out of nice questions, leave them off, as uselesse at last. Antoninus Pius, for his desire to search to the least differences, was called *Cumini sector*, the Carver of cummine seed. One need not be so accurate: for as soon shall one scowr the spots out of the moon, as all ignorance out of man. When Eunomius the Heretick vaunted that he knew God and his divinity, S. * Basil gravells him in 21 questions about the body of an ant or pismire: so dark is mans understanding. I wonder therefore at the boldnesse of some, who as if they were Lord Mashalls of the Angels place them in ranks and files. Let us not believe them here, but rather go to heaven to confute them.

* *Cambdens Elisab. anno.* 1576.

* *Epist.* 168. *quæ est ad Eunomium.*

12 *He neither multiplies needlesse, nor compounds necessary Controversies.* Sure they light on a labour in vain, who seek to make a bridge of reconciliation over the μέγα χάσμα betwixt Papists and Protestants; for though we go 99 steps, they (I mean their Church) will not come one to give us a meeting. And as for the offers of Clara's and private men (besides that they seem to be more of the nature of baits then gifts) they may make large profers, without any Commission to treat, and so the Romish Church not bound to pay their promises. In * Merionethshire in Wales there are high mountains,

* *Giraldus Camb. in descr. of Wales.*

mountains, whoſe hanging tops come ſo cloſe together that ſhepherds on the tops of ſeverall hills may audibly talk together,yet will it be a dayes journey for their bodies to meet, ſo vaſt is the hallowneſſe of the vallies betwixt them. Thus upon ſound ſearch ſhall we find a grand diſtance and remoteneſſe betwixt Popiſh and Proteſtant tenents to reconcile them, which at the firſt view may ſeem near, and tending to an accomodation.

13 *He is reſolute and ſtable in fundamentall points of Religion.* Theſe are his fixed poles,and axletree about which he moves, whileſt they ſtand unmoveable. Some ſail ſo long on the Sea of controverſies, toſſ'd up and down, to and fro, *Pro* and *Con*, that the very ground to them ſeems to move, and their judgements grow ſcepticall and unſtable in the moſt ſettled points of Divinity. When he cometh to Preach, eſpecially if to a plain Auditory, with the Paracelſians he extracts an oyl out of the drieſt and hardeſt bodies, and knowing that knotty timber is unfit to build with, he edifies people with eaſie and profitable matter.

CHAP. 5.

Chap. 5.

The life of Dr. VVhitaker.

WIlliam Whitaker born at Holm in the County of Lancaſter of good parentage, eſpecially by his mothers ſide, allied to two worſhipfull families. His reverend unckle, Alexander Nowell, Dean of S. Pauls (the firſt fruits of the Engliſh Confeſſours in the dayes of Queen Marie, who after her death firſt return'd into England from beyond the Seas) took him young from his parents, ſent him firſt to Pauls

School, thence to Trinity Colledge in Cambridge; where he ſo profited in his ſtudies, that he gave great promiſes of his future perfection.

I paſſe by his youthfull exerciſes, never ſtriving for the garland, but he wonne and wore it away. His prime appearing to the world, was when he ſtood for the Profeſſours place againſt two Competitours, in age farre his ſuperiours. But the ſeven Electours in the Univerſitie who were to chooſe the Emperour of the Schools, preferring a golden head before ſilver hairs, conferr'd the place on Whitaker; and the ſtrict form of their Election hath no room for corruption. He ſo well acquitted himſelf in the place that he anſwered expectation, the ſtrongeſt opponent in all diſputes and lectures, and by degrees taught envie to admire him.

By this time the Papiſts began to aſſault him, and the Truth. Firſt Campian, one fitter for a Trumpeter then a Souldier, whoſe beſt ability was that he could boaſt in good Latine, being excellent at the flat hand of Rhetorick (which rather gives pats then blows) but he could not bend his fiſt to diſpute. Whitaker both in writing and diſputing did teach him, that it was eaſier to make then maintain a challenge againſt our Church; and in like manner he handled both Duræus, and Sanders, who ſucceſsively undertook the ſame cauſe, ſolidly confuting their arguments.

But theſe Teazers, rather to rouze then pinch the Game, onely made Whitaker find his ſpirits. The fierceſt dog is behind even Bellarmine himſelf, a great ſcholar, and who wanted nothing but a good cauſe to defend, and generally writing ingeniouſly, uſing ſometimes ſlenting, ſeldome down-right railing. Whitaker gave him all fair quarter, ſtating the queſtion betwixt them, yielding all which the other in reaſon could ask, and agreeing on terms to fall out with him, plaid fairly but fiercely on him, till the other forſook the field.

Bellarmine

Bellarmine had no mind to reinforce his routed arguments, but rather consigned over that service to a new Generall, Stapleton an English man: He was born the same * yeare and moneth wherein S^r. Thomas More was beheaded, an observation little lesse then mysticall with the Papists, as if God had substituted him to grow up in the room of the other for the support of the Catholick cause. If Whitaker in answering him put more gall then usuall into his ink, Stapleton (whose mouth was as foul as his cause) first infected him with bitternesse: and none will blame a man for arming his hands with hard and rough gloves, who is to meddle with bryers and brambles.

* *Pitzeus, De illust. Angl. scrip. Ætat. 16. pag. 796.*

Thus they baited him constantly with fresh dogs: None that ran at him once desired a second course at him; and as * one observes, *Cum nullo hoste unquam conflixit, quem non fudit & fugavit.*

* *Davenant. in Præfat. De Judice & Norma fidei.*

He filled the Chair with a gracefull presence, so that one needed not to do with him as * Luther did with Melanchthon when he first heard him reade, abstract the opinion and sight of his stature and person, lest the meannesse thereof should cause an undervaluing of him: for our Whitakers person carried with it an excellent port. His style was manly for the strength, maidenly for the modesty, and elegant for the phrase thereof; shewing his skill in spinning a fine thred out of course wool, for such is controversiall matter. He had by his second wife, a modest woman, eight children. It being true of him also, what is said of the famous Lawyer * Andreas Tiraquillus, *singulis annis singulos libros & liberos Reipublicæ dedit.*

* *In epist. ad Spalatinum.*

* *Thuanus, obit. doct. vir. anno 1558.*

My Father hath told me, that he often wished that he might lose so much Learning as he had gotten in after-supper studies, on condition he might gain so much strength as he had lost thereby. Indeed his body was strongly built for the naturall temper, and well repair'd by his temperate diet and recreations; but first he foundred the foundation of this house by immoderate study, and at last the roof was set on fire by a hot disease.

The unhappy controversie was then started, Whether justifying faith may be lost. And this thorny question would not suffer our Nightingale to sleep. He was sent for up by Arch-bishop Whitgift to the conference at Lambeth, after which returning home, unseasonable riding, late studying, and night-watching brought him to a burning-fever, to which his body was naturally disposed, as appeared by the mastery of rednesse in his complexion. Thus lost he the health of his body, in maintaining, That the health of the soul could not be lost. All agreed that he should be let bloud; which might then easily have been done, but was deferred by the fault of some about him, till it was too late. Thus, when God intends to cut a mans life off, his dearest friends by dangerous involuntarie mistakes shall bring the knife. He died in the 47. yeare of his age, *Anno Dom.* 1595. and in S. Johns Colledge (whereof he was Master) was solemnly interred, with the grief of the University, and whole Church of God.

Chap. 6.

Chap. 6.

The true Church Antiquary.

HE is a traveller into former times, whence he hath learnt their language and faſhions. If he meets with an old manuſcript, which hath the mark worn out of its mouth, and hath loſt the date, yet he can tell the age thereof either by the phraſe or character.

He baits at middle Antiquity, but lodges not till he comes at that which is ancient indeed. Some ſcoure off the ruſt of old inſcriptions into their own ſouls, cankering themſelves with ſuperſtition, having read ſo often *Orate pro anima*, that at laſt they fall a praying for the departed; and they more lament the ruine of Monaſteryes, then the decay and ruine of Monks lives, degenerating from their ancient piety and painfulneſſe. Indeed a little skill in Antiquity inclines a man to Popery; but depth in that ſtudy brings him about again to our religion. A Nobleman who had heard of the extreme age of one dwelling not farre off, made a journey to viſit him, and finding an aged perſon ſitting in the chimney-corner, addreſſed himſelf unto him with admiration of his age, till his miſtake was rectified: for, *Oh S^r*, (ſaid the young-old man) *I am not he whom you ſeek for, but his ſonne; my father is farther off in the field.* The ſame errour is daily cõmitted by the Romiſh Church, adoring the reverend brow and gray hairs of ſome ancient Ceremonyes, perchance but of ſome ſeven or eight hundred years ſtanding in the Church, and miſtake theſe for their fathers, of farre greater age in the Primitive times. Maxime 1.

He deſires to imitate the ancient Fathers, as well in their Piety, as in their Poſtures. Not onely conforming his hands and knees, but chiefly his heart to their 2 pattern. O the holinesse of their living and painfulnesse of their preaching! how full were they of mortified thoughts, and heavenly meditations! Let us not make the ceremoniall part of their lives onely Canonicall, and the morall part thereof altogether Apocrypha, imitating their devotion not in the finenesse of the stuff, but onely in the fashion of the making.

3 *He carefully marks the declination of the Church from the Primitive purity.* Observing how sometimes humble devotion was contented to lie down, whilest proud superstition got on her back. Yea not onely Frederick the Emperour, but many a godly Father some hundreds of years before held the Pope s stirrop, and by their well-meaning simplicity gave occasion to his future greatnesse. He takes notice how their Rhetorical hyperboles were afterwards accounted the just measure of dogmaticall truths; How plain people took them at their word in their funerall apostrophes to the dead; How praying for the departed brought the fuell, under which after-ages kindled the fire of Purgatory; How one Ceremony begat another, there being no bounds in will-worship, wherewith one may sooner be wearied then satisfied; the inventours of new Ceremonyes endeavouring to supply in number, what their conceits want in solidity; How mens souls being in the full speed and career of the Historicall use of Pictures could not stop short, but must lash out into superstition, vailing their bonnets to Rome in civill courtesie, when making honourable mention thereof, are interpreted by modern Papists to have done it in adoration of the idole of the Popes infallibility. All these things he ponders in his heart, observing both the times and places, when and where they happened.

4 *He is not zealous for the introducing of old uselesse Ceremonies.* The mischief is, some that are most violent to bring

bring ſuch in, are moſt negligent to preach the cautions in uſing them; and ſimple people, like Children in eating of fiſh, ſwallow bones and all to their danger of choking. Beſides, what is obſerved of horſe-hairs, that lying nine dayes in water they turn to ſnakes; ſo ſome Ceremonies though dead at firſt, in continuance of time quicken, get ſtings, and may do much miſchief, eſpecially if in ſuch an age wherein the meddling of ſome have juſtly awaked the jealouſie of all. When many Popiſh tricks are abroad in the countrey; if then men meet with a Ceremony which is a ſtranger, eſpecially if it can give but a bad account of it ſelf, no wonder if the watch take it up for one on ſuſpicion.

He is not peremptory but conjecturall in doubtfull mat- 5
ters. Not forcing others to his own opinion; but leaving them to their own libertie; not filling up all with his own conjectures to leave no room for other men: nor tramples he on their credits, if in them he finds ſlips and miſtakes. For here our ſouls have but one eye (the Apoſtle ſaith, *we know in part*) be not proud if that chance to come athwart thy ſeeing ſide, which meets with the blind ſide of another.

He thankfully acknowledgeth thoſe by whom he hath profited. 6
Baſe natured they, who when they have quenched their own thirſt, ſtop up, at leaſt muddy, the fountain. But our Antiquary, if he be not the firſt Founder of a commendable conceit, contents himſelf to be a Benefactour to it in clearing and adorning it.

He affects not phancy-full ſingularity in his behaviour: Nor 7
cares he to have a proper mark in writing of words, to diſguiſe ſome peculiar letter from the ordinary character. Others, for fear travellers ſhould take no notice that skill in Antiquity dwells in ſuch an head, hang out an antique hat for the ſigne, or uſe ſome

obſolete

obſolete garb in their garments, geſtures, or diſcourſe.

8 *He doth not ſo adore the Ancients as to deſpiſe the Modern.* Grant them but dwarfs, yet ſtand they on giants ſhoulders, and may ſee the further. Sure, as ſtout champions of Truth follow in the rere, as ever march'd in the front. Beſides, as * one excellently obſerves, *Antiquitas ſeculi juventus mundi.* Theſe times are the ancient times, when the world is ancient; and not thoſe which we count ancient *ordine retrogrado*, by a computation backwards from our ſelves.

* *Sr. Fran. Ba on Advance. of learn. p. 46.*

Chap. 7.

The generall Artiſt.

I Know the generall cavill againſt generall learning is this, that *aliquis in omnibus eſt nullus in ſingulis*. He that ſips of many arts, drinks of none. However we muſt know, that all learning, which is but one grand Science, hath ſo homogeneall a body, that the parts thereof do with a mutuall ſervice relate to, and communicate ſtrength and luſtre each to other. Our Artiſt knowing language to be the key of learning, thus begins.

Maxime 1 *His tongue being but one by nature he gets cloven by art and induſtry.* Before the confuſion of Babel, all the world was one continent in language; ſince divided into ſeverall tongues, as ſeverall ilands. Grammer is the ſhip, by benefit whereof we paſſe from one to another, in the learned languages generally ſpoken in no countrey. His mother-tongue was like the dull muſick of a monochord, which by ſtudy he turns into the harmony of ſeverall inſtruments.

2 *He firſt gaineth skill in the Latine and Greek tongues.* On the

the credit of the former alone, he may trade in diſcourſe over all Chriſtendome: But the Greek, though not ſo generally ſpoken, is known with no leſſe profit, and more pleaſure. The joynts of her compounded words are ſo naturally oyled, that they run nimbly on the tongue; which makes them though long never tedious, becauſe ſignificant. Beſides, it is full and ſtately in ſound: onely it pities our Artiſt to ſee the vowels therein rackt in pronouncing them, hanging oftentimes one way by their native force, and haled another by their accents which countermand them.

Hence he proceeds to the Hebrew, the mother-tongue of the world. More pains then quickneſſe of wit is required to get it, and with daily exerciſe he continues it. Apoſtacy herein is uſuall to fall totally from the language by a little neglect. As for the Arabick, and other Orientall languages, he rather makes ſallies and incurſions into them, then any ſolemn ſitting down before them. 3

Then he applies his ſtudy to Logick, and Ethicks. The latter makes a mans ſoul mannerly & wiſe; but as for Logick, that is the armory of reaſon, furniſhed with all offenſive and defenſive weapons. There are Syllogiſmes, long ſwords; Enthymems, ſhort daggers; Dilemma's, two-edged ſwords that cut on both ſides; Sorites, chain-ſhot: And for the defenſive, Diſtinctions, which are ſhields; Retortions, which are targets with a pike in the midſt of them, both to defend and oppoſe. From hence he raiſeth his ſtudies to the knowledge of Phyſicks, the great hall of Nature, and Metaphyſicks the cloſet thereof; and is carefull not to wade therein ſo farre, till by ſubtle diſtinguiſhing of notions he confounds himſelf. 4

He is skilfull in Rhetorick, which gives a ſpeech colour, as Logick doth favour, and both together beauty. Though ſome condemne Rhetorick as the mother of lies, ſpeaking more then the truth in Hyperboles, leſſe in her Mioſis, 5 otherwiſe in her metaphors, contrary in her ironies; yet is there excellent uſe of all theſe, when diſpoſed of with judgement. Nor is he a ſtranger to Poetry, which is muſick in words; nor to Muſick, which is poetry in ſound: both excellent ſauce, but they have liv'd and died poore, that made them their meat.

6 *Mathematicks he moderately ſtudieth to his great contentment.* Uſing it as ballaſt for his ſoul, yet to fix it not to ſtall it; nor ſuffers he it to be ſo unmannerly as to juſtle out other arts. As for judiciall Aſtrology (which hath the leaſt judgement in it) this vagrant hath been whipt out of all learned corporations. If our Artiſt lodgeth her in the out-rooms of his ſoul for a night or two, it is rather to heare then believe her relations.

7 *Hence he makes his progreſſe into the ſtudy of Hiſtory.* Neſtor, who lived three ages, was accountedthe wiſeſt man in the world. But the Hiſtorian may make himſelf wiſe by living as many ages as have paſt ſince the beginning of the world. His books enable him to maintain diſcourſe, who beſides the ſtock of his own experience may ſpend on the common purſe of his reading. This directs him in his life, ſo that he makes the ſhipwracks of others ſea-marks to himſelf; yea accidents which others ſtart from for their ſtrangenes, he welcomes as his wonted acquaintance, having found preſidents for them formerly. Without Hiſtory a mans ſoul is purblind, ſeeing onely the things which almoſt touch his eyes.

8 *He is well ſeen in Chronology, without which Hiſtory is but an heap of tales.* If by the Laws of the land he is counted a Naturall, who hath not wit enough to tell twenty, or to tell his * age; he ſhall not paſſe with me for wiſe in learning, who cannot tell the age of the world, and count hundreds of years: I mean not ſo critically, as to ſolve all doubts ariſing thence; but that he may be able to give ſome tolerable account thereof. He is alſo acquainted

* *Fits Herbert de nat.brev.de Idiota inquiren.*

quainted with Coſmography, treating of the world in whole joynts; with Chorography, ſhredding it into countries; and with Topography, mincing it into particular places.

Thus taking theſe Sciences in their generall latitude, he hath finiſhed the round circle or golden ring of the arts; onely he keeps a place for the diamond to be ſet in, I mean for that predominant profeſsion of Law, Phyſick, Divinity, or State-policie, which he intends for his principall Calling hereafter.

CHAP. 8.

Iulius Cæſar SCALIGER. *a great Reſtorer of Learninge. He died at Agen in France. An^o. Dni. 1558. aged 75 yeares.* W.M. ſculp:

CHAP. 8.

The life of JULIUS SCALIGER.

I Know my choice herein is liable to much exception. Some will make me the pattern of ignorance, for making this Scaliger the pattern of the generall Artiſt, whoſe own ſonne Joſeph might have been his father in many arts. But all things conſidered, the choice will appear well adviſed, even in ſuch variety of examples. Yet let him know that undertakes to pick out the beſt ear amongſt an acre of wheat, that

he

he ſhall leave as good if not a better behind him, then that which he chooſeth.

He was born *Anno* 1484. in Italie, at the Caſtle of Ripa upon lacus Benacus, now called *Lago di Garda*, of the illuſtrious and noble family of the Scaligers, Princes, for many hundreds of years, of Verona, till at laſt the Venetians outed them of their ancient inheritance. Being about eleven years old, he was brought to the Court of Maximilian Emperour of Germany, where for ſeventeen years together he was taught learning, and military diſcipline. I paſſe by his valiant performances atchieved by him, ſave that this one action of his is ſo great and ſtrong, it cannot be kept in ſilence, but will be recorded.

In the cruel battel at Ravenna betwixt the Emperour and the French, he not onely bravely fetch'd off the dead bodies of Benedictus and Titus his father and brother, but alſo with his own hands reſcued the Eagle (the ſtandard Imperiall) which was taken by the enemies. For which his proweſſe Maximilian knighted him, and with his own hands put on him the golden ſpurres, and chain, the badges of knight-hood.

Amidſt theſe his Martiall employments he made many a clandeſtine match with the Muſes, and whileſt he expected the tides and returns of buſineſſe, he fill'd up the empty places of leiſure with his ſtudies. Well did the Poets feigne Pallas Patroneſſe of arts and armes, there being ever good intelligence betwixt the two Profeſsions, and as it were but a narrow cut to ferry over out of one into the other. At laſt Scaliger ſounded a retreat to himſelf from the warres, and wholly applyed himſelf to his book, eſpecially after his wandring life was fixed by marriage unto the beautifull Andietta Lobeiaca, with whom he lived at Agin, near Montpeliar in France.

His Latine was twice refined, and moſt criticall, as appears by his own writings, and notes on other Authours. He was an accurate Grecian, yet began to ſtudy it, when well nigh fourty years old, when a mans tongue is too ſtiff to bow to words. What a torture was it to him who flowed with ſtreams of matter then to learn words, yea letters, drop by drop? But nothing was unconquerable to his pains, who had a golden wit in an iron body. Let his book of Subtilties witneſſe his profound skill in Logick, and Naturall Philoſophy.

His skill in Phyſick was as great, as his practice therein was happy; in ſo much that he did many ſtrange and admirable cures. Heare how a * noble and learned pen doth commend him:

* *Stephanus Boetius Regius Senator Burdigolæ ad Vidum Braſſacum Præſidem.*

Non hunc feſellit ulla vis recondita
Salubris herbæ, ſaltibus ſi quam aviis
Celat nivoſus Caucaſus, ſeu quam procul
Riphæa duro contigit rupes gelu.
Hic jamq; ſpectantes ad orcum non ſemel
Animas repreſſit victor, & membris ſuis
Hærere ſuccis compulit felicibus,
Nigriq; avaras Ditis eluſit manus.

On ſnowy Caucaſus there grew no root
Of ſecret power, but he was privy to't;
On cold Riphean hills no ſimple grew,
But he the force thereof and virtue knew.
Wherewith (apply'd by his ſucceſſefull art)
Such ſullen ſouls as would this world depart,
He forc'd ſtill in their bodies to remain,
And from deaths doore fetch'd others back again.

As for his skill in Phyſiognomy, it was wonderfull. I know ſome will ſay, that cannot be read in mens faces which was never wrote there, and that he that ſeeks to find the diſpoſition of mens ſouls in the figures of their bodies, looks for letters on the backſide of of the book. Yet is it credibly * averred that he never look'd on his infant-ſonne Audectus but with grief, as ſorrow ſtruck with ſome ſad ſigne of ill ſucceſſe he ſaw in his face: which child at laſt was found ſtifled in bed with the embraces of his nurce being faſt aſleep.

* *In vita Jul. Scalig. p.* 54.

In Mathematicks he was no Archimedes, though he ſhewed his skill therein with the beſt advantage, and ſtood therein on his tiptoes, that his learning might ſeem the taller.

But in Poetry his over-meaſure of skill might make up this defect, as is atteſted by his book *de Arte Poetica.* Yet his own Poems are harſh, and unſmooth, (as if he rather ſnorted then *ſlept* on Parnaſſus) and they ſound better to the brain then the eare. Indeed his cenſure in Poetry was incomparable; but he was more happy in repairing of Poems then in building them from the ground, which ſpeaks his judgement to be better then his invention.

What ſhall I ſpeak of his skill in Hiſtory? whoſe own actions were a ſufficient Hiſtory. He was excellently verſ'd in the paſſages of the world, both modern and ancient. Many modern languages, which departed from Babel in a confuſion, met in his mouth in a method, being skilfull in the Sclavonick tongue, the Hungarian, Dutch, Italian, Spaniſh, and French.

But theſe his excellent parts were attended with prodigious pride; and he had much of the humour of the Ottomans in him, to kill all his brethren, and cry down all his equalls, which were corrivalls with him in the honour of arts, which was his principall quarrell with Cardan. Great was his ſpight at Eraſmus, the morning-ſtarre of learning, and one by whom Julius himſelf had profited, though afterwards he ſought to put out that candle whereat he had lighted his own. In the bickering betwixt them, Eraſmus pluckt Scali-

ger

ger by the long locks of his immoderate boaſting, and touched him to the quick (a proud man lies pat for a jeering mans hand to hit) yea Eraſmus was a badger in his jeeres, where he did bite he would make his teeth meet. Nor came Scaliger behind him in railing. However afterward Scaliger repented of his bitterneſſe, and before his death was * reconciled unto him.

* *Thuan. obit. Illuſtr. Anno.* 1558.

Thus his learning, being in the circuit of arts, ſpread ſo wide, no wonder if it lay thinne in ſome places. His parts were nimble, that ſtarting ſo late he overtook, yea overran his equalls: ſo that we may ſafely conclude that making abatement for his military avocations, and late applying himſelf to ſtudy, ſcarce any one is to be preferred before him for generality of humane learning. He died *Anno* 1558. in the 75.yeare of his age.

CHAP. 9.
The faithfull Miniſter.

WE ſuppoſe him not brought up by hand onely in his own countrey ſtudies, but that he hath ſuckt of his Mother Univerſity, and throughly learnt the arts: Not as S. * Rumball, who is ſaid to have ſpoken as ſoon as he was born, doth he preach as ſoon as he is Matriculated. Conceive him now a Graduate in arts, and entred into orders, according to the ſolemn form of the Church of England, and preſented by ſome Patrone to a paſtorall charge, or place equivalent, and then let us ſee how well he diſchargeth his office.

* *Camb. Brit. in Northamptonſhire.*

Maxime 1

He endeavours to get the generall love and good will of his pariſh. This he doth not ſo much to make a benefit of them, as a benefit for them, that his miniſtry may be more effectuall; otherwiſe he may preach his own heart out, before he preacheth any thing into theirs.

The

The good conceit of the Physician is half a cure, and his practice will scarce be happy where his person is hated; yet he humours them not in his Doctrine to get their love: for such a spanniel is worse then a dumbe dog. He shall sooner get their good will by walking uprightly, then by crouching and creeping. If pious living and painfull labouring in his calling will not win their affections, he counts it gain to lose them. As for those which causelessely hate him, he pities and prayes for them: and such there will be; I should suspect his preaching had no salt in it, if no gald horse did winse

2 *He is strict in ordering his conversation.* As for those who clense blurres with blotted fingers, they make it the worse. It was said of one who preach'd very well, & liv'd very ill, *That when he was out of the Pulpit, it was pity he should ever go into it, & when he was in the Pulpit, it was pity he should ever come out of it:* But our Minister lives Sermons. And yet I deny not but dissolute men, like unskilfull horsemen which open a gate on the wrong side, may by the virtue of their office open heaven for others, and shut themselves out.

3 *His behaviour towards his people is grave and courteous.* Not too austere and retired; which is laid to the charge of good Mr * Hooper the martyr, that his rigidnesse frighted people from consulting with him. Let *your light* (saith Christ) *shine before men*; whereas over reservednesse makes the brightest virtue burn dimme. Especially he detesteth affected gravity (which is rather on men then in them) whereby some belie their register-book, antedate their age to seem farre older then they are, and plait and set their brows in an affected sadnesse. Whereas S * Anthony the Monk might have been known among hundreds of his order by his cheerfull face, he having ever (though a most mortified man) a merry countenance.

* *Fox, Acts and Mon. in his life.*

* *Athanasius in ejus vita.*

4 *He doth not clash Gods ordinances together about precedency.* Not making odious comparisons betwixt Prayer and

Preaching, Preaching and Catechising, Publick prayer and Private, Premeditate prayer and *Ex tempore*. When at the taking of new Carthage in Spain two Souldiers contended about the Murall crown (due to him who first climbed the walls) so that the whole army was thereupon in danger of division, * Scipio the Generall said, He knew that they both got up the wall together, and so gave the Scaling crown to them both. Thus our Minister compounds all controversies betwixt Gods ordinances, by praysing them all, practising them all, and thanking God for them all. He counts the reading of Common-prayers to prepare him the better for preaching; and as one said, if he did first toll the bell on one side, it made it afterwards ring out the better in his Sermons.

* *Plutarch in Scipio's. life, pag.* 1807.

5 *He carefully Catechiseth his people in the elements of religion.* Except he hath (a rare thing) a flock without lambs, all of old sheep; and yet even Luther did not scorn to professe himself *Discipulum Catechismi*, a scholar of the Catechisme. By this Catechising the Gospel first got ground of Popery; and let not our Religion now grown rich be ashamed of that which first gave it credit and set it up, lest the Jesuites beat us at our own weapon. Through the want of this Catechising many which are well skilled in some dark out-corners of Divinity have lost themselves in the beaten road thereof.

6 *He will not offer to God of that which costs him nothing*; but takes pains aforehand for his Sermons. * Demosthenes never made any oration on the sudden; yea being called upon he never rose up to speak, except he had well studied the matter: and he was wont to say, *That he shewed how he honoured and reverenced the people of Athens because he was carefull what he spake unto them.* Indeed if our Minister be surprised with a sudden occasion, he counts himself rather to be excused then commended, if premeditating onely the bones of his Sermon he clothes

* *Plutarch in the life of Demosth.*

clothes it with flesh *ex tempore.* As for those, whose long custome hath made preaching their nature, that they can discourse Sermons without study, he accounts their examples rather to be admired then imitated.

Having brought his Sermon into his head, he labours to bring it into his heart, before he preaches it to his people. Surely that preaching which comes from the soul most works on the soul. Some have questioned ventriloquie, when men strangely speak out of their bellies, whether it can be done lawfully or no: might I coin the word *cordiloquie*, when men draw the doctrines out of their hearts, sure all would count this lawfull and commendable. 7

He chiefly reproves the raigning sins of the time, and place he lives in. We may observe that our Saviour never inveighed against Idolatry, Usury, Sabbath-breaking amongst the Jews; not that these were not sins, but they were not practised so much in that age, wherein wickednesse was spun with a finer thred: and therefore Christ principally bent the drift of his preaching against spirituall Pride, Hypocrisie, and Traditions then predominant amongst the people. Also our Minister confuteth no old Heresies which time hath confuted; nor troubles his Auditory with such strange, hideous cases of Conscience, that it is more hard to find the case then the resolution. In publick reproving of sinne, he ever whips the vice, and spares the person. 8

He doth not onely move the bread of life, and tosse it up and down in generalities, but also breaks it into particular directions: drawing it down to cases of Conscience, that a man may be warranted in his particular actions, whether they be lawfull or not. And he teacheth people their lawfull liberty as well as their restraints and prohibitions; for amongst men it is as ill taken to turn back favours, as to disobey commands. 9

The places of Scripture he quotes are pregnant and pertinent. 10

As for heaping up of many quotations, it ſmacks of a vain oſtentation of memory. Beſides, it is as impoſſible that the hearer ſhould profitably retain them all, as that the preacher hath ſeriouſly peruſed them all: yea, whileſt the auditours ſtop their attention, and ſtoop down to gather an impertinent quotation, the Sermon runs on, and they loſe more ſubſtantiall matter.

11 *His ſimiles and illuſtrations are alwayes familiar, never contemptible.* Indeed reaſons are the pillars of the fabrick of a Sermon, but ſimilitudes are the windows which give the beſt light. He avoids ſuch ſtories whoſe mention may ſuggeſt bad thoughts to the auditours, and will not uſe a light compariſon to make thereof a grave application, for fear leſt his poyſon go farther then his antidote.

12 *He provideth not onely wholſome but plentifull food for his people.* Almoſt incredible was the painfulneſſe of Baronius, the compiler of the voluminous Annals of the Church, who for thirty years together preached * three or foure times aweek to the people. As for our Miniſter, he preferreth rather to entertain his people with wholſome cold meat which was on the table before, then with that which is hot from the ſpit, raw and half roaſted. Yet in repetition of the ſame Sermon, every edition hath a new addition, if not of new matter of new affections. *Of whom,* ſaith S. Paul, *we have told you often, and now we tell you weeping.*

* *The words being ſomwhat ambiguous are thus,* In audiendis confeſſionibus, & ſermonibus ad populum ter in hebdomada quatérve habendis per triginta & ampliùs annos diligentiſſimâ aſſiduitate laboravit, *Spondanus in vita Baronii, pag.* 2. *part.* 7.

13 *He makes not that wearisome, which ſhould ever be welcome.* Wherefore his Sermons are of an ordinary length except on an extraordinary occaſion. What a gift had John * Haſelbach, Profeſſour at Vienna, in tediouſneſſe? who being to expound the Prophet Eſay to his auditours read twenty one years on the firſt Chapter, and yet finiſhed it not.

* *Mercator Atlas in the deſcrip. of Auſtria.*

14 *He counts the ſucceſſe of his Miniſtry the greateſt preferment.* Yet herein God hath humbled many painfull paſtours, in

in making them to be clouds to rain, not over Arabia the happy, but over the ſtonie or deſert: ſo that they may complain with the Herdsman in the Poet,

Heu mihi, quam pingui macer eſt mihi taurus in arvo?

My ſtarveling bull,
Ah woe is me,
In paſture full,
How lean is he?

Yet ſuch Paſtours may comfort themſelves that great is their reward with God in heaven, who meaſures it not by their ſucceſſe but endeavours. Beſides, though they ſee not, their people may feel benefit by their Miniſtry. Yea the preaching of the Word in ſome places is like the planting of woods, where though no profit is received for twenty years together, it comes afterwards. And grant, that God honours thee not to build his temple in thy pariſh, yet thou maiſt with David provide metall and materialls for Solomon thy ſucceſſour to build it with.

To ſick folks he comes ſometimes before he is ſent for, as 15
counting his vocation a ſufficient calling. None of his flock ſhall want the extreme unction of Prayer and Counſell. Againſt the Communion eſpecially he endeavours that Janus his temple be ſhut in the whole pariſh, and that all be made friends.

He is never plaintiff in any ſuit but to be rights defendant. 16
If his dues be detained from him, he grieves more for his pariſhioners bad conſcience then his own damage. He had rather ſuffer ten times in his profit, then once in his title, where not onely his perſon, but poſterity is wronged: And then he proceeds fairly and ſpeedily to a tryall, that he may not vex and weary others, but right himſelf. During his ſuit he neither breaks off nor ſlacks offices of courteſie to his adverſary; yea though he loſeth his ſuit, he will not alſo loſe his charity. Chiefly he is reſpectfull to his Patrone, that as

 he

he presented him freely to his living, so he constantly presents his Patrone in his prayers to God.

17 *He is moderate in his tenets and opinions.* Not that he gilds over lukewarmnesse in matters of moment with the title of discretion, but withall he is carefull not to entitle violence in indifferent and in concerning matters to be zeal. Indeed men of extraordinary tallnesse, (though otherwise little deserving) are made porters to lords, & those of unusuall littlenesse are made ladies dwarfs, whilest men of moderate stature may want masters. Thus many notorious for extremities may find favourers to preferre them, whilest moderate men in the middle truth may want any to advance them. But what saith the Apostle? *If in this life onely we had hope we are of all men the most miserable.*

18 *He is sociable and willing to do any courtesie for his neighbour Ministers.* He willingly communicates his knowledge unto them. Surely the gifts and graces of Christians lay in common, till base envy made the first enclosure. He neither slighteth his inferiours, nor repineth at those who in parts and credit are above him. He loveth the company of his neighbour Ministers. Sure as ambergreece is nothing so sweet in it self, as when it is compounded with other things; so both godly and learned men are gainers by communicating themselves to their neighbours.

19 *He is carefull in the discreet ordering of his own family.* A good Minister and a good father may well agree together. When a certain Frenchman came to visit * Melanchthon, he found him in his stove with one hand dandling his child in the swadling-clouts, and in the other hand holding a book and reading it. Our Minister also is as hospitable as his estate will permit, and makes every almes two by his cheerfull giving it. He loveth also to live in a well-repaired house, that he may serve God therein more cheerfully. A Clergieman who built his house from the ground,

* *Pantaleon de Illustr. Germ. in vita Melanch.*

ground wrote in it this counſell to his ſucceſſour,

If thou doſt find an houſe built to thy mind
Without thy coſt,
Serve thou the more God and the poore;
My labour is not loſt.

Lying on his deathbed he bequeaths to each of his pariſhioners 20
his precepts and example for a legacie: and they in requitall erect every one a monument for him in their hearts. He is ſo farre from that baſe jealouſie that his memory ſhould be outſhined by a brighter ſucceſſour, and from that wicked deſire that his people may find his worth by the worthleſneſſe of him that ſucceeds, that he doth heartily pray to God to provide them a better Paſtour after his deceaſe. As for outward eſtate, he commonly lives in too bare paſture to die fat: It is well if he hath gathered any fleſh, being more in bleſsing then bulk.

WILLIAM PERKINS *The Learned, pious, and painfull Preacher of Gods word, at St Andrewes in* Cambridge *where He died Anno Dni. 1602. Aged 44. yeares.*
W.M. sculp:

Chap. 10.

The life of Mr Perkins.

William Perkins, born at Marſton nigh Coventry in Warwickſhire, was afterwards brought up in Chriſt-Colledge in Cambridge, where he ſo well profited in his ſtudies that he got the grounds of all liberall Arts, and in the 24. of Queen Elizabeth was choſen fellow of that Colledge, the ſame yeare wherein Doctour Andrew Willet (one of admirable induſtry) and Doctour Richard Clark (whoſe learned

learned Sermons commend him to posterity) were elected into the same Society.

There goeth an uncontroll'd tradition, that Perkins, when a young scholar, was a great studier of Magick, occasioned perchance by his skill in Mathematicks. For ignorant people count all circles above their own sphere to be conjuring, and presently cry out those things are done by black art for which their dimme eyes can see no colour in reason. And in such cases, when they cannot flie up to heaven to make it a Miracle, they fetch it from hell to make it Magick, though it may lawfully be done by naturall causes. True it is he was very wild in his youth till God(the best Chymick who can fix quicksilver it self) gratiously reclaim'd him.

After his entrance into the Ministry, the first beam he sent forth shined to those *which sat in darknesse and the shadow of death*, I mean the prisoners in the castle of Cambridge, people (as generally in such places) living in England out of Christendome, wanting the means of their salvation, bound in their bodies, but too loose in their lives, yea often branded in their flesh, and seared in their consciences. Perkins prevailed so farre with their jaylour, that the prisoners were brought (fetter'd) to the Shire-house hard by, where he preached unto them every Lords day. Thus was the prison his parish, his own Charity his Patron presenting him unto it, and his work was all his wages. Many an Onesimus here he begat, and as the instrument freed the prisoners from the captivity of sinne. When this began to be known, some of good quality of the neighbouring parishes became his auditours, and counted it their feast to feed out of the prisoners basket. Hence afterwards he became Preacher of S. Andrews parish in Cambridge, where he continued to the day of his death.

His Sermons were not so plain but that the piously

learned did admire them, nor ſo learned but that the plain did underſtand them. What was ſaid of Socrates, That he firſt humbled the towring ſpeculations of Philoſophers into practice and morality; ſo our Perkins brought the ſchools into the Pulpit, and unſhelling their controverſies out of their hard ſchool-terms, made thereof plain and wholſome meat for his people. For he had a capacious head with angles winding, and roomthy enough to lodge all controverſiall intricaſies; and, had not preaching diverted him from that way, he had no doubt attained to eminency therein. An excellent Chirurgeon he was at joynting of a broken ſoul, and at ſtating of a doubtfull conſcience. And ſure in Caſe-divinity Proteſtants are defective. For (ſave that a Smith or two of late have built them forges, and ſet up ſhop) we go down to our enemies to ſharpen all our inſtruments, and are beholden to them for offenſive and defenſive weapons in Caſes of Conſcience.

He would pronounce the word *Damne* with ſuch an emphaſis as left a dolefull Echo in his auditours ears a good while after. And when Catechiſt of Chriſt-Colledge, in expounding the Commandments, applied them ſo home, able almoſt to make his hearers hearts fall down, and hairs to ſtand upright. But in his older age he altered his voice, and remitted much of his former rigidneſſe, often profeſsing that to preach mercie was that proper office of the Miniſters of the Goſpell.

S. W. Mr. of S. C. C.

Some object that his Doctrine, referring all to an abſolute decree, hamſtrings all induſtry, and cuts off the ſinews of mens endeavours towards ſalvation. For aſcribing all to the wind of Gods ſpirit, (which bloweth where it liſteth) he leaveth nothing to the oars of mans diligence, either to help or hinder to the attaining of happineſſe, but rather opens a wide doore to licentious ſecurity. Were this the hardeſt objection againſt

againſt Perkins his doctrine, his own life was a ſufficient anſwer thereunto, ſo pious, ſo ſpotleſſe, that Malice was afraid to bite at his credit, into which ſhe knew her teeth could not enter.

He had a rare felicity in ſpeedy reading of books, and as it were but turning them over would give an exact account of all conſiderables therein. So that as it were riding poſt thorow an Authour, he took ſtrict notice of all paſſages, as if he had dwelt on them particularly, peruſing books ſo ſpeedily, one would think he read nothing; ſo accurately, one would think he read all.

He was of a cheerfull nature and pleaſant diſpoſition: Indeed to mere ſtrangers he was reſerved and cloſe, ſuffering them to knock a good while before he would open himſelf unto them; but on the leaſt acquaintance he was merry and very familiar.

Beſides his aſsiduity in preaching he wrote many books, extant at this day. And pity it was, that he ſet not forth more of them himſelf; for though ſome of his Orphan works lighted on good Guardians, yet all were not ſo happy; and indeed no nurſe for a child to the own mother.

He dyed in the 44. yeare of his age of a violent fit of the ſtone. It hath been reported that he dyed in the conflict of a troubled conſcience; which admit were ſo, had been no wonder. For God ſometimes ſeemingly leaves his Saints when they leave the world, plunging them on their death-beds in deep temptations, and caſting their ſouls down to hell, to rebound the higher to heaven. Beſides, the devil is moſt buſie on the laſt day of his Term; and a Tenant to be outed cares not what miſchief he doth. But here was no ſuch matter. Indeed he alwayes cryed out *Mercy Mercy*: which ſome ſtanders by miſinterpreted for deſpair, as if he felt not Gods favour, becauſe he call'd for it: whereas Mercy is a Grace which they hold the faſteſt,

S. W. *ut priùs.*

that most catch after it. 'Tis true that many on lesse reason have expressed more confidence of their future happinesse, and have delivered themselves in larger speeches concerning the same. But who could expect a long oration from him, where every word was accented with pain in so sharp a disease.

His funeralls were solemnly and sumtuously perform'd of the sole charges of Christ-Colledge, which challenged, as she gave him his breeding, to pay for his buriall; the University and Town lovingly contending which should expresse more sorrow thereat. Doctour Mountague, afterwards Bishop of Winchester, preached his Funerall-Sermon, and excellently discharg'd the place, taking for his Text, *Moses my servant is dead.*

He was of a ruddy complexion, very fat and corpulent, lame of his right hand; and yet this Ehud with a lefthanded pen did stab the Romish Cause, and * as one saith,

Hugh Holland in his Icones.

Dextera quantumvis fuerat tibi manca, docendi
Pollebas mira dexteritate tamen.

Though nature thee of thy right hand bereft,
Rightwell thou writest with thy hand that's left.

He was born the first, and dyed the last yeare of Queen Elisabeth, so that his life streamed in equall length with her reigne, and they both had their fountains, and falls together.

I must not forget, how his books after his death were translated into most modern Christian languages. For though he excellently improved his talent in the English tongue, yet forreiners thought it but wrapt up in a napkin, whilest folded in an unknown language. Wherefore some translated the main body of his works into French, Dutch, and Italian; and his books speak more tongues, then the Maker ever understood. His *Reformed Catholick* was done into Spanish, and no Spaniard ever since durst take up that

gantlet

gantlet of defiance our Champion cast down: yea their Inquisition rather chose to answer it with tortures, then arguments.

Chap. 11.

The good Parishioner.

WE will onely describe his Church-reference; his Civill part hath and shall be met with under other Heads. Conceive him to live under such a faithfull Minister as before was character'd, as, either judging charitably that all Pastours are such, or wishing heartily that they were.

Though near to the Church he is not farre from God. Like unto Justus, Acts 18.8. *One that worshipped God, and his house joyned hard to the Synagogue.* Otherwise if his distance from the church be great, his diligence is the greater to come thither in season. *Maxime* 1

2 *He is timely at the beginning of Common prayer.* Yet as *Tullie Charged some dissolute people for being such sluggards that they never saw the sunne rising or setting, as being alwayes up after the one, and abed before the other; so some negligent people never heare prayers begun, or sermon ended: the Confession being past before they come, and the Blessing not come before they are passed away.

* *De finibus boni & mali, lib.* 2.

3 *In sermon he sets himself to heare God in the Minister.* Therefore divesteth he himself of all prejudice, the jaundise in the eyes of the soul presenting colours false unto it. He hearkens very attentively: 'Tis a shame when the Church it self is *Cœmeterium*, wherein the living sleep above ground as the dead do beneath.

4 *At every Point that concerns himself, he turns down a leaf in his heart*; and rejoyceth that Gods word hath peirc'd him, as hoping that whilest his soul smarts it heals. And as it is no manners for him that hath good venison

nison before him, to ask whence it came, but rather fairly to fall to it; so hearing an excellent Sermon, he never enquires whence the Preacher had it, or whether it was not before in print, but falls aboard to practise it.

5 *He accuseth not his Minister of spight for particularizing him.* It does not follow that the archer aimed, because the arrow hit. Rather our Parishioner reasoneth thus; If my sinne be notorious, how could the Minister misse it? if secret, how could he hit it without Gods direction? But foolish hearers make even the bells of Aarons garments *to clink as they think*. And a guilty conscience is like a whirlpool, drawing in all to it self which otherwise would passe by. One, causelessely disaffected to his Minister, complained that he in his last Sermon had personally inveighed against him, and accused him thereof to a grave religious Gentleman in the parish: *Truly*, said the Gentleman, *I had thought in his Sermon he had meant me, for it touched my heart*. This rebated the edge of the others anger.

6 *His Tithes he payes willingly with cheerfulnesse.* How many part with Gods portions grudgingly, or else pinch it in the paying. * *Decimum*, the Tenth, amongst the Romanes was ever taken for what was best or biggest. It falls out otherwise in paying of Tithes, where the least and leanest are shifted off to make that number.

* *Fluctus Decimus*, pro *maximo*. Ovidio & Lucano.

7 *He hides not himself from any Parish-office which seeks for him.* If chosen Churchwarden, he is not busily-idle, rather to trouble then reform, presenting all things but those which he should. If Overseer of the poore, he is carefull the rates be made indifferent (whose inequality oftentimes is more burthensome then the summe) and well disposed of. He measures not peoples wants by their clamorous complaining, and dispenseth more to those that deserve then to them that onely need relief.

He

He is bountifull in contributing to the repair of Gods houſe. 8 For though he be not of their opinion, who would have the Churches under the Goſpell conform'd to the magnificence of Solomons Temple (whoſe porch would ſerve us for a Church) and adorn them ſo gaudily, that devotion is more diſtracted then raiſed, and mens ſouls rather dazeled, then lightened; yet he conceives it fitting that ſuch ſacred places ſhould be handſomly and decently maintained: The rather becauſe the climactericall yeare of many Churches from their firſt foundation, may ſeem to happen in our dayes; ſo old, that their ruine is threatned if not ſpeedily repaired. 9

He is reſpectfull to his Miniſters widow and poſterity for his ſake. When the onely daughter of Peter Martyr was, through the riot and prodigality of her debauched husband, brought to extreme poverty, the *State of Zurick, out of gratefull remembrance of her Father, ſupported her with bountifull maintenance. My prayers ſhall be, that Miniſters widows, and children may never ſtand in need of ſuch relief, and may never want ſuch relief when they ſtand in need.

* *Thuan obit. vir. doct. Anno.* 1562.

Chap. 12.

The good Patron.

THat in the Primitive times (though I dare not ſay generally in all Churches) if not the ſole choyce, at leaſt the conſent of the people was required in appointing of Miniſters, may partly appear out of * Scripture, more plainly out of * Cyprian, and is confeſſed by reverend * Dr. Whitgift. Theſe popular elections were well diſcharged in thoſe purer times, when men being ſcoured with conſtant perſecution had little leaſure to ruſt with factions, and when there were no baits for Corruption; the places of Miniſters being then of great pains and perill, and

* Acts 14.23. χειροτονήσαντες
* *Lib.* 1.*epiſt.*4
* *Defence of the Anſwer to the Admonition. pag.* 164.

& ſmall profit. But diſſenſion creeping in,in after-ages (the eyes of common people at the beſt but dimme through ignorance being wholly blinded with partiality) it may ſeem their right of election was either devolved to, or aſſumed of the Biſhop of the Dioces, who * onely was to appoint Curates in every pariſh. Afterwards to invite lay-men to build and endow Churches, the Biſhops departed with their right to the lay Patrons according to the verſe,

* *Concil. Toletan. Anno* 589. *Can.* 9. *Synod. Antiochen. Can.* 24.*and* 2. *Concil.Gangrenſe Can.* 7. *and* 8.

Patronum faciunt Dos,Aedificatio,Fundus.

A Patron's he that did endow with lands,
Or built the Church, or on whoſe ground it ſtands.

It being conceived reaſonable that he who payed the Churches portion, ſhould have the main ſtroke in providing her an husband. Then came Patronages to be annexed to Mannours, and by ſale or deſcent to paſſe along with them ; nor could any juſtly complain thereof, if all Patron s were like him we deſcribe.

Maxime 1 *He counts the Living his to diſpoſe, not to make profit of.* He fears more to lapſe his conſcience, then his Living, fears more the committing then the diſcovery of Simony.

2 *A Benefice he ſometimes giveth ſpeedily, never raſhly.* Some are long in beſtowing them out of ſtate, becauſe they love to have many ſuiters ; others out of covetouſneſſe will not open their wares till all their chapmen are come together, pretending to take the more deliberation.

3 *He is deaf to opportunity, if wanting deſert.* Yet is he not of the mind of Tamberlane the Scythian King, who never gave Office to any that ſought for it : for deſiring proceeds not alwayes from want of deſerving ; yea God himſelf likes well that his favours ſhould be ſued for. Our Patron chiefly reſpects piety,ſufficiency, and promiſe of painfulneſſe, whereby he makes his election. If he can by the ſame deed provide for Gods houſe

and his own familie, he counts it lawfull, but on no terms will preferre his dearest and nearest sonne or kinsman if unworthy

4 *He hates not onely direct simony, or rather Gehazisme, by the string, but also that which goes about by the bow.* Ancient Councels present us with severall forms hereof. I find how the Patrons sonnes and nephews were wont to feed upon the Incumbent, and eat out the presentation in great banquets and dinners, till at last the Palentine Councel brought a voyder to such feasts, and made a canon against them. But the former ages were bunglers to the cunning contrivance of the simony-engineers of our times. *O my soul come thou not into their secrets.* As if they cared not to go to hell, so be it were not the nearest way, but that they might fetch a farre compasse round about. And yet father * Campian must not carry it so clearly, who taxeth the Protestants for maintaining of simony. We confesse it a personall vice amongst us, but not to be charged as a Church-sinne, which by penall Laws it doth both prohibit and punish. Did Rome herein look upon the dust behind her own doores, she would have but little cause to call her neighbour slut. What saith the Epigram?

Concil. Palent. Anno 1322. Constit. 14.

* *Vid. Videl. Comment. in Epist. Ignatii ad Trallenses.*

An Petrus fuerat Romæ sub judice lis est;
Simonem Romæ nemo fuisse negat.

That Peter was at Rome, there's strife about it;
That Simon was there, none did ever doubt it.

5 *He hates corruption not onely in himself, but his servants.* Otherwise it will do no good for the Master to throw bribes away, if the Men catch them up at the first rebound, yea before ever they come to the ground. * Cambden can tell you what Lord-Keeper it was in the dayes of Queen Elizabeth, who though himself an upright man was hardly spoken of for the basenesse of his servants in the sale of Ecclesiasticall preferments.

* *In the life of Queen Elizab. Anno Dom. 1596.*

O *When*

6 *When he hath freely bestowed a Living, he makes no boasts of it.* To do this were a kind of ſpirituall ſimony, to ask and receive applauſe of others; as if the commonneſſe of faulting herein made a right, and the rarity of giving things freely merited *ex condigno* a generall commendation. He expects nothing from the Clerk he preſented but his prayers to God for him, reſpectfull carriage towards him, and painfulneſſe in his Calling, who having gotten his place freely may diſcharge it the more faithfully: whereas thoſe will ſcarce afford to feed their ſheep fat, who rent the paſture at too high a rate.

To conclude, let Patrons imitate this particular example of King William Rufus, who (though ſacrilegious in other acts) herein diſcharged a good conſcience. Two Monks came to him to buy an Abbots place of him, ſeeking to outvie each other in offering great ſummes of money, whileſt a third Monk ſtood by, and ſaid nothing. To whom ſaid the King, What wilt thou give for the place. Not a penny, anſwered he, for it is againſt my conſcience; but here I ſtay to wait home on him whom your Royall pleaſure ſhall deſigne Abbot. Then quoth the King, Thou of the three beſt deſerveſt the place, and ſhalt have it, and ſo beſtowed it on him.

CHAP. 13.

Chap. 13.

The good Landlord.

IS one that lets his land on a reasonable rate, so that the Tenant by employing his stock, and using his industry, may make an honest livelihood thereby, to maintain himself and his children.

Maxime 1 *His rent doth quicken his Tenant but not gall him.* Indeed 'tis observed, that where Landlords are very easy, the Tenants (but this is *per Accidens*, out of their own lazinesse) seldome thrive, contenting themselves to make up the just measure of their rent, and not labouring for any surplusage of estate. But our Landlord puts some metall into his Tenants industry, yet not grating him too much, lest the Tenant revenge the Landlords cruelty to him upon his land.

2 *Yet he raiseth his rents (or fines equivalent) in some proportion to the present price of other commodities.* The plenty of money makes a seeming scarcity of all other things, and wares of all sorts do daily grow dear. If therefore our Landlord should let his rents stand still as his Grandfather left them, whilest other wares dayly go on in price, he must needs be cast farre behind in his estate.

3 *What he sells or sets to his Tenant, he suffers him quietly to enjoy according to his covenants.* This is a great joy to a Tenant, though he buyes dear to possesse without disturbance. A strange example there was of Gods punishing a covetous Landlord at * Rye in Sussex, *Anno* 1570. He having a certain marish, wherein men on poles did dry their fishnets, received yearly of them a sufficient summe of money, till not content therewith he caused his servant to pluck up the poles, not suffering the fishermen to use them any longer, except they would compound at a greater rate. But it came to passe the same night that the sea breaking in

* *Holinshed* p. 1224.

covered the ſame mariſh with water,and ſo it ſtill continueth.

4 *He deteſts and abhorres all incloſure with depopulation.* And becauſe this may ſeem a matter of importance, we will break it into ſeverall propoſitions.

1 *Incloſure may be made without depopulating.* Infinites of examples ſhew this to be true. But depopulation hath caſt a ſlander on incloſure, which becauſe often done with it, people ſuſpect it cannot be done without it.

2 *Incloſure made without depopulating is injurious to none.* I mean if proportionable allotments be made to the poore for their commonage, and free & leaſeholders have a conſiderable ſhare with the lord of the mannour.

3 *Incloſure without depopulating is beneficiall to private perſons.* Then have they moſt power and comfort to improve their own parts, and for the time, and manner thereof may mould it to their own conveniencie. The Monarch of one acre will make more profit thereof then he that hath his ſhare in fourty in common.

4 *Incloſure without depopulating is profitable to the Commonwealth.* If injurious to no private perſon, and profitable to them all, it muſt needs be beneficiall to the Commonwealth,which is but the *Summa totalis* of ſundry perſons, as ſeverall figures. Beſides, if a Mathematician ſhould count the wood in the hedges, to what a mighty forreſt would it amount? This underwood ſerves for ſupplies to ſave timber from burning, otherwiſe our wooden walls in the water muſt have been ſent to the fire. Adde to this the ſtrength of an incloſed Countrey againſt a forrein invaſion. Hedges and counterhedges (having in number what they want in height and depth) ſerve for barracadoes, and will ſtick as birdlime in the wings of the horſe, and

and ſcotch the wheeling about of the foot. Small reſiſtance will make the enemy to earn every mile of ground as he marches. Object not, That incloſure deſtroyes tillage, the ſtaff of a countrey, for it need not all be converted to paſturage. Cain and Abel may very well agree in the Commonwealth, the Plowman and Shepherd part the incloſures betwixt them.

5 *Incloſure with depopulation is a canker to the Commonwealth.* It needs no proof: wofull experience ſhews how it unhouſes thouſands of people, till deſperate need thruſts them on the gallows. Long ſince had this land been ſick of a pluriſie of people, if not let blood in their Weſtern Plantations.

6 *Incloſure with depopulation endammageth the parties themſelves.* 'Tis a paradox and yet a truth, that reaſon ſhews ſuch incloſures to be gainfull, and experience proves them to be loſſe to the makers. It may be, becauſe God being φιλάνθρωπος, a Lover of man, mankind, and mens ſociety, and having ſaid to them, *Multiply and increaſe*, counts it an affront unto him, that men depopulate, and whereas bees daily ſwarm, men make the hives fewer. The margin ſhall direct you to the * Authour that counts eleven mannours in Northamptonſhire thus incloſed: which towns have vomited out (to uſe his own expreſsion) and unburthened themſelves of their former deſolating and depopulating owners, and I think of their poſterity.

* Mr Benthams *Chriſtian Conflict*, pag. 321.

He rejoyceth to ſee his Tenants thrive. Yea he counts it a great honour to himſelf, when he perceiveth that God bleſſeth their endeavours, and that they come forward in the world. I cloſe up all with this pleaſant ſtory. A Farmer rented a Grange generally reported to be haunted by Faries, and paid a ſhrewd rent for the ſame at 5 each half years end. Now a Gentleman asked him how he durst be ſo hardy as to live in the houſe, and whether no Spirits did trouble him. *Truth* (ſaid the Farmer) *there be two Saints in heaven vex me more then all the devils in hell, namely the Virgin Mary, and Michael the Arch-angel* ; on which dayes he paid his rent

CHAP. 14.

The good Maſter of a Colledge.

THe Jews *Anno* 1348. were baniſhed out of moſt countreys of Chriſtendome, principally for poyſoning of ſprings and * fountains. Grievous therefore is their offenſe, who infect Colledges, the fountains of learning and religion ; and it concerneth the Church and State, that the Heads of ſuch houſes be rightly qualified, ſuch men as we come to character.

* *Munſter de German. lib.* 3. *pag.* 457.

Maxime 1 *His learning if beneath eminency is farre above contempt.* Sometimes ordinary ſcholars make extraordinary good Maſters. every one who can play well on Apollo's harp cannot skilfully drive his chariot, there being a peculiar myſtery of Government. Yea as a little allay makes gold to work the better, ſo (perchance) ſome dulneſſe in a man makes him fitter to manage ſecular affairs ; and thoſe who have climbed up Parnaſſus but half way better behold worldly buſineſſe (as lying low and nearer to their ſight) then ſuch as have climbed up to the top of the mount.

2 *He not onely keeps the Statutes (in his Study) but obſerves them* : for the maintaining of them will maintain him, if he be queſtioned. He gives them their true dimenſions, not racking them for one, and ſhrinking them for another, but making his conſcience his daily Viſitour. He that breaks the Statutes, and thinks to rule better by his own diſcretion, makes many gaps in the hedge, and then ſtands to ſtop one of them with a

ſtake

ſtake in his hand. Beſides, thus to confound the will of the dead Founders, is the ready way to make living mens charitie (like S[r] Hugh Willoughby in diſcovering the Northern paſſage) to be frozen to death, and will diſhearten all future Benefactours.

He is principall Porter, and chief Chappell-monitour. For where the Maſter keeps his chamber alwayes, the ſcholars will keep theirs ſeldome, yea perchance may make all the walls of the Colledge to be gate. He ſeeks to avoid the inconvenience when the gates do rather divide then confine the ſcholars, when the Colledge is diſtinguiſhed (as France into *Cis & Tranſalpina*) into the part on this, and on the otherſide of the walls. As for out-lodgings (like galleries, neceſſary evils in populous Churches) he rather tolerates then approves them. 3

In his Elections he reſpecteth merit, not onely as the condition but as the cauſe thereof. Not like Leofricus Abbot of S. Albans, who would ſcarce admit any into his Covent though well deſerving, except he was a * Gentleman born. He more reſpects literature in a ſcholar, then great mens letters for him. A learned Maſter of a Colledge in Cambridge (ſince made a reverend Biſhop, and, to the great grief of good men and great loſſe of Gods Church, lately deceaſed) refuſed a Mandate for chooſing of a worthleſſe man fellow. And when it was expected, that at the leaſt he ſhould have been outed of his Maſterſhip for this his contempt, King James highly commended him, and encouraged him ever after to follow his own conſcience, when the like occaſion ſhould be given him. 4

* *Math. Pariſ. in 23. Abbat. S. Alban. pag. 42.*

He winds up the Tenants to make good muſick, but not to break them. Sure Colledge-lands were never given to fat the Tenants and ſterve the ſcholars, but that both might comfortably ſubſiſt. Yea generally I heare the Muſes commended for the beſt Landladies, and a Colledge-leaſe is accounted but as the worſt kind of freehold. 5

He

6 *He is observant to do all due right to Benefactours.* If not piety, policy would dictate this unto him. And though he respects not Benefactours kinsmen, when at their first admission they count themselves born heirs apparent to all preferment which the house can heap on them, and therefore grow lazy & idle; yet he counts their alliance, seconded with mediocrity of desert, a strong title to Colledge-advancement.

7 *He counts it lawfull to enrich himself, but in subordination to the Colledge good.* Not like Varus, Governour of Syria, who came poore into the countrey, and found it rich, but departed thence rich, and left the countrey poore. Methinks 'tis an excellent commendation which Trinity Colledge in Cambridge in her records bestows on Doctour Still once Master thereof. *Se ferebat Patremfamilias providum,* ἀγαθὸν κουρότροφον, *nec Collegio gravis fuit aut onerosus.*

8 *He disdains to nourish dissension amongst the members of his house.* Let Machiavills Maxime, *Divide & regnabis,* if offering to enter into a Colledge-gate, sink thorow the grate, and fall down with the durt. For besides that the fomenting of such discords agrees not with a good conscience, each party will watch advantages, and Pupils will often be made to suffer for their Tutours quarrells: *Studium partium* will be *magna pars studiorum,* and the Colledge have more rents then revenues.

9 *He scorneth the plot, to make onely dunces Fellows, to the end he may himself command in chief.* As thinking that they who know nothing, will do any thing, and so he shall be a figure amongst cyphers, a bee amongst drones. Yet oftentimes such Masters are justly met with, and they find by experience, that the dullest horses are not easiest to be reined. But our Master endeavours so to order his elections, that every Scholar may be fit to make a Fellow, and every Fellow a Master.

Chap. 14.
The life of Dr. Metcalf.

NIcholas Metcalf Doctour of Divinity, extracted out of an ancient and numerous family of Gentry in Yorkshire, was Archdeacon of Rochester, & Chaplain to John Fisher the Bishop thereof; by whom this our Doctour was employed to issue forth the monies for the building of S. Johns Colledge in Cambridge. For Margaret Countesse of Richmond and Derby intending to graft S. Johns Colledge into the old stock of S. Johns Hospitall, referr'd all to the Bishop of Rochester, and he used Metcalf as an agent in all proceedings which did concern that Foundation: which will inferre him to be both a wise and an honest man.

Some make him to be but meanly * learned; and * one telleth us a long storie how a Sophister put a fallacie upon him, *a sensu diviso ad sensum compositum*, and yet the Doctours dimme eyes could not discern it. But such trifles were beneath him; and what wonder is it if a Generall long used in governing an armie, hath forgotten his school-play, and Fencers rules, to put by every thrust?

* *Ascham: Schoolmaster*, 2. *Book*, *fol.* 47.
* *Lively in his Chron. of Persian Monarch. p.* 196.

Doubtlesse, had not his learning been sufficient, Bishop Fisher, a great clerk himself, would not have placed him to govern the Colledge. But we know that some count all others but dry scholars, whose learning runneth in a different channell from their own: and it is possible, that the great distance betwixt men in matter of Religion might hinder the new learning in one to see the old learning in the other.

But grant that Metcalf, with Themistocles, could not fiddle, yet he could make a little city a great one: though dull in himself, he could whet others by his encouragement. He found the Colledge spending ſcarce two hundred marks by the yeare, he left it ſpending a * thouſand marks and more. For he not onely procured and ſettled many donations, and by-foundations (as we term them) of Fellowſhips, and Scholarſhips, founded by other; but was a Benefactour himſelf, *Pro certis ornamentis & structuris in Capella, & pro ædificatione ſex Camerarum a tergo Coquinæ*, &c. as it is evidenced in the Colledge books. He counted the Colledge his own home, and therefore cared not what coſt he beſtowed on it: not like thoſe Maſters, who making their Colledges as ſteps to higher advancement will trample on them to raiſe up themſelves, and uſing their wings to flie up to their own honour, cannot afford to ſpread them to brood their Colledge. But the thriving of the nourcery, is the beſt argument to prove the skill and care of the nource. See what ſtore of worthy men the houſe in his time did yield:

* *Aſcham. in loco priùs citato.*

William Cecill, *Lord Burly*,
S[r]. John Cheek,
Walter Haddon. } *Stateſmen.*

Biſhop of
Ralph Bain, — *Coventrie and Lichfield*
John Chriſtopherſon, — *Chicheſter*,
Robert Horn, — *Winton*,
James Pilkinton, — *Dureſme*,
John Tailour, — *Lincoln*,
Thomas Watſon. — *Lincoln*.

Roger Aſcham,
George * Bullock,
Roger * Hutchinſon,
Alban Langdale,
John Seaton. } *Learned writers.*

* *Pitzæus de Scriptor. Angli. pag. 773.*
* *Baleus de Scriptor. Anglicanis.*

Hugh Fitz-Herbert,
William Jreland,
Laurence Pilkinton,
---------Tomſon,
Henry Wright. } *Learned Men.*

With

With very many more. For though I dare not ſay that all theſe were old enough to bear fruit in Metcalfs time, yet ſure I am by him they were inoculated, and in his dayes admitted into the Colledge.

Yet for all theſe his deſerts Metcalf in his old age was expell'd the Colledge, and driven out when he could ſcarce go. A new generation grew up (advanced by him) whoſe active ſpirits ſtumbled at his gravity (young ſeamen do count ballaſt needleſſe yea burthenſome in a ſhip)and endeavoured his removall. It appears not what particular fault they laid to his charge. Some think that the Biſhop of Rocheſter his good lord being put to death, occaſioned his ruine, Fiſhers misfortune being Metcalfs higheſt miſdemeanour. He ſunk with his Patron, and when his ſunne was ſet it was preſently night with him: for according to the Spaniſh proverb, * *where goes the bucket, there goes the rope*, where the principall miſcarries, all the dependants fall with him.

* *Yrà la ſoga con el calderon.*

Others conceive it was for his partiality in preferring Northern men, as if in his compaſſe there were no points but ſuch onely as looked to the North, advancing alone his own countrey-men, and more reſpecting their need then deſerts. Indeed long * before, I find William Millington firſt Provoſt of Kings Colledge put out of his place, for his partiality in electing Yorkſhire men.

* 1446. *Manuſcrip Hutcher. Coll. Regal.*

But herein Metcalf is ſufficiently juſtified: for he found Charity hotteſt in the cold countrey, *Northern men were moſt * partiall* (ſaith one) *in giving lands to the Colledge, for the furtherance of learning.* Good reaſon therefore Northern Scholars ſhould be moſt watered there, where Northern Benefactours rained moſt.

* *Aſcham. in loco citato.*

Well, good old Metcalf muſt forſake the Houſe. Methinks the bluſhing bricks ſeem aſham'd of their ingratitudes, and each doore, window, and caſement in the Colledge, was a mouth to plead for him.

But what ſhall we ſay? Mark generally the grand deſervers in States, and you ſhall find them loſe their luſtre before they end their life. The world, out of covetouſneſſe to ſave charges to pay them their wages, quarrelling with them, as if an over-merit were an offence. And whereas ſome impute this to the malignant influence of the heavens, I aſcribe it rather to a peſtilent vapour out of the earth; I mean, That rather men then ſtarres are to be blamed for it.

He was twenty years Maſter, and on the 4 day of June 1537. went out of his office, and it ſeems dyed ſoon after: his Epitaph is faſtned on a piece of braſſe on the wall, in the Colledge-Chappell. We muſt not forget that all who were great doers in his expulſion, were great ſufferers afterwards, and dyed all in great * miſerie. There is difference betwixt prying into Gods ſecrets, and being ſtark blind: Yea I queſtion whether we are not bound to look where God points by ſo memorable a judgement, ſhewing that thoſe branches moſt juſtly whithered which pluck'd up their own root.

* Omnes qui Metcalfi excludendi autores exſtiterunt, multis adverſæ fortunæ procellis (ſive divinâ ultione ſeu fato ſuo) jactati, de gradu dejecti & deturbati, inglorii mortem obierunt exemplo memorabili, *Caius lib. 1. Hiſt. Cantabr. pag. 75, & 76.*

CHAP. 16.

Chap. 16.

The good Schoolmaſter.

THere is ſcarce any profeſsion in the Commonwealth more neceſſary, which is ſo ſlightly performed. The reaſons whereof I conceive to be theſe: firſt, young ſcholars make this calling their refuge, yea perchance before they have taken any degree in the Univerſity, commence Schoolmaſters in the countrey, as if nothing elſe were required to ſet up this profeſsion but onely a rod and a ferula. Secondly, others who are able uſe it onely as a paſſage to better preferment, to patch the rents in their preſent fortune, till they can provide a new one, and betake themſelves to ſome more gainfull calling. Thirdly, they are diſheartned from doing their beſt with the miſerable reward which in ſome places they receive, being Maſters to the children, and ſlaves to their parents. Fourthly, being grown rich, they grow negligent, and ſcorn to touch the ſchool, but by the proxie of an Uſher. But ſee how well our Schoolmaſter behaves himſelf.

His genius inclines him with delight to this profeſsion. *Maxime* 1 Some men had as lieve be ſchoolboyes as Schoolmaſters, to be tyed to the ſchool as Coopers Dictionary, and Scapula's Lexicon are chained to the desk therein; and though great ſcholars, and skilfull in other arts, are bunglers in this: But God of his goodneſſe hath fitted ſeverall men for ſeverall callings, that the neceſsities of Church, and State, in all conditions may be provided for. So that he who beholds the fabrick thereof may ſay, God hewed out this ſtone, and appointed it to lie in this very place, for it would fit none other ſo well, and here it doth moſt excellent. And thus God mouldeth ſome for a Schoolmaſters life, undertaking it with deſire and delight, and diſcharging it with dexterity and happy ſucceſſe.

2 *He ſtudieth his ſcholars natures as carefully as they their books*; and ranks their diſpoſitions into ſeverall forms. And though it may ſeem difficult for him in a great ſchool to deſcend to all particulars, yet experienced Schoolmaſters may quickly make a Grammar of boyes natures, and reduce them all (ſaving ſome few exceptions) to theſe generall rules.

1 Thoſe that are ingenious and induſtrious. The conjunction of two ſuch Planets in a youth preſage much good unto him. To ſuch a lad a frown may be a whipping, and a whipping a death; yea where their Maſter whips them once, ſhame whips them all the week after. Such natures he uſeth with all gentleneſſe.

2 Thoſe that are ingenious and idle. Theſe think with the hare in the fable, that running with ſnails (ſo they count the reſt of their ſchool-fellows) they ſhall come ſoon enough to the Poſt, though ſleeping a good while before their ſtarting.Oh, a good rod would finely take them napping.

3 Thoſe that are dull and diligent. Wines the ſtronger they be the more lees they have when they are new. Many boyes are muddy-headed till they be clarified with age,and ſuch afterwards prove the beſt. Briſtoll diamonds are both bright, and ſquared and pointed by Nature, and yet are ſoft and worthleſſe; whereas orient ones in India are rough and rugged naturally. Hard rugged and dull natures of youth acquit themſelves afterwards the jewells of the countrey, and therefore their dulneſſe at firſt is to be born with, if they be diligent. That Schoolmaſter deſerves to be beaten himſelf, who beats Nature in a boy for a fault. And I queſtion whether all the whipping in the world can make their parts, which are naturally ſluggiſh, riſe one minute before the houre Nature hath appointed. Thoſe

4 Thoſe that are invincibly dull and negligent alſo. Correction may reform the latter, not amend the former. All the whetting in the world can never ſet a raſours edge on that which hath no ſteel in it. Such boyes he conſigneth over to other profeſsions. Ship-wrights and boatmakers will chooſe thoſe crooked pieces of timber, which other carpenters refuſe. Thoſe may make excellent merchants and mechanicks which will not ſerve for Scholars.

He is able, diligent, and methodicall in his teaching ; not 3
leading them rather in a circle then forwards. He minces his precepts for children to ſwallow, hanging clogs on the nimbleneſſe of his own ſoul, that his Scholars may go along with him.

He is, and will be known to be an abſolute Monarch in his 4
ſchool. If cockering Mothers proffer him money to purchaſe their ſonnes an exemption from his rod (to live as it were in a peculiar, out of their Maſters juriſdiction) with diſdain he refuſeth it, and ſcorns the late cuſtome in ſome places of commuting whipping into money, and ranſoming boyes from the rod at a ſet price. If he hath a ſtubborn youth, correction-proof, he debaſeth not his authority by conteſting with him, but fairly if he can puts him away before his obſtinacy hath infected others.

He is moderate in inflicting deſerv'd correction. Many a 5
Shoolmaſter better anſwereth the name of παιδοτρίβης then παιδαγωγὸς, rather tearing his ſcholars fleſh with whipping, then giving them good education. No wonder if his ſcholars hate the Muſes, being preſented unto them in the ſhapes of fiends and furies. Junius complains *de inſolenti* carnificina* of his Schoolmaſter, by whom *conſcindebatur flagris ſepties aut octies in dies ſingulos*. Yea heare the lamentable verſes of poore Tuſſer in his own life:

* *In his life, of his own writing.*

From

From Pauls I went, to Eaton sent,
To learn straightwayes the Latine phrase,
Where fifty three stripes given to me
At once I had.
For fault but small, or none at all,
It came to passe thus beat I was;
*See, * Vdal, see the mercy of thee*
To me poore lad.

* *Nich. Vdal Schoolmaster of Eaton in the Reigne of King Henry the eight.*

Such an Orbilius marres more Scholars then he makes: Their Tyranny hath caused many tongues to stammer, which spake plain by nature, and whose stuttering at first was nothing else but fears quavering on their speech at their Masters presence. And whose mauling them about their heads hath dull'd those who in quicknesse exceeded their Master.

6 *He makes his school free to him, who sues to him* in forma pauperis. And surely Learning is the greatest alms that can be given. But he is a beast, who because the poore Scholar cannot pay him his wages, payes the Scholar in his whipping. Rather are diligent lads to be encouraged with all excitements to Learning. This minds me of what I have heard concerning M^r^. Bust, that worthy late Schoolmaster of Eaton, who would never suffer any wandring begging Scholar (such as justly the Statute hath ranked in the forefront of Rogues) to come into his school, but would thrust him out with earnestnesse (however privately charitable unto him) lest his school-boyes should be disheartned from their books, by seeing some Scholars after their studying in the University preferr'd to beggery.

7 *He spoyls not a good school to make thereof a bad Colledge,* therein to teach his Scholars Logick. For besides that Logick may have an action of trespasse against Grammar for encroaching on her liberties, Syllogismes are Solecismes taught in the school, and oftentimes they are forc'd afterwards in the University to unlearn the fumbling skill they had before.

Out of his school he is no whit pedanticall in carriage or dis-course; contenting himself to be rich in Latine, though he doth not gingle with it in every company wherein he comes. 8

To conclude, Let this amongst other motives make Schoolmasters carefull in their place, that the eminencies of their Scholars have commended the memories of their Schoolmasters to posterity, who otherwise in obscurity had altogether been forgotten. Who had ever heard of R. * Bond in Lancashire but for the breeding of learned Ascham his Scholar? or of * Hartgrave in Brundly school, in the same County, but because he was the first did teach worthy Doctour Whitaker. Nor do I honour the memory of Mulcaster for any thing so much, as for his Scholar, that gulf of learning, Bishop Andrews. This made the Athenians, the day before the great feast of Theseus their founder, to sacrifice a ramme to the memory of * Conidas his Schoolmaster that first instructed him.

* *Grant. in vit. Ascham. pag. 629.*

* *Ashton in the life of Whitaker, pag. 29.*

* *Plutar. in vit. Thesei.*

Chap. 17.
The good Merchant

IS one who by his trading claspeth the iland to the continent, and one countrey to another. An excellent gardiner, who makes England bear wine, and oyl, and spices; yea herein goes beyond Nature in causing that *Omnis fert omnia tellus.* He wrongs neither himself, nor the Commonwealth, nor private chapmen which buy commodities of him. As for his behaviour towards the Commonwealth, it farre surpasses my skill to give any Rules thereof; onely this I know, that to export things of necessity, and to bring in forrein needlesse toyes, makes a rich Merchant, and a poore Kingdome: for the State loseth her radicall moysture, and gets little better then sweat in exchange, except the neceſſaries which are exported be exceeding plentifull, which then though neceſſary in their own nature become ſuperfluous through their abundance. We will content our ſelves to give ſome generall advertiſements concerning his behaviour towards his chapmen, whom he uſeth well in the quantity, quality, and price of the commodities he ſells them.

Maxime 1. *He wrongs not the buyer in Number, Weight, or Meaſure.* Theſe are the Land-marks of all trading, which muſt not be removed: for ſuch coſenage were worſe then open felony. Firſt, becauſe they rob a man of his purſe, & never bid him ſtand. Secondly, becauſe highway-thieves defie, but theſe pretend juſtice. Thirdly, as much as lies in their power, they endeavour to make God acceſſary to their coſenage, deceiving by pretending his weights. For God is the principall clark of the market, *All the*

*Prov. 16.11. * *weights of the bag are his work.*

2 *He never warrants any ware for good but what is ſo indeed.* Otherwiſe he is a thief, and may be a murtherer, if ſelling ſuch things as are apply'd inwardly. Beſides, in ſuch a caſe he counts himſelf guilty if he ſelleth ſuch wares as are bad, though without his knowledge, if avouching them for good; becauſe he may, profeſſeth, & is bound to be Maſter in his own myſtery, and therefore in conſcience muſt recompence the buyers loſſe, except he gives him an Item to buy it at his own adventure.

3 *He either tells the faults in his ware, or abates proportionably in the price he demands*: for then the low value ſhews the viciouſneſſe of it. Yet commonly when Merchants depart with their commodities, we heare (as in funerall orations) all the virtues but none of the faults thereof.

4 *He never demands out of diſtance of the price he intends to take*: If not alwayes within the touch, yet within the reach of what he means to ſell for. Now we muſt know there be foure ſeverall prices of vendible things. Firſt, the Price of the market, which ebbes and flows

according to the plenty or ſcarcity of coyn, commodities, and chapmen. Secondly, the Price of friendſhip, which perchance is more giving then ſelling, and therefore not ſo proper at this time. Thirdly, the Price of fancie, as twenty pounds or more for a dog or hauk, when no ſuch inherent worth can naturally be in them, but by the buyers and ſellers fancie reflecting on them. Yet I believe the money may be lawfully taken. Firſt, becauſe the ſeller ſometimes on thoſe terms is as loth to forgo it, as the buyer is willing to have it. And I know no ſtandard herein whereby mens affections may be meaſured. Secondly, it being a matter of pleaſure, and men able and willing, let them pay for it, *Volenti non fit injuria.* Laſtly, there is the Price of coſenage, which our Merchant from his heart deteſts and abhorres.

He makes not advantage of his chapmans ignorance, chiefly if referring himſelf to his honeſty: where the ſellers conſcience is all the buyers skill, who makes him both ſeller and judge, ſo that he doth not ſo much ask as order what he muſt pay. When one told old Biſhop Latimer that the Cutler had coſened him, in making him pay twopence for a knife not (in thoſe dayes) worth a peny; *No*, quoth Latimer, *he coſen'd not me but his own conſcience.* On the other ſide S. * Auguſtine tells us of a ſeller, who out of ignorance asked for a book farre leſſe then it was worth, and the buyer (conceive himſelf to be the man if you pleaſe) of his own accord gave him the full value thereof. 5

* *Lib.* 13. *de Trinitat. c.* 3.

He makes not the buyer pay the ſhot for his prodigality; as when the Merchant through his own ignorance or ill husbandry hath bought dear, he will not bring in his unneceſſary expences on the buyers ſcore: and in ſuch a caſe he is bound to ſell cheaper then he bought. 6

Selling by retail he may juſtifie the taking of greater gain: becauſe of his care, pains, and coſt of fetching thoſe 7 wares from the fountain, and in parcelling and dividing them. Yet because retailers trade commonly with those who have least skill what they buy, and commonly sell to the poorer sort of people, they must be carefull not to grate on their necessity.

But how long shall I be retailing out rules to this Merchant? It would employ a Casuist an apprentiship of years: take our Saviours whole-sale rule, *Whatsoever ye would have men do unto you, do you unto them; for this is the Low, and the Prophets.*

Chap. 18.

The good Yeoman

IS a Gentleman in Ore, whom the next age may see refined; and is the wax capable of a gentile impression, when the Prince shall stamp it. Wise Solon (who accounted * Tellus the Athenian the most happy man for living privately on his own lands) would surely have pronounced the English Yeomanry, a fortunate condition, living in the temperate Zone, betwixt greatnesse and want, an estate of people almost peculiar to England. France and Italy are like a die, which hath no points betwixt sink and ace, Nobility and Pesantry. Their walls though high, must needs be hollow, wanting filling-stones. Indeed Germany hath her Boores, like our Yeomen, but by a tyrannicall appropriation of Nobility to some few ancient families, their Yeomen are excluded from ever rising higher to clarifie their bloods. In England the Temple of Honour is bolted against none, who have passed through the Temple of Virtue: nor is a capacity to be gentile denyed to our Yeoman, who thus behaves himself.

* *Herodotus lib. 1. pag. 12*

Maxime 1 *He wears russet clothes, but makes golden payment*, having tinne in his buttons, and silver in his pocket. If he chance to appear in clothes above his rank, it is to grace

grace ſome great man with his ſervice, and then he bluſheth at his own bravery. Otherwiſe he is the ſureſt landmark, whence forreiners may take aim of the ancient Engliſh cuſtomes; the Gentry more floting after forrein faſhions.

In his houſe he is bountifull both to ſtrangers, and poore people. 2
Some hold, when Hoſpitality dyed in England, ſhe gave her laſt groan amongſt the Yeomen of Kent. And ſtill at our Yeomans table you ſhall have as many joints as diſhes: No meat diſguiſ'd with ſtrange ſauces; no ſtraggling joynt of a ſheep in the midſt of a paſture of graſſe, beſet with ſallads on every ſide, but ſolid ſubſtantiall food; no ſerviters (more nimble with their hands then the gueſts with their teeth) take away meat, before ſtomachs are taken away. Here you have that which in it ſelf is good, made better by the ſtore of it, and beſt by the welcome to it.

He hath a great ſtroke in making a Knight of the ſhire. 3
Good reaſon, for he makes a whole line in the ſubſidie-book, where whatſoever he is rated he payes without any regret, not caring how much his purſe is let blood, ſo it be done by the adviſe of the phyſicians of the State.

He ſeldome goes farre abroad, and his credit ſtretcheth further then his travell. 4
He goes not to London, but *ſe defendendo*, to ſave himſelf of a fine, being returned of a Jurie, where ſeeing the King once, he prayes for him ever afterwards.

In his own countrey he is a main man in Juries. 5
Where if the Judge pleaſe to open his eyes in matter of law, he needs not to be led by the noſe in matters of fact. He is very obſervant of the Judges *item*, when it follows the truths *inprimis*; otherwiſe (though not mutinous in a Jurie) he cares not whom he diſpleaſeth ſo he pleaſeth his own conſcience.

He improveth his land to a double value by his good husbandry. 6
Some grounds that wept with water, or frown'd with

thorns, by draining the one, and clearing the other, he makes both to laugh and ſing with corn. By marle and limeſtones burnt he bettereth his ground, and his induſtry worketh miracles, by turning ſtones into bread. Conqueſt and good husbandry both inlarge the Kings Dominions: The one by the ſword, making the acres more in number; the other by the plough, making the ſame acres more in value. Solomon ſaith, *The King himſelf is maintained by husbandry.* Pythis * a King having diſcovered rich mines in his kingdome, employed all his people in digging of them, whence tilling was wholly neglected, inſomuch as a great famine enſued. His Queen, ſenſible of the calamities of the countrey, invited the King her husband to dinner, as he came home hungry from overſeeing his workmen in the mines. She ſo contrived it, that the bread and meat were moſt artificially made of gold; and the King was much delighted with the conceit thereof, till at laſt he called for reall meat to ſatisfie his hunger. *Nay,* ſaid the Queen, *if you employ all your ſubjects in your mines, you muſt expect to feed upon gold, for nothing elſe can your kingdome afford.*

* *Plutarch. de virtut. mulierum, exemplo ultimo.*

7 *In time of famine he is the Joſeph of the countrey, and keeps the poore from ſterving.* Then he tameth his ſtacks of corn, which not his covetouſneſſe but providence hath reſerv'd for time of need, and to his poore neighbours abateth ſomewhat of the high price of the market. The neighbour gentry court him for his acquaintance, which he either modeſtly waveth, or thankfully accepteth, but no way greedily deſireth. He inſults not on the ruines of a decayed Gentleman, but pities and relieves him: and as he is called *Goodman*, he deſires to anſwer to the name, and to be ſo indeed.

8 *In warre, though he ſerveth on foot, he is ever mounted on an high ſpirit:* as being a ſlave to none, and a ſubject onely to his own Prince. Innocence and independance make a brave ſpirit: Whereas otherwiſe one muſt

ask

ask his leave to be valiant on whom he depends. Therefore if a State run up all to Noblemen and Gentlemen, so that the husbandmen be onely mere labourers, or cottagers, (which * one calls but hous'd beggers) it may have good Cavalry, but never good bands of foot; so that their armies will be like those birds call'd *Apodes*, without feet, alwayes onely flying on their wings of horse. Wherefore to make good Infantry, it requireth men bred, not in a servile or indigent fashion, but in some free and plentifull manner. Wisely therefore did that knowing Prince, King Henry the seventh, provide laws for the increase of his Yeomanry, that his kingdome should not be like to Coppice-woods, where the staddles being left too thick, all runs to bushes and briers, and there's little clean underwood. For enacting, that houses used to husbandry should be kept up with a competent proportion of land, he did secretly sow Hydra's teeth, whereupon (according to the Poets fiction) should rise up armed men for the service of this kingdome.

* *Bacons Henry. 7. pag.* 74.

Chap. 19.

The Handicrafts-man.

HE is a necessary member in a Common-wealth: For though Nature, which hath armed most other creatures, sent man naked into the world, yet in giving him hands and wit to use them, in effect she gave him Shells, Scales, Paws, Claws, Horns, Tusks, with all offensive and defensive weapons of Beasts, Fish and Fowl, which by the help of his hands in imitation he may provide for himself, and herein the skill of our Artisan doth consist.

His trade is such whereby he provides things necessary for mankind. What S. * Paul saith of the naturall, is also true of

Maxime 1.

* 1. *Cor.* 12.

of the politick body, thoſe members of the body are much more neceſſary which ſeem moſt feeble. Mean trades for profit, are moſt neceſſary in the State; and a houſe may better want a gallery then a kitchin. The Philiſtins knew this when they maſſacred all the ſmiths in Iſrael (who might worſe be ſpared then all the uſerers therein) and whoſe hammers nail the Commonwealth together, being neceſſary both in peace and warre.

2 *Or elſe his trade contributeth to mans lawfull pleaſure.* God is not ſo hard a maſter, but that he alloweth his ſervants ſauce (beſides hunger) to eat with their meat.

3 *But in no caſe will he be of ſuch a trade which is a mere Pander to mans luſt*; and onely ſerves their wantonneſſe (which is pleaſure runne ſtark mad) and fooliſh curioſity. Yet are there too many extant of ſuch profeſsions, which, one would think, ſhould ſtand in dayly fear leſt the world ſhould turn wiſe, and ſo all their trades be caſhierd, but that (be it ſpoken to their ſhame) 'tis as ſafe a tenure to hold a livelyhood by mens ryot, as by their neceſsity.

4 *The wares he makes ſhew good to the eye, but prove better in the uſe.* For he knows if he ſets his mark (the Towerſtamp of his credit) on any bad wares, he ſets a deeper brand on his own conſcience. Nothing hath more debaſed the credit of our Engliſh cloth beyond the ſeas, then the deceitfulneſſe in making them, ſince the Fox hath crept under the fliece of the Sheep.

5 *By his ingenuouſneſſe he leaves his art better then he found it.* Herein the Hollanders are excellent, where children get their living, when but newly they have gotten their life, by their induſtrie. Indeed Nature may ſeem to have made thoſe Netherlanders the younger brethren of mankind, allowing them little land, and that alſo ſtanding in dayly fear of a double deluge, of the ſea

and

and the Spaniard: but ſuch is their painfulneſſe and ingenuity, hating lazineſſe as much as they love liberty, that what commodities grow not on their Countrey by nature they graft on it by art, and have wonderfully improved all making of Manufactures, Stuffes, Clocks, Watches: theſe latter at firſt were made ſo great and heavy, it was rather a burden then an ornament to wear them, though ſince watches have been made as light and little, as many that were them make of their time.

He is willing to communicate his skill to poſterity. An in- 6
vention though found is loſt if not imparted. But as it is reported of ſome old toads, that before their death they ſuck up the gelly in their own heads (which otherwiſe would be hardned into a pretious ſtone) out of ſpight, that men ſhould receive no benifit thereby; ſo ſome envious Artiſans will have their cunning die with them, that none may be the better for it, and had rather all mankind ſhould loſe, then any man gain by them.

He ſeldome attaineth to any very great eſtate: except his 7
trade hath ſome outlets and excurſions into wholeſale and merchandize; otherwiſe mere Artificers cannot heap up much wealth. It is difficult for gleaners, without ſtealing whole ſheaves, to fill a barn. His chief wealth conſiſteth in enough, and that he can live comfortably, and leave his children the inheritance of their education.

Yet he is a grand Benefactour to the Commonwealth. En- 8
gland in former ages, like a dainty dame, partly out of ſtate, but more out of lazineſſe, would not ſuckle the fruit of her own body, to make the beſt to battle and improve her own commodities, but put them out to nurſe to the Netherlanders, who were well paid for their pains. In thoſe dayes the Sword and the Plough ſo took up all mens imployments that clothing was whollie neglected, and ſcarce any other webs to be

found in houſes, then what the ſpiders did make. But ſince ſhe hath ſeen and mended her errour, making the beſt uſe of her own wooll; and indeed the riches of a kingdome doth conſiſt in driving the home-commodities thereof as far as they will go, working them to their very perfection, imploying more handicrafts thereby. The ſheep feeds more with his fliece then his fleſh, doing the one but once, but the other once a yeare, many families ſubſiſting by the working thereof. Let not meaner perſons be diſpleaſed with reading thoſe verſes wherewith Queen Elizabeth her ſelf was ſo highly affected, when in the one and twentieth yeare of her *reigne ſhe came in progreſſe to Norwich, wherein a child, repreſenting the ſtate of the City, ſpake to her Highneſſe as followeth,

** Hollingſhead. pag. 1290.*

Moſt gratious Prince, undoubted Sovereigne Queen,
Our onely joy, next God, and chief defence,
In this ſmall ſhew our whole eſtate is ſeen,
The wealth we have, we find proceeds from hence:
The idle hand hath here no place to feed,
The painfull wight hath ſtill to ſerve his need.

Again, our ſeat denies us traffick here,
The ſea too near decides us from the reſt:
So weak we were within this dozen yeare,
That care did quench the courage of the beſt:
*But good advice hath taught theſe * little hands*
To rend in twain the force of pining bands.

** Sixteen little children were there preſented to her Majeſtie, eight ſpinning worſted, and eight knitting yarne hoſe.*

From combed wooll we draw this ſlender thred,
From thence the looms have dealing with the ſame,
And thence again in order do proceed
Theſe ſeverall works which skilfull art doth frame:
And all to drive dame Need into her cave
Our heads and hands together laboured have.

We

We bought before the things which now we ſell:
Theſe ſlender imps, their works do paſſe the waves:
Gods peace and thine we hold, and proſper well,
Of every mouth the hands the charges ſaves:
Thus through thy help, and aid of power divine
Doth Norwich live, whoſe hearts and goods are thine.

We have cauſe to hope that as we have ſeen the cities Dornicks and Arras brought over into England, ſo poſterity may ſee all Flaunders brought hither, I mean that their works ſhall be here imitated, and that either our land ſhall be taught to bear forrein commodities, or our people taught to forbear the uſing of them.

I ſhould now come to give the deſcription of the Day-Labourer (of whom we have onely a dearth in a plentifull harveſt) but ſeeing his character is ſo co-incident with the hired ſervant, it may well be ſpared. And now wee'l riſe from the hand to the arm, and come to deſcribe the Souldier.

Chap. 19.

The good Souldier.

A Souldier is one of a lawfull, neceſſary, commendable, and honourable profeſsion; yea God himſelf may ſeem to be one free of the company of Souldiers, in that he ſtyleth himſelf, *A man of warre.* Now though many hate Souldiers as the twigs of the rod Warre, wherewith God ſcourgeth wanton countreys into repentance, yet is their calling ſo needfull, that were not ſome Souldiers we muſt be all Souldiers, dayly imployed to defend our own, the world would grow ſo licentious.

He keepeth a clear and quiet conſcience in his breaſt, which otherwiſe will gnaw out the roots of all valour. For vicious Souldiers *Maxime* 1 diers are compaſſed with enemies on all ſides, their foes without them, and an ambuſh within them of fleſhly luſts, which, as S. Peter ſaith, *fight againſt the ſoul.* None fitter to go to warre, then thoſe who have made their peace with God in Chriſt; for ſuch a mans ſoul is an impregnable fort: It cannot be ſcaled with ladders, for it reacheth up to heaven; nor be broken by batteries, for it is walled with braſſe; nor undermined by pioners, for he is founded on a rock; nor betrayed by treaſon, for faith it ſelf keeps it; nor be burnt by granadoes, for he can quench the fiery darts of the devil; nor be forced by famine, for *a good conſcience is a continuall feaſt.*

2 *He chiefly avoids thoſe ſinnes, to which Souldiers are taxed as moſt ſubject.* Namely common ſwearing, which impayreth ones credit by degrees, and maketh all his promiſes not to be truſted; for he who for no profit will ſinne againſt God, for ſmall profit will treſpaſſe againſt his neighbour; drinking, whoring. When valiant Ziſca, near Pilſen in Bohemia, fought againſt his enemies, he commanded the women which followed his army, to caſt their kerchiefs and partlets on the ground, wherein their enemies being entangled by their ſpurres (for though horſmen, they were forced to alight, and fight on foot, through the roughneſſe of the place) were ſlain before they could * unlooſe their feet. A deep morall may be gathered hence, and women have often been the nets to catch and enſnare the ſouls of many Martiall men.

*Fox Acts and Monum pag. 646.

3 *He counts his Princes lawfull command to be his ſufficient warrant to fight.* In a defenſive warre, when his countrey is * hoſtilely invaded, 'tis pity but his neck ſhould hang in ſuſpence with his conſcience that doubts to fight; in offenſive warre, though the caſe be harder, the common Souldier is not to diſpute, but do * his Princes command. Otherwiſe

* In publicos hoſtes omnis homo miles, .. *Tertull. Apol. cap.* 2.

* *Ameſius. Caſ. Conſcien. lib.* 5. *cap.* 33.

wiſe Princes, before they leavie an army of Souldiers, muſt firſt leavy an army of Caſuiſts and Confeſſours to ſatisfie each ſcrupulous Souldier in point of right to the warre; and the moſt cowardly will be the moſt conſcientious, to multiply doubts eternally. Beſides, cauſes of warre are ſo complicated and perplex'd, ſo many things falling in the proſecution, as may alter the originall ſtate thereof, and private Souldiers have neither calling nor ability to dive into ſuch myſteries. But if the conſcience of a Counſellour or Commander in chief remonſtrates in himſelf the unlawfulneſſe of this warre, he is bound humbly to repreſent to his Prince his reaſons againſt it.

He eſteemeth all hardſhip eaſy through hopes of victory. 4
Moneys are the ſinews of war, yet if theſe ſinews ſhould chance to be ſhrunk, and pay caſually fall ſhort, he takes a fit of this convulſion patiently; he is contented though in cold weather his hands muſt be their own fire, and warm themſelves with working; though he be better armed againſt their enemies then the weather, and his corſlet wholler then his clothes; though he hath more Faſts and Vigills in his almanack then the Romiſh Church did ever enjoyn: he patiently endureth drougth for deſire of honour, and one thirſt quencheth another. In a word, though much indebted to his own back and belly, and unable to pay them, yet he hath credit with himſelf, and confidently runnes on ticket with himſelf, hoping the next victory will diſcharge all ſcores with advantage.

He looks at and alſo through his wages, at Gods glory, and his countreys good. 5
He counts his pay an honourable addition, but no valuable compenſation for his pains: for what proportion is there betwixt foure ſhillings a-week, and adventuring his life? I cannot ſee how their calling can be lawfull, who for greater wages will fight on any ſide againſt their own King and cauſe;

yea as false witnesses were hired against our blessed
Mat. 28. 15. * Saviour (money will make the mouths of men
plead against their Maker) so were the Giants now in
the world, who, as the Poets feigned, made warre
against God himself, and should they offer great pay,
they would not want mercenary Souldiers to assist
them.

6 *He attends with all readinesse on the commands of his Generall*; rendring up his own judgement in obedience to the will and pleasure of his Leader, and by an implicite faith believing all is best which he enjoyneth; lest otherwise he be served as the French Souldier was in Scotland some eighty years since, who first mounted the bulwark of a fort besieged, whereupon ensued the gaining of the fort: but Marescal de * Thermes, the French Generall, first knighted him, and then hanged him within an houre after, because he had done it without commandment.

* Hollman in his book of the Embassadour.

7 *He will not in a bravery expose himself to needlesse perill.* 'Tis madnesse to holloe in the ears of sleeping temptation, to awaken it against ones self, or to go out of his calling to find a danger: But if a danger meets him (as he walks in his vocation) he neither stands still, starts aside, nor steps backward, but either goes over it with valour, or under it with patience. All single Duels he detesteth, as having first no command in Gods Word; yea this arbitrary deciding causes by the sword subverts the fundamentall Laws of the Scripture: Secondly, no example in Gods Word, that of David and Goliah moving in an higher Sphere, as extraordinary: Thirdly, it tempts God to work a Miracle for mans pleasure, and to invert the course of nature, whereby otherwise the stronger will beat the weaker: Fourthly, each Dueller challengeth his King as unable or unwilling legally to right him, and therefore he usurps the office himself: Fifthly, if slaying, he hazards his neck to the halter; if slain, in heat of malice, without

without repentance, he adventures his ſoul to the devil.

Object. But there are ſome intricate caſes (as in Titles of land) which cannot otherwiſe be decided. Seeing therefore that in ſuch difficulties, the right in queſtion cannot be delivered by the midwifery of any judiciall proceedings, then it muſt (with Julius Cæſar in his mothers belly) be cut out and be determined by the ſword.

Anſw. Such a right may better be loſt, then to light a candle from hell to find it out, if the Judges cannot find a middle way to part it betwixt them. Beſides, in ſuch a caſe Duells are no *medium proportionatum* to find out the truth, as never appointed by God to that purpoſe. Nor doth it follow that he hath the beſt in right, who hath the beſt in fight; for he that reads the lawfulneſſe of actions by their events, holds the wrong end of the book upwards.

Object. But ſuppoſe an army of thirty thouſand Infidells ready to fight againſt ten thouſand Chriſtians, yet ſo that at laſt the Infidells are contented to try the day upon the valour of a ſingle Champion; whether in ſuch a caſe may not a Chriſtian undertake to combat with him, the rather becauſe the treble oddes before is thereby reduced to terms of equalitie, and ſo the victory made more probable.

Anſw. The victory was more probable before; becauſe it is more likely God will bleſſe his own means, then means of mans appointing: and it is his prerogative to give victory, as well by few as by many. Probability of conqueſt is not to be meaſured by the eye of humane reaſon, contrary to the ſquare of Gods Word. Beſides, I queſtion whether it be lawfull for a Chriſtian army to derive their right of fighting Gods battels to any ſingle man. For the title every man hath to promote Gods glory, is ſo inveſted and inherent in his own particular perſon, that he cannot paſſe it over to another. None may appear in Gods ſervice by an Atturney; and when Religion is at the ſtake, there muſt be no lookers on (except impotent people, who alſo help by their prayers) and every one is bound to lay his ſhoulders to the work. Laſtly, would to God no Duels might be fought till this caſe came into queſtion. But how many dayly fall out upon a more falſe, ſlight, and flitting ground, then the ſands of Callis whereon they fight : eſpecially, ſeeing there is an honourable Court appointed, or ſome other equivalent way, for taking up ſuch quarrells, and allowing reparations to the party injured.

Object. But Reputation is ſo ſpirituall a thing it is ineſtimable, and Honour falls not under valuation : Beſides, to complain to the civil Magiſtrate ſheweth no manhood, but is like a childs crying to his father, when he is onely beaten by his equall; and my enemies forc'd acknowledgement of his fault (enjoyn'd him by the Court) ſhews rather his ſubmiſsion to the laws then to me. But if I can civilize his rudeneſſe by my ſword, and chaſtize him into ſubmiſsion, then he ſings his penitentiall ſong in the true tune, and it comes naturally indeed.

Anſw. Honourable perſons in that Court are the moſt competent Judges of Honour, and though Credit be as tender as the apple of the eye, yet ſuch curious oculiſts can cure a blemiſh therein. And why, I pray, is it more diſgrace to repair to the Magiſtrate for redreſſe in Reputation, then to have recourſe to him in actions of treſpaſſe? The pretence of a forced ſubmiſsion is nothing, all ſubmiſsions having *aliquid violentum* in them ; and even

even the Evangelicall repentance of Gods ſervants hath a mixture of legall terrour frighting them thereto.

Object. But Gownmen ſpeak out of an antipathy they bear to fighting: ſhould we be rul'd by them, we muſt break all our ſwords into penknifes; and Lawyers, to inlarge their gains, ſend prohibitions to remove ſuits from the Camps to their Courts: Divines are not to be conſulted with herein, as ignorant of the principles of Honour.

Anſw. Indeed Honour is a word of courſe in the talk of roring boyes, and pure enough in it ſelf, except their mouths ſoil it by often uſing of it: But indeed God is the fountain of Honour, Gods Word the Charter of Honour, and godly men the beſt Judges of it; nor is it any ſtain of cowardlineſſe for one to fear hell and damnation.

We may therefore conclude that the laws of Duelling, as the laws of drinking, had their originall from the devil; and therefore the declining of needleſſe quarrels in our Souldier, no abatement of Honour. I commend his diſcretion and valour, who walking in London-ſtreetes met a gallant, who cryed to him a pretty diſtance beforehand, *I will have the wall? Yea* (anſwered he) *and take the houſe too, if you can but agree with the Landlord.* But when God, and his Prince, calls for him, our Souldier

Had rather die ten times then once ſurvive his credit. 8

Though life be ſweet, it ſhall not flatter the pallat of his ſoul, as with the ſweetneſſe of life to make him ſwallow down the bitterneſſe of an eternall diſgrace: He begrutcheth not to get to his ſide a probability of victory by the certainty of his own death, and flieth from nothing ſo much as from the mention of flying. And though ſome ſay he is a mad-man that will purchaſe Honour ſo dearly with his bloud, as that he cannot live to enjoy what he hath bought; our Souldier knows that he ſhall poſſeſſe the reward of his valour with God in heaven, and alſo making the world his executor, leave to it the rich inheritance of his memory.

9 *Yet in ſome caſes he counts it no diſgrace to yield, where it is impoſsible to conquer*; as when ſwarms of enemies crowd about him, ſo that he ſhall rather be ſtifled then wounded to death: In ſuch a caſe if quarter be offered him, he may take it with more honour then the other can give it; and if he throws up his deſperate game, he may happily winne the next, whereas if he playeth it out to the laſt, he ſhall certainly loſe it and himſelf. But if he be to fall into the hand of a barbarous enemy, whoſe giving him quarter is but repriving him for a more ignominious death, he had rather disburſe his life at the preſent, then to take day to fall into the hands of ſuch remorſleſſe creditours.

10 *He makes none the object of his cruelty, which cannot be the object of his fear.* Lyons they ſay (except forc'd with hunger) will not prey on women and children, * though I would wiſh none to try the truth hereof: the truly valiant will not hurt women or infants, nor will they be cruell to old men. What conqueſt is it to ſtrike him up, who ſtands but on one leg, and hath the other foot in the grave? But arrant cowards (ſuch as would conquer victory it ſelf, if it ſhould ſtand in their way as they flie) count themſelves never evenly match'd, except they have threefold oddes on their ſide, and eſteem their enemie never diſarmed till they be dead. Such love to ſhew a nature ſteep'd in gall of paſsion, and diſplay the ignoble tyrany of prevailing daſtards: theſe being thus valiant againſt no reſiſtance, will make no reſiſtance when they meet with true valour.

* *Plin. Nat. Hiſt. lib. 8. cap. 16.*

11 *He counts it murther to kill any in cold bloud.* Indeed in taking Cities by aſſault (eſpecially when Souldiers have

have ſuffered long in an hard ſiege) it is pardonable what preſent paſsion doth with a ſudden thruſt ; but a premeditated back-blow in cold bloud is baſe. Some excuſe there is for bloud enraged, and no wonder if that ſcaldeth which boyleth : but when men ſhall call a conſultation in their ſoul, and iſſue thence a deliberate act, the more adviſed the deed is, the leſſe adviſed it is, when men raiſe their own paſsions, and are not raiſed by them ; ſpecially if fair quarter be firſt granted ; an alms which he who gives to day may crave to morrow ; yea, he that hath the hilt in his hand in the morning, may have the point at his throat ere night.

12 *He doth not barbarouſly abuſe the bodies of his dead enemies.* We find that Hercules was the * firſt (the moſt valiant are ever moſt mercifull) that ever ſuffered his enemies to carry away their dead bodies, after they had been put to the ſword. Belike before his time they cruelly cut the corps in pieces, or caſt them to the wild beaſts.

* *Plutarch. in vita Theſei, Pagin.* 15.

13 *In time of plenty he provides for want hereafter.* Yet generally Souldiers (as if they counted one Treaſurer in an army were enough) ſo hate covetouſneſſe that they cannot affect providence for the future, and come home with more marks in their bodies then pence in their pockets.

14 *He is willing and joyfull to imbrace peace on good conditions.* The procreation of peace, and not the ſatisfying of mens luſts and liberties, is the end of warre. Yet how many, having warre for their poſſeſsion, deſire a perpetuity thereof! Wiſer men then King Henry the eights fool uſe to cry in fair weather, whoſe harveſt being onely in ſtorms, they themſelves deſire to raiſe them ; wherefore fearing peace will ſtarve, whom warre hath fatted, and to render themſelves the more uſefull they prolong diſcord to the utmoſt, and could wiſh when ſwords are once drawn that all ſcabbards might be cut aſunder.

He

15 *He is as quiet and painfull in peace, as couragious in warre.* If he hath not gotten already enough whereon comfortably to subsist, he rebetakes himself to his former calling he had before the warre began: the weilding of his sword hath not made him unweildie to do any other work, and put his bones out of joynt to take pains. Hence comes it to passe, that some take by-courses on the high-wayes, and death, whom they honourably sought for in the field, meets them in a worse place.

But we leave our Souldier, seeking by his virtues to ascend from a private place, by the degrees of Sergeant, Lieutenant, Captain, Colonell, till he comes to be a Generall, and then in the next book, God willing, you shall have his example.

Chap. 20.

The good Sea-Captain.

HIs Military part is concurrent with that of the Souldier already described: He differs onely in some Sea-properties, which we will now set down. Conceive him now in a Man of warre, with his letters of mart, well arm'd victuall'd and appointed, and see how he acquits himself.

Maxime 1 *The more power he hath, the more carefull he is not to abuse it.* Indeed a Sea-captain is a King in the Iland of a ship, supreme Judge, above appeal, in causes civill and criminall, and is seldome brought to an account in Courts of Justice on land, for injuries done to his own men at sea.

2 *He is carefull in observing of the Lords day.* He hath a watch in his heart though no bells in a steeple to proclaim that day by ringing to prayers. S[r] Francis Drake * in three years sailing about the world lost one whole day, which was scarce considerable in so long time. Tis to be feared some Captains at sea lose a day

* *Manuscr. of Mr. Fortescu, who went with him.*

day every week, one in ſeven, neglecting the Sabbath.

3 *He is as pious and thankfull when a tempeſt is paſt, as devout when 'tis preſent*: not clamorous to receive mercies, and tongue-tied to return thanks. Many mariners are calm in aſtorm, and ſtorm in a calm, bluſtring with oathes. In atempeſt it comes to their turn to be religious, whoſe piety is but a fit of the wind, and when that's allayed, their devotion is ended.

4 *Eſcaping many dangers makes him not preſumptuous to run into them.* Not like thoſe Sea-men who (as if their hearts were made of thoſe rocks they have often ſayled by) are ſo alwayes in death they never think of it. Theſe in their navigations obſerve that it is farre hotter under the Tropicks in the coming to the Line, then under the Line it ſelf, & in like manner they conceive that the fear & phancy in preparing for death is more terrible then death it ſelf, which makes them by degrees deſperately to contemne it.

5 *In taking a prize he moſt prizeth the mens lives whom he takes*; though ſome of them may chance to be Negroes or Savages. 'Tis the cuſtome of ſome to caſt them overbord, and there's an end of them: for the dumbe fiſhes will tell no tales. But the murder is not ſo ſoon drown'd as the men. What, is a brother by the half bloud no kinne? a Savage hath God to his father by creation, though not the Church to his mother, and God will revenge his innocent bloud. But our Captain counts the image of God neverthleſſe his image cut in ebony as if done in ivory, and in the blackeſt Moores he ſees the repreſentation of the King of heaven.

6 *In dividing the gains he wrongs none who took pains to get them.* Not ſhifting off his poore mariners with nothing, or giving them onely the garbage of the prize, and keeping all the fleſh to himſelf. In time of peace he quietly returns home, and turns not to the trade of

Pirates, who are the worſt ſea-vermine, and the devils water-rats.

7 *His voyages are not onely for profit, but ſome for honour and knowledge*; to make diſcoveries of new countreys, imitating the worthy Peter Columbus. Before his time the world was cut off at the middle; Hercules Pillars (which indeed are the navell) being made the feet, and utmoſt bounds of the continent, till his ſucceſſefull induſtry inlarged it.

Primus ab infuſis quod terra emerſerat undis
*Gen. 8. 11. *Nuncius adveniens ipſa * Columba fuit.*
Occiduis primus qui terram invenit in undis
Nuncius adveniens ipſe Columbus erat.

Our Sea-captain is likewiſe ambitious to perfect what the other began. He counts it a diſgrace, ſeeing all mankind is one familie, ſundry countreys but ſeverall rooms, that we who dwell in the parlour (ſo he counts Europe) ſhould not know the out-lodgings of the ſame houſe, and the world be ſcarce acquainted with it ſelf before it be diſſolved from it ſelf at the day of judgement.

8 *He daily ſees, and duly conſiders Gods wonders in the deep.* Tell me, ye Naturaliſts, who ſounded the firſt march and retreat to the Tide, *Hither ſhalt thou come, and no further?* why doth not the water recover his right over the earth, being higher in nature? whence came the ſalt, and who firſt boyled it, which made ſo much brine? when the winds are not onely wild in a ſtorm, but even ſtark mad in an herricano, who is it that reſtores them again to their wits, and brings them aſleep in a calm? who made the mighty whales, who ſwim in a ſea of water, and have a ſea of oyl ſwimming in them? who firſt taught the water to imitate the creatures on land? ſo that the ſea is the ſtable of horſe-fiſhes, the ſtall of kine-fiſhes, the ſtye of hog-fiſhes, the kennell of dog-fiſhes, and in all things the ſea the ape of the land. Whence growes the amber-greece

in

in the Sea? which is not ſo hard to find where it is, as to know what it is. Was not God the firſt ſhip wright? and all veſſels on the water deſcended from the loyns (or ribs rather) of Noahs ark; or elſe who durſt be ſo bold with a few crooked boards nayled together, a ſtick ſtanding upright, and a rag tied to it, to adventure into the ocean? what loadſtone firſt touched the loadſtone? or how firſt fell it in love with the North, rather affecting that cold climate, then the pleaſant Eaſt, or fruitfull South, or Weſt? how comes that ſtone to know more then men, and find the way to the land in a miſt?In moſt of theſe men take ſanctuary at *Occulta qualitas*, and complain that the room is dark, when their eyes are blind. Indeed they are Gods Wonders; and that Seaman the greateſt Wonder of all for his blockiſhneſſe, who ſeeing them dayly neither takes notice of them, admires at them, nor is thankfull for them.

Chap. 21.

The life of Sir Francis Drake.

** S^t. Francis Drake his nephew in the descript. of his third voyage, Epistle to the Reader.*

FRancis Drake was born nigh* south Tavestock in Devonshire, and brought up in Kent; God dividing the honour betwixt two Counties, that the one might have his birth, and the other his education. His Father, being a Minister, fled into Kent for fear of the Six Articles, wherein the sting of Popery still remained in England, though the teeth thereof were knock'd out, and the Popes Supremacy abolish-

abolished. Coming into Kent, he bound his sonne Francis apprentice to the Master of a small bark, which traded into France, and Zealand, where he underwent a hard service; and pains with patience in his youth did knit the joynts of his soul, and made them more solid and compacted. His Master dying unmarried, in reward of his industry, bequeath'd his bark unto him for a Legacie.

For some time he continued his Masters profession: But the Narrow Seas were a prison for so large a spirit, born for greater undertakings. He soon grew weary of his bark, which would scarce go alone but as it crept along by the shore: wherefore selling it, he unfortunately ventured most of his estate with Captain John Hawkins into the West Indies, whose goods *1567.* were taken by the Spaniards at S. John de Ulva, and he himself scarce escaped with life. The King of Spain being so tender in those parts, that the least touch doth wound him; and so jealous of the West Indies, his wife, that willingly he would have none look upon her, and therefore used them with the greater severity.

Drake was perswaded by the Minister of his ship that he might lawfully recover in value of the King of Spain, and repair his losses upon him any where else. The Case was clear in sea-divinity, and few are such Infidels, as not to believe doctrines which make for their own profit. Whereupon Drake, though a poore private man, hereafter undertook to revenge himself on so mighty a Monarch; who, as not contented that the Sun riseth and setteth in his dominions, may seem to desire to make all his own where he shineth. And now let us see how a dwarf, standing on the Mount of Gods providence, may prove an overmatch for a giant.

After two or three severall Voyages to gain intelligence in the West Indies, and some prizes taken, at last

last he effectually set forward from Plimouth with two ships, the one of seventy, the other twenty five tunnes, and seventy three men and boyes in both. He made with all speed and secrecy to Nombre de Dios, as loth to put the Town to too much charge (which he knew they would willingly bestow) in providing beforehand for his entertainment; which City was then the granary of the West Indies, wherein the golden harvest brought from Panama was hoarded up till it could be conveyed into Spain. They came hard aboard the shore, and lay quiet all night intending to attempt the Town in the dawning of the day.

But he was forced to alter his resolution, and assault it sooner; for he heard his men muttering amongst themselves of the strength and greatnesse of the Town: and when mens heads are once fly-blown with buzzes of suspicion, the vermine multiply instantly and one jealousie begets another. Wherefore he raised them from their nest before they had hatch'd their fears, and to put away those conceits, he perswaded them it was day-dawning when the Moon rose, and instantly set on the Town, and wonne it being unwalled. In the Market-place the Spaniards saluted them with a volley of shot; Drake returned their greeting with a flight of arrows, the best and ancient English complement, which drave their enemies away. Here Drake received a dangerous wound, though he valiantly conceal'd it a long time, knowing if his heart stooped, his mens would fall, and loth to leave off the action, wherein if so bright an opportunity once setteth, it seldome riseth again. But at length his men forced him to return to his ship, that his wound might be dressed, and this unhappy accident defeated the whole designe. Thus victory sometimes slips thorow their fingers, who have caught it in their hands.

But

But his valour would not let him give over the project as long as there was either life or warmth in it: And therefore having received intelligence from the Negroes, called Symerons, of many mules-lading of gold and ſilver, which was to be brought from Panama, he leaving competent numbers to man his ſhips went on land with the reſt, and beſtowed himſelf in the woods by the way as they were to paſſe, and ſo intercepted and carried away an infinite maſſe of gold. As for the ſilver which was not portable over the mountains, they digged holes in the ground and hid it therein.

There want not thoſe who love to beat down the price of every honourable action, though they themſelves never mean to be chapmen. Theſe cry up Drakes fortune herein to cry down his valour; as if this his performance were nothing, wherein a golden opportunity ran his head with his long forelock into Drakes hands beyond expectation. But certainly his reſolution and unconquerable patience deſerved much praiſe, to adventure on ſuch a deſigne, which had in it juſt no more probability then what was enough to keep it from being impoſſible: yet I admire not ſo much at all the treaſure he took, as at the rich and deep mine of Gods providence.

Having now full fraughted himſelf with wealth, and burnt at the Houſe of Croſſes above two hundred thouſand pounds worth of Spaniſh Merchandiſe, he returned with honour and ſafety into England, and ſome * years after undertook that his famous voyage about the world, moſt accurately deſcribed by our Engliſh Authours: and yet a word or two thereof will not be amiſſe. * 1577. *Decemb.* 13.

Setting forward from Plimouth, he bore up for Caboverd, where near to the Iland of S. Jago he took priſoner Nuno-da-Silva, an experienc'd Spaniſh pilot, whoſe direction he uſed in the coaſts of Braſil and Magellan

Magellan ſtraits, and afterwards ſafely landed him at Guatulco in New Spain. Hence they took their courſe to the iland of Brava, and hereabouts they met with thoſe tempeſtuous winds, whoſe onely praiſe is, that they continue not above an houre, in which time they change * all the points of the compaſſe. Here they had great plenty of rain, poured (not as in other places, as it were out of ſives, but) as out of ſpouts, ſo that a but of water falls down in a place : which notwithſtanding is but a courteous injury in that hot climate farre from land,and where otherwiſe freſh water cannot be provided : then cutting the Line, they ſaw the face of that heaven which earth hideth from us, but therein onely three * ſtarres of the firſt greatneſſe, the reſt few and ſmall compared to our Hemiſphere, as if God, on purpoſe, had ſet up the beſt and biggeſt candles in that room wherein his civileſt gueſts are entertained.

** Manuſc. of Geor. Forteſcue who went the voyage with Sr Fran. Drake.*

**Cambd Eliza. Anno* 1580. *p.* 323.

Sayling the South of Braſile, he afterwards paſſed the * Magellan ſtraits, and then entred *Mare pacificum*, came to the Southermoſt land at the height of 55 ½ latitude ; thence directing his courſe Northward, he pillaged many Spaniſh Towns, and took rich prizes of high value in the kingdomes of Chily, Peru, and New Spain. Then bending Eaſtwards, he coaſted China, and the Moluccoes, where by the King of Ternate, a true Gentleman Pagan, he was moſt honourably entertain'd : The King told them, They and he were all of one religion in this reſpect,that they believed * not in Gods made of ſtocks and ſtones as did the Portugalls. He furniſh'd them alſo with all neceſſaries that they wanted.

**Auguſt.* 20. 1578.

** Manuſcri. Geor. Forteſcue*

On the ninth of * January following,his ſhip,having a large wind and a ſmooth ſea,ran a ground on a dangerous ſhole, and ſtrook twice on it,knocking twice at the doore of death, which no doubt had opened the third time.Here they *ſtuck from eight a clock at night till

* 1579.

**Hacluits voyage,p.*741. 3. *vol.*

till foure the next afternoon, having ground too much, and yet too little to land on, and water too much, and yet too little to ſail in. Had God (*who*, as the wiſe-man ſaith, Prov. 30. 4. *holdeth the winds in his fiſt*) but opened his little finger, and let out the ſmalleſt blaſt, they had undoubtedly been caſt away; but there blew not any wind all the while. Then they conceiving aright that the beſt way to lighten the ſhip, was firſt to eaſe it of the burthen of their ſinnes by true repentance, humbled themſelves by faſting under the hand of God: Afterwards they received the Communion, dining on Chriſt in the Sacrament, expecting no other then to ſup with him in heaven: Then they caſt out of their ſhip ſix great pieces of ordinance, threw over-board as much wealth as would break the heart of a Miſer to think on't, with much ſuger, and packs of ſpices, making a caudle of the ſea round about: Then they betook themſelves to their prayers, the beſt lever at ſuch a dead lift indeed, and it pleaſed God that the wind, formerly their mortall enemy, became their friend, which changing from the Starboard to the Larboard of the ſhip, and riſing by degrees, cleared them off to the ſea again, for which they returned unfeigned thanks to almighty God.

By the Cape of good hope and weſt of Africa he returned ſafe into England, and landed at * Plimouth, (being almoſt the firſt of thoſe that made a thorow-light through the world) having in his whole voyage, though a curious ſearcher after the time, loſt one day through the variation of ſeverall Climates. He feaſted the Queen in his ſhip at Dartford, who Knighted him for his ſervice: yet it grieved him not a little, that ſome prime * Courtiers refuſed the gold he offer'd them, as gotten by piracy. Some of them would have been loth to have been told, that they had *Aurum Tholoſanum* in their own purſes. Some think that they did it to ſhew that their envious pride was above their covetouſneſſe,

* *Novemb.* 3 1580.

* *Camb. Eliza. Anno ut prius, pag.* 127.

T who

who of set purpose did blur the fair copy of his performance, because they would not take pains to write after it.

1585. I passe by his next *West Indian voyage, wherein he took the Cities of S. Jago, S. Domingo, Carthagena, and S. Augustine in Florida: as also his service performed in 88, wherein he with many others helped to the waining of that half Moon, which sought to govern all the motion of our Sea. I hast to his last Voyage.

1595. Queen Elizabeth perceiving that the onely way to make the Spaniard a criple for ever, was to cut his Sinews of warre in the West Indies, furnished S[r] Francis Drake, and S[r] John Hawkins with six of her own ships, besides 21 ships and Barks of their own providing, containing in all 2500 Men and Boyes, for some service on America. But, alas, this voyage was marr'd before begun. For so great preparations being too big for a cover, the King of Spain knew of it, and sent a Caravall of adviso to the West Indies, so that they had intelligence * three weeks before the Fleet set forth of England, either to fortifie, or remove their treasure; whereas in other of Drakes Voyages not two of his own men knew whither he went; and managing such a designe is like carrying a Mine in warre, if it hath any vent, all is spoyled. Besides, Drake and Hawkins being in joynt Commission hindred each other. The later took himself to be inferiour rather in successe then skill, and the action was unlike to prosper when neither would follow, and both could not handsomly go abreast. It vexed old Hawkins that his counsell was not followed, in present sayling to America, but that they spent time in vain in assaulting the Canaries; and the grief that his advice was slighted (say some) was the cause of his death. Others impute it to the sorrow he took, for the taking of his Bark called the Francis, which five Spanish Frigates had intercepted: But whē the same heart hath two mortall wounds given it together, 'tis hard to say which of them killeth. Drake

* *Hacluits voyage, 3. vol. pag. 583.*

Drake continued his courſe for Port-Rico, and riding within the roade, a ſhot from the Caſtle entred the ſteerage of the ſhip, took away the ſtool from under him as he ſate at ſupper, wounded Sr Nicholas Clifford and Brute Brown to death. *Ah dear * Brute* (ſaid Drake) *I could grieve for thee but now is no time for me to let down my ſpirits.* And indeed a Souldiers moſt proper bemoaning a friends death in warre is in revenging it. And ſure, as if grief had made the Engliſh furious, they ſoon after fired five Spaniſh ſhips of two hundred tunnes apiece, in deſpight of the Caſtle.

* *From the mouth of Henr. Drake Eſquire there preſent, my dear and worthy pariſhioner lately deceaſed.*

America is not unfitly reſembled to an Houre-glaſſe, which hath a narrow neck of land (ſuppoſe it the hole where the ſand paſſeth) betwixt the parts thereof, Mexicana & Pervana. Now the Engliſh had a deſigne to march by land over this Iſthmus from Port-Rico to Panama, where the Spaniſh treaſure was layd up. St Thomas Baskervile, Generall of the land-forces, undertook the ſervice with ſeven hundred and fifty armed men. They marched through deep wayes, the Spaniards much annoying them with ſhot out of the woods. One fort in the paſſage they aſſaulted in vain, and heard that two others were built to ſtop them, beſides Panama it ſelf. They had ſo much of this breakfaſt, they thought they ſhould ſurfet of a dinner and ſupper of the ſame. No hope of conqueſt, except with cloying the jaws of Death, and thruſting men on the mouth of the Canon. Wherefore fearing to find the Proverb true, That Gold may be bought too dear, they returned to their ſhips. Drake afterwards fired Nombre de Dios, and many other petty Towns (whoſe treaſure the Spaniards had conveyed away) burning the empty casks, when their precious liquour was runne out before, and then prepared for their returning home.

Great was the difference betwixt the Indian cities

now from what they were when Drake first haunted these coasts : At first the Spaniards here were safe and secure, counting their treasure sufficient to defend it self, the remotenesse thereof being the greatest (almost onely) resistance, and the fetching of it more then the fighting for it. Whilest the King of Spain guarded the head and heart of his dominions in Europe, he left his long legs in America open to blows, till finding them to smart, being beaten black and blew by the English, he learned to arm them at last, fortifying the most important of them to make them impregnable.

Now began S[r] Francis his discontent to feed upon him. He conceived that expectation, a mercilesse usurer, computing each day since his departure exacted an interest and return of honour and profit proportionable to his great preparations, and transcending his former atchievements. He saw that all the good which he had done in this voyage, consisted in the evill he had done to the Spaniards afarre off, whereof he could present but small visible fruits in England. These apprehensions accompanying if not causing the disease of the flux wrought his sudden * death. And sicknesse did not so much untie his clothes, as sorrow did rend at once the robe of his mortality asunder. He lived by the sea, died on it, and was buried in it. Thus an ex-tempore performance (scarce heard to be begun before we hear it is ended) comes off with better applause, or miscarries with lesse disgrace, then a long studied and openly premeditated action. Besides, we see how great spirits, having mounted to the highest pitch of performance, afterwards strain and break their credits in striving to go beyond it. Lastly, God oftentimes leaves the brightest men in an eclipse, to shew that they do but borrow their lustre from his reflection. We will not justifie all the actions of any man, though of a tamer profession then a

** January 28. 1595.*

Sea-

Sea-Captain, in whom civility is often counted preciſeneſſe. For the main, we ſay that this our Captain was a religious man towards God and his houſes (generally ſparing Churches where he came) chaſt in his life, juſt in his dealings, true of his word, and mercifull to thoſe that were under him, hating nothing ſo much as idleneſſe: And therefore leſt his ſoul ſhould ruſt in peace, at ſpare houres he brought freſh water to Plimouth. Carefull he was for poſterity (though men of his profeſsion have as well an ebbe of riot, as a flote of fortune) and providently raiſed a worſhipfull Family of his kinred. In a word, ſhould thoſe that ſpeak againſt him faſt till they fetch their bread where he did his, they would have a good ſtomach to eat it.

Chap. 22.

The good Herald.

HE is a Warden of the temple of Honour. Mutuall neceſsity made mortall enemies agree in theſe Officers; the lungs of Mars himſelf would be burnt to pieces having no reſpiration in a truce. Heralds therefore were invented to proclaim peace or warre, deliver meſſages about ſummons of forts, ranſoming of captives, burying the dead, and the like.

He is grave and faithfull in diſcharging the ſervice he is imployed in. The names which Homer gives the Grecian Ceryces, excellently import their virtues in diſcharging their office: One was called Aſphalio, *ſuch an one as made ſure work*; another Eurybates, *cunning and ſubtle*; a third Theotes, from his piety and godlineſſe; a fourth Stentor, from his loud and audible pronouncing of meſſages. Therefore of every Heathen ſacrifice the * tongue was cut out, and given to the Heralds, to ſhew that liberty of ſpeech in all places was allowed them. *Maxime* 1

* *Sr. Hen. Spelman Gloſſar. de verbo* Herald.

2 *He imbitters not a distastfull message to a forrein Prince by his indiscretion in delivering it.* Commendable was the gravity of Guien King of arms in France, and Thomas Bevolt Clarenceaux of England, sent by their severall Princes to defie Charles the Emperour. For after leave demanded and obtained to deliver the message with safe conduct to their persons, they delivered the Emperour the lie in writing, and defying him were sent home safe with rewards. It fared worse with a foolish French Herald, sent from the Count of Orgell to challenge combat with the Count of Cardonna, Admiral of Arragon, where instead of wearing his Coat of Arms the Herald was attired in a long linen garment, painted with some dishonest actions, imputed to the said Count of Cardonna. But Ferdinand King of Arragon caused the Herald to be whipt naked through the streets * of Barcelona, as a punishment of his presumption. Thus his indescretion remitted him to the nature of an ordinary person, his Armour of proof of publick credence fell off, and he left naked to the stroke of justice, no longer a publick Officer, but a private offender. Passe we now from his use in warre to his imployment in peace.

Span. Hist. in the life of Ferdinand.

3 *He is skilfull in the pedigrees and descents of all ancient Gentry.* Otherwise, to be able onely to blazon a Coat doth no more make an Herald, then the reading the titles of Gally-pots makes a Physician. Bring our Herald to a Monument, *ubi jacet epitaphium*, and where the Arms on the Tombe are not onely crest-fallen, but their colours scarce to be discerned, and he will tell whose they be, if any certainty therein can be rescued from the teeth of Time. But how shamefull was the ignorance of the French * Heralds some fourty years since, who at a solemn entertainment of Queen Mary of Florence, wife to King Henrie the fourth, did falsly devise and blazon both the Arms of Florence, and the Arms of the Daulphin of France, now King thereof.

* *Andr. Favin (a Parisian Advocate) in his Theatre of Honour, 1. book 4. chap. pag. 35*

He

He carefully preſerveth the memories of extinguiſh'd Families, of ſuch Zelophehads, who dying left onely daughters. He is more faithfull to many ancient Gentlemen then their own Heirs were, who ſold their lands, and with them (as much as in them lay) their memories, which our Herald carefully treaſureth up. 4

He reſtoreth many to their own rightfull Arms. An Heir is a Phenix in a familie, there can be but one of them at the ſame time. Hence comes it often to paſſe, that younger brothers of gentile families live in low wayes, clouded often amongſt the Yeomanry; and yet thoſe under-boughs grow from the ſame root with the top-branches. It may happen afterwards that by induſtry they may advance themſelves to their former luſtre; and good reaſon they ſhould recover their ancient enſignes of honour belonging unto them: For the river Anas in Spain, though running many miles under ground, when it comes up again is ſtill the ſame river which it was before. And yet 5

He curbs their Vſurpation who unjuſtly entitle themſelves to ancient Houſes. Hierophilus a*Ferrier in Rome pretended himſelf to be nephew to C. Marius, who had ſeven times been Conſul, and carried it in ſo high a ſtrain that many believed him, and ſome companies in Rome accepted him for their Patron. Such want not amongſt us, who in ſpight of the ſtock will engraff themſelves into noble bloods, and thence derive their pedegree. Hence they new mould their names, taking from them, adding to them, melting out all the liquid letters, torturing mutes to make them ſpeak, and making vowels dumbe to bring it to a fallacious Homonomy at the laſt, that their names may be the ſame with thoſe noble Houſes they pretend to. By this trick (to forbear dangerous inſtances, if affinity of ſound makes kinred) Lutulentus makes himſelf kinne to Luculentus, dirt to light, and Anguſtus to Auguſtus, ſome narrow-hearted Peaſant, to ſome large-ſpirited Prince, 6

* *Valer. Max. lib.9.cap.16.*

Prince, except our good Herald marre their mart, and diſcover their forgery. For well he knows where indeed the names are the ſame (though alter'd through variety of writing in ſeverall ages, and diſguiſ'd by the liſping of vulgar people, who miſcall hard French Sirnames) and where the equivocation is untruly affected.

7 *He aſsignes honourable Arms to ſuch as raiſe themſelves by deſerts.* In all ages their muſt be as well a beginning of new Gentry, as an ending of ancient. And let not *Linea*, when farre extended in length, grow ſo proud as to ſcorn the firſt *Punctum* which gave it the originall. Our Herald knows alſo to cure the ſurfet of Coats, and unſurcharge them, and how to waſh out ſtained colours, when the merits of Poſterity have outworn the diſgraces of their Anceſtours.

8 *He will not for any profit favour wealthy unworthineſſe.* If a rich Clown (who deſerves that all his ſhield ſhould be the Baſe point) ſhall repair to the Herald-office, as to a drapers ſhop, wherein any Coat may be bought for money, he quickly finds himſelf deceived. No doubt if our Herald gives him a Coat, he gives him alſo a badge with it.

CHAP. 23.

WILLIAM CAMBDEN Clarenciaux *king of* Armes. *He dyed at Westminster Anno Dñi* 1623. *Aged* 74 *yeares* W *Marshall sculp*.

Chap. 23.

The life of Mr W. Cambden.

William Cambden was born *Anno* 1550 in old Baily, in the City of London. His Father, Sampson Cambden, was descended of honest parentage in Staffordshire; but by his Mothers side he was extracted from the worshipfull family of the * Curwens in Cumberland.

* A quibus nobis (absit invidia) genus maternum, *Cambd. Brit. in Cumber.*

He was brought up first in Christ-Church, then in Pauls School in London, and at fifteen years of age

V went

went to Magdalen Colledge in Oxford, and thence to * Broadgates Hall, where he first made those short Latine Graces, which the Servitours still use. From hence he was removed, and made student of Christ Church, where he profited to such eminency, that he was preferred to be Master of Westminster School, a most famous seminarie of learning.

* *Ex Parentatione Degorii Wheat.*

For whereas before, of the two grand Schools of England, one sent all her Foundation-scholars to Cambridge, the other all to Oxford, the good Queen (as the Head equally favouring both Breasts of Learning and Religion) divided her Scholars here betwixt both Universities, which were enriched with many hope full plants sent from hence, through Cambdens learning, diligence, and clemency. Sure none need pity the beating of that Scholar, who would not learn without it under so meek a Master.

His deserts call'd him hence to higher employments. The Queen first made him Richmond Herald, and then Clarenceaux King of Arms. We reade how Dionysius first King of Sicily turn'd afterwards a Schoolmaster in his old age. Behold here Dionysius inverted, one that was a Schoolmaster in his youth become a King(of Arms) in his riper years, which place none ever did or shall discharge with more integrity. He was a most exact Antiquary, witnesse his worthy work, which is a comment on three kingdomes; and never was so large a text more briefly, so dark a text more plainly expounded. Yea what a fair garment hath been made out of the very shreds and Remains of that greater Work?

It is most worthy observation with what diligence he inquired after ancient places, making Hue and Crie after many a City which was run away, and by certain marks and tokens pursuing to find it; as by the situation on the *Romane high-wayes, by just distance from other ancient cities, by some affinity of name, by

* *Watlin* } *street* *Ermin* }

by tradition of the inhabitants, by Romane coyns digged up, and by ſome appearance of ruines. A broken urn is a whole evidence, or an old gate ſtill ſurviving, out of which the city is run out. Beſides, commonly ſome new ſpruce town, not farre off, is grown out of the aſhes thereof, which yet hath ſo much naturall affection, as dutifully to own thoſe reverend ruines for her Mother.

By theſe and other means he arrived at admirable knowledge, and reſtored Britain to her ſelf. And let none tax him for preſumption in conjectures where the matter was doubtfull; for many probable conjectures have ſtricken the fire, out of which Truths candle hath been lighted afterwards. Beſides, conjectures, like parcells of unknown ore, are ſold but at low rates: If they prove ſome rich metall, the buyer is a great gainer; if baſe, no looſer, for he payes for it accordingly.

His candour and ſweet temper was highly to be commended, gratefully acknowledging thoſe by whom he was aſsiſted in the work (in ſuch a caſe confeſsion puts the difference betwixt ſtealing and borrowing) and ſurely ſo heavy a log needed more levers then one. He honourably mentioneth ſuch as differ from him in opinion; not like thoſe Antiquaries, who are ſo ſnarling one had as good diſſent a mile as an hairs breadth from them.

Moſt of the Engliſh ancient Nobility and Gentry he hath unpartially obſerved. Some indeed object that he * claws and flatters the Grandees of his own age, extolling ſome families rather great then ancient, making them to flow from a farre fountain becauſe they had a great channell, eſpecially if his private friends. But this cavil hath more of malice then truth: indeed 'tis pitty he ſhould have a tongue, that hath not a word for a friend on juſt occaſion; and juſtly might the ſtream of his commendations run broader, where meeting

* *Hugh Holland in the life of the Earl of Leiceſter.*

with a confluence of desert and friendshi p in the same party. For the main, his pen is sincere and unpartiall, and they who complain that Grantham steeple stands awry will not set a straiter by it.

Some say that in silencing many gentile families, he makes baulks of as good ground as any he ploweth up. But these again acquit him, when they consider that it is not onely difficult but impossible to anatomize the English Gentry so exactly, as to shew where every smallest vein thereof runs. Besides, many Houses, conceived to be by him omitted, are rather rightly placed by him, not where they live, but whence they came. Lastly, we may perceive that he prepared another work on purpose for the English Gentry.

I say nothing of his learned Annalls of Queen Elizabeth, industriously performed. His very enemies (if any) cannot but commend him. Sure he was as farre from loving * Popery, as from hating Learning, though that aspersion be generall on Antiquaries; as if they could not honour hoary hairs, but presently themselves must doat.

* *These words he wrote in the beginning of his Testament*, Christi solius meritis & satisfactione spem omnem salutis meæ semper niti profiteor.

His liberality to Learning is sufficiently witnessed in his Founding of an History-Professour in Oxford, to which he gave the mannour of Bexley in Kent, worth in present a hundred and fourty pounds, but (some years expired) foure hundred pounds *per Annum*, so that he merited that distich,

Est tibi pro Tumulo, Cambdene, Britannia tota,
Oxonium vivens est Epigramma tibi.

The Military part of his office he had no need to imploy, passing it most under a peaceable Prince. But now having lived many years in honour and esteem, death at last, even contrarie to *Jus Gentium*, kill'd this worthy Herald, so that it seems, Mortality, the Law of Nature, is above the Law of Arms. He died *Anno* 1623. the ninth of November, in the seventie fourth yeare of his age.

CHAP. 24.

Chap. 24.
The true Gentleman.

WE will conſider him in his Birth, Breeding, and Behaviour.

He is extracted from ancient and worſhipfull parentage. Maxime 1
When a Pepin is planted on a Pepin-ſtock, the fruit
growing thence is called a *Renate, a moſt delicious (* Draitons Poliolbion, p.298.)
apple, as both by Sire and Damme well deſcended.
Thus his bloud muſt needs be well purified who is
gentilely born on both ſides. 2

If his birth be not, at leaſtwiſe his qualities are generous.
What if he cannot with the Hevenninghams of Suffolk country *five and twenty Knights of his familie, or (* Weavers fun. mon. pag. 854.)
tell *ſixteen Knights ſucceſsively with the Tilneys of (* Idem. p.818.)
Norfolk, or with the Nauntons ſhew where their Anceſtours had *ſeven hundred pound a yeare before or at (* Idem p.758.)
the conqueſt; yet he hath endeavoured by his own deſerts to ennoble himſelf. Thus Valour makes him ſonne to Cæſar, Learning entitles him kinſman to Tully, & Piety reports him nephew to godly Conſtantine. It graceth a Gentleman of low deſcent & high deſert, when he will own the meanneſſe of his parentage. How ridiculous is it when many men brag, that their families are more ancient then the Moon, which all know are later then the ſtarre which ſome ſeventy years ſince ſhined in Caſsiopea. But if he be generouſly born, ſee how his parents breed him. 3

He is not in his youth poſſeſt with the great hopes of his poſſeſsion. No flatterer reads conſtantly in his ears a ſurvey of the lands he is to inherit. This hath made many boyes thoughts ſwell ſo great they could never be kept in compaſſe afterwards. Onely his Parents acquaint him that he is the next undoubted Heir to correction, if misbehaving himſelf; and he finds no more favour from his Schoolmaſter then his Schoolmaster finds diligence in him, whose rod respects persons no more then bullets are partiall in a battel.

4 *At the University he is so studious as if he intended Learning for his profession.* He knowes well that cunning is no burthen to carry, as paying neither portage by land, nor poundage by sea. Yea though to have land be a good First, yet to have learning is the surest Second, which may stand to it when the other may chance to be taken away.

5 *At the Innes of Court he applyes himself to learn the Laws of the kingdome.* Object not, Why should a Gentleman learn law, who if he needeth it may have it for his money, and if he hath never so much of his own, he must but give it away. For what a shame is it for a man of quality to be ignorant of Solon in our Athens, of Lycurgus in our Sparta? Besides, law will help him to keep his own, and besteed his neighbours. Say not, that there be enough which make this their set practice: for so there are also many masters of defence by their profession; and shall private men therefore learn no skill at their weapons.

As for the Hospitality, the Apparell, the Travelling, the Companie, the Recreations, the Marriage of Gentlemen, they are described in severall Chapters in the following Book. A word or two of his behaviour in the countrey.

6 *He is courteous and affable to his neighbours.* As the sword of the best tempered mettall is most flexible; so the truly generous are most pliant and courteous in their behaviour to their inferiours.

7 *He delights to see himself, and his servants well mounted:* therefore he loveth good Horsemanship. Let never any forrein Rabshakeh send that brave to our Jerusalem, offering *to lend her * two thousand horses, if she be able for her part to set riders upon them.* We know how Darius got the Persian Empire from the rest of his fellow Peeres,

* 2. Kings. 18. 23.

Peeres, by the firſt neighing of his generous ſteed. It were no harm if in ſome needleſſe ſuits of intricate precedencie betwixt equall Gentlemen, the priority were adjudged to him who keeps a ſtable of moſt ſerviceable horſes.

8 *He furniſheth and prepareth himſelf in peace againſt time of warre.* Leſt it be too late to learn when his skill is to be uſed. He approves himſelf couragious when brought to the triall, as well remembring the cuſtome which is uſed at the Creation of Knights of the Bath, wherein the Kings Maſter-Cook * cometh forth, & preſente his great knife to the new-made Knights, admoniſhing them to be faithfull and valiant, otherwiſe he threatens them that that very knife is prepared to cut off their ſpurres.

* *M. Selden in his titles of Honour, pag.* 820

9 *If the Commiſſion of the Peace finds him out, he faithfully diſcharges it.* I ſay, Finds him out; for a publick Office is a gueſt which receives the beſt uſage from them who never invited it. And though he declined the Place, the countrey knew to prize his worth, who would be ignorant of his own. He compounds many petty differences betwixt his neighbours, which are eaſier ended in his own Porch then in Weſtminſter-hall: for many people think, if once they have fetched a warrant from a Juſtice, they have given earneſt to follow the ſuit, though otherwiſe the matter be ſo mean that the next nights ſleep would have bound both parties to the peace, and made them as good friends as ever before. Yet

10 *He connives not at the ſmothering of puniſhable faults.* He hates that practice, as common as dangerous amongſt countrey people, who having received again the goods which were ſtollen from them, partly out of fooliſh pity, and partly out of covetouſneſſe to ſave charges in proſecuting the law, let the thief eſcape unpuniſhed. Thus whileſt private loſſes are repaired, the wounds to the Commonwealth (in the breach of the Laws)

Laws) are left uncured : And thus petty Larceners are encouraged into Felons, and afterwards are hang'd for pounds, becauſe never whipt for pence, who, if they had felt the cord, had never been brought to the halter.

11 *If choſen a Member of Parliament he is willing to do his Countrey ſervice.* If he be no Rhetorician to raiſe affections, (yea Barnabas was a * greater ſpeaker then S. Paul himſelf) he counts it great wiſdome to be the good manager of Yea and Nay. The ſlow pace of his judgement is recompenced by the ſwift following of his affections, when his judgement is once ſoundly inform'd. And here we leave him in conſultation, wiſhing him with the reſt of his honourable Society all happy ſucceſſe.

* *Acts* 14.12.

The

The Holy State.

THE THIRD BOOK. Containing Generall Rules.

Chap. I. *Of Hospitality.*

Hospitality is threefold: for ones familie; this is of Necessity: for strangers; this is Courtesie: for the poore; this is Charity. Of the two latter.

To keep a disorderly house is the way to keep neither house nor lands. For whilest they keep the greatest roaring, their state steals away in the greatest silence. Yet when many consume themselves with secret vices, then Hospitality bears the blame: whereas it is not the Meat but the Sauce, not the Supper but the Gaming after it, doth undoe them. Maxime 1.

Measure not thy entertainment of a guest by his estate, but thine own. Because he is a Lord, forget not that thou art but a Gentleman: otherwise if with feasting him thou breakest thy self, he will not cure thy rupture, and (perchance) rather deride then pitie thee. 2

When provision (as we say) groweth on the same, it is miraculously multiplied. In Northamptonshire all the rivers of the County are bred in it, besides those (Ouse and Charwell) it lendeth and sendeth into other shires: So the good Housekeeper hath a fountain of wheat in his field, mutton in his fold, &c. both to serve himself, 3 and ſupply others. The expence of a feaſt will but breath him, which will tire another of the ſame eſtate who buyes all by the penny.

4 *Mean mens palates are beſt pleaſed with fare rather plentifull then various, ſolid then dainty.* Dainties will coſt more, and content leſſe, to thoſe that are not Criticall enough to diſtinguiſh them.

5 *Occaſionall entertainment of men greater then thy ſelf is better then ſolemn inviting them.* Then ſhort warning is thy large excuſe: whereas otherwiſe, if thou doſt not overdo thy eſtate, thou ſhalt underdo his expectation, for thy feaſt will be but his ordinary fare. A King of France was often pleaſed in his hunting wilfully to loſe himſelf, to find the houſe of a private Park-keeper; where going from the School of State-affairs, he was pleaſed to make a play-day to himſelf. He brought ſauce (Hunger) with him, which made courſe meat dainties to his palate. At laſt the Park-keeper took heart, and ſolemnely invited the King to his houſe, who came with all his Court, ſo that all the mans meat was not a morſell for them: *Well* (ſaid the Park-keeper) *I will invite no more Kings*; having learnt the difference between Princes when they pleaſe to put on the viſard of privacie, and when they will appear like themſelves, both in their Perſon and Attendants.

6 *Thoſe are ripe for charitie which are withered by age or impotencie.* Eſpecially if maimed in following their calling; for ſuch are Induſtries Martyrs, at leaſt her Confeſſours. Adde to theſe thoſe that with diligence fight againſt poverty, though neither conquer till death make it a drawn battel. Expect not, but prevent their craving of thee; for God forbid the heavens ſhould never rain till the earth firſt opens her mouth, ſeing ſome grounds will ſooner burn then chap.

7 *The Houſe of correction is the fitteſt Hoſpital for thoſe Cripples, whoſe legs are lame through their own lazineſſe.* Surely King Edward the ſixth was as truly charitable in granting

Bridewell

Bridewell for the puniſhment of ſturdy Rogues, as in giving S. Thomas Hoſpitall for the relief of the Poore. I have done with the ſubject, onely I deſire rich men to awaken Hoſpitality, which * one ſaith ſince the yeare 1572 hath in a manner been laid aſleep in the grave of Edward Earl of Darby.

* *Cambd.Eliſ. Anno* 1573.

Chap. 2.

Of Jeſting.

HArmleſſe mirth is the beſt cordiall againſt the conſumption of the ſpirits: wherefore Jeſting is not unlawfull if it treſpaſſeth not in Quantity, Quality, or Seaſon.

It is good to make a Jeſt, but not to make a trade of Jeſting. *Maxime* 1.
The Earl of Leiceſter, knowing that Queen Elizabeth was much delighted to ſee a Gentleman dance well, brought the Maſter of a dancing-ſchool to dance before her: *Piſh* (ſaid the Queen) *it is his profeſſion, I will not ſee him.* She liked it not where it was a Maſter-quality, but where it attended on other perfections. The ſame may we ſay of Jeſting.

*Jeſt not with the two-edged * ſword of Gods Word.* Will 2
nothing pleaſe thee to waſh thy hands in, but the Font? or to drink healths in, but the Church Chalice? And know the whole art is learnt at the firſt admiſsion, and profane Jeſts will come without calling. If in the troubleſome dayes of King Edward the fourth a Citizen in Cheap-ſide was executed as a traitour, for ſaying he would make his ſonne heir to the * Crown, though he onely meant his own houſe, having a Crown for the ſigne; more dangerous it is to wit-wanton it with the Majeſtie of God. Wherefore if without thine intention, and againſt thy will, by chancemedly thou hitteſt Scripture in ordinary diſcourſe, yet fly to the city of refuge, and pray to God to forgive thee.

* Μάχαιραν δίστομον, *Heb.* 4.11.

* *Speed in Edward the* 4.

Wanton Jeſts make fools laugh, and wiſe men frown. 3
Seeing

Seeing we are civilized Engliſh men, let us not be naked Salvages in our talk. Such rotten ſpeeches are worſt in withered age, when men runne after that ſinne in their words which flieth from them in the deed.

4 *Let not thy Jeſts like mummie be made of dead mens fleſh.* Abuſe not any that are departed; for to wrong their memories is to robbe their ghoſts of their winding-ſheets.

5 *Scoff not at the naturall defects of any which are not in their power to amend.* Oh 'tis crueltie to beat a cripple with his own crutches. Neither flout any for his profeſsion if honeſt though poore and painfull. Mock not a Cobler for his black thumbes.

6 *He that relates another mans wicked Jeſt with delight, adopts it to be his own.* Purge them therefore from their poyſon. If the prophaneneſſe may be ſever'd from the wit, it is like a Lamprey, take out the ſtring in the back, it may make good meat: But if the ſtaple conceit conſiſts in prophaneneſſe, then it is a viper, all poyſon, and meddle not with it.

7 *He that will loſe his friend for a Jeſt deſerves to die a begger by the bargain.* Yet ſome think their conceits, like muſtard, not good except they bite. We reade that all thoſe who were born in England the yeare after the beginning of the great mortality * 1349. wanted their foure Cheek-teeth. Such let thy Jeſts be, that they may not grind the credit of thy friend, and make not Jeſts ſo long till thou becomeſt one.

* *Tho. Walſingam in eodem anno.*

8 *No time to break Jeſts when the heart-ſtrings are about to be broken.* No more ſhewing of wit when the head is to be cut off. Like that dying man, who, when the Prieſt coming to him to give him extreme unction, asked of him where his feet were, anſwered, *at the end of my legs.* But at ſuch a time Jeſts are an unmannerly *crepitus ingenii*: And let thoſe take heed who end here with Democritus, that they begin not with Heraclitus hereafter.

CHAP. 3.

CHAP. 3.
Of Self-praysing.

HE *whose own worth doth speak need not speak his own worth.* Such boasting sounds proceed from emptinesse of desert: whereas the Conquerours in the Olympian games did not put on the Laurells on their own heads, but waited till some other did it. Onely Anchorets that want company may crown themselves with their own commendations. Maxime 1

It sheweth more wit but no lesse vanity to commend ones self not in a strait line but by reflection. Some sail to the port of their own praise by a side-wind: as when they dispraise themselves, stripping themselves naked of what is their due, that the modesty of the beholders may cloth them with it again; or when they flatter another to his face, tosing the ball to him that he may throw it back again to them; or when they commend that quality, wherein themselves excell, in another man (though absent) whom all know farre their inferiour in that faculty; or lastly (to omit other ambushes men set to surprise praise) when they send the children of their own brain to be nursed by another man, and commend their own works in a third person, but if chalenged by the company that they were Authours of them themselves, with their tongues they faintly deny it, and with their faces strongly affirm it. 2

Self-praising comes most naturally from a man when it comes most violently from him in his own defence. For though modesty binds a mans tongue to the peace in this point, yet being assaulted in his credit he may stand upon his guard, and then he doth not so much praise as purge himself. One braved a Gentleman to his face that in skill and valour he came farre behind him; *Tis true* (said the other) *for when I fought with you, you* 3 *ran away before me*. In ſuch a caſe, it was well return'd, and without any juſt aſperſion of pride.

4 *He that falls into ſin is a man; that grieves at it, is a ſaint; that boaſteth of it, is a devil.* Yet ſome glory in their ſhame, counting the ſtains of ſin the beſt complexion for their ſouls. Theſe men make me believe it may be true what Mandevil writes of the Isle of Somabarre, in the Eaſt Indies, that all the Nobility thereof brand their faces with a hot iron in token of honour.

5 *He that boaſts of ſinnes never committed is a double devil.* Many brag how many gardens of virginity they have defloured, who never came near the walls thereof, lying on thoſe with whom they did never lie, and with ſlanderous tongues committing rapes on chaſte womens reputations. Others (who would ſooner creep into a ſcabbard then draw a ſword) boaſt of their robberies, to uſurp the eſteem of valour : Whereas firſt let them be well whipt for their lying, and as they like that, let them come afterward and entitle themſelves to the gallows.

Chap. 4.
Of Travelling.

IT is a good accompliſhment to a man, if firſt the ſtock be well grown whereon Travell is graffed, and theſe rules obſerved Before, In, and After his going abroad.

Maxime 1. *Travell not too early before thy judgement be riſen*; leſt thou obſerveſt rather ſhews then ſubſtance, marking alone Pageants, Pictures, beautifull Buildings, &c.

2 *Get the Language (in part) without which key thou ſhalt unlock little of moment*. It is a great advantage to be ones own interpreter. Object not that the French tongue learnt in England muſt be unlearnt again in France; for it is eaſier to adde then begin, and to pronounce then to ſpeak.

Be

Be well settled in thine own Religion, lest, travelling out of England into Spain, thou goest out of Gods blessing into the warm Sunne. They that go over maids for their Religion, will be ravish'd at the sight of the first Popish Church they enter into. But if first thou be well grounded, their fooleries shall rivet thy faith the faster, and Travell shall give thee Confirmation in that Baptisme thou didst receive at home. 3

Know most of the rooms of thy native countrey before thou goest over the threshold thereof. Especially seeing England presents thee with so many observables. But late Writers lack nothing but age, 'and home-wonders but distance to make them admired. 'Tis a tale what * Josephus writes of the two pillars set up by the sonnes of Seth in Syria, the one of brick, fire-proof; the other of stone, water-free, thereon engraving many heavenly matters to perpetuate learning in defiance of time. But it is truly moralized in our Universities, Cambridge (of Brick) and Oxford (of Stone) wherein Learning and Religion are preserved, and where the worst Colledge is more sight-worthy then the best Dutch Gymnasium. First view these, and the rest home-rarities; not like those English, that can give a better account of Fountain-bleau then Hampton-Court, of the Spaw then Bath, of Anas in Spain then Mole in Surrey. 4

* *Antiqu. Jud. lib. 1. cap. 3.*

Travell not beyond the Alps. Mr. * Ascham did thank God that he was but nine dayes in Italie, wherein he saw in one citie (Venice) more liberty to sinne, then in London he ever heard of in nine years. That some of our Gentry have gone thither, and returned thence without infection, I more praise Gods providence then their adventure. 5

* *In his preface to his Schoolmaster.*

To travell from the sunne is uncomfortable. Yet the northern parts with much ice have some crystall, and want not their remarkables. 6

If thou wilt see much in a little, travell the Low countreys. Holland is all Europe in an Amsterdam-print, for 7 for Minerva, Mars, and Mercurie, Learning, Warre, and Traffick.

8 *Be wise in choosing Objects, diligent in marking, carefull in remembring of them*: yet herein men much follow their own humours. One askt a Barber, who never before had been at the Court, what he saw there? *Oh* (said he) *the King was excellently well trimm'd!* Thus Merchants most mark forrein Havens, Exchanges, and Marts; Souldiers note Forts, Armories, and Magazines; Scholars listen after Libraries, Disputations, and Professours; Statesmen observe Courts of justice, Counsells, &c. Every one is partiall in his own profession.

9 *Labour to distill and unite into thy self the scatterd perfections of severall Nations.* But (as it was said of one, who with more industry then judgement frequented a Colledge-Library, and commonly made use of the worst notes he met with in any Authours, *that he weeded the Library*) many weed forrein Countries, bringing home Dutch Drunkennes, Spanish Pride, French Wantonnesse and Italian Atheisme. As for the good herbs, Dutch Industry, Spanish Loyalty, French Courtesie, and Italian Frugality, these they leave behind them. Others bring home just nothing; and because they singled not themselves from their Countreymen, though some years beyond Sea, were never out of England.

10 *Continue correspondency with some choyce forrein friend after thy return.* As some Professour or Secretary, who virtually is the whole University, or State. 'Tis but a dull Dutch fashion, their *Albus Amicorum*, to make a dictionary of their friends names: But a select-ed familiar in every Countrey is usefull, betwixt you there may be a Letter-exchange. Be sure to return as good wares as thou receivest, and acquaint him with the remarkables of thy own Countrey, and he will willingly continue the trade, finding it equally gainfull.

Let

Let discourse rather be easily drawn, then willingly flow from thee. That thou mayest not seem weak to hold, or desirous to vent news, but content to gratifie thy friends. Be sparing in reporting improbable truths, especially to the vulgar, who insteed of informing their judgements will suspect thy credit. Disdain their pevish pride who rail on their native land (whose worst fault is that it bred such ungratefull fools) and in all their discourses preferre forrein countreys, herein shewing themselves of kinne to the wild Irish in loving their Nurses better then their Mothers. 11

Chap. 5.

Of Company.

Companie is one of the greatest pleasures of the nature of man. For the beams of joy are made hotter by reflection, when related to another; and otherwise gladnesse it self must grieve for want of one to expresse itself to. *Maxime* 1.

It is unnaturall for a man to court and hug solitarinesse. It is observed, that the farthest Ilands in the world are so seated that there is none so remote but that from some shore of it another Iland or Continent may be discerned: As if hereby Nature invited countreys to a mutuall commerce one with another. Why then should any man affect to environ himself with so deep and great reservednesse, as not to communicate with the societie of others? And though we pity those who made solitarinesse their refuge in time of persecution, we must condemne such as chuse it in the Churches prosperity. For well may we count him not well in his wits, who will live alwayes under a bush, because others in a storm shelter themselves under it. 2

Yet a desert is better then a debauch'd companion. For the wildnesse of the place is but uncheerfull, whilest the 3 wildneſſe of bad perſons is alſo infectious. Better therefore ride alone then have a thiefs company. And ſuch is a wicked man, who will rob thee of pretious time, if he doth no more miſchief. The Nazarites who might drink no wine were alſo forbidden (Numb. 6. 3.) to eat grapes, whereof wine is made. We muſt not onely avoid ſinne it ſelf, but alſo the cauſes and occaſions thereof: amongſt which bad company (the limetwigs of the devil) is the chiefeſt, eſpecially, to catch thoſe natures which like the good-fellow planet Mercury are moſt ſwayed by others.

4 *If thou beeſt caſt into bad company, like Hercules, thou muſt ſleep with thy club in thine hand, and ſtand on thy guard.* I mean if againſt thy will the tempeſt of an unexpected occaſion drives thee amongſt ſuch rocks ; then be thou
** Cambd. Brit. in Merioneth.* like the river * Dee in Merionethſhire in Wales, which running through Pimble meere remains entire, and mingles not her ſtreames with the waters of the lake. Though with them, be not of them ; keep civil communion with them, but ſeparate from their ſinnes. And if againſt thy will thou fall'ſt amongſt wicked men, know to thy comfort thou art ſtill in thy calling, and therefore in Gods keeping, who on thy prayers will preſerve thee.

5 *The company he keeps is the comment, by help whereof men expound the moſt cloſe and myſticall man*; underſtanding him for one of the ſame religion, life, and manners with his aſſociates. And though perchance he be not ſuch an one, 'tis juſt he ſhould be counted ſo for converſing with them. Auguſtus Ceſar came thus to diſcern his two daughters inclinations : for being once at a pub-
** Sueton. in August. Cæſ.* lick Shew, where much people was preſent, he * obſerved that the grave Senatours talked with Livia, but looſe Youngſters and riotous perſons with Julia.

9 *He that eats cherries with Noblemen ſhall have his eyes ſpirted out with the ſtones.* This outlandiſh Proverb hath in it an Engliſh truth, that they who conſtantly con-

verſe

verſe with men farre above their eſtates ſhall reap ſhame and loſſe thereby: If thou payeſt nothing, they will count thee a ſucker, no branch; a wen, no member of their companie: If in payments thou keepeſt pace with them, their long ſtrides will ſoon tire thy ſhort legs. The Bevers in New England, when ſome ten of them together draw a ſtick to the building of their lodging, ſet the * weakeſt Bevers to the lighter end of the log, and the ſtrongeſt take the heavieſt part thereof: whereas men often lay the greateſt burthen on the weakeſt back; and great perſons, to teach meaner men to learn their diſtance, take pleaſure to make them pay for their companie. I except ſuch men, who having ſome excellent qualitie are gratis very welcome to their betters; ſuch a one, though he payes not a penny of the ſhot, ſpends enough in lending them his time and diſcourſe.

* *Wood in his deſcription of New England.*

7 *To affect alwayes to be the beſt of the companie argues a baſe diſpoſition.* Gold alwayes worn in the ſame purſe with ſilver loſes both of the colour and weight; and ſo to converſe alwayes with inferiours degrades a man of his worth. Such there are that love to be the Lords of the companie, whileſt the reſt muſt be their Tenants: as if bound by their leaſe to approve, praiſe, and admire, whatſoever they ſay. Theſe knowing the lowneſſe of their parts love to live with dwarfs, that they may ſeem proper men. To come amongſt their equalls, they count it an abbridgement of their freedome, but to be with their betters, they deem it flat ſlavery.

8 *It is excellent for one to have a Library of Scholars, eſpecially if they be plain to be read.* I mean of a communicative nature, whoſe diſcourſes are as full as fluent, and their judgements as right as their tongues ready: ſuch mens talk ſhall be thy Lectures. To conclude, Good Company is not onely profitable whileſt a man lives, but ſometimes when he is dead. For he that was buried

* 2. Kings. 13. 21. with the bones of * Elisha, by a Posthumous miracle of that Prophet, recovered his life by lodging with such a grave-fellow.

Chap. 6.

Of Apparell.

CLothes are for Necessity; warm cloths for Health; cleanly for Decency; lasting for Thrift; and rich for Magnificence. Now there may be a fault in their Number, if too various; Making, if too vain; Matter; if too costly; and Mind of the wearer, if he takes pride therein. We come therefore to some generall directions.

Maxime 1 *It's a chargeable vanity to be constantly clothed above ones purse, or place.* I say Constantly; for perchance sometimes it may be dispensed with. A Great man, who himself was very plain in apparell, checkt a Gentleman for being over fine: who modestly answered, *Your Lordship hath better clothes at home, and I have worse.* But sure no plea can be made when this Luxury is grown to be ordinary. It was an arrogant act of *Hubert Archbishop of Canterbury, who, when King John had given his Courtiers rich Liveries, to Ape the Lion, gave his servants the like, wherewith the King was not a little offended. But what shall we say to the riot of our age, wherein (as Peacocks are more gay then the Eagle himself) subjects are grown braver then their Sovereigne?

* Math. Paris in Joan. Anno. 1201.

2 *'Tis beneath a wise man alwayes to wear clothes beneath men of his rank.* True, there is a state sometimes in decent plainnesse. When a wealthy Lord at a great Solemnity had the plainest apparell, *O* (said one) *if you had markt it well his sute had the richest pockets.* Yet it argues no wisdome, in clothes alwayes to stoop beneath his condition. When Antisthenes saw Socrates in a torn coat, he shewed a hole thereof to the people; *And loe* (quoth

(quoth he) *through this I see Socrates his pride.*

3 *He shews a light gravity who loves to be an exception from a generall fashion.* For the received custome in the place where we live is the most competent judge of decency; from which we must not appeal to our own opinion. When the French Courtiers mourning for their King * Henrie the second had worn cloth a whole yeare, all silks became so vile in every mans eyes, that if any was seen to wear them, he was presently accounted a Mechanick or Countrey-fellow.

* *Mont.* 1. *book, chap.* 4.

4 *It's a folly for one Proteus-like never to appear twice in one shape.* Had some of our Gallants been with the * Israelites in the wildernesse, when for fourty years their clothes waxed not old, they would have been vexed, though their clothes were whole, to have been so long in one fashion. Yet here I must confesse, I understand not what is reported of Fulgentius, that he used the same garment Winter and Summer, and never alter'd his * clothes, *etiam in Sacris peragendis.*

* *Deuterono.* 29. 5.

* *Vincentius. Spec. lib.* 10. *cap.* 105.

5 *He that is proud of the russling of his silks, like a mad man, laughs at the ratling of his fetters.* For indeed, Clothes ought to be our remembrancers of our lost innocency. Besides, why should any brag of what's but borrowed? Should the Estrige snatch off the Gallants feather, the Beaver his hat, the Goat his gloves, the Sheep his sute, the Silk-worm his stockings, and Neat his shoes (to strip him no farther then modesty will give leave) he would be left in a cold condition. And yet 'tis more pardonable to be proud, even of cleanly rags, then (as many are) of affected slovennesse. The one is proud of a molehill, the other of a dunghill.

To conclude, Sumptuary laws in this land to reduce apparell to a set standard of price, and fashion, according to the severall states of men, have long been wish'd, but are little to be hoped for. Some think private mens superfluity is a necessary evill in a State, the floting of fashions affording a standing maintenance to many thousands which otherwise would be at a losse for a livelihood, men maintaining more by their pride then by their charitie.

Chap. 7.

Of Building.

HE that alters an old house is tied as a translatour to the originall, and is confin'd to the phancie of the first builder. Such a man were unwise to pluck down good old building, to erect (perchance) worse new. But those that raise a new house from the ground are blame worthy if they make it not handsome, seeing to them Method and Confusion are both at a rate. In building we must respect Situation, Contrivance, Receipt, Strength, and Beauty. Of Situation.

Maxime 1. *Chiefly choose a wholesome aire.* For aire is a dish one feeds on every minute, and therefore it need be good. Wherefore great men (who may build where they please, as poore men where they can) if herein they preferre their profit above their health, I referre them to their Physicians to make them pay for it accordingly.

2 *Wood and water are two staple commodities where they may be had.* The former I confesse hath made so much iron, that it must now be bought with the more silver, and grows daily dearer. But 'tis as well pleasant as profitable to see a house cased with trees, like that of Anchises in Troy.

* *Virgil* 2. *Æneid.* 32.

--------- quanquam secreta parentis*
Anchisæ domus arboribusq; obtecta recessit.

The worst is, where a place is bald of wood, no art can make it a periwig. As for water, begin with Pindars beginning, ἄριστον μὲν ὕδωρ. The fort of * Gogmagog Hills nigh Cambridge is counted impregnable but for want of water, the mischief of many

* *Camb. Brit. in Cambridge-shire.*

ny houſes where ſervants muſt bring the well on their ſhoulders.

Next a pleaſant proſpect is to be reſpected. A medly view (ſuch as of water and land at Greenwich) beſt entertains the eyes, refreſhing the wearied beholder with exchange of objects. Yet I know a more profitable proſpect, where the owner can onely ſee his own land round about. 3

A fair entrance with an eaſie aſcent gives a great grace to a building: where the Hall is a preferment out of the Court,the Parlour out of the Hall; not (as in ſome old buildings) where the doores are ſo low Pygmies muſt ſtoop, and the rooms ſo high that Giants may ſtand upright. But now we are come to Contrivance. 4

Let not thy common rooms be ſeverall, nor thy ſeverall rooms be common. The Hall (which is a Pandocheum) ought to lie open,and ſo ought Paſſages and Stairs (provided that the whole houſe be not ſpent in paths) Chambers and Cloſets are to be private and retired. 5

Light (Gods eldeſt daughter) is a principall beauty in a building: yet it ſhines not alike from all parts of Heaven. An Eaſt-window welcomes the infant beams of the Sun, before they are of ſtrength to do any harm, and is offenſive to none but a ſluggard. A South-window in ſummer is a chimny with a fire in't,and needs the ſchreen of a curtain.In a Weſt-window in ſummer time towards night, the Sun grows low and over familiar with more light then delight. A North-window is beſt for Butteries and Cellars, where the beere will be ſower for the Suns ſmiling on it. Thorow-lights are beſt for rooms of entertainment, and windows on one ſide for dormitories. As for Receipt, 6

A houſe had better be too little for a day then too great for a yeare. And it's eaſier borrowing of thy neighbour a brace of chambers for a night, then a bag of money for a twelvemonth. It is vain therefore to proportion the receipt to an extraordinary occaſion, as thoſe who 7

by

by overbuilding their houſes have dilapidated their lands, and their ſtates have been preſſ'd to death under the weight of their houſe. As for Strength,

8 *Countrey-houſes muſt be Subſtantives, able to ſtand of themſeves.* Not like City-buildings ſupported by their neighbours on either ſide. By Strength we mean ſuch as may reſiſt Weather and Time, not Invaſion, Caſtles being out of date in this peaceable age. As for the making of motes round about, it is queſtionable whether the fogs be not more unhealthfull, then the fiſh brings profit, or the water defence. Beauty remains behind as the laſt to be regarded, becauſe houſes are made to be lived in not lookt on.

9 *Let not the Front look aſquint on a ſtranger, but accoſt him right at his entrance.* Uniformity alſo much pleaſeth the eye; and 'tis obſerved that free-ſtone, like a fair complexion, ſooneſt waxeth old, whileſt brick keeps her beauty longeſt.

10 *Let the office-houſes obſerve the due diſtance from the manſion-houſe.* Thoſe are too familiar which preſume to be of the ſame pile with it. The ſame may be ſaid of ſtables and barns; without which a houſe is like a city without outworks, it can never hold out long.

11 *Gardens alſo are to attend in their place:* When God (Geneſis 2. 9) planted a garden Eaſtward, he made to grow out of the ground every tree pleaſant to the ſight, and good for food. Sure he knew better what was proper to a garden then thoſe, who nowadayes therein only feed the eyes, and ſtarve both taſt and ſmell.

To conclude, in Building rather believe any man then an Artificer in his own art for matter of charges, not that they cannot but will not be faithfull. Should they tell thee all the coſt at the firſt, it would blaſt a young Builder in the budding, and therefore they ſooth thee up till it hath coſt thee ſomething to confute them. The ſpirit of Building firſt poſſeſſed people after the floud,

floud, which then caused the confusion of languages, and since of the estate of many a man.

Chap. 8.

Of Anger.

ANger is one of the sinews of the soul; he that wants it hath a maimed mind, and with Jacob sinew-shrunk in the hollow of his thigh must needs halt. Nor is it good to converse with such as cannot be angry, and with the Caspian sea never ebbe nor flow. This Anger is either Heavenly, when one is offended for God: or Hellish, when offended with God and Goodnes: or Earthly, in temporall matters. Which Earthly Anger (whereof we treat) may also be Hellish, if for no cause, no great cause, too hot, or too long.

Be not angry with any without a cause. If thou beest, thou must not onely, as the Proverb saith, be appeas'd without amends (having neither cost nor damage given thee) but, as our Saviour * saith, be in danger of the judgement. *Maxime* 1.

*Matth 5.22.

2 *Be not mortally angry with any for a veniall fault.* He will make a strange combustion in the state of his soul, who at the landing of every cockboat sets the beacons on fire. To be angry for every toy debases the worth of thy anger; for he who will be angry for any thing, will be angry for nothing.

3 *Let not thy anger be so hot, but that the most torrid zone thereof may be habitable.* Fright not people from thy presence with the terrour of thy intolerable impatience. Some men like a tiled house are long before they take fire, but once on flame there is no coming near to quench them.

4 *Take heed of doing irrevocable acts in thy passion.* As the revealing of secrets, which makes thee a bankrupt for society ever after: neither do such things which done once are done for ever, so that no bemoaning can

amend them. Sampsons hair grew again, but not his eyes: Time may restore some losses, others are never to be repaird. Wherefore in thy rage make no Persian decree which cannot be revers'd or repeald; but rather Polonian laws which (they say) last but three dayes: Do not in an instant what an age cannot recompence.

5 *Anger kept till the next morning, with * Manna, doth putrifie and corrupt.* Save that Manna corrupted not at all, and anger most of all, kept the next Sabbath. S. Paul * saith, *Let not the Sunne go down on your wrath*; to carry news to the Antipodes in another world of thy revengefull nature. Yet let us take the Apostles meaning, rather then his words, with all possible speed to depose our passion, not understanding him so literally that we may take leave to be angry till Sunset: then might our wrath lengthen with the dayes; and men in Greenland, where day lasts above a quarter of a yeare, have plentifull scope of revenge. And as the English (by command from William the Conquerer) alwayes raked up their fire, and put out their candles, when the * Curfew-bell was rung; let us then also quench all sparks of anger and heat of passion.

* Exod. 16.24.
* Ephes. 4.26.
* Cowels Interpreter out of Stows Annals.

6 *He that keeps anger long in his bosome giveth place to the * devil.* And why should we make room for him, who will crowd in too fast of himself? Heat of passion makes our souls to chappe, and the devil creeps in at the cranies; yea a furious man in his fits may seem possess'd with a devil, fomes, fumes, tears himself, is deaf, and dumbe in effect, to heare or speak reason: sometimes wallows, stares, stamps, with fiery eyes and flaming cheeks. Had Narcissus himself seen his own face when he had been angry, he could never have fallen in love with himself.

* Ephes. 4.27.

CHAP. 9.

Chap. 9.

Of Expecting Preferment.

THere are as many ſeverall tenures of Expectation as of Poſſeſsion, ſome nearer, ſome more remote, ſome grounded on ſtrong, others on weaker reaſons. (As for a groundleſſe Expectation, it is a wilfull ſelf-deluſion.) We come to inſtructions how men ſhould manage their hopes herein.

Hope not for impoſsibilities. For though the object of hope be *Futurum poſsibile*, yet ſome are ſo mad as to feed their Expectation on things, though not in themſelves, yet to them impoſsible, if we conſider the weakneſſe of the means whereby they ſeek to attain them. He needs to ſtand on tiptoes that hopes to touch the moon; and thoſe who expect what in reaſon they cannot expect, may expect. Maxime 1.

Carefully ſurvey what proportion the means thou haſt bear to the end thou expecteſt. Count not a Courtiers promiſe of courſe a ſpecialty that he is bound to preferre thee: Seeing Complements oftentimes die in the ſpeaking, why ſhould thy hopes (grounded on them) live longer then the hearing? perchance the text of his promiſe intended but common courteſies, which thy apprehenſion expounds ſpeedy and ſpeciall favours. Others make up the weakneſſe of their means with conceit of the ſtrength of their deſerts, fooliſhly thinking that their own merits will be the undoubted Patrons to preſent them to all void Benefices. 2

The heir apparent to the next preferment may be diſinherited by an unexpected accident. A Gentleman, ſervant to the Lord Admirall Howard, was ſuiter to a Lady above his deſerts, grounding the confidence of his ſucceſſe on his relation to ſo honourable a Lord; which Lord gave the Anchor as badge of his office, and therefore this ſuiter wrote in a window, 3

If I be bold,
The anchor is my hold.

But his corrivall to the ſame Miſtris coming into the ſame room wrote under,

Yet fear the worſt:
What if the Cable burſt?

Thus uſeleſſe is the Anchor of hope (good for nothing but to deceive thoſe that relie on it) if the cable or ſmall cords of means and cauſes whereon it depends fail and miſcarry. Daily experience tenders too many examples. A Gentleman who gave a Baſilisk for his Arms or Creſt promiſed to make a young kinſman of his his heir, which kinſman to ingratiate himſelf painted a Baſilisk in his ſtudy, and beneath it theſe verſes,

Falleris aſpectu Baſiliſcum occidere, Plini,
Nam vitæ noſtræ ſpem Baſiliſcus alit.
The Baſilisk's the onely ſtay,
My life preſerving ſtill;
Pliny, thou li'dſt when thou didſt ſay
The Baſilisk doth kill.

But this rich Gentleman dying fruſtrated his expectation, and bequeathed all his eſtate to another, whereupon the Epigram was thus altered,

Certe aluit, ſed ſpe vana, ſpes vana venenum:
Ignoſcas, Plini, verus es Hiſtoricus.
Indeed vain hopes to me he gave,
Whence I my poiſon drew:
Pliny, thy pardon now I crave,
Thy writings are too true.

4 *Proportion thy expences to what thou haſt in poſſeſsion, not to thy expectancies.* Otherwiſe he that feeds on wind muſt needs be griped with the Collick at laſt. And if the Ceremoniall law forbad the Jews to ſeeth a kid in the mothers milk, the law of good husbandry forbids us to eat a kid in the mothers belly, ſpending our pregnant hopes before they be delivered.

Imbrue not thy soul in bloudy wishes of his death who parts thee and thy preferment. A murther the more common, because one cannot be arraigned for it on earth. But those are charitable murtherers which wish them in heaven, not so much that they may have ease at their journeys end, but because they must needs take death in the way. 5

In earthly matters expectation takes up more joy on trust, then the fruition of the thing is able to discharge. The Lion is not so fierce as painted; nor are matters so fair as the pencill of the expectant limmes them out in his hopes. They forecount their wives fair, fruitfull, and rich, without any fault; their children witty, beautifull, and dutifull, without any frowardnesse: and as S. Basil held that roses in paradise before mans fall grew without prickles, they abstract the pleasures of things from the troubles annexed to them, which when they come to enjoy, they must take both together. Surely a good unlook'd for is a virgin happinesse; whereas those who obtain what long they have gazed on in expectation, onely marry what themselves have defloured before. 6

When our hopes break let our patience hold: relying on Gods providence without murmuring, who often provides for men above what we can think or desire. When Robert * Holgate could not peaceably enjoy his small living in Lincolneshire, because of the litigiousnesse of a neighbouring Knight, coming to London to right himself he came into the favour of King Henrie the eighth, and got by degrees the Archbishoprick of York. Thus God sometimes defeats our hopes, or disturbs our possession of lesser favours, thereby to bestow on his servants better blessings, if not here, hereafter. 7

* *Godwin in his Catal. of Archbishops of York.*

CHAP. 10.

Of Memory.

IT is the treaſure-houſe of the mind, wherein the monuments thereof are kept and preſerved. Plato makes it the mother of the Muſes. * Ariſtotle ſets it one degree further, making Experience the mother of Arts, Memory the parent of Experience. Philoſophers place it in the rere of the head; and it ſeems the mine of Memory lies there, becauſe there naturally men dig for it, ſcratching it when they are at a loſſe. This again is twofold: one, the ſimple retention of things; the other, a regaining them when forgotten.

* *Metaphyſ. lib.* 1 *cap.* 1.

Maxime 1 *Brute creatures equall, if not exceed, men in a bare retentive Memory.* Through how many labyrinths of woods, without other clue of threed then naturall inſtinct, doth the hunted hare return to her muce? How doth the little bee, flying into ſeverall meadows and gardens, ſipping of many cups, yet never intoxicated, through an ocean (as I may ſay) of air, ſteddily ſteer her ſelf home, without help of card or compaſſe. But theſe cannot play an aftergame, and recover what they have forgotten, which is done by the mediation of diſcourſe.

2 *Artificiall memory is rather a trick then an art, and more for the gain of the teacher then profit of the learners.* Like the toſsing of a pike, which is no part of the poſtures and motions thereof, and is rather for oſtentation then uſe, to ſhew the ſtrength and nimbleneſſe of the arm, and is often uſed by wandring Souldiers as an introduction to beg. Underſtand it of the artificiall rules which at this day are delivered by Memory-mountebanks; for ſure an art thereof may be made (wherein as yet the world is defective) and that no more deſtructive to naturall Memory then ſpectacles are to eyes, which girls in Holland wear from 12 years of age. But till this

this be found out, let us obſerve theſe plain rules.

Firſt ſoundly infix in thy mind what thou deſireſt to remember. What wonder is it if agitation of buſineſſe jog that out of thy head, which was there rather tack'd then faſtned? whereas thoſe notions which get in by *violenta poſſesſio* will abide there till *ejectio firma*, ſickneſſe or extreme age, diſpoſſeſſe them. It is beſt knocking in the nail overnight, and clinching it the next morning. 3

Overburthen not thy Memory to make ſo faithfull a ſervant a ſlave. Remember Atlas was weary. Have as much reaſon as a Camell, to riſe when thou haſt thy full load. Memory, like a purſe, if it be over full that it cannot ſhut, all will drop out of it: Take heed of a gluttonous curioſitie to feed on many things, leſt the greedineſſe of the appetite of thy Memory ſpoyl the digeſtion thereof. Beza's caſe was peculiar and memorable; being above foureſcore years of age he perfectly could ſay by heart any Greek Chapter in * S. Pauls Epiſtles, or any thing elſe which he had learnt long before, but forgot whatſoever was newly told him; his Memory like an inne retaining old gueſts, but having no room to entertain new. 4

* *Thuan. obit. doct. virorum. pag.* 384.

Spoyl not thy Memory with thine own jealouſie, nor make it bad by ſuſpecting it. How canſt thou find that true which thou wilt not truſt? S. Auguſtine tells us of his friend Simplicius, who being ask'd, could tell all Virgills verſes backward and forward, and yet the ſame party, * vowed to God, that he knew not that he could do it till they did try him. Sure there is conceal'd ſtrength in mens Memories, which they take no notice of. 5

* *Teſtatus eſt Deum, neſciſſe ſe hoc poſſe ante illud experimentum*, Auguſt. Tom. 7. lib. de anima & ejus orig. cap. 7.

Marſhall thy notions into a handſome method. One will carrie twice more weight truſt and pack'd up in bundles, then when it lies untowardly flapping and hanging about his ſhoulders. Things orderly fardled up under heads are moſt portable. 6

Adventure not all thy learning in one bottom, but divide it betwixt 7 *betwixt thy Memory and thy Note-books.* He that with Bias carries all his learning about him in his head will utterly be beggerd and bankrupt, if a violent disease, a mercilesse thief, should rob and strip him. I know some have a Common-place against Common-place-books, and yet perchance will privately make use of what publickly they declaim against. A Common-place-book contains many Notions in garison, whence the owner may draw out an army into the field on competent warning.

8 *Moderate diet and good aire preserve Memory*; but what aire is best I dare not define, when such great ones differ. * Some say a pure and subtle aire is best, another commends a thick and foggy aire. For the * Pisans sited in the fennes and marish of Arnus have excellent memories, as if the foggy aire were a cap for their heads.

*Plato, Aristotle, Tully.

*Singulari valent memoriâ quo urbs crassiore fruatur aere, *Mercat. Atlas in Tusia.*

9 *Thankfulnesse to God for it continues the Memory*: whereas some proud people have been visited with such oblivion, that they have forgotten their own names. Staupitius Tutour to Luther, and a godly man, in a vain ostentation of his memory repeated Christs Genealogie (Matth. 1.) by heart in his Sermon, but being out about the Captivity of Babylon, *I see* (saith*he) *God resisteth the proud*, and so betook himself to his book. Abuse not thy Memory to be Sinnes Register, nor make advantage thereof for wickednesse. Excellently * Augustine, *Quidam vero pessimi memoria sunt mirabili, qui tanto pejores sunt, quanto minus possunt, quæ male cogitant, oblivisci.*

* *Melchior Adamus in vita Staupitii, pag.* 20.

* *De civ. Dei lib.* 7. *cap.* 3.

CHAP. II.

CHAP. II.
Of Phancie.

IT is an inward Senſe of the ſoul, for a while retaining and examining things brought in thither by the Common ſenſe. It is the moſt boundles and reſtleſſe faculty of the ſoul: for whileſt the Underſtanding and the Will are kept as it were in *Libera Cuſtodia* to their objects of *Verum* & *Bonum*, the Phancie is free from all engagements: it digs without ſpade, ſails without ſhip, flies without wings, builds without charges, fights without bloudſhed, in a moment ſtriding from the centre to the circumference of the world, by a kind of omnipotencie creating and annihilating things in an inſtant; and things divorced in Nature are married in Phancie as in a lawleſſe place. It is alſo moſt reſtleſſe: whileſt the Senſes are bound, and Reaſon in a manner aſleep, Phancie like a ſentinell walks the round, ever working, never wearied. The chief diſeaſes of the Phancie are, either that they are too wild and high-ſoaring, or elſe too low and groveling, or elſe too deſultory and overvoluble. Of the firſt.

If thy Phancie be but a little too rank, age it ſelf will correct it. Maxime 1 To lift too high is no fault in a young horſe, becauſe with travelling he will mend it for his own eaſe. Thus lofty Phancies in young men will come down of themſelves, and in proceſſe of time the overplus will ſhrink to be but even meaſure. But if this will not do it, then obſerve theſe rules.

Take part alwayes with thy Judgement againſt thy Phancie in 2 *any thing wherein they ſhall diſſent.* If thou ſuſpecteſt thy conceits too luxuriant, herein account thy ſuſpicion a legall conviction, and damne whatſoever thou doubteſt of. Warily Tullie, *Bene monent, qui vetant quicquam facere, de quo dubitas, æquum ſit an iniquum.*

Take the adviſe of a faithfull friend, and ſubmit thy inventions 3 *to his censure.* When thou pennest an oration, let him have the power of *Index expurgatorius*, to expunge what he pleaseth; and do not thou like a fond mother crie if the child of thy brain be corrected for playing the wanton. Mark the arguments and reasons of his alterations, why that phrase least proper, this passage more cautious and advised, and after a while thou shalt perform the place in thine own person, and not go out of thy self for a censurer. If thy Phancie be too low and humble,

4 *Let thy judgement be King but not Tyrant over it, to condemne harmlesse yea commendable conceits.* Some for fear their orations should giggle will not let them smile. Give it also liberty to rove, for it will not be extravagant. There is no danger that weak folks if they walk abroad will straggle farre, as wanting strength.

5 *Acquaint thy self with reading Poets, for there Phancie is in her throne*; and in time the sparks of the Authours wit will catch hold on the Reader, and inflame him with love, liking, and desire of imitation. I confesse there is more required to teach one to write then to see a coppy: however there is a secret force of fascination in reading Poems to raise and provoke Phancie. If thy Phancie be over voluble, then

6 *Whip this vagrant home to the first object whereon it should be settled.* Indeed nimblenesse is the perfection of this faculty, but levity the bane of it. Great is the difference betwixt a swift horse, and a skittish, that will stand on no ground. Such is the ubiquitary Phancie, which will keep long residence on no one subject, but is so courteous to strangers that it ever welcomes that conceit most which comes last; and new species supplant the old ones, before seriously considered. If this be the fault of thy Phancie, I say whip it home to the first object, whereon it should be settled. This do as often as occasion requires, and by degrees the fugitive servant will learn to abide by his work without running away.

Acquaint

7 *Acquaint thy self by degrees with hard and knotty studies*, as School-divinity, which will clog thy overnimble Phancie. True, at the first it will be as welcome to thee as a prison, and their very solutions will seem knots unto thee. But take not too much at once, lest thy brain turn edge. Taste it first as a potion for Physick, and by degrees thou shalt drink it as beer for thirst: Practice will make it pleasant. Mathematicks are also good for this purpose: If beginning to try a Conclusion, thou must make an end, lest thou losest thy pains that are past, and must proceed seriously and exactly. I meddle not with those Bedlam-phancies, all whose conceits are antiques, but leave them for the Physician to purge with hellebore.

8 *To clothe low-creeping matter with high-flown language is not fine Phancie, but flat foolerie.* It rather loads then raises a Wren, to fasten the feathers of an Estridge to her wings. Some mens speeches are like the high mountains in Ireland, having a durty bog in the top of them; the very ridge of them in high words having nothing of worth, but what rather stalls then delights the Auditour.

9 *Fine Phancies in manufactures invent engines rather pretty then usefull*; and commonly one trade is too narrow for them. They are better to project new wayes then to prosecute old, and are rather skilfull in many mysteries then thriving in one. They affect not voluminous inventions, wherein many years must constantly be spent to perfect them, except there be in them variety of pleasant employment.

10 *Imagination (the work of the Phancie) hath produc'd reall effects.* Many serious and sad examples hereof may be produced: I will onely insist on a merry one. A Gentleman having led a company of children beyond their usuall journey, they began to be weary, and joyntly cried to him to carry them; which because of their multitude he could not do, but told them he would

provide them horſes to ride on. Then cutting little wands out of the hedge as nagges for them, and a great ſtake as a gelding for himſelf, thus mounted Phancie put mettall into their legs, and they came cheerfully home.

11 *Phancie runs moſt furiouſly when a guilty Conſcience drives it.* One that owed much money, and had many Creditours, as he walked London-ſtreets in the evening, a tenterhook catch'd his cloak. *At whoſe ſuit?* ſaid he, conceiving ſome Bailiff had arreſted him. Thus guilty Conſciences are afraid where no fear is, and count every creature they meet a Serjeant ſent from God to puniſh them.

CHAP. 12.
Of Naturall Fools.

THey have the caſes of men, and little elſe of them beſides ſpeech and laughter. And indeed it may ſeem ſtrange that *Riſibile* being the propertie of man alone, they who have leaſt of man ſhould have moſt thereof, laughing without cauſe or meaſure.

Maxime 1 *Generally Nature hangs out a ſigne of ſimplicity in the face of a Fool;* and there is enough in his countenance for an Hue and Crie to take him on ſuſpicion: or elſe it is ſtamped on the figure of his body; their heads ſometimes ſo little, that there is no room for wit; ſometimes ſo long, that there is no wit for ſo much room.

2 *Yet ſome by their faces may paſſe currant enough till they cry themſelves down by their ſpeaking.* Thus men know the bell is crackt, when they heare it toll'd; yet ſome that have ſtood out the aſſault of two or three queſtions, and have anſwered pretty rationally, have afterwards of their own accord betrayed and yielded themſelves to be fools.

3 *The oathes and railing of Fools is oftentimes no fault of theirs but their teachers.* The Hebrew word *Barac* ſignifies to bleſſe,

blesse, and to curse; and 'tis the speakers pleasure if he use it in the worst acception. Fools of themselves are equally capable to pray and to swear; they therefore have the greatest sinne who by their example or otherwise teach them so to do.

One may get wisdome by looking on a Fool. In beholding him, think how much thou art beholden to him that suffered thee not to be like him: Onely Gods pleasure put a difference betwixt you. And consider that a Fool and a Wiseman are alike both in the starting-place, their birth, and at the post, their death; onely they differ in the race of their lives. 4

It is unnaturall to laugh at a Naturall. How can the object of thy pity be the subject of thy pastime? I confesse sometimes the strangenesse, and, as I may say, witty simplicity of their actions may extort a smile from a serious man, who at the same time may smile at them and sorrow for them. But it is one thing to laugh at them *in transitu*, a snap and away, and another to make a set meal in jeering them, and as the Philistines to send for Sampson to make them sport. 5

To make a trade of laughing at a Fool is the highway to become one. Tullie confesseth that whilest he laughed at one * Hircus a very ridiculous man, *dum illum rideo pene factus sum ille*: And one telleth us of Gallus Vibius, a man first of great eloquence, and afterwards of great madnesse, which seized not on him so much by accident as his own affectation, so long * mimically imitating mad men that he became one. 6

* *Epist. lib.* 2. *Epist.* 9.

* Dum insanos imitatur, quod assimulabat ad vivum redegit, *Rhodiginus Antiq. lib.* 11. *c.* 13.

Many have been the wise speeches of fools, though not so many as the foolish speeches of wise men. Now the wise speeches of these silly souls proceed from one of these reasons: Either because talking much, and shooting often, they must needs hit the mark sometimes, though not by aim, by hap: Or else because a Fools *mediocriter* is *optime*; Sense from his mouth, a Sentence; and a tole- 7 rable ſpeech cri'd up for an Apothegme: Or laſtly, becauſe God may ſometimes illuminate them, and (eſpecially towards their death) admit them to the poſſeſsion of ſome part of reaſon. A poore begger in Paris being very hungry ſtayed ſo long in a Cooks ſhop, who was diſhing up of meat, till his ſtomach was ſatisfied with the onely ſmell thereof. The cholerick covetous Cook demanded of him to pay for his breakfaſt. The pooreman denyed it, and the controverſie was referr'd to the deciding of the next man that ſhould paſſe by, which chanced to be the moſt notorious Idiot in the whole City. He on the relation of the matter determined that the poore mans money ſhould be put betwixt two empty diſhes, and the Cook ſhould be recompenced with the gingling of the poore mans money, as he was ſatisfied with the onely ſmell of the Cooks meat. And this is affirmed by * credible Writers, as no fable but an undoubted fact. More waggiſh was that of a rich landed Fool, whom a Courtier had begg'd, and carried about to wait on him. He coming with his maſter to a Gentlemans houſe where the picture of a Fool was wrought in a fair ſuit of arras, cut the picture out with a penknife. And being chidden for ſo doing, *You have more cauſe* (ſaid he) *to thank me, for if my maſter had ſeen the picture of the Fool, he would have begg'd the hangings of the King as he did my lands.* When the ſtanders by comforted a Naturall which lay on his death-bed, and told him that foure proper fellows ſhould carry his body to the Church: *Yea* (quoth he) *but I had rather by half go thither my ſelf*; and then prayed to God at his laſt gaſp not to require more of him then he gave him.

** Jo. And. Panor. Barba. & alii indè ad noſtram. Hiero. Franc. in lib. furioſ. de reg. juris ff. Boer. deciſ. 23 n 58. Mantic. de conject. ult. v. lib. 2. Tit. 5. n. 8. Corſet. ſing. verbi Teſtamentum.*

As for a Changeling, which is not one child changed for another, but one child on a ſudden much changed from it ſelf; and for a Jeſter, which ſome count a neceſſary evil in a Court (an office which none but he that hath wit can perform, and

none

and none but he that wants wit will perform) I conceive them not to belong to the present subject.

Chap. 13.

Of Recreations.

Recreation is a second Creation, when wearinesse hath almost annihilated ones spirits. It is the breathing of the soul, which otherwise would be stifled with continuall businesse. We may trespasse in them, if using such as are forbidden by the Lawyer, as against the statutes; Physician, as against health; Divine, as against conscience.

Be well satisfied in thy Conscience of the lawfulnesse of the recreation thou usest. Some fight against Cockfighting, Maxime 1
and bait Bull and Bearbaiting, because man is not to be a common Barretour to set the creatures at discord; and seeing Antipathy betwixt creatures was kindled by mans sinne, what pleasure can he take to see it burn? Others are of the contrary opinion, and that Christianity gives us a placard to use these sports; and that mans Charter of dominion over the creatures enables him to employ them as well for pleasure as necessity. In these, as in all other doubtfull recreations, be well assured first of the legality of them. He that sinnes against his Conscience sinnes with a witnesse.

Spill not the morning (the quintessence of the day) in recreations. For sleep it self is a recreation; adde not therefore 2
sauce to sauce; and he cannot properly have any title to be refresh'd, who was not first faint. Pastime, like wine, is poyson in the morning. It is then good husbandry to sow the head, which hath lain fallow all night, with some serious work. Chiefly intrench not on the Lords day to use unlawfull sports; this were to spare thine own flock, and to sheere Gods lambe.

Let thy recreations be ingenious, and bear proportion with 3
thine age. If thou saist with Paul, *When I was a child I did as*

as a child, ſay alſo with him, *But when I was a man I put away childiſh things*. Wear alſo the childs coat, if thou uſeſt his ſports.

4 *Take heed of boiſterous and overviolent exerciſes.* Ringing oftentimes hath made good muſick on the bells, and put mens bodies out of tune, ſo that by overheating themſelves they have rung their own paſsing-bell.

5 *Yet the ruder ſort of people ſcarce count any thing a ſport which is not loud and violent.* The Muſcovite women eſteem none loving husbands except they beat their wives. 'Tis no paſtime with country Clowns that cracks not pates, breaks not ſhins, bruiſes not limbes, tumbles and toſſes not all the body. They think themſelves not warm in their geeres, till they are all on fire; and count it but dry ſport, till they ſwim in their own ſweat. Yet I conceive the Phyſicians rule in exerciſes, *Ad ruborem* but *non ad ſudorem*, is too ſcant meaſure.

6 *Refreſh that part of thy ſelf which is moſt wearied.* If thy life be ſedentary, exerciſe thy body; if ſtirring and active, recreate thy mind. But take heed of couſening thy mind, in ſetting it to do a double task under pretence of giving it a play-day, as in the labyrinth of Cheſſe, and other tedious and ſtudious Games.

7 *Yet recreations diſtaſtfull to ſome diſpoſitions relliſh beſt to others.* Fiſhing with an angle is to ſome rather a torture then a pleaſure, to ſtand an houre as mute as the fiſh they mean to take: yet herewithall * Doctour Whitaker was much delighted. When ſome Noblemen had gotten William Cecill Lord Burleigh and Treaſurer of England to ride with them a hunting, & the ſport began to be cold; What call you this, ſaid the Treaſurer? Oh now ſaid they the dogs are at a fault. Yea quoth the Treaſurer, take me again in ſuch a fault, and Ile give you leave to puniſh me. Thus as ſoon may the ſame meat pleaſe all palats, as the ſame ſport ſuit with all diſpoſitions.

* *In his life writ by Mr. Aſhton.*

8 *Running, Leaping, and Dancing, the deſcants on the plain ſong*

ſong of walking, are all excellent exercises. And yet thoſe are the beſt recreations which beſides refreſhing enable, at leaſt diſpoſe, men to ſome other good ends. Bowling teaches mens hands and eyes Mathematicks, and the rules of Proportion : Swimming hath ſav'd many a mans life, when himſelf hath been both the wares, and the ſhip : Tilting and Fencing is warre without anger ; and manly ſports are the Grammer of Military performance.

But above all Shooting is a noble recreation, and an half Li- 9
berall art. A rich man told a poore man that he walked to get a ſtomach for his meat : *And I,* ſaid the poore man, *walk to get meat for my ſtomach.* Now Shooting would have fitted both their turns ; it provides food when men are hungry, and helps digeſtion when they are full. King Edward the ſixth (though he drew no ſtrong bow) ſhot very well, and when once John Dudley Duke of Northumberland commended him for hitting the mark ; *You ſhot better* (quoth the King) *when you ſhot off my good uncle Protectours head.* But our age ſees his Succeſſour exceeding him in that art, whoſe eye like his judgement is clear and quick to diſcover the mark, and his hands as juſt in Shooting as in dealing aright.

Some ſports being granted to be lawfull, more propend to be ill 10
then well uſed. Such I count Stage-playes, when made alwayes the Actours work, and often the Spectatours recreation. * Zeuxis the curious picturer painted a boy holding a diſh full of grapes in his hand, done ſo lively that the birds being deceived flew to peck the grapes. But Zeuxis in an ingenious choller was angry with his own workmanſhip *Had I* (ſaid he) *made the boy as lively as the grapes the birds would have been afraid to touch them.* Thus two things are ſet forth to us in Stage-playes : ſome grave ſentences, prudent counſells, and puniſhment of vitious examples ; and with theſe deſperate oathes, luſtfull talk, and riotous acts are ſo perſonated

* *Plin. nat. Hiſt. lib.* 35. *cap.* 10.

ſonated to the life, that wantons are tickled with delight, and feed their palats upon them. It ſeems the goodneſſe is not portrayed out with equall accents of livelineſſe as the wicked things are: otherwiſe men would be deterr'd from vitious courſes, with ſeeing the wofull ſucceſſe which follows them. But the main is, wanton ſpeeches on ſtages are the devils ordinance to beget badneſſe; but I queſtion whether the pious ſpeeches ſpoken there be Gods ordinance to increaſe goodneſſe, as wanting both his inſtitution and benediction.

11 *Choak not thy ſoul with immoderate pouring in the cordiall of pleaſures.* The Creation laſted but ſix dayes of the firſt week: Prophane they whoſe Recreation laſts ſeven dayes every week. Rather abbridge thy ſelf of thy lawfull liberty herein; it being a wary rule which S. * Gregory gives us, *Solus in illicitis non cadit, qui ſe aliquando & a licitis caute reſtringit.* And then Recreations ſhall both ſtrengthen labour, and ſweeten reſt, and we may expect Gods bleſsing and protection on us in following them, as well as in doing our work: For he that ſaith grace for his meat, in it prayes alſo to God to bleſſe his ſauce unto him. As for thoſe that will not take lawfull pleaſure, I am afraid they will take unlawfull pleaſure, and by lacing themſelves too hard grow awry on one ſide.

* *Lib.* 5. *moral. & Homil.* 35. *ſupra Evang.*

CHAP. 14.

Chap. 14.
Of Tombes.

TOmbes are the clothes of the dead: a Grave is but a plain suit, and a rich Monument is one embroyder'd. Most moderate men have been carefull for the decent interment of their corps. Few of the fond mind of Arbogastus an Irish Saint, and Bishop of Spires in Germany, who would be buried near the * Gallows in imitation of our Saviour, whose grave was in mount Calvary near the place of execution.

* *Warræus de Scriptor. Hiber. pag. 26.*

Maxime 1

Tis a provident way to make ones Tombe in ones life-time; both hereby to prevent the negligence of heirs, and to mind him of his mortality. * Virgil tells us that when bees swarm in the aire, and two armies meeting together fight as it were a set battel with great violence, cast but a little dust upon them and they will be quiet,

* *Georgic. lib. 4.*

Hi motus animorum, atque hæc certamina tanta
Pulveris exigui jactu compressa quiescunt.
These stirrings of their minds and strivings vast,
If but a little dust on them be cast,
Are straitwayes stinted, and quite overpast.

Thus the most ambitious motions and thoughts of mans mind are quickly quell'd when dust is thrown on him, whereof his fore-prepared Sepulchre is an excellent remembrancer.

2 *Yet some seem to have built their Tombes, therein to bury their thoughts of dying*, never thinking thereof, but embracing the world with greater greedinesse. A Gentleman made choice of a fair stone, and intending the same for his Grave-stone, caused it to be pitched up in a field a pretty distance from his house, and used often to shoot at it for his exercise. *Yea but* (said a wag that stood by) *you would be loath Sir to hit the mark*: And so are many unwilling to die who notwithstanding have erected their Monuments.

3 *Tombes ought in ſome ſort to be proportioned not to the wealth but deſerts of the party interred.* Yet may we ſee ſome rich man of mean worth loaden under a tombe big enough for a Prince to bear. There were Officers appointed in the * Grecian Games, who alwayes by publick authority did pluck down the Statues erected to the Victours, if they exceeded the true ſymmetrie and proportion of their bodies. We need ſuch nowadayes to order Monuments to mens merits, chiefly to reform ſuch depopulating Tombes as have no good fellowſhip with them, but engroſſe all the room, leaving neither ſeats for the living, nor graves for the dead. It was a wiſe and thrifty law which * Reutha King of Scotland made, That Noblemen ſhould have ſo many pillars, or long pointed ſtones ſet on their ſepulchres, as they had ſlain enemies in the warres. If this order were alſo enlarged to thoſe who in peace had excellently deſerved of the Church or Commonwealth, it might well be revived.

* *Lucian.* περὶ εἰκόνων.

* *Hector Boeth in the life of King Reutha.*

4 *Overcoſtly Tombes are onely baits for Sacriledge.* Thus Sacriledge hath beheaded that peereleſſe Prince King Henrie the fift, the body of whoſe Statue on his Tombe in Weſtminſter was covered over with ſilver plate guilded, and his head of* maſſy ſilver ; both which now are ſtollen away : Yea hungry palats will feed on courſer meat. I had rather *Mr Stow then I ſhould tell you of a Nobleman who ſold the monuments of Noblemen, in S. Auguſtines Church in Broadſtreet, for an hundred pound, which coſt many thouſands, and in the place thereof made fair ſtabling for horſes ; as if Chriſt who was born in a ſtable ſhould be brought into it the ſecond time. It was not without cauſe in the Civill Law that a wife might be divorc'd, from her husband, if ſhe could prove him to be one that had * broken the Sepulchres of the dead : For it was preſum'd he muſt needs be a tyrannicall husband to his wife, who had not ſo much mercy as to ſpare the aſhes of the departed.

* *J. Speed in the end of Henry the 5.*

* *In the deſcript. of London, Broad-ſtreet-ward, pag.* 184.

* Si nimirum ſepulchrorum diſſolutorem eſſe probaverit, *Kirkman. de funer. Roman. lib.* 3. *c.* 26. *ex cod. de repudiis.*

The

The ſhorteſt, plaineſt, & trueſt Epitaphs are beſt. I ſay, the 5
Shorteſt; for when a Paſſenger ſees a Chronicle written on a Tombe, he takes it on truſt, ſome Great man lies there buried, without taking pains to examine who he is. M[r] Cambden in his Remains preſents us with examples of Great men that had little * Epitaphs. And when once I ask'd a witty Gentleman, an honoured friend of mine, what Epitaph was fitteſt to be written on M[r] Cambdens Tombe. Let it be, ſaid he,

CAMBDENS REMAINS.

* *as,* Fui Caius. Scaligeri quod reliquum eſt. Depoſitum Cardinalis Poli, *&c.*

I ſay alſo the Plaineſt; for except the ſenſe lie above ground, few will trouble themſelves to dig for't. Laſtly, it muſt be True: Not as as in ſome Monuments, where the red veins in the marble may ſeem to bluſh at the falſhoods written on it. He was a witty man that firſt taught a ſtone to ſpeak, but he was a wicked man that taught it firſt to lie.

To want a Grave is the cruelty of the living, not the miſery of 6
the dead. An Engliſh Gentleman not long ſince did lie on his death-bed in Spain, and the Jeſuites did flock about him to pervert him to their Religion. All was in vain. Their laſt argument was, If you will not turn Romane Catholick, then your body ſhall be unburied. *Then* (anſwered he) *I'le ſtink*, and ſo turned his head and dyed. Thus love, if not to the dead, to the living will make him, if not a grave, a hole: and it was the Beggers Epitaph,

Nudus eram vivus, mortuus ecce tegor.
Naked I liv'd, but being dead,
Now behold I'm covered.

A good Memory is the beſt Monument. Others are ſubject 7
to Caſualty and Time, and we know that the Pyramids themſelves doting with age have forgotten the names of their Founders. To conclude, Let us be carefull to provide reſt for our ſouls, and our bodies will provide reſt for themſelves. And let us not be herein like unto Gentlewomen, which care not to

keep the inside of the orenge, but candy and preserve onely the outside thereof.

CHAP. 15.
Of Deformitie.

DEformitie is either Naturall, Voluntary, or Adventitious, being either caused by Gods unseen Providence (by men nicknamed, Chance)or by mans Cruelty. We will take them in order.

Maxime 1 *If thou beest not so handsome as thou wouldest have been thank God thou art no more unhandsome then thou art.* 'Tis his mercie thou art not the mark for passengers fingers to point at, an Heteroclite in Nature, with some member defective or redundant. Be glad that thy clay-cottage hath all the necessary rooms thereto belonging, though the outside be not so fairly playstered as some others.

2 *Yet is it lawfull and commendable by Art to correct the defects and deformities of Nature.* Ericthonius being a goodly man from the girdle upwards, but, as the Poets feigne, having downwards the body of a * Serpent (moralize him to have had some defect in his feet) first invented charets, wherein he so sate that the upper parts of him might be seen, and the rest of his body concealed. Little heed is to be given to his * lying pen, who maketh Anna Bollen, Mother to Queen Elizabeth, the first finder out and wearer of Ruffes, to cover a wen she had in her neck. Yet the matter's not much, such an addition of Art being without any fraud or deceit.

* *Servius in illud Virgilii lib. 3. Georg* Primus Ericthonius, *&c.*

* *Sanders de schism. Anglic. lib. 1. pag. 17.*

Mock not at those who are misshapen by Nature. There is the same reason of the poore and of the deformed; he that despiseth them despiseth God that made them. A poore man is a picture of Gods own making, but set in a plain frame, not guilded : a deformed man is also his workmanship, but not drawn with

with even lines and lively colours : The former, not ſor want of wealth, as the latter not for want of skill, but both for the pleaſure of the maker. As for *Ariſtotle,who would have parents expoſe their deformed children to the wide world without caring for them, his opinion herein,not onely deform'd but moſt monſtrous, deſerves rather to be expoſed to the ſcorn and contempt of all men.

* *Lib. 7.Polit. ca 16.*

Some people handſome by Nature have wilfully deformed themſelves. Such as wear Bacchus his colours in their faces, ariſing not from having, but being, bad livers. When the woman (the firſt of Kings, the 3. and 21.) conſidered the child that was laid by her, *Behold*, ſaid ſhe, *it was not my ſonne which I did bear.* Should God ſurvey the faces of many men and women, he would not own and acknowledge them for thoſe which he created : many are ſo altered in colour, and ſome in ſex, women to men, and men to women in their monſtrous, faſhions , ſo that they who behold them cannot by the evidence of their apparell give up their verdict of what ſex they are. It is moſt ſafe to call the uſers of theſe hermaphroditicall faſhions, Franciſſes, and Philips, names agreeing to both ſexes. 4

Confeſſours which wear the badges of truth are thereby made the more beautifull; though deformed in time of Perſecution for Chriſts ſake through mens malice. This made Conſtantine the Great to * kiſſe the hole in the face of Paphnutius, out of which the Tyrant Maximinus had bored his eye for the profeſsion of the faith, the good Emperour making much of the ſocket even when the candle was put out. Next theſe, wounds in warre are moſt honourable : Halting is the ſtatelieſt march of a Souldier ; and 'tis a brave ſight to ſee the fleſh of an Ancient as torn as his Colours. He that mocks at the marks of valour in a Souldiers face, is likely to live 5

* *Ruffin. lib.1. cap. 4.*

to

to have the brands of juſtice on his own ſhoulders.

6 *Nature oftentimes recompenceth deform'd bodies with excellent wits.* Witneſſe Æſop, then whoſe Fables children cannot reade an eaſier, nor men a wiſer book; for all latter Moralliſts do but write comments upon them. Many jeering wits who have thought to have rid at their eaſe on the bowed backs of ſome Cripples, have by their unhappy anſwers been unhorſ'd and thrown flat on their own backs. A jeering Gentleman commended a Begger who was deformed and little better then blind for having an excellent eye, *True* (ſaid the Begger) *for I can diſcern an honeſt man from ſuch a knave as you are.*

7 *Their ſouls have been the Chappells of ſanctity, whoſe bodies have been the Spitolls of deformity.* An * Emperour of Germany coming by chance on a Sunday into a Church, found there a moſt misſhapen Prieſt, *pene portentum Naturæ*, inſomuch as the Emperour ſcorn'd and contemn'd him. But when he heard him reade thoſe words in the Service, *For it is he that made us and not we our ſelves*, the Emperour check'd his own proud thoughts, and made inquiry into the quality and condition of the man, and finding him on examination to be moſt learned and devout, he made him Archbiſhop of Colen, which place he did excellently diſcharge.

*Guliel.Malm. lib. 2. cap. 10.

CHAP. 16.

Chap. 16.

Of Plantations.

PLantations make mankind broader, as Generation makes it thicker. To advance an happy Plantation the Undertakers, Planters, and Place it ſelf muſt contribute their endeavours.

Let the prime Undertakers be men of no ſhallow heads, nor narrow fortunes. Such as have a reall Eſtate, ſo that if defeated in their adventure abroad, they may have a retreating place at home, and ſuch as will be contented with their preſent loſſe to be benefactours to poſterity. But if the Prince himſelf be pleaſed not onely to wink at them with his permiſsion, but alſo to ſmile on them with his encouragement, there is great hope of ſucceſſe: for then he will grant them ſome immunities and priviledges. Otherwiſe (Infants muſt be ſwathed not laced) young Plantations will never grow, if ſtraitned with as hard Laws as ſettled Common-wealths. Maxime 1

Let the Planters be honeſt, skilfull, and painfull people. For if they be ſuch as leap thither from the gallows, can any hope for cream out of ſcumme? when men ſend (as I may ſay) Chriſtian Savages to Heathen Savages. It was rather bitterly then falſely ſpoken concerning one of our Weſtern Plantations (conſiſting moſt of diſſolute people) *That it was very like unto England, as being ſpit out of the very mouth of it.* Nor muſt the Planters be onely honeſt but induſtrious alſo. What hope is there that they who were drones at home will be bees abroad, eſpecially if farre off from any to overſee them. 2

Let the place be naturally ſtrong, or at leaſtwiſe capable of fortification. For though at the firſt Planters are ſufficiently fenced with their own povertie, and though at the beginning their worſt enemies will ſpare them out 3 of pity to themselves, their spoyl not countervailing the cost of spoyling them; yet when once they have gotten wealth, they must get strength to defend it. Here know Ilands are easily shut, whereas Continents have their doores ever open, not to be bolted without great charges. Besides, unadvised are those Planters, who having choice of ground, have built their Towns in places of a servile nature, as being overawed and constantly commanded by some hills about them.

4 *Let it have a Self-sufficiency, or some Staple commoditie to ballance traffique with other countreys.* As for a Self-sufficiencie few countreys can stand alone, and such as can for matter of want, will for wantonnesse lean on others. Staple commodities are such as are never out of fashion, as belonging to a mans Being, Being with comfort, Being with delight, the Luxury of our age having made superfluities necessary. And such a place will thrive the better, when men may say with Isaac, * *Rehoboth, Now the Lord hath made room for us*, when new Colonies come not in with extirpation of the Natives; for this is rather a Supplanting then a Planting.

* Gen. 26. 22.

5 *Let the Planters labour to be loved and feard of the Natives.* With whom let them use all just bargaining, being as naked in their dealings with them as the other in their going, keeping all covenants, performing all promises with them: Let them embrace all occasions to convert them, knowing that each Convert is a conquest; and it is more honour to overcome Paganisme in one, then to conquer a thousand Pagans. As for the inscription of a Deity in their hearts it need not be new written, but onely new scowred in them.. I am confident that America (though the youngest sister of the foure) is now grown marriageable, and daily hopes to get Christ to her husband, by the Preaching of the Gospel. This makes me attentively to listen after some Protestant first-fruits, in hope the harvest will ripen afterwards.

Chap. 17.
Of Contentment.

IT is one property which (they ſay) is required of thoſe who ſeek for the Philoſophers ſtone, that they muſt not do it with any covetous deſire to be rich ; for otherwiſe they ſhall never find it. But moſt true it is that whoſoever would have this jewell of Contentment (which turns all into Gold, yea Want into Wealth) muſt come with minds deveſted of all ambitious and covetous thoughts, elſe are they never likely to obtain it. We will deſcribe Contentment firſt negatively:

It is not a ſenſeleſſe ſtupidity what becomes of our outward eſtates. God would have us take notice of all accidents which from him happen to us in worldly matters. Had the Martyrs had the dead palſie before they went to the ſtake to be burnt, their ſuffrings had not been ſo glorious. Maxime 1

It is not a word-braving, or ſcorning of all wealth in diſcourſe. Generally thoſe who boaſt moſt of Contentment have leaſt of it. Their very boaſting ſhews that they want ſomething,and baſely beg it, namely Commendation. Theſe in their language are like unto kites in their flying, which mount in the aire ſo ſcornfully, as if they diſdaind to ſtoop for the whole earth, fetching about many ſtately circuits : but what is the Spirit theſe conjurers with ſo many circles intend to raiſe ? a poore chicken, or perchance a piece of carrion : And ſo the height of the others proud boaſting will humble it ſelf for a little baſe gain. 2

But it is an humble and willing ſubmitting our ſelves to Gods pleaſure in all conditions. One obſerveth (how truly I diſpute not) that the French naturally have ſo elegant and gracefull a carriage, that what poſture of body ſoever in their ſalutations, or what faſhion of attire ſoe- 3 ver they are pleaſed to take on them it doth ſo beſeem them,that one would think nothing can become them better. Thus Contentment makes men carry themſelves gracefully in wealth, want, in health, ſickneſſe, freedome, fetters, yea what condition ſoever God allots them.

4 *It is no breach of Contentment for men to complain that their ſufferings are unjust, as offered by men*: provided they allow them for juſt, as proceeding from God, who uſeth wicked mens injuſtice to correct his children. But let us take heed that we bite not ſo high at the handle of the rod, as to faſten on his hand that holds it; our diſcontentments mounting ſo high as to quarrell with God himſelf.

5 *It is no breach of Contentment for men by lawfull means to ſeek the removall of their miſerie, and bettering of their estate.* Thus men ought by induſtrie to endeavour the getting of more wealth, ever ſubmitting themſelves to Gods will. A lazy hand is no argument of a Contented heart. Indeed he that is idle, and followeth after vain perſons ſhall have enough, but how? Prov. 28. 19. *Shall have poverty enough.*

6 *Gods Spirit is the best Schoolmaster to teach Contentment*: A Schoolmaſter who can make good Scholars, and warrant the ſucceſſe as well as his endeavour. The School of Sanctified afflictions is the beſt place to learn Contentment in: I ſay, Sanctified; for naturally, like reſty horſes, we go the worſe for the beating, if God bleſſe not afflictions unto us.

7 *Contentment conſisteth not in adding more fuell, but in taking away ſome fire*: not in multiplying of wealth,but in ſubſtracting mens deſires. Worldly riches, like nuts, teare many clothes in getting them, ſpoil many teeth in cracking them, but fill no belly with eating them, obſtructing onely the ſtomach with toughnes, and filling the guts with windineſſe: Yea our ſouls may ſooner ſurfet then be ſatisfied with earthly things. He that at firſt

first thought ten thousand pound too much for any one man, will afterwards think ten millions too little for himself.

8 *Men create more discontents to themselves, then ever happened to them from others.* We reade of our Saviour that at the buriall of Lazarus, John 11. 33. Ἐτάραξεν ἑαυτὸν, *He troubled himself,* by his spirit raising his own passions, though without any ataxie or sinfull disturbance. What was an act of power in him, is an act of weaknesse in other men: *Man disquieteth himself in vain,* with many causelesse and needlesse afflictions.

9 *Pious meditations much advantage Contentment in adversitie.* Such as these are, to consider first, that more are beneath us then above us; secondly, many of Gods dear Saints have been in the same condition; thirdly, we want rather superfluities then necessities; fourthly, the more we have the more we must account for; fifthly, earthly blessings through mans corruption are more prone to be abused then well used. In some fenny places in England, where they are much troubled with gnats, they use to hang up dung in the midst of the room for a bait for the gnats to flie to, and so catch them with a net provided for the purpose. Thus the devil ensnareth the souls of many men by alluring them with the muck and dung of this world, to undo them eternally; sixthly, we must leave all earthly wealth at our death, *and riches avail not in the day of wrath.* But as some use to fill up the stamp of light gold with dirt, thereby to make it weigh the heavier; so it seems some men load their souls with thick clay, to make them passe the better in Gods ballance, but all to no purpose; seventhly, the lesse we have, the lesse it will grieve us to leave this world; lastly, it is the will of God, and therefore both for his glory and our good, whereof we ought to be assured. I have heard how a Gentleman travelling in a misty morning ask'd of a Shepherd (such men

being generally skill'd in the Physiognomie of the Heavens) what weather it would be? *It will be*, said the Shepherd, *what weather shall please me*: and being courteously requested to expresse his meaning, *Sir* (saith he) *it shall be what weather pleaseth God, and what weather pleaseth God, pleaseth me*. Thus Contentment maketh men to have even what they think fitting themselves, because submitting to Gods will and pleasure.

To conclude, A man ought to be like unto a cunning Actour, who if he be enjoyned to represent the person of some Prince or Nobleman, does it with a grace and comlinesse; if by and by he be commanded to lay that aside, and play the Begger, he does that as willingly and as well. But as it happened in a Tragedy (to spare naming the Person and Place) that one being to act Theseus, in *Hercules Furens*, coming out of Hell, could not for a long time be perswaded to wear old sooty clothes proper to his part, but would needs come out of Hell in a white Satin doublet: so we are generally loath, and it goes against flesh and blood, to live in a low and poore estate, but would fain act in richer and handsomer clothes, till Grace, with much adoe, subdues our rebellious stomachs to Gods will.

Chap. 18.

Of Books.

SOlomon ſaith truly, *Of making many Books there is no end,* ſo inſatiable is the thirſt of men therein : as alſo endles is the deſire of many in buying and reading them. But we come to our Rules.

It is a vanity to perſwade the World one hath much learning by getting a great library. As ſoon ſhall I believe every one is valiant that hath a well furniſh'd armoury. I gueſſe good houſekeeping by the ſmoking, not the number of the tunnels, as knowing that many of them (built merely for uniformity) are without chimnies, and more without fires. Once a dunce, void of learning but full of Books, flouted a library-leſſe Scholar with theſe words, *Salve Doctor ſine libris* : But the next day the Scholar coming into this jeerers ſtudy crowded with Books, *Salvete libri* (ſaith he) *ſine Doctore.* Maxime 1

Few Books well ſelected are beſt. Yet as a certain Fool bought all the pictures that came out, becauſe he might have his choice ; ſuch is the vain humour of many men in gathering of Books : yet when they have done all, they miſſe their end, it being in the Editions of Authours as in the faſhions of clothes, when a man thinks he hath gotten the lateſt and neweſt, preſently another newer comes out. 2

Some Books are onely curſorily to be taſted of. Namely firſt Voluminous Books, the task of a mans life to reade them over ; ſecondly, Auxiliary Books, onely to be repair'd to on occaſions ; thirdly, ſuch as are mere pieces of Formality, ſo that if you look on them you look thorow them ; and he that peeps thorow the caſement of the Index ſees as much as if he were in the houſe. But the lazineſſe of thoſe cannot be excuſed who perfunctorily paſſe over Authours of conſequence, and onely trade in their Fables and Contents. Theſe like 3

City-

City-Cheaters having gotten the names of all countrey Gentlemen, make ſilly people believe they have long lived in thoſe places where they never were, and flouriſh with skill in thoſe Authours they never ſeriouſly ſtudied.

4 *The Genius of the Authour is commonly diſcovered in the Dedicatory epiſtle.* Many place the pureſt grain in the mouth of the ſack for chapmen to handle or buy: And from the dedication one may probably gueſſe at the Work, ſaving ſome rare and peculiar exceptions. Thus when once a Gentleman admired how ſo pithy, learned, and witty a dedication was match'd to a flat, dull, fooliſh book; *In truth*, ſaid another, *they may be well match'd together, for I profeſſe they are nothing a kinne.*

5 *Proportion an houres meditation to an houres reading of a ſtaple Authour.* This makes a man maſter of his learning, and diſpirits the book into the Scholar. The King of Sweden never * filed his men above ſix deep in one company, becauſe he would not have them lie in uſeleſſ cluſters in his Army, but ſo that every particular Souldier might be drawn out into ſervice. Books that ſtand thinne on the ſhelves, yet ſo as the owner of them can bring forth every one of them into uſe, are better then farre greater libraries.

* *Wards Animadver. of warre ſect. 17 lib. 2. cap. 5.*

6 *Learning hath gained moſt by thoſe books by which the Printers have loſt.* Arius Montanus in printing the Hebrew Bible (commonly called the Bible of the King of Spain) much waſted himſelf, and was accuſed in the Court of Rome for his good deed, and being cited thither, * *Pro tantorum laborum præmio vix veniam impetravit.* Likewiſe Chriſtopher Plantin by printing of his curious interlineary Bible in Anwerp, through the unſeaſonable * exactions of the Kings Officers, ſunk and almoſt ruin'd his eſtate. And our worthy Engliſh Knight, who ſet forth the golden-mouth'd Father in a ſilver print, was a looſer by it.

* *Thuanus obit. vir. Doct. Anno 1598.*

* *Idem in eodem oper. Anno 1589.*

7 *Whereas fooliſh Pamphlets prove moſt beneificall to the Printers.*

ters. When a French Printer complain'd that he was utterly undone by Printing a ſolid ſerious book of Rablais concerning Phyſick, Rablais to make him recompence made that his jeſting ſcurrilous Work which repair'd the Printers loſſe with advantage. Such books the world ſwarms too much with. When one had ſet out a witleſſe Pamphlet,writing *Finis* at the end thereof, another wittily wrote beneath it,

--------Nay there thou li ſt, my friend,
In Writing fooliſh books there is no end.

And ſurely ſuch ſcurrilous ſcandalous papers do more then conceivable miſchief.Firſt their luſciouſneſſe puts many palats out of taſte, that they can never after relliſh any ſolid and wholſome Writers : ſecondly, they caſt dirt on the faces of many innocent perſons, which dryed on by continuance of time can never after be waſhed off : thirdly, the Pamphlets of this age may paſſe for Records with the next (becauſe publickly uncontrolled) and what we laugh at, our children may believe : fourthly, grant the things true they jeer at , yet this muſick is unlawfull in any Chriſtian Church,to play upon the ſinnes and miſeries of others, the fitter object of the Elegies then the Satyrs of all truly religious.

But what do I ſpeaking againſt multiplicity of books in this age, who treſpaſſe in this nature my ſelf ? What was a * learned mans complement may ſerve for my confeſſion and concluſion, *Multi mei ſimiles hoc morbo laborant, ut cum ſcribere neſciant tamen a ſcribendo temperare non poſſint.*

* *Eraſmus in præfat. in* 3. *ſeriem* 4. *Tomi Hieron. pag.* 408.

Chap. 19.

CHAP. 19.

Of Time-serving.

THere be foure kinds of Time-ſerving: firſt, out of Chriſtian diſcretion, which is commendable; ſecond, out of humane infirmity, which is more pardonable; third, and fourth, out of ignorance, or affection, both which are damnable: of them in order.

Maxime 1 *He is a good Time-ſerver that complyes his manners to the ſeverall ages of this life*: pleaſant in youth, without wantonneſſe; grave in old age without frowardneſſe. Froſt is as proper for winter, as flowers for ſpring. Gravity becomes the ancient; and a green Chriſtmas is neither handſome nor healthfull.

2 *He is a good Time-ſerver that finds out the fitteſt opportunity for every action.* God hath made a *time for every thing under the ſunne*, ſave onely for that, which we do at all times, to wit Sinne.

3 *He is a good Time-ſerver that improves the preſent for Gods glory, and his own ſalvation.* Of all the extent of time, onely the inſtant is that which we can call ours.

4 *He is a good Time-ſerver that is pliant to the times in matters of mere indifferency.* Too blame are they whoſe minds may ſeem to be made of one entire bone without any joynts: they cannot bend at all, but ſtand as ſtiffly in things of pure indifferency, as in matters of abſolute neceſsity.

5 *He is a good Time-ſerver that in time of perſecution neither betrayes Gods cauſe, nor his own ſafety.* And this he may do,

1 By lying hid both in his perſon and practice: though he will do no evil he will forbear the publick doing of ſome good. He hath as good cheer in his heart, though he keeps not open houſe, and will not publickly broch his Religion,

on, till the palat of the times be better in taste to rellish it. *The * Prudent shall keep silence in that time, for it is an evil time.* Though according to S. Peters command we are to *give a * reason of our hope to every one that asketh*; namely, that asketh for his instruction, but not for our destruction, especially if wanting lawfull Authority to examine us. * *Ye shall be brought* saith Christ (no need have they therefore to run) *before Princes for my sake.*

* Annos. 5. v. 13.

* 1. Pet. 3. 15.

* Matth. 10. 18.

2 By flying away : if there be no absolute necessity of his staying, no scandall given by his flight; if he wants strength to stay it out till death; and lastly, if God openeth a fair way for his departure: otherwise, if God bolts the doores and windows against him, he is not to creep out at the top of the chimney, and to make his escape by unwarrantable courses. If all should flie, Truth would want champions for the present; if none should flie, Truth might want champions for the future. We come now to Time-servers out of infirmity.

Heart of oke hath sometimes warp'd a little in the scorching heat of persecution. Their want of true courage herein cannot be excused. Yet many censure them for surrendring up their forts after a long siege, who would have yielded up their own at the first summons. Oh, there is more required to make one valiant, then to call Cranmer or Jewell Coward, as if the fire in Smithfield had been no hotter, then what is painted in the Book of Martyrs. 6

Yet afterwards they have come into their former straightnesse & stiffnesse. The troops which at first rather wheeld about then ran away have come in seasonable at last. Yea their constant blushing for shame of their former cowardlinesse hath made their souls ever after look more modest and beautifull. Thus Cranmer (who subscribed to Popery) grew valiant afterwards, and 7 thrust his right hand which subscribed first into fire, so that that hand dyed (as it were) a malefactour and all the rest of his body dyed a martyr.

8 *Some have served the times out of mere Ignorance.* Gaping for company, as others gap'd before them, *Pater noster*, or, Our Father. I could both sigh and smile at the witty simplicity of a poore old woman who had lived in the dayes of Queen Marie, and Queen Elizabeth, and said her prayers dayly both in Latine and English, and *Let God*, said she, *take to himself which he likes best.*

9 *But worst are those who serve the times out of mere Affectation.* Doing as the times do, not because the times do as they should do, but merely for sinister respects, to ingratiate themselves. We reade of an Earl of * Oxford fined by King Henrie the seventh fifteen thousand marks for having too many Retainers. But how many Retainers hath Time had in all ages ? and Servants in all offices ? yea and Chaplains too ?

* *Lord Bacon in Henry seventh, p.* 211.

10 *It is a very difficult thing to serve the times* ; they change so frequently, so suddenly, and sometimes so violently from one extreme to another. The times under Dioclesian were Pagan ; under Constantine, Christian ; under Constantius, Arian ; under Julian, Apostate ; under Jovian, Christian again, and all within the age of man, the term of seventie years. And would it not have wrench'd and spraind his soul with short turning, who in all these should have been of the Religion *for the time being?*

11 *Time-servers are oftentimes left in the lurch.* If they do not onely give their word for the times in their constant discourses, but also give their bands for them, and write in their defence. Such, when the times turn afterwards to another extreme, are left in the briers, and come off very hardly from the bill of their hands ; If they turn again with the times none will trust them ; for who will make a staff of an osier ?

12 *Miserable will be the condition of such Time-servers when*

their

their Master is taken from them. When as the Angel ſwore Rev. 10. 6. that *Time ſhall be no longer.* Therefore is it beſt ſerving of him who is eternity, a Maſter that can ever protect us.

To conclude, he that intends to meet with one in a great Fair, and knows not where he is, may ſooner find him by ſtanding ſtill in ſome principall place there, then by traverſing it up and down. Take thy ſtand on ſome good ground in Religion,and keep thy ſtation in a fixed poſture, never hunting after the times to follow them, and an hundred to one, they will come to thee once in thy lifetime.

CHAP. 20.

Of Moderation.

MOderation *is * the ſilken ſtring running through the pearl-chain of all virtues.* It appears both in Practice, and Judgement : we will inſiſt on the latter, and deſcribe it firſt negatively :

* *Biſhop Hall of Chriſtian Moderation, pag. 6.*

Maxime 1

Moderation is not an halting betwixt two opinions, when the through-believing of one of them is neceſſary to ſalvation . no pity is to be ſhown to ſuch voluntary cripples. We reade (Acts 27. 12.) of an Haven in Crete *which lay towards the South-Weſt, and towards the North-Weſt* : ſtrange, that it could have part of two oppoſite points, North and South, ſure, it muſt be very winding. And thus ſome mens ſouls are in ſuch intricate poſtures, they lay towards the Papiſts,and towards the Proteſtants ; ſuch we count not of a moderate judgement, but of an immoderate unſettledneſſe.

2

Nor is it a lukewarmneſſe in thoſe things wherein Gods glory is concernd. Herein it's a true Rule, * *Non amat qui non zelat.* And they that are thus lukewarm here ſhall be too hot hereafter in that oven wherein *Dow-bak'd cakes* ſhall be burnt.

* *Auguſtin. contra Adamant. cap. 13.*

3

But it is a mixture of diſcretion and charity in ones judgement.

 Diſcretion

Discretion puts a difference betwixt things absolutely necessary to salvation to be done and believed, and those which are of a second sort and lower form, wherein more liberty and latitude is allowed. In maintaining whereof, the stiffnesse of the judgement is abated, and suppled with charity towards his neighbour. The lukewarm man eyes onely his own ends, and particular profit; the moderate man aims at the good of others, and unity of the Church.

4 *Yet such moderate men are commonly crush'd betwixt the extreme parties on both sides.* But what said Ignatius? * *I am Christs wheat, and must be ground with the teeth of beasts, that I may be made Gods pure manchet.* Saints are born to suffer, and must take it patiently. Besides, in this world generally they get the least preferment; it faring with them as with the guest that sat in the midst of the table, who could reach to neither messe, above or beneath him:

> *Esuriunt Medii, Fines bene sunt saturati;*
> *Dixerunt stulti, Medium tenuere beati.*
> Both ends o'th' table furnish'd are with meat,
> Whilst they in middle nothing have to eat.
> They were none of the wisest well I wist,
> Who made blisse in the middle to consist.

Yet these temporall inconveniences of moderation are abundantly recompenced with other better benefits: for

1 A well inform'd judgement in it self is a preferment. Potamon began a sect of Philosophers called * Ἐκλέκτικοι, who wholly adher'd to no former sect, but chose out of all of them what they thought best. Surely such Divines, who in unimporting controversies extract the probablest opinions from all Professions, are best at ease in their minds.

2 As the moderate mans temporall hopes are not great so his fears are the lesse. He fears not to have

* Ireneus lib. 5.

* Diog. Laert in fine Proœmii.

have the ſplinters of his party (when it breaks) flie into his eyes, or to be buried under the ruines of his ſide if ſuppreſt. He never pinn'd his religion on any mans ſleeve, no, not on *the Arme of fleſh*, and therefore is free from all dangerous engagements.

3 His conſcience is clear from raiſing Schiſmes in the Church. The Turks did uſe to wonder much at our Engliſh men for * pinking or cutting their clothes, counting them little better then mad for their pains to make holes in whole cloth, which time of it ſelf would tear too ſoon. But grant men may doe with their own garments, as their phancy adviſeth them: yet woe be to ſuch who willingly cut and rend the ſeamleſſe Coat of Chriſt with diſſentions.

* *Bidulph. in his travell to Jeruſalem, pag.* 98.

4 His religion is more conſtant and durable; being here, *in via*, in his way to Heaven, and jogging on a good Travellers pace he overtakes and out-goes many violent men, whoſe over-hot ill-grounded Zeal was quickly tired.

5 In matters of moment indeed none are more Zealous. He thriftily treaſur'd up his ſpirits for that time, who if he had formerly rent his lungs for every trifle, he would have wanted breath in points of importance.

6 Once in an age the moderate man is in faſhion, Each extreme courts him, to make them friends; and ſurely he hath a great advantage to be a Peace-maker betwixt oppoſite parties. Now whileſt, as we have ſaid, moderate men are conſtant to themſelves,

Violent men reel from one extremity to another. Who would think that the Eaſt and Weſt Indies were ſo near together, whoſe names ſpeak them at diametricall oppoſition? And yet their extremities are either the ſame Continent, or parted with a very narrow Sea.

As

As the world is round, ſo we may obſerve a circulation in opinions, and Violent men turn often round in their tenets.

6 *Pride is the greateſt enemy to Moderation.* This makes men ſtickle for their opinions, to make them fundamentall: Proud men having deeply ſtudied ſome additionall point in Divinity, will ſtrive to make the ſame neceſſary to ſalvation, to enhanſe the value of their own worth and pains; and it muſt be fundamentall in religion, becauſe it is fundamentall to their reputation. Yea as love doth deſcend, and men doat moſt on their Grandchildren, ſo theſe are indulgent to the deductions of their deductions, and conſequentiall inferences to the ſeventh generation, making them all of the foundation, though ſcarce of the building of religion. * Ancient Fathers made the Creed *ſymbolum*, the ſhot and totall ſumme of Faith. Since which how many arrearages, and after-reckonings have men brought us in? to which if we will not pay our belief, our ſouls muſt be arreſted without bail upon pain of damnation. Next to Pride popular Applauſe is the greateſt foe Moderation hath, and ſure they who ſail with that wind have their own vain glory for their Haven.

* *Irenæus cap. 2. 5. Tertull. de virgin. velan. Hilarius ad Conſtant. Auguſt. Taur. Maxim. Serm. de ſymbolo. Auguſt. Serm. 2. & 108 1. De Tempore.*

To cloſe up all, Let men on Gods bleſſing ſoundly, yet wiſely, whip and laſh Lukewarmneſſe and Time-ſerving, their thongs will never flie in the face of true Moderation, to do it any harm; for however men may undervalue it, that * Father ſpake moſt truly, *Si virtutum finis ille ſit maximus, qui plurimorum ſpectat profectum, Moderatio prope omnium pulcherrima eſt.*

* *Ambroſ. de pœniten. contra Novat. lib. 1. cap. 1*

CHAP. 21.

Chap. 21.

Of Gravity.

GRavity is the ballaſt of the ſoul, which keeps the mind ſteddy. It is either true, or counterfeit.

Naturall dulneſſe, and heavineſſe of temper, is ſometimes miſtaken for true Gravity. In ſuch men in whoſe conſtitutions one of the tetrarch Elements *fire* may ſeem to be omitted. Theſe ſometimes not onely cover their defects, but get praiſe : Maxime 1

Sæpe latet vitium proximitate boni.

They do wiſely to counterfeit a reſervedneſſe, and to keep their cheſts alwayes lock'd, not for fear any ſhould ſteal treaſure thence, but leſt ſome ſhould look in, and ſee that there is nothing within them. But they who are born Eunuchs deſerve no ſuch great commendation for their chaſtity. Wonder not ſo much that ſuch men are grave, but wonder at them if they be not grave.

Affected Gravity paſſes often for that which is true: I mean with dull eyes, for in it ſelf nothing is more ridiculous. When one ſhall uſe the preface of a mile, to bring in a furlong of matter, ſet his face and ſpeech in a frame, and to make men believe it is ſome pretious liquour, their words come out drop by drop : Such mens viſards do ſometimes fall from them, not without the laughter of the beholders. One was called *Gravity* for his affected ſolemneſſe, who afterwards being catch'd in a light prank was ever after to the day of his death called *Gravity-levity* . 2

True Gravity expreſſeth it ſelf in Gate, Geſture, Apparell, and Speech. Vox * *quædam eſt animi, corporis motus.* As for Speech, Gravity enjoyns it, 3

1 Not to be over much. *In* * *the multitude of words there wanteth not ſinne.* For of neceſsity many of them muſt be idle, whoſe beſt commendation is that

* *Ambroſ. de offic. lib.* 1. *cap.* 18.

* *Prov.*10.19.

* Greg. moral. lib. 7. cap. 17.

they are good for nothing. Beſides, * *Dum otioſa verba cavere negligimus, ad noxia pervenimus.* And great talkers diſcharge too thick to take alwayes true aim; beſides, it is odious in a company. A man full of words, who took himſelf to be a Grand wit, made his brag that he was the leader of the diſcourſe in what company ſoever he came, and *None*, ſaid he, *dare ſpeak in my preſence, if I hold my peace. No wonder*, anſwered one, *for they are all ſtruck dumbe at the miracle of your ſilence.*

*Fox Martyrs, pag. 1079.

2 To be wiſe and diſcreet, Coloſsians 4. 6. *Let your ſpeech be alwayes with grace, ſeaſoned with ſalt. Alwayes*, not onely ſometimes in the company of godly men. * Tindals being in the room hindred a juggler that he could not play his feats: (A Saints preſence ſtops the devils elbow-room to do his tricks) and ſo ſome wicked men are awed into good diſcourſe, whileſt pious people are preſent. But it muſt be alwayes *ſeaſoned with ſalt*, which is the *primum vivens & ultimum moriens* at a feaſt, firſt brought, and laſt taken away, and ſet in the midſt as moſt neceſſary thereunto. *With ſalt*, that is with wiſdome and diſcretion, *non ſalibus, ſed ſale*; nor yet with ſmarting jeeres, like thoſe whoſe diſcourſe is *fire-ſalt*, ſpeaking conſtant ſatyrs to the diſgrace of others.

4 *That may be done privately without breach of Gravity, which may not be done publickly.* As when a father makes himſelf his childs rattle, ſporting with him till the father hath devour'd the wiſeman in him.

Equitans in arundine longa.
In ſtead of ſtately ſteed,
Riding upon a reed.

Making play unto him, that one would think he kill'd his own diſcretion, to bring his child aſleep. Such caſes are no treſpaſſe on Gravity, and married men may claim their priviledge, *to be judged by their*

Peeres

Peeres, and may herein appeal from the cenſuring verdict of batchelours.

5 *Nature in men is ſometimes unjuſtly taxed for a treſpaſſe againſt Gravity.* Some have active ſpirits, yea their ordinary pace is a race. Others have ſo ſcornfull a carriage, that he who ſeeth them once may think them to be all pride, whileſt he that ſeeth them often knows them to have none. Others have perchance a misbeſeeming garb in geſture which they cannot amend; that fork needing ſtrong tines wherewith one muſt thruſt away nature. A fourth ſort are of a merry cheerfull diſpoſition; and God forbid all ſuch ſhould be condemned for lightneſſe. O let not any envious eye diſinherit men of that which is their * *Portion in this life*, comfortably to enjoy the bleſsings thereof. Yet Gravity muſt prune though not root out our mirth.

* *Eccles* 7.18.

6 *Gratious deportment may ſometimes unjuſtly be accuſed of lightneſſe.* Had one ſeen David * dancing before the Ark, * Eliah in his praying-poſture when he put his head betwixt his legs, perchance he might have condemn'd them of unfitting behaviour. Had he ſeen * Peter and John poſting to Chriſts grave, * Rhodia running into the houſe, he would have thought they had left their Gravity behind them. But let none blame them for their ſpeed untill he knows what were their ſpurres, and what were the motives that urged them to make ſuch haſte. Theſe their actions were the true concluſions, following from ſome inward premiſſes in their own ſouls; and that may be a ſyllogiſme in grace, which appears a ſoleciſme in manners.

* 2. *Sam.* 6. 16.
* 1. *Kings* 18. 42.
* *John* 20. 14.
* *Acts* 12. 14

7 *In ſome perſons Gravity is moſt neceſſary.* Viz. in Magiſtrates and Miniſters. One * Palevizine an Italian Gentleman, and kinſman to Scaliger, had in one night all his haire chang'd from black to gray. Such an alteration ought there to be in the heads of every one that enters into Holy Orders, or Pub-

* *Scaliger de ſubtil. pag.* 18.

lick Office, metamorphos'd from all lightnesse to Gravity.

8 *God alone is the giver of true Gravity.* No man wants so much of any grace as he hath to spare; and a constant impression of Gods omnipresence is an excellent way to fix mens souls. Bishop Andrews ever placed the picture of* Mulcaster his Schoolmaster over the doore of his study (whereas in all the rest of his house you should scarce see a picture) as to be his Tutour and Supervisour. Let us constantly apprehend Gods being in presence, and this will fright us into staied behaviour.

* *Vid. in the funerall serm. on him, pag.* 18.

Chap. 22.

Of Marriage.

SOme men have too much decried Marriage, as if she the mother were scarce worthy to wait on Virginity her daughter, and as if it were an advancement for Marriage to be preferr'd before fornication, and praise enough for her to be adjudged lawfull. Give this holy estate her due, and then we shall find,

Maxime 1 *Though batchelours be the strongest stakes, married men are the best binders in the hedge of the Commonwealth.* 'Tis the Policy of the Londoners when they send a ship into the Levant or Mediterranean sea, to make every marriner therein a merchant, each seaman adventuring somewhat of his own, which will make him more wary to avoid, and more valiant to undergo dangers. Thus married men, especially if having posterity, are the deeper sharers in that state wherein they live, which engageth their affections to the greater loyalty.

2 *It is the worst clandestine marriage when God is not invited to it.* Wherefore beforehand beg his gratious assistance. Marriage shall prove no lottery to thee, when the

hand of providence chuseth for thee, who, if drawing a blank, can turn it into a prize by sanctifying a bad wife unto thee.

Deceive not thy self by overexpecting happinesse in the married estate. Look not therein for contentment greater then God will give, or a creature in this world can receive, namely to be free from all inconveniences. Marriage is not like the hill Olympus, ὅλος λαμπρὸς, *wholly clear*, without clouds; yea expect both wind and storms sometimes, which when blown over, the aire is the clearer, and wholsomer for it. Make account of certain cares and troubles which will attend thee. Remember the nightingales which sing onely some moneths in the spring, but commonly are silent when they have hatch'd their egges, as if their mirth were turned into care for their young ones. Yet all the molestations of Marriage are abundantly recompenced with other comforts which God bestoweth on them, who make a wise choice of a wife, and observe the following rules. 3

Let Grace and Goodnesse be the principall loadstone of thy affections. For love which hath ends will have an end, whereas that which is founded in true virtue will alwayes continue. Some hold it unhappy to be married with a diamond ring, perchance (if there be so much reason in their folly) because the diamond hinders the roundnesse of the ring, ending the infinitenesse thereof, and seems to presage some termination in their love, which ought ever to endure, and so it will, when it is founded in religion. 4

Neither chuse all, nor not at all for Beauty. A cried-up Beauty makes more for her own praise then her husbands profit. They tell us of a floting Iland in Scotland: but sure no wise pilot will cast anchor there, lest the land swimme away with his ship. So are they served (and justly enough) who onely fasten their love on fading Beauty, and both fail together. 5

6 *Let there be no great disproportion in age.* They that marry ancient people merely in expectation to bury them, hang themselves in hope that one will come and cut the halter. Nor is Gods ordinance but mans abusing thereof taxed in this homely expression, used by the Apostle himself. If Virginity enforced above the parties power be * termed by S. Paul 1. Cor. 7. 35. a *snare or halter*, marriage is no better when against ones will, for private respects.

* Ὀυχ ἵνα βρόχον ὑμῖν ἐπιβάλω, 1. Cor. 7. 35.

7 *Let wealth in its due distance be regarded.* There be two towns in the land of Liege called Bovins and Dinant, the inhabitants whereof bear almost an incredible hatred one to another, and yet notwithstanding their children usually marry together; and the * reason is, because there is none other good town, or wealthy place near them. Thus parents for a little pelf often marry their children to those whose persons they hate; and thus union betwixt families is not made, but the breach rather widened the more.

* *Phil. Com. lib.* 2. *cap.* 1.

This shall serve for a Conclusion. A Batchelour was saying, *Next to no wife, a good wife is best. Nay*, said a Gentlewoman, *next to a good wife, no wife is the best.* I wish to all married people the outward happinesse which * *Anno* 1605 happened to a couple in the city of Delph in Holland, living most lovingly together seventy five years in wedlock, till the man being one hundred and three, the woman ninety nine years of age, died within three houres each of other, and were buried in the same grave.

* *Thuan. de obit. vir doct. in eod. Anno. pag.* 385.

CHAP. 23.
Of Fame.

FAme is the echo of actions, resounding them to the world, save that the echo repeats onely the last part, but Fame relates all and often more then all.

Fame sometimes hath created something of nothing. She hath made whole countreys more then ever Nature did, especially near the Poles, and then hath peopled them likewise with inhabitants of her own invention, Pygmies, Giants, and Amazons : Yea Fame is sometimes like unto a kind of Mushrom, which * Pliny recounts to be the greatest miracle in nature, because growing and having no root, as Fame no ground of her reports. *Maxime* 1

Fame often makes a great deal of a little. Absalom kill'd one of Davids sonnes, and * Fame kill'd all the rest; and generally she magnifies and multiplies matters. Loud was that lie which that bell told hanging in a clock-house at Westminster, and usually rung at the Coronation and Funeralls of Princes, having this inscription about it, 2

King Edward made me
thirty thousand and three,
Take me down and weigh me
and more shall you find me.

But when this bell was taken down at the doomsday of Abbeys, this and two more were found not to weigh * twenty thousand. Many relations of Fame are found to shrink accordingly.

Some Fames are most difficult to trace home to their form: and those who have sought to track them, have gone rather in a circle then forward, and oftentimes through the doubling of reports have return'd back again where they began. Fame being a bastard or *filia populi*, 'tis very hard to find her father, and ofttimes she hath 3

* *In miraculis vel maximum est Tubera nasci & vivere sine ulla radice, Plin. Nat. Hist. lib. 19. cap. 2.*

* 2. *Sam.* 13. 30.

* *Stowes survey of London, pag.* 528.

hath rather all then any for her firſt Authours.

4 *Politicians ſometimes raiſe Fames on purpoſe.* As that ſuch things are done already, which they mean to do afterwards. By the light of thoſe falſe fires they ſee into mens hearts, and theſe falſe rumours are true ſcouts to diſcover mens diſpoſitions. Beſides, the deed (though ſtrange in it ſelf) is done afterwards with the leſſe noiſe, men having vented their wonder beforehand, and the ſtrangeneſſe of the action is abated, becauſe formerly made ſtale in report. But if the rumour ſtartles men extremely,and draws with it dangerous conſequences, then they can preſently confute it, let their intentions fall and proſecute it no further.

5 *The Papall ſide of all Fame-merchants drive the moſt gainfull trade,* as that worthy * Knight hath given us an exact ſurvey thereof. But long before them, ſtrange was that plot of Stratocles, who gave it out that he had gotten a victory, and the conſtant report thereof continued three dayes, and then was confuted ; and Stratocles being charged with abuſing his people with a lie, *Why* (ſaid * he) *are ye angry with me for making you paſſe three dayes in mirth and jollity more then otherwiſe you ſhould ?*

* *S. Edward Sandys view of the weſt Religions, pag.* 100.

* *Plutarchs Πολίτικα παραγγέλματα.*

6 *Incredible is the ſwiftneſſe of Fame in carrying reports.* Firſt ſhe creeps thorow a village, then ſhe goes thorow a town, then ſhe runs thorow a city, then ſhe flyes thorow a countrey, ſtill the farther the faſter. Yea Chriſt who made the dumbe ſpeak, made not tell-tale Fame ſilent, though charging thoſe he cured to hold their peace, * *but ſo much the more went there a Fame abroad of him.* Yea ſome things have been reported ſoon as ever they were done at impoſsible diſtance. The overthrow of Perſeus was brought out of Macedon to Rome in * foure dayes. And in Domitians time a report was brought two thouſand five hundred miles in one day. In which accidents,

* *Luke* 5. 15.

* *Livy. lib.*45. *juxta princip.*

1 Fame takes poſt on ſome other advantage. Thus the

the overthrow of the Sabines was known at Rome *prius pene quam nunciari poſsit*, by the means of the * arms of the Sabines drowned in the river of Tiber, and carried down by the tide to Rome. And thus *Anno* * 1568 the overthrow which the Spaniards gave the Dutch at the river of Ems was known at Grunning before any horſeman could reach thither, by the multitude of the Dutch caps which the river brought down into the city. But theſe conveiances are but ſlugs to make ſuch miraculous ſpeed: wherefore ſometimes reports are carried,

* Livy, lib. 1.

*Famian. Strada de Bello Belgic. lib. 5. pag. 456.

2 By the miniſtration of Spirits. The devils are well at leiſure to play ſuch pranks, and may do it in a frolick. And yet they would ſcarce be the carriers except they were well payed for the portage, getting ſome profit thereby (doing of miſchief is all the profit they are capable of) and do harm to ſome by the ſuddenneſſe of thoſe reports. Or elſe

3 The Fame is antedated and raiſ'd before the fact, being related at gueſſe before 'twas acted. Thus ſome have been cauſleſſely commended for early riſing in the morning, who indeed came to their journeys end over night. If ſuch foremade reports prove true, they are admired and regiſtred; if falſe, neglected and forgotten: as thoſe onely which eſcaped ſhipwrack hung up *votivas tabulas*, tablets with their names in thoſe Haven-towns where they came aſhore. But as for thoſe who are drowned, their memorialls are drowned with them.

Generall reports are ſeldome falſe. Vox populi vox Dei. A body of that greatneſſe hath an eye of like clearneſſe, and it is impoſsible that a wanderer with a counterfeit paſſe ſhould paſſe undiſcovered. 7

A fond Fame is beſt confuted by neglecting it. By *Fond* underſtand 8

derſtand ſuch a report as is rather ridiculous then dangerous if believed. It is not worth the making a Schiſme betwixt News-mongers to ſet up an antifame againſt it. Yea ſeriouſly and ſtudiouſly to endeavour to confute it, will grace the rumour too much, and give ſuſpicion that indeed there is ſome reality in it. What madneſſe were it to plant a piece of ordinance to beat down an aſpen leaf, which having alwayes the palſie, will at laſt fall down of it ſelf. And Fame hath much of the ſcold in her; the beſt way to ſilence her is to be ſilent, and then at laſt ſhe will be out of breath with blowing her own trumpet.

9 *Fame ſometimes reports things leſſe then they are.* Pardon her for offending herein, ſhe is guilty ſo ſeldome. For one kingdome of Scotland, which (they ſay) Geographers deſcribe an hundred miles too ſhort, moſt Northern countreys are made too large. Fame generally overdoes, underdoes but in ſome particulars. The Italian proverb hath it, *There is leſſe honeſty, wiſdome, and money in men then is counted on*: yet ſometimes a cloſe churl, who locks his coffers ſo faſt Fame could never peep into them, dyeth richer then he was reported when alive. None could come near to feel his eſtate; it might therefore cut fatter in his purſe, then was expected. But Fame falls moſt ſhort in thoſe Tranſcendents, which are above her Predicaments; as in * Solomons wiſdome: *And behold one half was not told me: thy wiſdome and proſperity exceedeth the Fame that I heard.* But chiefly in fore-reporting the Happineſſe in heaven, which eye hath not ſeen, nor ear heard, neither hath it entred into the heart of man to conceive.

* 1 *Kings.* 10. 7.

CHAP. 24.

Chap. 24.

Of the Antiquity of Churches and Necessity of them.

WE will consider their Antiquity amongst the Jews, Heathen, and Christians. Now Temples amongst the Jews were more or lesse ancient as the acception of the word is straiter or larger.

Take Temple for a covered standing Structure, and the Jews had none till the time of Solomon, which was from the beginning of the * world about two thousand nine hundred thirty two yeares : till then they had neither leave nor libertie to build a Temple. For the Patriarchs, Abraham, Isaac, and Jacob, lived in Pilgrimage; their posterity in Egypt in persecution; their children in the Wildernesse in constant travelling ; their Successours in Canaan in continuall warrefare, till the dayes of Solomon. *Maxime* 1

* *Vid. Chron. Helvici.*

Take Templum *for* tectum * amplum, *a large place covered to serve God therein, and the Tabernacle was a moveable Temple,* built by Moses in the wildernesse about the yeare of the world two thousand foure hundred fiftie five. Yea we find Gods Spirit styling this Tabernacle a Temple, 1. Sam. 1. 9. *Ely the Priest sate upon a seat by a pillar of the Temple.* 1. Sam. 3. 3. *Before the lamp of the Lord went out in the Temple.* Such a portable Church Constantine * had carried about with him when he went to warre. 2

* *Isidorus lib. 15. cap 14.*

* *Socrates lib. 1. cap. 14. & Sozomen. lib. 1. cap. 8.*

Gods children had places with Altars to serve God in before they had any Temples. Such Altars seem as ancient as Sacrifices, both which are twins ; and in Relatives find one and find both. Indeed the first Altar we reade of in Scripture is that which Noah built after the Flood : But heare what a * Learned man saith thereof, *Non tamen existimandum toto illo tempore, quo ante diluvium pii homines* 3

* *Rivet. in Genes. pag. 275.*

Deo sacrificarunt Altarium usum fuisse incognitum. Potius id credendum, Noachum sequutum fuisse exemplum eorum, qui eum præcesserant, imo morem inolitum.

4 *The Jews besides the Temple had many other Synagogues,* serving instead of Chappells of ease to the mother Church at Jerusalem. In the new Testament (the Temple yet standing) 'tis plain that Christ often graced such Synagogues with his presence and preaching; and 'tis * probable they were in use ever since Josuahs time, when the land was first inhabited with Israelites, and that the Levites dispersed all over the land did teach the people therein: Otherwise Palestine was a great Parish, and some therein had an hundred miles to Church; besides, peoples souls were poorely fed having but three meals in a yeare, being but thrice to appear at Jerusalem.

* Hospinian. de orig. Temp c. 4.

5 *Many Heathen Temples were ancienter then that of Solomons.* Amongst which Pagan Temples there is much justling for precedency, though some think that of Apis in Egypt shews the best evidence for her seniority, wherein was worshipped an Oxe, of whose herd (not to say breed) was the Calf which the Israelites worshipped in the wildernesse, being made in imitation thereof. But the Heathen had this grosse conceit that their Gods were affixt to their Statues, as their Statues were confin'd in their Temples: So that in effect they did not so much build Temples for their Gods, as thereby lay Nets to catch them in, inviting them thither as into a Pallace, and then keeping them there as in a Prison.

6 *Most civilized Heathen Nations had Temples for their Gods.* I say, *Most*, for the Persians are said to have none at all. Perchance it was because they chiefly worshipped the Sunne, and then according to the generall opinion of fixing Deities to their Temples, it was in vain to erect any structure therein to restrain and keep his Ubiquitary beams. And yet that the Persians were wholly

Temple-lesse will hardly be believed, seeing the Assyrians on this side(* Senacherib was killed worshipping in the house of Nisroch his God) and the Indians on the other side of them had their Temples erected, as some will have it, by Bacchus their Dionysius: yea we find a Temple in Persia dedicated to * Nanea in the time of Antiochus, and though it may be pretended that the influence of the Grecian Empire on the Persians had then spiced them with a smack of Grecisme, yet Nanea will scarce be proved any Grecian Deity: not to say any thing of the Temple of Bell. *Civilized*: for as for the Scythian wandring Nomades, Temples sorted not with their condition, as wanting both civility and settlednesse: and who can expect Churches from them, who had no houses for themselves? Lastly I say, *Nation*: for the Stoicks onely, a conceited sect, forbad any building of Temples, either out of derision of the common conceit that Deities were kept in durance in their Temples; or else out of humour, because they counted the generall practice of other men a just ground for their contrary opinion. And now we come to the Antiquity of Christian Churches, and crave leave of the Reader, that we may for a while dissolve our continued discourse into a dialogue.

* 2 *Kings* 19. 37.

* 2. *Maccabees* 1. 13. *vide etiam.* 1. *Maccab.* 6. 2.

A. I am much perplexed to find the beginning of Christian Churches in the Scripture. There I find the Saints meeting *in the house of Marie the mother of Mark*; *in the School of Tyrannus*; *in an upper Chamber*; but can see no foundation of a Church, I mean of a place and structure separated and set apart solely for Divine Service.

B. That the Saints had afterwards Churches in your sense is plain: 1. Cor. 11. 22. *Have ye not Houses to eat and drink in, or despise ye the Church of God, and shame them that have not?* Here the opposition is a good exposition of the Apostles meaning, and the Antithesis betwixt *Houses* and *Church*

 speaks

ſpeaks them both to be locall ; ſo that S. Paul thought their materiall Church *deſpiſed*, that is abuſed and unreverenc'd, by their lay-meetings of Love-feaſts therein.

A. By your favour, S[r], the Apoſtle by *Church* meaneth there the aſſembly or ſociety of Gods ſervants, as appears by what followeth, *or deſpiſe ye the Church of God, and ſhame them that have not ? Them*, and not *that*, not ſpeaking of the Place but Perſons : The latter words of the Apoſtle comment on the former, ſhewing how to ſhame thoſe who had not (that is, to neglect and upbraid the poore) is *to deſpiſe the Church of God*.

B. Pardon me S[r] : for the Apoſtle therein accuſeth the Corinthians of a ſecond fault. *Imprimis* he chargeth them for deſpiſing Gods materiall Church ; *Item*, for ſhaming their poore brethren in their Love-feaſts. The particle *And* ſheweth the addition of a new charge, but no expounding or amplifying of the former. But, S[r], ſuſpending our judgements herein, let us deſcend to the Primitive times before Conſtantine, we ſhall there find Churches without any contradiction.

A. Not ſo neither : Herein alſo the trumpet of Antiquity giveth a very uncertain ſound : Indeed we have but little left of the ſtory of thoſe times wherein Chriſtian books were as much perſecuted as men, and but a few Confeſſour-records eſcaping martyrdome are come to our hands. Yea God may ſeem to have permitted the ſuppreſsion of primitive Hiſtory, leſt men ſhould be too ſtudious in reading, and obſervant in practiſing the cuſtomes of that age, even to the neglecting and undervaluing of his written Word.

B. Yet how ſlenderly ſoever thoſe Primitive times

are ſtoried, there is enough in them to prove the Antiquity of Churches. I will not inſtance on the decrees of Evariſtus, Hyginus, and other Popes in the firſt three hundred years about the conſecrating of Churches, becauſe their authority is ſuſpected as antedated; and none are bound to believe that the Gibeonites came from ſo far a Countrey as their mouldy bread & clouted ſhoes did pretend. Churches are plainly to be found in Tertullian, two hundred years after Chriſt; and Euſebius * witneſſeth that before the time of Diocleſian the Chriſtians had Churches, which the Tyrant cauſed to be deſtroyed.

A. But * Origen, Minutius Felix, Arnobius, and Lactantius, being preſſ'd by the Heathen that Chriſtians had no Churches, anſwered by way of confeſsion, yielding that they had none. This is the difficulty perplexeth me. It was a bloody ſpeech of Abner, *Let the young men riſe up and play before us*: But worſe is their cruelty who make ſport at the falling out of the old men, when the reverend brows of Antiquity knock one againſt another, and Fathers thus extremely differ in matters of fact.

B. Why, S[r]? A charitable diſtinction may reconcile them: if by *Churches*, ſtately magnificent Fabricks be meant, in that acception the Chriſtians had no Churches; but ſmall Oratories and Prayer-places they then had, though little, low and dark, being ſo fearfull of perſecution they were jealous the Sunne-beams ſhould behold them: and indeed ſtately Churches had but given a fairer aim to their Enemies malice to hit them. Such an homely place learned S[r] Henrie Spelman * preſents us with, which was firſt founded at Glaſtenbury, thatched and wattled: And

* *Hiſt. Eccles. lib.* 8. *c.* 1, & 2.

* *Origen. lib.* 4. *contra Celſum*, Objicit nobis Celſus quod non habeamus Imagines aut Aras aut Templa. *Idem lib.* 8. *contra Celſum*, Celſus & Aras & Simulacra & Delubra ait nos diffugere quo minùs fundentur. *Arnobius lib.* 4 *contra Gen.* Accuſatis nos quòd nec Templa habeamus, nec Imagines nec Aras. *Minut. Felix pag.* 73. Putatis autem nos occultare quod colamus ſi Delubra et Aras non habemus. *Lactantius*, Quid ſibi Templa, quid Aræ volunt, quid denique ipſa Simulacra, &c.

* *De Conciliis Brittan. pag.* 11.

And let not our Churches now grown men look with a ſcornfull eye on their own picture, when babes in their ſwadling clothes. And no wonder if Gods Houſe

Erubuit domino cultior eſſe ſuo,

The Church did bluſh more glory for to have
Then had her Lord.He begg'd, ſhould ſhe be brave?

Chriſt himſelf being then cold, and hungry, and naked in his afflicted members. Such a mean Oratory Tertullian calls * *Triclinium Chriſtianorum*, the Parlour or Three-bed-room of the Chriſtians.

* *Adverſus Gentes,cap.3.9.*

A. But it ſeems not to conſiſt with Chriſtian ingenuity for the fore-named Fathers abſolutely to deny their having of Churches, becauſe they had onely poore ones.

B. Take then another Anſwer, namely in denying they had no Temples, they meant it in the ſame notion wherein they were interrogated, to wit, they had no Temples like the Pagans for Heathen Gods, no *clauſtra Numinum*, wherein the Deity they ſerved was impriſoned. Or may we not ſay that in that age the Chriſtians had no Churches generally, though they might have them in ſome places ? the elevation of their happineſſe being varied according to ſeverall climates : And Chriſtendome then being of ſo large an extent, it might be ſtormy with perſecution in one countrey, and fair weather in another. We come now to the Neceſsity.

7 *There is no abſolute neceſsity that Chriſtians ſhould have Churches.* No neceſsity at all in reſpect of God, no abſolute neceſsity in reſpect of men, when perſecution hinders the erecting of them : In ſuch a caſe any place is made a Church for the time being, as any private houſe where the King and his Retinue meet is preſently made the Court.

Chriſtians

Christians have no direct precept to build Churches under the Gospel. I say *direct*: For the Law of God, which commands a publick Sanctification of a Sabbath, must needs, by * way of necessary consequence, imply a set, known, and publick Place. Besides, Gods command to Moses and Solomon to build a Temple in a manner obligeth us to build Churches. In which command observe the body and the soul thereof. The body thereof was Ceremoniall and mortall, yea dyed, and is buried in our Saviours grave: The soul thereof is Morall and eternall, as founded in Nature, and is alwayes to endure. Thus S. Paul finds a constant bank for Ministers Maintenance lockt up in a Ceremoniall Law, *Thou shalt not muzzle the mouth of the Ox that treadeth out the corn.* The Apostle on the Morality couched therein founded the *Charter of endowment* for Ministers in the Gospel. Besides, God hath left a warrant dormant with his Church, *Let all things be done decently and in order.* And this ties Christians to the building of Churches for their publick Assemblies, whereby not onely Decency but Piety is so much advanced, especially in these three respects: 8

* Ut communes fidelibus preces Deus verbo suo edicit, sic & Templa publica ipsis peragendis destinata esse oportet, *Calvin. instit. lib. 3. cap. 20. num. 30.*

1 Hereby the same meat serves to feed many guests, one Pastour instructing many people in the same place.

2 Devotion is increased with company. Their praises are the louder; and musick is sweetest in a full consort: their prayers are the stronger, besetting God as it were in a round, and not suffering him to depart till he hath blessed them.* *Hæc vis grata deo.*

*Tertull. Apol.

3 The very Place it self, being dedicated to Gods service, is a Monitour to them *Hoc agere*, & stirres up pious thoughts in them. Say not, it is but lame Devotion that cannot mount without the help of such a wooden stock; rather 'tis lame indeed which is not rais'd though having the advantage thereof.

Gg *Those*

9 *Those that may, must frequent the publick Churches.* Such as nowadayes are ambitious of conventicles are deeply guilty: for as it had been desperate madnesse in time of persecution publickly to resort to Divine Service, so it is no lesse unthankfulnesse to God now to serve him in woods and holes, not taking notice of the liberty of the Gospel, which he gratiously hath vouchsafed; yea such people in effect deny the King to be Defender of the Faith, but make him a Persecuter rather, in that they dare not avouch the truth in the face of his Authority. If it be good they do (thanks be to God) it may be done any where; if bad, it must be done no where. Besides, by their voluntary private meetings, they give occasions to many to supect their actions there: And grant them unjustly traduced for their behaviour therein, yet can they not justly be excused, because they invite slaunderous tongues to censure them, in not *providing for honest things in the sight of men*, and clearing Gods service as well from the suspicion as from the guilt of any dishonesty.

We should now come to speak of the Holinesse, Reverence, Decency, and Magnificencie of Churches: But herein I had rather heare the judgements of other men. Let it serve instead of a conclusion to observe that Solomons Temple was the statelyest structure that ever was or shall be in the world; built by the wealthyest, contrived by the wisest King in seven years (now counted the life of a man) by an army of Workmen, no fewer then * one hundred fourtie three thousand three hundred, of the soundest timber, most pretious stones, most proper metall, as the nature of the things required; either the strongest, Brasse; or the richest, Gold: In a word, Earth gave it most costly matter, and Heaven it self most curious workmanship, God directing them. And though Solomon had no mines of Gold and Silver in his own land, yet had he the spoils and gifts of the neighbouring nations, and once

* 1. *Kings* 5. 15, 16.

once in three years the golden land of Ophir came ſwimming to Hieruſalem. God being the Landlord of the earth, Solomon was then his Receiver, to whom the World payed in her rent, to build his Temple. And was not he a moſt wealthy King, *in whoſe dayes ſilver was nothing accounted of*; ſeeing in our dayes the commander of both Indyes hath ſo much braſſe coin currant in his Court? As for Joſephus his conceit, that the ſecond edition of the Temple by Zorobabel, as it was new forrelled and filleted with gold by Herod, was a ſtatelier volume then that firſt of Solomon, it is too weak a ſurmiſe to have a confutation faſtned to it.

And yet we will not deny but the world hath ſeen greater buildings for the Piles and Fabricks, as may appear by this parrallel.

1	2	3
Gods Temple, built at *Hieruſalem by Solomon.*	*Diana's Temple,* built at *Epheſus by the Kings of Aſia.*	*Sepulcher Church,* built on *Mount Calvary by Conſtantine.*
Long 60, Broad 20, High 30 } cubits. [a]	Long 425, Broad 220, High 60 } foot. [b]	Long, Broad, High } [c] We find no ſet dimenſion but hyperbolicall expreſſions of it.

4	5	6
S. Sophia's Church, built at *Conſtantinople by Juſtinian.*	*S. Pauls Church,* built at *London by King Ethelbert.*	*Turkiſh Mosque,* built at *Fez.*
Long 260, Broad 75, High 180 } foot. [d]	Long 690, Broad 130, High 102 } foot. [e]	Long 150, Broad 80, High } Florentine Cubits. [f]

But when the Reader hath with his eyes ſurveyed theſe Temples, and findeth them to exceed Solomons, yet let him remember, firſt, that there is nothing more uncertain then the meaſures uſed in ſeverall countreys; one countreys ſpan may be another countreys cubit, and

[a] *2. Chron. 3. 3.*
[b] *Plin. nat. Hiſt. lib. 36. cap. 14.*
[c] *Euſebius lib. 3 de vit. Conſtantini, c. 24.* ὕψ⊙ ἄπειρον μῆκ⊙ πλεῖστα πλάτος εὐρυνόμενον.
[d] *Evagrius lib. 4. cap. 30.*
[e] *Namely in the body of the Church beſides the ſteeple, Cambd. Britt. in Middleſex.*
[f] *The height we find not, but it is a mile and half in compaſſe, Leo Africanus, lib. 3. pag. 126.*

and the toe of one countrey as big as the foot of another: secondly, that in Solomons Temple great Cubits were meant *Primæ mensuræ*, 2. Chron. 3. 3. thirdly, that we see most of these structures onely through the magnifying glasse of Fame, or else by the eyes of Travellers, who usually count the best they ever saw to be the best was ever seen, yea in charity will lend a Church some hundreds of feet to help out the dimension thereof, as Bellonius a modern eye-witnesse counteth * three hundred sixtie five doores in the present Church of Sophia, which hath but foure, as an exact * Traveller hath observed. Lastly, whilest humane Historians will overlash for the honour of their own Nations, we know it must needs be true what Truth hath written of Solomons Temple.

*Lib. 1. observ. cap. 76.

* G. Sandys Travells, pag. 32.

Chap. 25.

Of Ministers maintenance.

Maintenance of Ministers ought to be Plentifull Certain, and in some sort Proportionable to their deserts. It should be Plentifull, because

Maxime 1

Their education was very chargeable to fit them for their profession, both at School, and in the University: their books very dear, and those which they bought in Folio shrink quickly into Quarto's, in respect of the price their executours can get for them. Say not that Scholars draw needlesse expences on themselves by their own lavishnesse, and that they should rather lead a Fashion of thrift, then follow one of riot; for let any equall man tax the bill of their necessary charges, and it amounts to a great Summe, yea though they be never so good husbands. Besides, the prizes of all commodities daily rise higher; all persons and professions are raised in their manner of living: Scholars therefore, even against their wills, must otherwhiles be involved in the generall expensivenesse of the times, it being impossible

poſsible that one ſpoke ſhould ſtand ſtill when all the wheel turns about.

Ob. But many needleſſely charge themſelves in living too long in the Univerſity, ſucking ſo long of their Mother, they are never a whit the wiſer for it; whileſt others not ſtaying there ſo long, nor going through the porch of humane Arts, but entring into Divinity at the poſtern, have made good Preachers, providing their people wholſome meat, though not ſo finely dreſt.

Anſw. Much good may it do their very hearts that feed on it. But how neceſſary a competent knowledge of thoſe Sciences is for a perfect Divine, is known to every wiſe man. Let not mens ſuffering be counted their fault, nor thoſe accuſed to *ſtand idle in the market whom no man hath hired.* Many would leave the Univerſity ſooner, if called into the countrey on tolerable conditions.

Becauſe Miniſters are to ſubſiſt in a free, liberal, & comfortable way. Balaam the falſe Prophet rode with his * two men; Gods Levite had * one man: Oh let not the Miniſters of the Goſpel be ſlaves to others, and ſervants to themſelves! They are not to prie into gain through every ſmall chink. It becomes them rather to be acquainted with the natures of things, then with the prizes, and to know them rather as they are in the world then as they are in the market. Otherwiſe, if his means be ſmall, and living poore, neceſsity will bolt him out of his own ſtudy, and ſend him to the barn, when he ſhould be at his book, or make him ſtudy his Eaſter-book more then all other Writers. Hereupon ſome wanting what they ſhould have at home, have done what they ſhould not abroad. 2

* *Numb.* 22. 22.

* *Judges.* 19. 11.

Becauſe Hoſpitality is expected at their hands. The poore come to their houſes, as if they had intereſt in them, and the Miniſters can neither receive them nor refuſe them. 3

them. Not to relieve them, were not Christianity,and to relieve them, were worse then Infidelity, because therein they wrong their providing for their own family. Thus sometimes are they forced to be Nabals against their will; yet it greiveth them to send away the people empty. But what shall they do, seeing they cannot multiply their loaves and their fishes? Besides, Clergie-men are deeply rated to all payments. Oh that their profession were but as highly prized, as their estate is valued.

4 *Because they are to provide for their Posterity*, that after the death of their parents they may live, though not in an high, yet in an honest fashion, neither leaving them to the wide world, nor to a narrow cottage.

5 *Because the Levites in the Old Testament had plentifull provision.* Oh 'tis good to be Gods Pensioner, for he giveth his large allowance. They had Cities and Suburbs (houses and glebeland) Tithes, Freewill-offerings, and their parts in First-fruits, and Sacrifices. Do the Ministers of the Gospel deserve worse wages for bringing better tidings? Besides, the Levites places were hereditary, and the Sonne sure of his Fathers house and land without a Faculty *ad succedendum patri.*

6 *Because the Papists in time of Popery gave their Priests plentifull means.* Whose Benefactours, so bountifull to them, may serve to condemne the covetousnesse of our age towards Gods Ministers, in such who have more knowledge, and should have more religion.

Ob. But the great means of the Clergie in time of Popery was rather wrested then given. The Priests melted mens hearts into charity with the Scarefire of Purgatory: And for justice now to give back what holy fraud had gotten away, is not Sacriledge but Restitution. And when those grand and vast Donations were given to the Church,

Church, there was (as ſome ſay) a voyce of Angels heard from heaven, ſaying, *Hodie venenum in Eccleſiam Chriſti cecidit.*

Anſw. If poyſon then fell into the Church, ſince hath there a ſtrong antidote been given to expell it, eſpecially in Impropriations. Diſtinguiſh we betwixt ſuch Donations given to uſes in themſelves merely unlawfull and ſuperſtitious, as Praying for the dead, and the like; and thoſe which *in Genere* were given to Gods Service, though *in Specie* ſome ſuperſtitious end were annexed thereto. And grant the former of theſe to be void in their very granting, yet the latter ought to be rectified and reduced to the true uſe, and in no caſe to be alienated from God. Plato ſaith that in his time it was a Proverb amongſt Children, Τῶν ὀρθῶς δοθέντων οὐκ ἔστιν ἀφαίρεσις, *Things that are truly given muſt not be taken away again.* Sure, as our Saviour ſet a child in the midſt of his Diſciples to teach them humility, ſo nowadayes a child need be ſet in the midſt of ſome men to teach them juſtice. Excellently * Luther, *Niſi ſupereſſet ſpolium Aegypti, quod rapuimus Papæ, omnibus Miniſtris Verbi fame pereundum eſſet; quod ſi ſuſtentandi eſſent de contributione populi, miſere profecto ac duriter viverent. Alimur ergo de ſpoliis Aegypti collectis ſub Papatu, & hoc ipſum tamen quod reliquum eſt diripitur à Magiſtratu: ſpoliantur Parochiæ & Scholæ, non aliter ac ſi fame necare nos velint.*

* In his Comment on the 47. of Geneſ. pag. 631.

Ob. But in the pure Primitive times the Means were leaſt, and Miniſters the beſt: And nowadayes, does not wealth make them lazy, and poverty keep them painfull? like Hawks they flie beſt when ſharp. The beſt way to keep the ſtream of the Clergie ſweet and clear is to fence out the tide of wealth from coming unto them.

Anſw.

Answ. Is this our thankfulnesse to the God of heaven, for turning persecution into peace,in pinching his poore Ministers? When the Commonwealth now makes a feast, shall neither Zadok the Priest,nor Nathan the Prophet, be invited to it? that so the footsteps of Primitive persecution may still remain in these peaceable times, amongst the Papists, in their needlesse burning of candles; and amongst the Protestants, in the poore means of their Ministers. And what if some turn the spurres unto Virtue into the stirrups of Pride, grow idle, and insolent? let them soundly suffer for it themselves on Gods blessing; but let not the bees be sterved that the drones may be punished.

7 *Ministers Maintenance ought to be certain*; lest some of them meet with Labans for their Patrons and parishioners; changing their wages ten times; and at last, if the fear of God doth not fright the, send them away empty.

8 *It is unequall that there should be an equality betwixt all Ministers Maintenance.* Except that first there were made an equality betwixt all their Parts, Pains, and Piety. Parity in means will quickly bring a levell and flat in Learning; and few will strive to be such spirituall Musicians, to whom David directeth many Psalms, *To him that excelleth*, but will even content themselves with a Canonicall sufficiency, and desiring no more then what the Law requires: More learning would be of more pains, and the same profit, seeing the *mediocriter* goeth abreast with *optime*.

Ob. But neither the best, nor the most painfull and learned get the best preferment. Sometimes men of the least, get Livings of the best worth; yea such as are not worthy to be the curates to their curates, and *crassa Ingenia* go away with *opima Sacerdotia*.

Answ. Thus it ever was, and will be. But is this dust onely to be found in Churches, and not in Civill

Civill Courts? Is merit everywhere elſe made the exact ſquare of preferment? or did ever any urge, that all Offices ſhould be made champian for their profits, none higher then other? ſuch corruption will ever be in the Church, except there were a Law (ridiculous to be made, and impoſsible to be kept) that men ſhould be no men, but that all Patrons or people in their Election or Preſentations of Miniſters ſhould wholly deveſt themſelves of by-reſpects of kinred, friendſhip, profit, affection, and merely chuſe for deſert: and then ſhould we have all things ſo well ordered, ſuch Paſtours and ſuch people, the Church in a manner would be Triumphant, whileſt Militant. Till then, though the beſt livings light not alwayes on the ableſt men, yet as long as there be ſuch preferments in the Church, there are ſtill encouragements for men to endeavour to excell, all hoping, and ſome hapning on advancement.

Ob. But Miniſters ought to ſerve God merely for love of himſelf; and pity but his eyes were out that ſquints at his own ends in doing Gods work.

Anſw. Then ſhould Gods beſt Saints be blind; for Moſes himſelf had *an eye to the recompence of reward.* Yea Miniſters may look not onely on their eternall but on their temporall reward, as motives to quicken their endeavours. And though it be true, that grave and pious men do ſtudy for learning ſake, and embrace virtue for it ſelf, yet it is as true that youth (which is the ſeaſon when learning is gotten) is not without ambition, nor will ever take pains to excell in any thing, when there is not ſome hope of excelling others in reward and dignity. And what reaſon is it that whileſt Law and Phyſick bring great portions to ſuch as marry them, Divinity their elder ſiſter ſhould onely be put off with her own beauty? In after-ages men will rather bind their ſonnes to one gainfull, then to ſeven liberall Sciences: onely the loweſt of the people would be made Miniſters, which cannot otherwiſe ſubſiſt; and it will be bad when Gods Church is made a Sanctuary onely for men of deſperate eſtates to tak e refuge in it.

However, let every Miniſter take up this reſolution, *To preach the word, to be inſtant in ſeaſon, out of ſeaſon, reprove, rebuke, exhort with all long-ſuffering and doctrine.* If thou haſt competent means comfortably to ſubſiſt on, be the more thankfull to God the fountain, to man the channell; painfull in thy place, pitifull to the poore, cheerfull in ſpending ſome, carefull in keeping the reſt. If not, yet tire not for want of a ſpurre: do ſomething for love, and not all for money; for love of God, of goodneſſe, of the godly, of a good conſcience. Know 't is better to want means, then to detain them; the one onely ſuffers, the other deeply ſinnes: and it is as dangerous a perſecution to religion, to draw the fewell from it, as to caſt water on it. Comfort thy ſelf that another world will pay this worlds debts, *and great is thy reward with God in heaven.* A reward, in reſpect of his promiſe; a gift, in reſpect of thy worthleſneſſe: And yet the leſſe thou lookeſt at it, the ſurer thou ſhalt find it, if labouring with thy ſelf to ſerve God for himſelf, in reſpect of whom even heaven it ſelf is but a ſiniſter end.

To

To the Reader.

THese Generall Rules we have placed in the middle, that the Books on both ſides may equally reach to them; becauſe all Perſons therein are indifferently concerned.

The Holy State.

THE FOURTH BOOK.

Chap. I.
The Favourite.

A Favourite is a Court-diall, whereon all look whileſt the King ſhines on him, and none, when it is night with him. A Minion differs from a Favourite: for He acts things by his own will and appetite, as a Favourite by the judgement and pleaſure of his Prince. Theſe again are twofold: either ſuch as relie wholly on their Kings favour, or ſuch as the King partly relies on their wiſdome, loving them rather for uſe then affection. The former are like pretty wands in a Princes hand, for him to play with at pleaſure; the latter, like ſtaves, whereon he leans and ſupports himſelf in State-affairs.

God is the originall Patron of all preferment, all dignities being in his diſpoſall. Promotion (* ſaith David) *comes neither from the Eaſt, nor from the West, nor yet from the South.* The word here tranſlated *South*, in the Hebrew ſignifies the Deſert; and ſuch a courſe liſt bounded Paleſtine both on the South and * North, ſo that in effect preferment bloweth from no point of the Compaſſe. True, every man is, *fortunæ ſuæ faber*, the Smith to beat out his own

Maxime 1

* *Pſal.* 75.7.

* *Tremellius on the verſe.*

fortunes ; but God first doth give him coals, iron, and anvil before he can set up his trade.

2 *The first inlet into a Princes knowledge is half way into his favour.* Indeed the heat of the sunne pierceth into the innermost bowells of the earth, but onely the surface thereof is guilded with his beams : So though the influence of the Princes protection reacheth the utmost and obscurest man in his dominions, yet onely some few, who lie on the top of the heap of his subjects, can be graced with his favour. He therefore that is known to his Prince, starts in the half way of his race to honour. A notable fellow, and a souldier to Alexander, finding this first admission to be the greatest difficulty, put feathers into his nose and eares, and danced about the Court in an antique fashion, till the strangenesse of the Shew brought the King himself to be a spectatour. Then this Mimick throwing off his disguize, *S^r^* (said he to the King) *thus I first arrive at your Majesties notice in the fashion of a fool, but can do you service in the place of a wise-man, if you please to employ me.*

3 *'Tis the easier for them to leap into preferment, who have the rise of noble bloud* : such get their honour with more ease, and keep it with lesse envie, which is busiest in maligning of upstarts. Nor is it any hinderance unto him, but rather an advantage, if such a Nobleman be of an ancient family, decayed in estate through the fault of his Ancestours ; for such, Princes count the object as well of their pity as favour, and it an act as well of charity as bounty to relieve and raise them : But those are in some sort born Favourites, and succeed by descent to a Princes affection (rather as a debt then a gift) whose parents have formerly suffered in the Princes or his predecessours behalf. This made Queen Elizabeth first reflect on the Lord Norris, (for in the peaceable beginning of her reigne the Martiall spirits of his sonne were not yet raised) because his father dyed her mothers Martyr, to attest her innocencie in the reigne of King Henry the eighth.

Severall

Severall doores open to preferment, but the King keeps the key of them all. Some have been advanced for their Faces, their Beauty; their Heads, their Wisdome; their Tongues, their Eloquence; their Hands, their Valour; their Bloud, their Nobility; their Feet, their Nimblenesse, and Comlinesse in dancing; but all is ultimately resolv'd on the Princes pleasure. 4

Happy the Favourite that is raised without the ruine of another: as those which succeed in a dead place, who draw lesse envy of competitours, in keeping others out of the Kings favour, then those that cast one out of the possession thereof. Also he that climbeth up by degrees stands more firmly in favour, as making his footing good as he goes. 5

Sometimes the Princes favour is all the known worth in the Favourite. I say, *known*: for he is an Infidel that believes not more then he sees, and that a rationall Prince will love where he sees no lovelinesse. Surely Charles the ninth of France beheld some worth in Albertus Tudius (an Hucksters sonne, to whom in five years, besides other honours, he gave six hundred thousand crowns) though some affirm all the good the King got by him, was to learn to * swear by the Name of God. Except we will say, that Kings desire in some to shew as the absolutenesse of their power, to raise them from nothing, so of their will also, to advance them for nothing. But Princes have their grounds reard above the flats of common men, and who will search the reasons of their actions must stand on an equall basis with them. 6

* *Camerarius, med. Hist. cap.* 4.

Some Kings to make a jest have advanced a man in earnest. When amongst many Articles exhibited to King Henrie the seventh by the Irish against the Earl of Kildare, the last was, * *Finally, all Ireland cannot rule this Earl. Then* (quoth the King) *shall this Earl rule all Ireland*; and made him Deputie thereof. But such accidents are miraculous; and he shall sterve that will not eat till such Manna is dropt into his mouth. 7

* *Camb. Rem. pag.* 171.

But

8 *But by what lawfull means soever he hath gotten his advancement, he standeth but in a slippery place*; and therefore needs constantly to wear ice-spurres, for he rather glides then goes, and is in continuall fear to be crush'd from above by his Princes anger, and undermin'd from beneath by his fellow-subjects envie. Against both which see how he fenceth himself.

9 *He prayseth God for preferring him, and prayeth to him to preserve him.* His Greatnesse must needs fall which is not founded in Goodnesse. First he serveth his God in heaven, and then his Master on earth. The best way to please all, or to displease them with least danger, is to please him who is all in all.

10 *Next he studieth the alphabet of his Princes disposition*: whose inclination when found out is half fitted. Then he applyes himself to please his naturall, though not vitious, humours, never preferring himself before his Prince in any thing, wherein he desires or conceiveth himself to excell. Nero, though indeed but a Fidler, counted himself as well Emperour of Musick as of Rome; and his Followers too grossely did sooth him up in the admiration of his skill in that Art. But the most temperate Princes love to taste the sweetnesse of their own praises (if not overluscious with flattery) where their own deserts lay the groundwork, and their Favourites give the varnish to their commendations.

11 *Bluntnesse of speech hath becom'd some, and made them more acceptable*: Yea this hath been counted Freeheartednesse, in Courtiers; Conscience and Christian simplicity, in Clergiemen; Valour, in Souldiers. *I love thee the better* (said Queen Elizabeth to Archbishop Grindall) *because you live unmarried. And I, Madam,* (replyed Grindall) *because you live unmarried love you the worse*. But those, who make musick with so harsh an instrument, need have their bow well rosend before, and to observe Time and Place, lest that gall which would tickle at other times.

He leaveth his Prince alwayes with an appetite, and never gluts him with his company. Sometimes taking occasion to depart, whilest still his staying might be welcome. Such intermissions render him more gratious ; yet he absents himself neither farre, nor long, lest he might seem to neglect. Though he doth not alwayes spurre up close to the Kings side (to be constantly in his presence) he never lagges so farre behind, as to be out of distance. Long absence hath drawn the curtain betwixt a Favourite and his Sovereigne, and thereby hath made room for others to step in betwixt them. 12

He doth not boldly engrosse and limit his Masters favour to himself. He is willing his Prince should shine beside him, but especially thorow him, on others. Too covetous are they who, not content to be sole heirs to their Princes favour, grudge that any pensions should be allotted to their younger brethren. Why should it not as well be Treason to confine a Princes affection, as to imprison his person ? 13

He makes provident yet moderate use of his Masters favour. Especially if he be of a various nature, and loveth exchange, counting it not to stand with the state of a King to wear a Favourite thredbare. Too blame they, who thinking it will be continuall summer with them (as in the countrey under the Æquator) will not so much as frostnip their souls with a cold thought of want hereafter, and provide neither to oblige others, nor to maintain themselves : As bad they on the other side, who like those who have a lease, without impeachment of waste, speedily to expire, whip and strip, and rap and rend, whatsoever can come to their fingers. 14

He makes his estate invisible by purchasing reversions, and in remote countreys. He hath a moderate estate in open view, that the world may settle their looks on't (for if they see nothing they will suspect the more) and the rest farre off and hereafter. The eyes of envy can never be- 15 witch that which it doth not ſee. Theſe Reverſions will be ripe for his heir, by that time his heir ſhall be ripe for them, and the money of diſtracted revennues will meet entirely in one purſe.

6 *Having attained to a competent height, he had rather grow a buttreſſe broader, then a ſtorie higher.* He fortifieth himſelf by raiſing outworks, and twiſting himſelf by inter-marriages of his kinred into noble Families: his Countenance will give all his Kinſwomen beauty. Some Favourites, whoſe heels have been tript up by their adverſaries, have with their hands held on their Allies, till they could recover their feet again.

17 *He makes not Great men dance envidious attendance to ſpeak with him.* Oh whileſt their heels cool how do their hearts burn? Wherefore in the midſt of the Term of his buſineſſe he makes himſelf a vacation to ſpeak with them. Indeed ſome difficulty of acceſſe and conference begets a reverence towards them in common people (who will ſuſpect the ware not good if cheap to come by) and therefore he values himſelf in making them to wait: Yet he loves not to over-linger any in an afflicting hope, but ſpeedily diſpatcheth the fears or deſires of his expecting Clients.

18 *He loveth a good name, but will not wooe or court it otherwiſe, then as it is an attendant on honeſty and virtue.* But chiefly he avoydeth the ſweet poyſon of Popularity, wherewith ſome have ſwollen till they have broken. Eſpecially, he declines the entertainment of many Martialiſts, the harſh counſell of ſouldiers being commonly untunable to the Court-way. The immoderate reſorting of military men to a Favourite (chiefly if by any palliation he pretends to the Crown) is like the flocking of ſo many ravens and vulturs which foretell his funerall.

19 *He preſerves all inferiour Officers in the full rights and priviledges of their places.* Some are ſo boyſterous, no ſeverals will hold them, but lay all Offices common to their

their power, or elſe are ſo buſie, that making many circles in other mens profeſsions, they raiſe up ill ſpirits in them, and for every finger they needleſſely thruſt into other mens matters, ſhall find an hand againſt them, when occaſion ſhall ſerve. As bad are they, who leaping over meaner perſons to whom the buſineſſe is proper, bring it *per ſaltum* to themſelves, not ſuffering matters to run along in a legall channell, but in a by-ditch of their own cutting, ſo drawing the profit to themſelves, which they drein from others.

If accuſed by his adverſaries, he flies with ſpeed to his Princes 20
perſon. No better covert for a hunted Favourite to take to: where if innocent, with his loyall breath he eaſily diſpels all vapours of ill ſuggeſtions; if guilty, yet he is half acquitted, becauſe judged by the Prince himſelf, whoſe compaſsion he moves by an ingenuous confeſsion. But if this Sanctuary-doore be bolted againſt him, then his ruine is portended, and not long after.

He is a fiſh on the dry ſhore when the tide of his Maſters 21
love hath left him; ſo that if he be not the more wiſe, he will be made a prey to the next that finds him. Severall are the cauſes of Favourites falls, proceeding either from the Kings pleaſure, their enemies malice, or their own default: different the degrees and manner of their ruine: ſome when grown too great are ſhifted under honourable colours of employment into a forrein aire, there to purge and leſſen; others receive their condemnation at home. But how bad ſoever his caſt be, ſee how he betters it by good playing it.

He ſubmits himſelf, without conteſting, to the pleaſure of his 22
Prince. For being a Tenant at will to the favour of his Sovereigne, it is vain to ſtrive to keep violent poſſeſsion when his Landlord will out him. Such ſtruggling makes the hook of his enemies malice ſtrike the deeper into him. And whileſt his adverſaries ſpurre him with injuries on purpoſe to make him ſpring out into

rebellious practices, he reins in his pasſions with the ſtronger patience.

23 *If he must down, he ſeeks to fall eaſily, and if poſsible, to light on his legs.* If ſtript out of his robes, he ſtrives to keep his clothes; looſing his honour, yet to hold his lands, if not them, his life; and thanks his Prince for giving him whatſoever he takes not away from him.

To conclude, A Favourite is a trade, whereof he that breaks once ſeldome ſets up again. Rare are the examples of thoſe who have compounded and thrived well afterwards. Mean men are like underwood, which the Law calls *ſylva cædua, quæ* * *ſucciſa renaſcitur*, being cut down it may ſpring again, but Favourites are like okes, which ſcarce thrive after (to make timber)being lopt,but if once cut down never grow more.If we light on any who have flouriſhed the ſecond time, impute it to their Princes pleaſure to croſſe the common obſervation, and to ſhew that nothing is paſt cure with ſo great a chirurgion, who can even ſet a broken Favourite.

* *Lynwood lib.* 3. *cap.* Quanquam exſolventibus.

Now to ſhew the inconſtancie of Greatneſſe not ſupported with virtue, we will firſt inſiſt in a remarkable pattern in holy Scripture. Next will we produce a parallel of two Favourites in our Engliſh Court, living in the ſame time, and height of honour with their Sovereigne, the one through his vitiouſneſſe ending in miſery, the other by his virtuous demeanour ſhining bright to his death: for I count it a wrong to our Countrey to import preſidents out of forrein Hiſtories, when our home-Chronicles afford us as plentifull and proper examples.

CHAP. 2.

Chap. 2.
The life of Haman.

Haman the ſonne of Amedatha, of the kinred of Agag, and people of Amalek, was highly favoured by Ahaſuerus Emperour of Perſia. I find not what pretious properties he had, ſure he was a pearl in the eye of Ahaſuerus, who commanded all his ſubjects to do lowly reverence unto him : onely Mordecai the Jew excepted himſelf from that rule, denying him the payment of ſo humble an obſervance.

I fathome not the depth of Mordecai's refuſall : perchance Haman interpreted this reverence farther then it was intended, as a divine honour, and therefore Mordecai would not blow wind into ſo empty a bladder, and be acceſſary to puff him up with ſelf-conceit ; or becauſe Amalek was the devils firſt-fruits, which firſt brake the peace with Iſrael, and God commanded an antipathy againſt them ; or he had ſome private countermand from God not to reverence him. What ever it was, I had rather accuſe my ſelf of ignorance, then Mordecai of pride.

Haman ſwells at this neglect. Will not his knees bow ? his neck ſhall break with an halter. But oh,this was but poore and private revenge : one lark will not fill the belly of ſuch a vultur. What if Mordecai will not ſtoop to Haman, muſt Haman ſtoop to Mordecai to be revenged of him alone ? wherefore he plotteth with the Kings ſword to cut off the whole Nation of the Jews.

Repairing to Ahaſuerus, he requeſted that all the Jews might be deſtroyed. He backs his petition with three arguments : firſt, It was a ſcattered Nation ; had they inhabited one entire countrey, their extirpation would have weakned his empire, but being diſperſed, though kill'd every where, they would have been miſſed no where;ſecondly,his Empire would be more uniform when this irregular people, not obſerving his Laws, were taken away ; thirdly, ten thouſand talents Haman would pay into the bargain into the Kings Treaſure.

What, out of his own purſe ? I ſee his pride was above his covetouſneſſe ; and ſpightfull men count their revenge a purchaſe which cannot be overbought : or perchance this money ſhould ariſe out of the confiſcation of their goods. Thus Ahaſuerus ſhould lock all the Jews into his cheſt, and by help of Hamans Chymiſtry convert them into ſilver.

See how this grand deſtroyer of a whole Nation pleads the Kings profit. Thus our punie depopulatours alledge for their doings the Kings and countreys good; and we will believe them, when they can perſwade us that their private coffers are the Kings exchequer. But never any wounded the Commonwealth,but firſt they kiſſ'd it, pretending the publick good.

Hamans ſilver is droſſe with Ahaſuerus : onely his pleaſure is currant with him. If Haman will have it ſo, ſo it ſhall freely be ; he will give him and not ſell him his favour. 'Tis wofull when great Judges ſee parties accuſed by other mens eyes, but condemne them by their own mouthes : and now Poſts were ſent thorow out all Perſia to execute the Kings cruell decree.

I had almoſt forgotten how before this time Mordecai had diſcovered the treaſon,which two of the Kings Chamberlains had plotted againſt him ; which good ſervice of his,though not preſently paid, yet was ſcored up in the Chronicles, not rewarded but recorded, where it ſlept till a due occaſion did awake it. Perchance Hamans envy kept it from the Kings knowledge ; and Princes ſometimes to reward the deſert of men want not mind, but minding of it

To proceed : See the Jews all pitifully penſive, and

faſting

faſting in ſackcloth and aſhes, even to Queen Eſther her ſelf, which (unknown to Haman) was one of that nation. And to be brief, Eſther invites Ahaſuerus and Haman to a banquet (whoſe life ſhall pay the reckoning) and next day they are both invited to a ſecond entertainment.

Mean time Haman provides a gallows of fifty cubits high to hang Mordecai on. Five cubits would have ſerv'd the turn ; and had it took effect, the height of the gallows had but ſet his ſoul ſo much the farther on his journey towards heaven. His ſtomach was ſo ſharp ſet , he could not ſtay till he had din'd on all the Jews, but firſt he muſt break his faſt on Mordecai ; and fit it was this bell-weather ſhould be ſacrificed before the reſt of the flock : wherefore he comes to the Court to get leave to put him to death.

The night before Ahaſuerus had paſſed without ſleep. The Chronicles are called for, either to invite ſlumber, or to entertain waking with the leſſe tediouſneſſe. Gods hand in the margin points the Reader to the place where Mordecai's good ſervice was related ; and Ahaſuerus asketh Haman (newly come into the preſence) what ſhall be done to the man whom the King will honour ?

Haman being now (as he thought) to meaſure his own happineſſe, had been much too blame if he made it not of the largeſt ſize. He cuts out a garment of honour, royall both for matter and making, for Mordecai to wear. By the Kings command he becomes Mordecai's Herauld and Page, lacquying by him riding on the Kings ſteed (who he hoped by this time ſhould have mounted the wooden horſe) and then penſive in heart haſts home to bemoan himſelf to his friends. Hamans wife proves a true Propheteſſe, preſaging his ruine. If the feet of a Favourite begin to ſlip on the ſteep hill of Honour, his own weight will down with him to the bottome : once paſt noon with him, it is preſently night.

For

For at the next feaſt Ahaſuerus is mortally incenſ'd againſt him for plotting the death of Eſther, with the reſt of her people. (For had his project ſucceeded, probably the Jew had not been ſpared for being a Queen, but the Queen had been killed for being a Jew.) Haman in a careleſſe ſorrowfull poſture, more minding his life then his luſt, had caſt himſelf on the Queens bed. *Will he force the Queen alſo* (ſaid Ahaſuerus) *before me in the houſe*? Theſe words rang his paſsing-bell in the Court, and according to the Perſian faſhion they covered his face, putting him in a winding ſheet that was dead in the Kings favour. The next news we hear of him is, that by exchange Haman inherits the gibbet of Mordecai, and Mordecai the houſe and greatneſſe of Haman, the decree againſt the Jews being generally reverſed.

CHAP. 3.

THOMAS WOLSEY Arch-Biſhop *of Yorke*, Chancelovr *of England* Cardinal *and* Legate *de Latere He Died at Leicester* Abby .*Anno* Dni 1529. *the* 29th *of November*. W.M. *ſculp*:

Chap. 3.

The life of Card. Wolsey.

THomas Wolſey was born at Ipſwich in Suffolk, whoſe father was a Butcher, and an * honeſt man, and was there brought up at ſchool, where afterwards he built a beautifull Colledge. From Ipſwich he went to Oxford, and from thence was preferred to be Schoolmaſter to the Marques of Dorſet's children, where he firſt learnt to be imperious over Noble bloud. By the ſtairs of a Parſonage or two he climbed

* Parentem habuit virum probum at lanium, *Pol. Virgil. pag.* 633.

up at laſt into the notice of Fox, Biſhop of Wincheſter, and was received to be his Secretary.

There was at that time a faction at Court betwixt Biſhop Fox and Thomas Howard, Earl of Surrey. The Biſhop being very old was ſcarce able to make good his party; yet it grieved him not ſo much to ſtoop to Nature as to the Earl his Corrivall: wherefore not able to manage the matter himſelf, he was contented to be the ſtock whereon Wolſey ſhould be graffed, whom he made heir to his favour, commending him to King Henrie the ſeventh for one fit to ſerve a King, and command others: And hereupon he was entertained at Court.

Soon after, when Henrie his ſonne came to the Crown, Wolſey quickly found the length of his foot, and fitted him with an eaſie ſhoe. He perſwaded him that it was good accepting of pleaſure whileſt youth tender'd it: let him follow his ſports, whileſt Wolſey would undertake every night briefly to repreſent unto him all matters of moment which had paſſed the Counſell-table. For Princes are to take State-affairs not in the maſſe and whole bulk of them, but onely the ſpirits thereof skilfully extracted. And hereupon the King referred all matters to Wolſey's managing, on whom he conferr'd the Biſhopricks of Dureſme, Wincheſter, and York, with ſome other ſpirituall promotions.

Nothing now hindred Wolſey's proſpect to overlook the whole Court but the head of Edward Stafford Duke of Buckingham, who was high in birth, honour, and eſtate. For as for Charles Brandon, Duke of Suffolk, he ſtood not in Wolſey's way, but rather beſides then againſt him: Brandon being the Kings companion in pleaſures, Wolſey his counſellour in policy; Brandon Favourite to Henrie, Wolſey to the King. Wolſey takes this Buckingham to task, who (otherwiſe a brave Gentleman) was proud and popular; and that

that tower is eaſily undermin'd whoſe foundation is hollow. His own folly with Wolſey's malice overthrew him. Vainglory ever lyeth at an open guard, and giveth much advantage of play to her enemies. The Duke is condemned of high treaſon, though rather corrivall with the King for his Clothes then his Crown, being exceſsively brave in apparell.

The ax that kills Buckingham frights all others, who turn conteſting into complying with our Archbiſhop, now Cardinall, Legate *à latere*, and Lord-Chancellour. All the Judges ſtood at the barre of his devotion. His diſpleaſure more feared then the Kings, whoſe anger though violent was placable ; the Cardinalls of leſſe furie, but more malice : yet in matters of Judicature he behaved himſelf commendably. I heare no widows ſighes, nor ſee orphans tears in our Chronicles cauſed by him : ſure in ſuch caſes wherein his private ends made him not a party, he was an excellent Juſticer, as being too proud to be bribed, and too ſtrong to be overborn.

Next he aſpires to the Triple Crown ; he onely wants Holineſſe, and muſt be Pope. Yet was it a great labour for a Tramountain to climbe over the Alps to S. Peters Chair ; a long leap from York to Rome, and therefore he needed to take a good riſe. Beſides he uſed Charles the fift, Emperour, for his ſtaff, gold he gave to the Romiſh Cardinalls, and they gave him golden promiſes, ſo that at laſt Wolſey perceived, both the Emperour and the Court of Rome delay'd and deluded him.

He is no fox whoſe den hath but one hole : Wolſey finding this way ſtopt, goes another way to work, and falls off to the French King, hoping by his help to obtain his deſires. However if he help not himſelf, he would hinder Charles the Emperours deſignes ; and revenge is a great preferment. Wherefore covertly he ſeeks to make a divorce betwixt Queen Katharine,

 Dowager,

Dowager, the Emperours Aunt, and King Henrie the eighth his Master.

Queen Katharines age was above her Husbands, her gravity above her age; more pious at her beads then pleasant in her bed, a better woman then a wife, and a fitter wife for any Prince then King Henrie. Wolsey by his instruments perswades the King to put her away, pleading they were so contiguous and near in kinred, they might not be made continuous (one flesh) in marriage, because she before had been wife to Prince Arthur the Kings brother. Besides, the King wanted a male heir, which he much desired.

Welcome whisperings are quickly heard. The King embraceth the motion: the matter is enter'd in the Romish Court, but long delayed; the Pope first meaning to divorce most of the gold from England in this tedious suit. But here Wolsey miscarried in the Master-piece of his policy. For he hoped upon the divorce of King Henrie from Queen Katharine his wife (which with much adoe was effected) to advance a marriage betwixt him and the King of France his sister, thinking with their nuptiall ring to wed the King of France eternally to himself, and mould him for farther designes: whereas contrary to his expectation King Henrie fell in love with Anna Bullen, a Lady whose beauty exceeded her birth (though honourable) wit her beauty, piety all; one for his love not lust, so that there was no gathering of green fruit from her till marriage had ripened it: whereupon the King took her to wife.

Not long after followed the ruine of the Cardinall, caused by his own vitiousnesse, heightned by the envy of his Adversaries. He was caught in a Premunire for procuring to be Legate *de latere*, and advancing the Popes power against the Laws of the Realm; and eight other Articles were framed against him, for which we report the Reader to our * Chronicles. The

* *Fox Acts & Monuments, p. 996.*

main

main was, his *Ego & Rex meus*, wherein he remembred his old profeſsion of a Schoolmaſter, and forgot his preſent eſtate of a Stateſman. But as for ſome things laid to his charge, his friends plead, that where potent malice is Promoter, the accuſations ſhall not want proof,though the proof may want truth. Well,the broad ſeal was taken from him, and ſome of his ſpirituall Preferments. Yet was he ſtill left Biſhop of Wincheſter, and Archbiſhop of York, ſo that the Kings goodneſſe hitherto might have ſeemd rather to eaſe him of burthenſome greatneſſe, then to have deprived him of wealth or honour : which whether he did out of love to Wolſey, or fear of the Pope, I interpoſe no opinion.

Home now went Wolſey into Yorkſhire, and lived at his Mannour of Cawood,where he wanted nothing the heart of man could deſire for contentment. But great minds count every place a priſon, which is not a Kings Court; and juſt it was that he which would not ſee his own happineſſe, ſhould therefore feel his own miſery. He provided for his enſtalling Archbiſhop State equivalent to a Kings Coronation, which his ambition revived other of his miſdemeanours,and by command from the King he was arreſted by the Earl of Northumberland, and ſo took his journeys up to London. By the way his ſoul was rackt betwixt different tidings ; now hoyſed up with hope of pardon, then inſtantly let down with news of the Kings diſpleaſure, till at Leiceſter his heart was broken with theſe ſudden and contrary motions. The Storie goes that he ſhould breath out his ſoul with ſpeeches to this effect, *Had I been as carefull to ſerve the God of Heaven, as I have to comply to the will of my earthly King, God would not have left me in mine old age, as the other hath done.*

His body ſwell'd after his death, as his mind did whileſt he was living, which with other ſymptomes gave the ſuſpicion that he poyſoned himſelf. It will ſuffice us to obſerve, If a Great man much beloved dyeth ſuddenly, the report goes that others poyſoned him: If he be generally hated, then that he poyſoned himſelf. Sure never did a Great man fall with leſſe pity. Some of his own ſervants with the feathers they got under him flew to other Maſters. Moſt of the Clergy (more pitying his Profeſsion then Perſon) were glad that the felling of this oke would cauſe the growth of much underwood.

Let Geometricians meaſure the vaſtneſſe of his mind by the footſteps of his Buildings, Chriſt-Church White-Hall, Hampton-Court: And no wonder if ſome of theſe were not finiſhed, ſeeing his life was rather broken off then ended. Sure King Henrie lived in two of his houſes, and lies now in the third, I mean his Tombe at Windſor. In a word, in his prime he was the bias of the Chriſtian world, drawing the bowl thereof to what ſide he pleaſed.

CHAP. 4.

The life of CHARLES BRANDON, *Duke of Suffolk.*

CHarles Brandon was ſonne to S^r^. William Brandon, Standerd-bearer to King Henry the ſeaventh, in whoſe quarrell he was ſlain in Boſworth field; wherefore the King counted himſelf bound in honour and conſcience to favour young Charles, whoſe father ſpent his laſt breath to blow him to the haven of victory, and cauſed him to be brought up with Prince Henrie, his ſecond ſonne.

The intimacy betwixt them took deep impreſsion in their tender years, which hardned with continuance of time proved indeleble. It was advanced by the ſympathy of their active ſpirits (men of quick and large-ſtriding minds loving to walk together) not to ſay, that the looſeneſſe of their youthfull lives made them

them the faster friends. Henry, when afterwards King, heaped honours upon him, created him Viscount L isle, and Duke of Suffolk.

Not long after some of the English Nobility got leave to go to the publick Tilting in Paris, and there behav'd themselves right valiantly, though the sullen French would scarce speak a word in their praise. For they conceived it would be an eternall impoverishing of the credit of their Nation, if the honour of the day should be exported by foreiners. But Brandon bare away the credit from all, fighting at Barriers with a giant Almain, till he made an earth-quake in that mountain of flesh, making him reel and * stagger, and many other courses at Tilt he performed to admiration. Yea, the Lords beheld him not with more envious, then the Ladies with gracious eyes, who darted more glaunces in love, then the other ranne spears in anger against him; especially Mary the French Queen, and sister to King Henry the eighth, who afterward proved his wife.

* *Hollinshed, pag* 833.

For after the death of Lewis the twelfth her husband, King Henry her brother imployed Charles Brandon to bring her over into England; who improved his service so well that he got her good will to marrie her. Whether his affections were so ambitious to climbe up to her, or hers so courteous as to descend to him (who had been * twice a widower before) let youthfull pennes dispute it: it sufficeth us, both met together. Then wrote he in humble manner to request King Henries leave to marrie his sister; but knowing that matters of this nature are never sure till finisht, and that leave is sooner got to do such attempts when done already; and wisely considering with himself that there are but few dayes in the Almanack, wherein such *Marriages come in*, and subjects have opportunity to wed Queens, he first married her * privately in Paris.

* *First married to Margaret Nevil, after to Anne, daughter to Sr Anthony Brown.*

* *Hollinshed, pag.* 836.

King Henrie after the acting of some anger, and

shewing

ſhewing ſome ſtate-diſcontent, was quickly contented therewith ; yea the world conceiveth that he *gave this woman to be married to this man*, in ſending him on ſuch an imployment. At Calis they were afterward re-married, or if you will their former private marriage publickly ſolemniz'd, and coming into England liv'd many years in honour and eſteem, no leſſe dear to his fellow-ſubjects then his Sovereigne. He was often imployed Generall in Martiall affairs, eſpecially in the warres betwixt the Engliſh and French, though the greateſt performance on both ſides was but mutuall indenting the Dominions each of other with inrodes.

When the divorce of King Henry from Queen Katharine was ſo long in agitation, Brandon found not himſelf a little agrieved at the Kings expence of time and money : for the Court of Rome in ſuch matters, wherein money is gotten by delayes, will make no more ſpeed then the beaſt in Braſil, which the Spaniards call *Pigritia*, which goes no farther in a fortnight then a man will caſt a ſtone. Yea Brandon well perceived that Cardinall Campeius and Wolſey in their Court at Bridewell, wherein the divorce was judicially handled, intended onely to produce a ſolemn Nothing, their Court being but the clock ſet according to the diall at Rome, and the inſtructions received thence. Wherefore knocking on the table, in the preſence of the two Cardinalls, he bound it with an oath, That *It was never well in England ſince Cardinalls had any thing to do therein* : And from that time forward, as an active inſtrument, he indeavoured the aboliſhing of the Popes power in England.

For he was not onely (as the Papiſts complain * of him) a principall agent in that Parliament, *Anno*. 1534. wherein the Popes ſupremacy was abrogated, but alſo a main means of the overturning of Abbeys, as conceiving that though the head was ſtruck off, yet as long

* *Sanderſ. de Schiſmate Anglicano*, p. 108.

as

as that neck and those shoulders remained there would be a continuall appetite of reuniting themselves. Herein his thoughts were more pure from the mixture of covetousnesse then many other imployed in the same service : For after that our eyes, justly dazled at first with the brightnesse of Gods Justice on those vitious fraternities, have somewhat recovered themselves, they will serve us to see the greedy appetites of some instruments to feed on Church-morsels.

He lived and dyed in the full favour of his Prince, though as Cardinall Pool observed, they who were highest in this Kings favour, their heads were nearest danger. Indeed King Henrie was not very tender in cutting off that joynt, and in his Reigne the ax was seldome wiped, before wetted again with Noble bloud. He dyed *Anno* 1544. much beloved, and lamented of all, for his bounty, humility, valour, and all noble virtues, since the heat of his youth was tamed in his reduced age, and lies buried at Windsor.

Chap. 5.

The wise Statesman.

TO describe the Statesman at large, is the subject rather of a Volume then a Chapter, and is as farre beyond my power, as wide of my profession. We will not lanch into the deep, but satisfie our selves to sail by the shore, and briefly observe his carriage towards God, his King, himself, home-persons, and forein Princes.

He counts the fear of God the beginning of wisdome; and therefore esteemeth no project profitable, which is not lawfull; nothing politick, which crosseth piety. Let not any plead for the contrary Hushai's dealing with Absalom, which strongly savour'd of double-dealing; for what is a question cannot be an argument, seeing *Maxime* 1 the lawfulnesse of his deed therein was never decided; and he is unwise that will venter the state of his soul on the litigious title of such an example. Besides, we must live by Gods precepts, not by the godlies practice. And though God causeth sometimes the sunne of successe to shine as well on bad as good projects, yet commonly wicked actions end in shame at the last.

2 *In giving counsell to his Prince, he had rather displease then hurt him.* Plain-dealing is one of the daintiest rarities can be presented to some Princes, as being novelty to them all times of the yeare. The Philosopher could say,* *Quid omnia possidentibus deest? Ille qui verum dicat.* Wherefore our Statesman seeks to undeceive his Prince from the fallacies of flatterers, who by their plausible perswasions have bolster'd up their crooked counsells, to make them seem straight in the Kings eyes.

* *Seneca de benefic. lib. 3. c. 30.*

3 *Yet if dissenting from his Sovereigne, he doth it with all humility and moderation.* It is neither manners nor wit to crosse Princes in their game, much lesse in their serious affairs. Yea, it may be Rebellion in a subject to give his Sovereigne loyall counsell, if proceeding from a spirit of contradiction and contempt, and uttered in audacious language. What do these but give wholsome Physick, wrapt up in poysoned papers?

4 *He is constant, but not obstinate in the advice he gives.* Some think it beneath a wise man to alter their opinion: A maxime both false and dangerous. We know what worthy Father wrote his own Retractation; and it matters not though we go back from our word, so we go forward in the truth and a sound judgement. Such a one changeth not his main opinion, which ever was this, to embrace that course which upon mature deliberation shall appear unto him the most advised. As for his carriage towards himself,

5 *He taketh an exact survey of his own defects and perfections.* As for the former, his weaknesses and infirmities he doth carefully and wisely conceal: sometimes he covers

covers them over with a cautious confidence, and presents a fair hilt, but keeps the sword in the sheath which wanteth an edge. But this he manageth with much art, otherwise, being betray'd, it would prove most ridiculous, and it would make brave musick to his enemies, to heare the hissing of an empty bladder when it is prick'd.

His known perfections he seeks modestly to cloud and obscure. 6
It is needlesse to shew the sunne shining, which will break out of it self. Not like our Phantasticks, who having a fine watch draw all occasions to draw it out to be seen. Yea, because sometimes he concealeth his sufficiency in such things, wherein others know he hath ability, he shall therefore be thought at other times to have ability in those matters wherein indeed he wants it, men interpreting him therein rather modestly to dissemble, then to be defective. Yet when just occasion is offer'd, he shews his perfections soundly, though seldome, and then graceth them out to the best advantage.

In discourse he is neither too free, nor overreserv'd, but ob- 7
serves a mediocrity. His hall is common to all comers, but his closet is lock'd. Generall matters he is as liberall to impart, as carefull to conceal importancies. Moderate liberty in speech inviteth and provoketh liberty to be used again, where a constant closenesse makes all suspect him: and his company is burthensome that liveth altogether on the expences of others, and will lay out nothing himself. Yea, who will barter intelligence with him, that returns no considerable ware in exchange?

He trusteth not any with a secret which may endanger his 8
estate. For if he tells it to his servant, he makes him his master; if to his friend, he enables him to be a foe, and to undo him at pleasure, whose secrecy he must buy at the parties own price, and if ever he shuts his purse, the other opens his mouth. Matters of inferiour conse-

quence he will communicate to a faſt friend, and crave his advice ; for two eyes ſee more then one, though it be never ſo big, and ſet(as in Polyphemus) in the middeſt of the forehead.

9 *He is carefull and provident in the managing of his private eſtate.* Excellently * Ambroſe, *An idoneum putabo qui mihi det conſilium, qui non dat ſibi?* Well may Princes ſuſpect thoſe Stateſmen not to be wiſe in the buſineſſe of the Common-wealth, who are fools in ordering their own affairs.Our Politician, if he enlargeth not his own eſtate, at leaſt keeps it in good repair. As for avaricious courſes, he diſdaineth them. S[r] Thomas More, though ſome years Lord-Chancellour of England, ſcarce left his ſonne * five and twenty pounds ayeare more then his father left him. And S[r] Henrie Sidney (father to S[r] Philip) being Lord Preſident of Wales and Ireland, got not * one foot of land in either Countrey, rather ſeeking after the common good then his private profit. I muſt confeſſe the laſt age produced an Engliſh Stateſman, who was the picklock of the cabinets of forein Princes, who, though the wiſeſt in his time and way, died poore and indebted to private men, though not ſo much as the whole Kingdome was indebted to him. But ſuch an accident is rare ; and a ſmall Hoſpitall will hold thoſe Stateſmen who have impaired their means,not by their private careleſneſſe, but carefulneſſe for the publick. As for his carriage towards Home-perſons,

* *Lib. 2. de offic. cap. 112.*

* *Sanderſ. de Schiſm. Anglic. pag. 118.*

* *Henry Lho'd, in the beginning of his Welch Chronicle.*

10 *He ſtudieth mens natures, firſt reading the Title-pages of them by the report of Fame:* but credits not Fames relations to the full. Otherwiſe, as in London-exchange one ſhall overbuy wares, who gives half the price at firſt demanded, ſo he that believeth the moity of Fame may believe too much. Wherefore to be more accurate,

11 *He reads the Chapters of mens natures (chiefly his concurrents and competitours) by the reports of their friends and foes,*

making

making allowance for their engagements, not believing all in the masse, but onely what he judiciously extracteth. Yet virtues confess'd by their foes, and vices acknowledged by their friends, are commonly true. The best intelligence, if it can be obtained, is from a fugitive Privado.

But the most legible Character and truest Edition wherein he reads a man is in his own occasionall openings: And that in these three cases. 12

1 When the party discloses himself in his wine: for though it be unlawfull to practise on any to make them drunk, yet no doubt one may make a good use of another mans abusing himself. What they say of the herb Lunaria ceremoniously gathered at some set times, that laid upon any lock, it makes it flie open, is most true of drunkennesse, unbolting the most important secrets.

2 When he discovereth himself in his passions. Physicians to make some small veins in their Patients arms plump and full, that they may see them the better to let them bloud, use to put them into hot water: so the heat of passion presenteth many invisible veins in mens hearts to the eye of the beholder; yea the sweat of anger washeth off their paint, and makes them appear in their true colours.

3 When accidentally they bolt out speeches unawares to themselves. More hold is then to be taken of a few words casually uttered, then of set solemn speeches, which rather shew mens arts then their natures, as endited rather from their brains then hearts. The drop of one word may shew more then the stream of an whole oration; and our Statesman by examining such fugitive passages (which have stollen on a sudden out of the parties mouth) arrives at his best intelligence.

13 *In Court-factions he keeps himself in a free neutrality.* Otherwise to engage himself needlessely were both folly and danger. When Francis the first, King of France, was consulting with his Captains how to lead his army * over the Alpes into Italy, whether this way or that way, Amarill his fool sprung out of a corner, where he sate unseen, and bade them rather take care which way they should bring their army out of Italy back again. Thus is it easie for one to interest and embarque himself in others quarrells, but much difficulty it is to be disengaged from them afterwards. Nor will our Statesman entitle himself a party in any feminine discords, knowing that *womens jarres breed mens warres.*

* *Pere de Lancre, of the uncertainty of things, lib. 2. fourth discourse*

14 *Yet he counts neutrality profanenesse in such matters wherein God, his Prince, the Church, or State are concern'd.* Indeed, *He that meddleth with strife not belonging unto him is like one that taketh a dog by the eares.* Yet if the dog worrieth a sheep, we may, yea ought to rescue it from his teeth, and must be champions for innocence when it is overborn with might. He that will stand neuter in such matters of moment, wherein his calling commands him to be a party, with Servilius in Rome, will please neither side: Of whom the Historian sayes, *P. Servilius medium se gerendo, nec plebis vitavit odium, nec apud Patres gratiam inivit.* And just it is with God, that they should be strained in the twist, who stride so wide as to set their legs in two opposite sides. Indeed an upright shoe may fit both feet, but never saw I glove that would serve both hands. Neutrality in matters of an indifferent nature may fit well, but never suit well in important matters, of farre different conditions.

Prov. 26. 17.

15 *He is the centre wherein lines of intelligence meet from all forein countreys.* He is carefull that his outlandish instructions be full, true, and speedy; not with the sluggard telling for news at noone, that the sunne is risen.

ſen. But more largely hereof in the Embaſſadour hereafter.

He refuſeth all underhand penſions from forein Princes. Indeed honourary rewards received with the approbation of his Sovereigne may be lawfull, and leſſe dangerous. For although even ſuch gifts tacitly oblige him by way of gratitude to do all good offices to that forein Prince whoſe Penſioner he is; yet his counſells paſſe not but with an open abatement, in regard of his known engagements, and ſo the State is armed againſt the advice of ſuch, who are well known to lean to one ſide. But ſecret penſions which flow from forein Princes, like the river Anas in Spain, under ground, not known or diſcerned, are moſt miſchievous. The receivers of ſuch will play under-board at the Counſell-table; and the eating and digeſting of ſuch outlandiſh food will by degrees fill their veins with outlandiſh bloud, even in their very hearts. 16

His Maſter-piece is in negotiating for his own Maſter with forein Princes. At Rhodes there was a contention betwixt Apelles and Protogenes, corrivalls in the Myſtery of Limming. Apelles with his pencill drew a very ſlender even line; Protogenes drew another more ſmall and ſlender in the midſt thereof with another colour: Apelles again with a third line of a different colour drew thorow the midſt of that Protogenes had made, * *Nullum relinquens amplius ſubtilitati locum.* Thus our Stateſman traverſeth matters, doubling and redoubling in his forein negotiations with the Politicians of other Princes, winding, and entrenching themſelves mutually within the thoughts each of other, till at laſt our Stateſman leaves no degree of ſubtlety to go beyond him. 17

* *Plin. nat. Hist. lib.* 34. *cap.* 10.

To conclude: Some plead that diſſembling is Lawfull in the State-craft, upon the preſuppoſition that men muſt meet with others which diſſemble. Yea they hold, that thus to counterfeit, *ſe defendendo*, againſt

a

a crafty corrivall, is no ſinne, but a juſt puniſhment on our adverſary, who firſt began it. And therefore Statesmen ſometimes muſt uſe crooked ſhoes, to fit hurl'd feet. Beſides, the honeſt Politician would quickly be begger'd, if, receiving black money from cheatours, he payes them in good ſilver, and not in their own coin back again. For my part, I confeſſe that herein I rather ſee what then whither to flie; neither able to anſwer their arguments, nor willing to allow their practice. But what ſhall I ſay? They need to have ſteddy heads who can dive into theſe gulfs of policy, and come out with a ſafe conſcience. I'le look no longer on theſe whirl-pools of State, leſt my pen turn giddy.

CHAP. 6.

WILLIAM CECIL *Baron of* Burgleigh & *Lord* Treaſurer *of England. He dyed Anno 1598. Aged 77 yeares.* W: *Marſhall ſculp:*

CHAP. 6.

The life of William Cecil *Lord Burleigh.*

WIlliam Cecil born at Bourn in Lincolnſhire, deſcended from the ancient and worſhipfull Family of the Sitſilts or Cecils of Alterynnis in Herefordſhire, on the confines of Wales; a name which a great * Antiquary thinks probably derived from the Romane *Cecilii.* No credit is to be given to their pens, who tax him with meanneſſe of birth, and whoſe malice is ſo generall againſt all goodneſſe, that it had been

* *Verſtegan, reſtitut. of decaid intelligence, pag.* 312.

a ſlander if this worthy man had not been ſlandred by them: The ſervant is not above his maſter; and we know what aſperſions their malice ſought to caſt on the Queen her ſelf.

He being firſt bred in S. Johns Colledge in Cambridge, went thence to Grayes Inne (and uſed it as an Inne indeed, ſtudying there in his Paſſage to the Court) where he attained good learning in the Laws: yet his skill in fencing made him not daring to quarrell, who in all his life-time neither * ſued any, nor was ſued himſelf. He was after Maſter of the Requeſts (the firſt that ever bare that office) unto the Duke of Sommerſet, Lord Protectour, and was knighted by King Edward the ſixth.

* *Cambd. Elizab. in Anno* 1598.

One * challengeth him to have been a main contriver of that act, and unnaturall will of King Edward the ſixth, wherein the King paſſing by his ſiſters, Marie and Elizabeth, entailed the Crown on Queen Jane; and that he furniſhed that act with reaſons of State, as Judge Montague filled it with arguments of Law. Indeed his hand wrote it, as Secretary of State, but his heart conſented not thereto; yea he openly * oppoſed it, though at laſt yielding to the greatneſſe of Northumberland, in an age wherein it was preſent drowning, not to ſwim along with the ſtream. But as the * Philoſopher tells us, that though the Planets be whirled about daily from Eaſt to Weſt by the motion of the *Primum mobile*, yet have they alſo a contrary proper motion of their own, from Weſt to Eaſt, which they ſlowly yet ſurely move at their leiſures: ſo Cecill had ſecret counter-endeavours againſt the ſtrain of the Court herein, and privately advanced his rightfull intentions againſt the foreſaid Dukes ambition; and we ſee that afterward Queen Marie not onely pardoned but employ'd him; ſo that towards the end of her reigne he ſtood in ſome twilight of her favour.

* S[r]. *John Hayward in his Edward ſixth*, p.417.

* *Cambden, ut priùs.*

* *Ariſtot. lib.* 2. *de cœlo cap.* 4. & 10.

As for S[r]. Edward Montague Lord chief Juſtice,

what

what he did was by command againſt his own will, as appears by his written proteſtation at his death, ſtill in the hands of his honourable poſterity. But whileſt in this army of offenders, the Nobility in the front made an eſcape for themſelves, Queen Maries diſpleaſure overtook the old Judge in the rere, the good old man being not able with ſuch ſpeed to provide for himſelf; yea though he had done nothing but by generall conſent and command, the reſt of the Lords laid load on him, deſirous that the Queens anger ſhould ſend him on an errand to the priſon, and thence to the ſcaffold, to excuſe themſelves from going on the ſame meſſage. However, after ſome impriſonment he was pardon'd; a ſufficient argument, that the Queen conceived him to concurre paſsively in that action.

In Queen Elizabeths dayes he was made Secretary of State, Maſter of the Wards, Lord Treaſurer, and at laſt after long ſervice Baron of Burleigh. For the Queen honoured her honours in conferring them ſparingly, thereby making Titles more ſubſtantiall, wherewith ſhe payed many for their ſervice. The beſt demonſtration of his care in ſtewarding her Treaſure was this, that the Queen, vying gold and ſilver with the King of Spain, had money or credit, when the other had neither; her Exchequer, though but a pond in compariſon, holding water, when his river, fed with a ſpring from the Indies, was dreined dry.

In that grand faction betwixt Leiceſter and Suſſex, he meddled not openly, though 'tis eaſie to tell whom he wiſh'd the beſt to. Indeed this cunning Wreſtler would never catch hold to grapple openly with Leiceſter (as having ſomewhat the diſadvantage of him both in height and ſtrength) but as they ran to their ſeverall goles, if they chanced to meet, Burleigh would fairly give him a trip, and be gone; and the Earl had many a rub laid in his way, yet never ſaw who put it there.

Tis true, the Sword-men accuſ'd him as too cold in the Queens credit, and backward in fighting againſt forein enemies. Indeed he would never engage the State in a warre, except neceſsity, or her Majeſties honour, ſounded the alarm : But no reaſon he ſhould be counted an enemie to the Sparks of Valour, who was ſo carefull to provide them fewel, and pay the Souldier. Otherwiſe, in vain do the brows frown, the eyes ſparkle, the tongue threaten, the fiſt bend, and the arm ſtrike, except the belly be fed.

The Queen reflected her favour highly upon him, counting him both her Treaſurer, and her principall Treaſure. She would cauſe him alwayes to ſit down in her preſence, becauſe troubled with the gout, and uſed to tell him: *My Lord, we make much of you, not for your bad legs, but for your good head.* This cauſed him to be much envied of ſome great ones at Court; and at one time no fewer then the * Marqueſſe of Wincheſter, Duke of Norfolk, Earls of Arundel, Northumberland, Weſtmerland, Pembroke and Leiceſter combining againſt him, taking advantage about his making over ſome moneys beyond ſea to the French Proteſtants, and on ſome other occaſions; S. Nicholas Throgmorton adviſed them firſt to clap him up in priſon, ſaying, that if he were once ſhut up, men would open their mouths to ſpeak freely againſt him. But the Queen underſtanding hereof, and ſtanding, as I may ſay, in the very priſon-doore, quaſh'd all their deſignes, and freed him from the miſchief projected againſt him.

* *Cambden, Elizab. Anno* 1579.

He was a good friend to the Church, as then eſtabliſhed by Law; he uſed to adviſe his eldeſt ſonne Thomas never to beſtow any great coſt, or to build any great houſe on an Impropriation, as fearing the foundation might fail hereafter. A Patron to both Univerſities, chiefly to Cambridge, whereof he was Chancellour; and though Rent-corn firſt grew in the

head

head of S[r] Thomas Smith, it was ripened by Burleighs aſsiſtance, whereby though the rents of Colledges ſtand ſtill, their revennues increaſe.

No man was more pleaſant and merry at meals; and he had a pretty wit-rack in himſelf, to make the dumbe to ſpeak, to draw ſpeech out of the moſt ſullen and * ſilent gueſt at his table, to ſhew his diſpoſition in any point he ſhould propound. For forein intelligence, though he traded ſometimes on the ſtock of Secretary Walſingham, yet wanted he not a plentifull bank of his own. At night when he put off his gown, he uſed to ſay, *Lie there*, *Lord Treaſurer*, and bidding adieu to all State-affairs, diſpoſed himſelf to his quiet reſt.

* *Hottoman in deſcrip. of the Embaſſadour witneſſeth ſo much, who had been at his table.*

Some looking on the eſtate he left, have wondered that it was ſo great, and afterwards wondred more that it was ſo little, having conſidered what Offices he had, and how long he enjoyed them. His harveſt laſted every day for above thirty years together, wherein he allowed ſome of his ſervants the ſame courteſie Boaz granted to Ruth, to glean even among the ſheaves, and to ſuffer ſome handfulls alſo to fall on purpoſe for them, whereby they raiſed great eſtates.

To draw to a concluſion: There aroſe a great queſtion in State, whether warre with Spain ſhould be continued, or a peace drawn up? The Sword and Gown-men brought weighty arguments on both ſides, ſtamping alſo upon them with their private intereſts, to make them more heavy: Burleigh was all againſt warre, now old, being deſirous to depart in peace, both private in his Conſcience, and publick in the State. But his life was determined before the queſtion was fully decided. In his ſickneſſe the Queen often viſited him, a good plaiſter to aſſwage his pain, but unable to prolong his life; ſo that, *Cum ſatis naturæ, ſatisque gloriæ, patriæ autem non ſatis vixiſſet*, in the ſeventy ſeventh yeare of his age, *Anno* 1598. he exchanged this

life

life for a better. God meaſured his outward happineſſe not by an ordinary ſtandard: How many great Undertakers in State ſet in a cloud, whereas he ſhined to the laſt? Herein much is to be aſcribed to the Queens conſtancy, who to confute the obſervation of Feminine fickleneſſe, where her favour did light it did lodge; more to his own temper and moderation, whereas violent & boyſterous meddlers in State cripple themſelves with aches in their age; moſt to Gods goodneſſe, who honoureth them that honour him. He ſaw Thomas his eldeſt ſonne richly married to an honourable coheir; Robert, able to ſtand alone in Court, having a competent portion of favour, which he knew thriftily to improve, being a pregnant proficient in State-diſcipline.

CHAP. 7.
The good Judge.

* *Lib. 2. cap. 1.*

THe good Advocate, whom we * formerly deſcribed, is ſince by his Princes favour, and own deſerts, advanced to be a Judge: which his place he freely obtained with S[r]. Auguſtine * Nicolls, whom King James uſed to call *the Judge that would give no money*. Otherwiſe they that buy Juſtice by wholeſale, to make themſelves ſavers muſt ſell it by retail.

* *Bolton in his funer. notes on him.*

Maxime 1 *He is patient and attentive in hearing the pleadings on both ſides*; and hearkens to the witneſſes, though tedious. He may give a waking teſtimony who hath but a dreaming utterance; and many countrey people muſt be impertinent, before they can be pertinent, and cannot give evidence about an hen, but firſt they muſt begin with it in the egge. All which our Judge is contented to hearken to.

2 *He meets not a teſtimony half-way, but ſtayes till it come at him*. He that proceeds on half-evidence, will not do quarter-juſtice. Our Judge will not go till he is lead.

If

If any ſhall brow-beat a pregnant witneſſe,on purpoſe to make his proof miſcarry, he checketh them, and helps the witneſſe that labours in his delivery. On the other ſide, he nips thoſe Lawyers, who under a pretence of kindneſſe to lend a witneſſe ſome words, give him new matter,yea clean contrary to what he intended.

3 *Having heard with patience, he gives ſentence with uprightneſſe.* For when he put on his robes, he put off his relations to any ; and like Melchiſedech becomes without pedigree. His private affections are ſwallowed up in the common cauſe, as rivers loſe their names in the ocean. He therefore allows no noted favourites, which cannot but cauſe multiplication of fees,and ſuſpicion of by-wayes.

4 *He ſilences that Lawyer who ſeeks to ſet the neck of a bad cauſe, once broken with a definitive ſentence* ; and cauſeth that contentious ſuits be ſpued out, as the ſurfets of Courts.

5 *He ſo hates bribes, that he is jealous to receive any kindneſſe above the ordinary proportion of friendſhip* ; leſt like the Sermons of wandring Preachers, they ſhould end in begging. And ſurely Integrity is the proper portion of a Judge. Men have a touch-ſtone whereby to try gold, but gold is the touch-ſtone whereby to trie men. It was a ſhrewd gird which Catulus gave the Romane Judges for acquitting Clodius a great malefactour, when he met them going home well attended with Officers ; *You do well* (quoth he) *to be well * guarded for your ſafety, leſt the money be taken away from you, you took for bribes.* Our Judge alſo deteſteth the trick of Mendicant Friers, who will touch no money themſelves, but have a boy with a bag to receive it for them.

* *Plutar. in the life of Cicero, pag.* 871.

6 *When he ſits upon life, in judgement he remembreth mercy.* Then (they ſay) a butcher may not be of the Jurie, much leſſe let him be the Judge. Oh let him take heed how he ſtrikes, that hath a dead hand. It was the

charge Queen Marie gave to Judge Morgan, chief Juſtice of the common Pleas, that notwithſtanding the old * errour amongſt Judges did not admit any witneſſe to ſpeak, or any other matter to be heard in favour of the adverſary, her Majeſtie being party; yet her Highneſſe pleaſure was that whatſoever could be brought in the favour of the Subject ſhould be admitted and heard.

* *Holinſhed in Queen Marie, pag.* 1112.

7 *If the cauſe be difficult, his diligence is the greater to ſift it out.* For though there be mention, Pſal. 37. 6. of righteouſneſſe as clear as the noon-day, yet God forbid that that innocency which is no clearer then twilight ſhould be condemned. And ſeeing ones oath commands anothers life, he ſearcheth whether malice did not command that oath: yet when all is done, the Judge may be deceived by falſe evidence. But blame not the hand of the diall, if it points at a falſe houre, when the fault's in the wheels of the clock which direct it, and are out of frame.

8 *The ſentence of condemnation he pronounceth with all gravity.* 'Tis beſt when ſteep'd in the Judges tears. He avoideth all jeſting on men in miſery: eaſily may he put them out of countenance, whom he hath power to put out of life.

9 *Such as are unworthy to live, and yet unfitted to die, he provides ſhall be inſtructed.* By Gods mercy, and good teaching, the reprive of their bodies may get the pardon of their ſouls, and one dayes longer life for them here may procure a bleſſed eternity for them hereafter, as may appear by this memorable Example. It happened about the yeare one thouſand five hundred and fiftie ſix in the town of * Weiſſenſtein in Germany that a Jew for theft he had comitted, was in this cruell manner to be executed: He was hang'd by the feet with his head downwards betwixt two dogs, which conſtantly ſnatch'd and bit at him. The ſtrangeneſſe of the torment moved Jacobus Andreas (a grave, moderate, and

* *Melchior Adamus in vit. Jac. Andreæ, pag.* 639.

and learned Divine as any in that age) to go to behold it. Coming thither he found the poore wretch, as he hung, repeating Verſes out of the Hebrew Pſalmes, wherein he cryed out to God for mercy. Andreas hereupon took occaſion to counſell him to truſt in Jeſus Chriſt the true Saviour of mankind: The Jew embracing the Chriſtian Faith, requeſted but this one thing, that he might be taken down and be baptized, though preſently after he were hanged again (but by the neck as Chriſtian malefactours ſuffered) which was accordingly granted him.

He is exact to do juſtice in civill Suits betwixt Sovereigne 10
and Subject. This will moſt ingratiate him with his Prince at laſt. Kings neither are, can, nor ſhould be Lawyers themſelves, by reaſon of higher State-employments, but herein they ſee with the eyes of their Judges, and at laſt will break thoſe falſe ſpectacles which (in point of Law) ſhall be found to have deceived them.

He counts the Rules of State and the Laws of the Realm mu- 11
tually ſupport each other. Thoſe who made the Laws to be not onely diſparate, but even oppoſite terms to maximes of Government, were true friends neither to Laws nor Government. Indeed *Salus Reip.* is *Charta maxima*: extremity makes the next the beſt remedy. Yet though hot waters be good to be given to one in a ſwound, they will burn his heart out who drinks them conſtantly, when in health. Extraordinary courſes are not ordinarily to be uſed, when not enforced by abſolute neceſſity.

And thus we leave our good Judge to receive a juſt reward of his integrity from the Judge of Judges, at the great Aſsize of the world.

Chap. 8.

The life of S^r. John Markham.

IOhn Markham was born at Markham in Nottinghamſhire, deſcended of an ancient and worthy familie. He employed his youth in the ſtudying of the Municipall Law of this realm, wherein he attained to ſuch eminencie, that King Edward the fourth Knighted him, and made him Lord chief * Juſtice of the Kings Bench in the place of Sr John Forteſcue, that learned and upright Judge, who fled away with King Henrie the ſixth.

* *13. Maii. 1. Edwardi. 4.*

Yet Forteſcue was not miſſ'd, becauſe Markham ſucceeded him : and that loſſe, which otherwiſe could not be repair'd, now could not be perceiv'd. For though theſe two Judges did ſeverally lean to the ſides of Lancaſter and York, yet both ſate upright in matters of Judicature.

We will inſtance and inſiſt on one memorable act of our Judge, which though ſingle in it ſelf, was plurall in the concernings thereof. And let the Reader know, that I have not been careleſſe to ſearch, though unhappy not to find, the originall Record, perchance aboliſhed on purpoſe, and ſilenced for telling tales to the diſgrace of great ones. We muſt now be contented to write this Story out of the Engliſh Chronicles; * and let him die of drought without pity, who will not quench his thirſt at the river, becauſe he cannot come at the fountain.

* *Fabian. pag. 497 &c. Holinſhed pag. 670. and Stow in 12. of Edward the fourth.*

King Edward the fourth having married into the family of the Woodvills (Gentlemen of more antiquity then wealth, and of higher ſpirits then fortunes) thought it fit for his own honour to beſtow honour upon them : But he could not ſo eaſily provide them of wealth, as titles. For honour he could derive from himſelf, like light from a candle, without any diminiſhing nifhing of his own luftre; whereas wealth flowing from him, as water from a fountain, made the fpring the fhallower. Wherefore he refolved to cut down fome prime fubjects, and to engraff the Queens kinred into their eftates, which otherwife like fuckers muft feed on the ftock of his own Exchequer.

There was at this time one Sr Thomas Cook, late Lord Maior of London, and Knight of the Bath, one who had well lick'd his fingers under Queen Margaret (whofe Wardroper he was, and cuftomer of Hampton) a man of a great eftate. It was agreed that he fhould be accufed of high Treafon, and a Commifsion of Oyer and Terminer granted forth to the Lord Maior, the Duke of Clarence, the Earl of Warwick, the Lord Rivers, Sr. John Markham, Sr. John Fogg, &c. to try him in Guild Hall: And the King by private inftructions to the Judge appear'd fo farre, that Cook, though he was not, muft be found guilty, and if the Law were too fhort, the Judge muft ftretch it to the purpofe.

The fault laid to his charge was for lending moneys to Queen Margaret, wife to King Henrie the fixth; the proof, was the confefsion of one Hawkins, who being rack'd in the Tower had confeffed fo much. The Counfell for the King, hanging as much weight on the fmalleft wier as it would hold, aggravated each particular, & by their Rhetoricall flafhes blew the fault up to a great height. Sr Thomas Cook pleaded for himfelf, that Hawkins indeed upon a feafon came to him, and requefted him to lend one thoufand marks, upon good fecurity. But he defired firft to know for whom the money fhould be: and underftanding it was for Queen Margaret, denyed to lend any money, though at laft the faid Hawkins defcended fo low as to require but one hundred pounds, and departed without any peny lent him.

Judge Markham in a grave fpeech did recapitulate,

ſelect and collate the materiall points on either ſide, ſhewing that the proof reached not the charge of high Treaſon, and miſpriſion of Treaſon was the higheſt it could amount to, and intimated to the Jurie, to be tender in matter of life, and diſcharge good conſciences.

The Jurie being wiſe men (whoſe apprehenſions could make up an whole ſentence of every nod of the Judge) ſaw it behoved them to draw up Treaſon into as narrow a compaſſe as might be, leſt it became their own caſe ; for they lived in a troubleſome world, wherein the cards were ſo ſhuffled, that two Kings were turn'd up trump at once, which amazed men how to play their games. Whereupon they acquitted the priſoner of high Treaſon, and found him guilty, as the Judge directed.

Yet it coſt S[r] Thomas Cook, before he could get his libertie, eight hundred pounds to the Queen, and eight thouſand pounds to the King : A ſumme in that age more ſounding like the ranſome of a Prince, then the fine of a Subject. Beſides, the Lord Rivers (the Queens Father) had, during his Impriſonment, deſpoyled his houſes, one in the city, another in the countrey of plate and furniture, for which he never received a penie recompence. Yet God righted him of the wrongs men did him, by bleſsing the remnant of his eſtate to him, and his poſterity, which ſtill flouriſh at Giddy Hall in Eſſex.

As for S[r] John Markham, the Kings diſpleaſure fell ſo heavy on him, that he was outed of his place, and S[r] Thomas Billing put in his room, though the one loſt that Office with more honour then the other got it ; and gloried in this, that though the King could make him no Judge, he could not make him no upright Judge. He lived privately the reſt of his dayes, having (beſides the eſtate got by his practice) fair lands by Margaret his wife, daughter and coheir

to

to S[r] Simon Leak * of Cotham in Nottinghamshire, whose Mother Joan was daughter and heir of S[r] John Talbot, of Swannington in Leicestershire.

* *Burtons Leicestershire, pag. 577.*

CHAP. 9.

The good Bishop.

HE is an Overseer of a Flock of Shepherds, as a Minister is of a Flock of Gods sheep. Divine providence and his Princes bounty advanced him to the Place, whereof he was no whit ambitious: Onely he counts it good manners to sit there where God hath placed him, though it be higher then he conceives himself to deserve, and hopes that he who call'd him to the Office hath or will in some measure fit him for it.

Maxime 1

His life is so spotlesse, that Malice is angry with him, because she cannot be angry with him: because she can find no just cause to accuse him. And as * Diogenes confuted him who denyed there was any motion, by saying nothing but walking before his eyes; so our Bishop takes no notice of the false accusations of people disaffected against his order, but *walks* on *circumspectly* in his calling, really refelling their cavils by his conversation. A Bishops bare presence at a marriage in his own diocesse, is by the Law interpreted for a licence; and what actions soever he graceth with his company, he is conceived to priviledge them to be lawfull, which makes him to be more wary in his behaviour.

* *Diogen. Laert. lib. 6. pag. 212. in vit. Diogenis.*

2

With his honour, his holinesse and humility doth increase. His great Place makes not his piety the lesse: farre be it from him that the glittering of the candlestick should dimme the shining of his candle. The meanest Minister of Gods word may have free accesse unto him: whosoever brings a good cause brings his own welcome with him. The pious poore may enter in at his wide

 gates,

gates, when not ſo much as his wicket ſhall be open to wealthy unworthineſſe.

3 *He is diligent and faithfull in preaching the Goſpel*: either by his pen, *Evangelizo manu & ſcriptione*, ſaith a ſtrict * Divine; or by his vocall Sermons (if age and other indiſpenſable occaſions hinder him not) teaching the Clergie to preach, and the Laity to live, according to the ancient * Canons. Object not that it is unfitting he ſhould lie Perdue, who is to walk the round, and that Governing as an higher employment is to ſilence his Preaching: For Preaching is a principall part of Governing, and Chriſt himſelf ruleth his Church by his Word. Hereby Biſhops ſhall govern hearts, and make men yield unto them a true and willing obedience, reverencing God in them. Many in conſumptions have recover'd their healths by returning to their native aire wherein they were born: If Epiſcopacy be in any declination or diminution of honour, the going back to the painfulneſſe of the primitive Fathers in Preaching, is the onely way to repair it.

* *Reinold de Idol. Rom. Eccles. Epiſt. dedicat.*

* *Concil. Toletan. 2. Cap. 2. Tom. 4. pag. 820. Concil. Conſtant. 6. Can. 19. Tom. 5. pag. 328. Concil. Aurel. Can. 33. pag. 723. and lately, Concil Trident. Seſſ 24. Can. 4*

4 *Painfull, pious, and peaceable Miniſters are his principall Favourites.* If he meets them in his way (yea he will make it his way to meet them) he beſtoweth all grace and luſtre upon them.

5 *He is carefull that Church-cenſures be juſtly and ſolemnly inflicted*: namely,

1. Admonition, when the Church onely chideth, but with the rod in her hand.
2. Excommunication, the Mittimus whereby the Malefactour is ſent to the gaolour of hell, and *delivered to Satan.*
3. Aggravation, whereby for his greater contempt, he is removed out of the gaole into the dungeon.
4. Penance, which is or ſhould be inward repentance, made viſible by open confeſſion, whereby the Congregation is ſatisfied for the publick offenſe given her.

5 Abſolution,

5 Absolution, which fetcheth the penitent out of hell, and opens the doore of heaven for him, which Excommunication had formerly lock'd, and Aggravation bolted against him.

As much as lies in his power, he either prevents or corrects those too frequent abuses, whereby offenders are not * *prick'd to the heart*, but let bloud in the purse; and when the Court hath her costs, the Church hath no damage given her, nor any reparation for the open scandall she received by the parties offence. Let the memory of Worthy Bishop Lake ever survive, whose hand had the true seasoning of a Sermon with Law and Gospel, and who was most fatherly grave in inflicting Church-censures: Such offenders as were unhappy in deserving, were happy in doing penance in his presence.

* *Acts* 2.37.

He is carefull and happy in suppressing of Heresies and Schismes. He distinguisheth of Schismaticks, as Phisicians do of Leprous people: Some are infectious, * others not; Some are active to seduce others, others quietly enjoy their opinions in their own consciences. The latter by his mildnesse he easily reduceth to the truth; whereas the Chirurgeons rigourously handling it, often breaks that bone quite off, which formerly was but out of joynt: Towards the former he useth more severity, yet endeavouring first to inform him aright, before he punisheth him. To use force first before people are fairly taught the truth, is to knock a nail into a board, without wimbling a hole for it, which then either not enters, or turns crooked, or splits the wood it pierceth. 6

* *The Leprosy Elephantiasis not infectious to the company.*

He is very mercifull in punishing offenders; both in matters of life and livelyhood, seing in S. Johns Language the same word * Βίος signifies both. He had rather draw tears, then bloud. It was the honour of the Romane State, as yet being Pagan, * *In hoc gloriari licet, nulli Gentium mitiores placuisse pœnas*: Yea for the first seventy years 7

* *Iohn.* 3 17.

* *Livius lib.* 1. *pag.* 20.

years (till the reigne of Ancus Martius) they were without a priſon. Clemency therefore in a Chriſtian Biſhop is moſt proper: O let not the *Starres of our Church* be herein turn'd to Comets, whoſe appearing in place of judicature preſageth to ſome death or deſtruction. I confeſſe that even Juſtice it ſelf is a kind of mercy: But God grant that my portion of mercy be not paid me in that coin. And though the higheſt deteſtation of ſinne beſt agreeth with Clergy-men, yet ought they to caſt a ſevere eye on the vice and example, and a mercifull eye on the perſon.

8 *None more forward to forgive a wrong done to himſelf.* Worthy Archbiſhop * Whitgift interceded to Queen Elizabeth for remitting of heavie fines laid on ſome of his Adverſaries (learning from Chriſt his Maſter to be a mediatour for them) till his importunity had angred the Queen, yea and till his importunity had pleaſ'd her again, and gave not over till he got them to be forgiven.

* *Cambd Elizab. in Anno* 1588. *p.* 538.

9 *He is very carefull on whom he layeth hands in Ordination*; leſt afterwards he hath juſt cauſe to beſhrew his fingers, and with Martianus, a Biſhop of Conſtantinople (who made Sabbatius a Jew and a turbulent man Prieſt) wiſh he had then rather laid his hand on the * briers, then ſuch a mans head. For the ſufficiency of Scholarſhip he goeth by his own eye; but for their honeſt life, he is guided by other mens hands, which would not ſo oft deceive him, were Teſtimonialls a matter of leſſe courteſie and more conſcience. For whoſoever ſubſcribes them enters into bond to God and the Church, under an heavy forfeiture, to avouch the honeſtie of the party commended; and, as Judah for Benjamin, they become *ſureties for the young man unto his father*. Nor let them think to void the band and make it but a blank with that clauſe, *ſo farre forth as we know*, or words to the like effect: For what ſaith the Apoſtle? *God is not mocked*.

* *Socrat. Eccleſ. Hiſt. lib.* 5. *cap.* 10.

He

He meddleth as little as may be with Temporall matters : ha- 10
ving little skill in them, and leſſe will to them. Not that he is unworthy to manage them, but they unworthy to be managed by him. Yea generally the moſt dexterous in ſpirituall matters are left-handed in temporall buſineſſe, and go but untowardly about them. Wherefore our Biſhop, with reverend * Andrews, *meddleth little in civill affairs, being out of his profeſſion and element.* Heaven is his vocation, and therefore he counts earthly employments avocations : except in ſuch caſes which lie (as I may ſay) in the Marches of Divinity, and have connexion with his calling ; or elſe when temporall matters meddle with him, ſo that he muſt rid them out of his way. Yet he rather admireth then condemneth ſuch of his brethren, who are ſtrengthned with that which would diſtract him, making the concurrence of ſpirituall and temporall power in them ſupport one another, and uſing worldly buſineſſe as their recreation to heavenly employment.

* *Funerall Serm. on him, pag. 19.*

If call'd to the Court he there doth all good offices, betwixt 11
Prince and people, ſtriving to remove all miſpriſions & diſaffections,& advancing unity and concord. They that think the Church may flouriſh when the Common-wealth doth wither may as well conceive that the brains may be ſound when *pia mater* is periſhed. When in the way of a Confeſſour he privately tells his Prince of his faults, he knows by Nathans parable, to go the neareſt way home by going farre about.

He improves his power with his Prince for the Churches good, 12
in maintaining both true religion and the maintenance thereof ; leſt ſome pretending with pious Ezechiah to beat down the brazen ſerpent,the occaſion of Idolatry, do indeed with ſacrilegious Ahaz take away the brazen bulls from the Laver, and ſet it on a pavement of ſtone. He jointly advanceth the pains and gains, the work and wages of Miniſters, which going together make a flouriſhing Clergy, with Gods bleſsing, and without mans envy.

13 *His mortified mind is no whit moved with the magnificent vanities of the Court*: no more then a dead corps is affected with a velvet herse-cloth over it. He is so farre from wondring at their pomps, that though he looks daily on them, he scarce sees them, having his eyes taken up with higher objects; and onely admires at such, as can admire such low matters. He is loved and feared of all; and his presence frights the Swearer either out of his oathes or into silence, and he stains all other mens lives with the clearnesse of his own.

14 *Yet he daily prayeth God to keep him in so slippery a place.* Elisha prayed that a double portion of Eliahs Spirit might rest upon him. A Father descanteth hereon, that a double portion of grace was necessary for Elisha, who was gratious at Court, lived in a plentifull way, and favoured of the Kings of Israel; whereas Eliah lived poorely, and privately: And more wisdome is requisite to manage prosperity then affliction.

15 *In his grave writings he aims at Gods glory, and the Churches peace*, with that worthy Prelate, the second Jewell of Salisbury, whose Comments and Controversies will transmit his memory to all Posterity:

Whose dying pen did write of *Christian Union,*
How Church with Church might safely keep *Communion.*
Commend his care, although the cure do misse;
The woe is ours, the happinesse is his:
Who finding discords daily to encrease,
Because he could not live, would die, in peace.

16 *He ever makes honourable mention of forein Protestant Churches*; even when he differs and dissents from them. The worst he wisheth the French Church is a Protestant King: not giving the left hand of Fellowship to them, and reserving his right for some other. Cannot Christs coat be of different colours, but also it must be of severall seams? railing one on another, till these Sisters, by bastardizing one another, make the Popish Church

Church the ſole heir to all truth. How often did reverend*Whitgift(knowing he had the farre better cheere) ſend a meſſe of meat from his own table to the Miniſters of Geneva? relieving many of them by bountifull contributions. Indeed Engliſh charity to forein Proteſtant Churches in ſome reſpect is payment of a debt: their children deſerve to be our welcome gueſts, whoſe Grandfathers were our loving hoſts in the dayes of Queen Mary.

* S. G. Paul. in his life, pag. 63, 64.

17 *He is thankfull to that Colledge whence he had his education.* He conceiv'd himſelf to heare his Mother-Colledge alwayes ſpeaking to him in the language of Joſeph to Pharaohs Butler, * *But think on me, I pray thee, when it ſhall be well with thee.* If he himſelf hath but little, the leſſe from him is the more acceptable: A drop from a ſpunge is as much as a tunne of water from a Mariſh. He beſtows on it Books, or Plate, or Lands or Building; and the Houſes of the Prophets rather lack watering then planting, there being enough of them, if they had enough.

* Gen. 40. 14.

18 *He is hoſpitable in his houſekeeping according to his eſtate.* His bounty is with diſcretion to thoſe that deſerve it: Charity miſtaken, which relieves idle people, like a dead corps, onely feeds the vermin it breeds. The rankneſſe of his houſekeeping produceth no riot in his Family. S. Paul calls a Chriſtian Family well ordered, * *a Church in their houſe.* If a private mans houſe be a Parochiall, a Biſhops may ſeem a Cathedrall Church, as much better as bigger, ſo decently all things therein are diſpoſed.

* Rom. 6. 5. Theoph. in locum.

We come now to give a double Example of a godly Biſhop: the firſt out of the Primitive times, the ſecond out of the Engliſh Church ſince the Reformation, both excellent in their ſeverall wayes.

CHAP. 10.

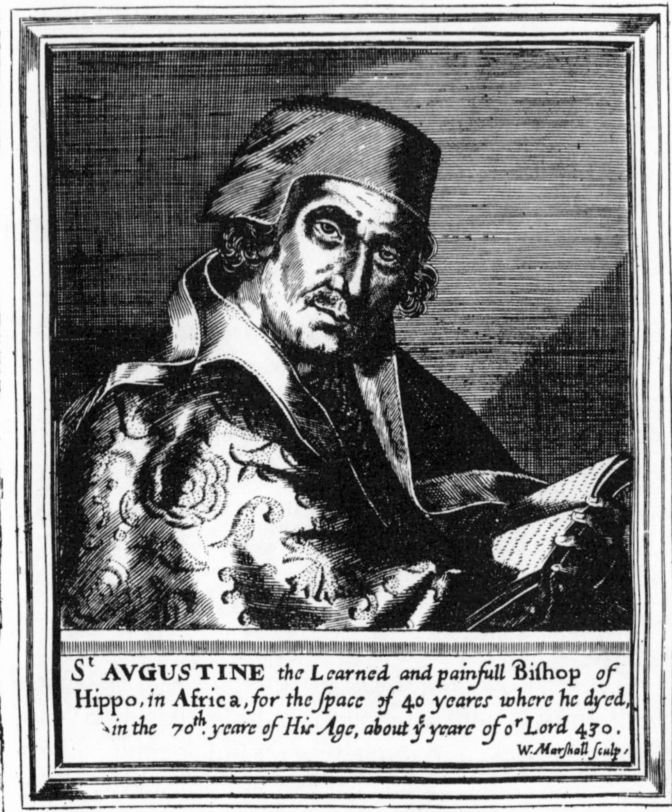

Chap. II.

The life of S. Augustine.

Auguſtine was born in the City of Tagaſta in Africa, of Gentile parentage, Patricius and Monica, though their means bore not proportion to their birth, ſo that the breeding of their ſonne at Learning much weakned their eſtate, in ſo much as Romanian a noble gentleman (all the world is bound to be thankfull to S. Auguſtines Benefactour) bountifully advanced his education.

It

It will be needleſſe to ſpeak of his youth, vitious in manners and erroneous in doctrine, eſpecially ſeeing he hath ſo largely accuſ'd himſelf in his *Confeſsions*. 'Tis tyranny to trample on him that proſtrates himſelf; and whoſe ſinnes God hath gratiouſly forgotten, let no man deſpightfully remember.

Being made a Presbyter in the Church of Hippo, this great favour was allowed him, to preach conſtantly, though in the preſence of * Valerius the Biſhop: whereas in that age to heare a Prieſt preach when that a Biſhop was in the Church, was as great a wonder as the Moon ſhining at mid-day. Yea godly Valerius, one that could do better then he could ſpeak, and had a better heart then tongue, (being a Grecian, and therefore not well underſtood of the Africans) procured Auguſtine in his life-time to be deſigned Biſhop of Hippo, and to be joyned * fellow-Biſhop with himſelf, though it was flatly againſt the Canons.

** Poſidonius in vit. Auguſt. cap 5.*

** Idem. cap. 8.*

For a Coadjutour commonly proves an hinderer, and by his envious claſhing doth often dig his Partners grave with whom he is joyn'd; beſides that ſuch a ſuperinſtallation ſeems an unlawfull bigamy, marrying two husbands at the ſame time to the ſame Church. Yea, S. Auguſtine himſelf, afterwards underſtanding that this was againſt the Conſtitutions of the Church, was ſorry thereat (though others thought his eminency above Canons, and his deſerts his diſpenſation) and deſiring that his ignorance herein ſhould not miſguide others, obtained that the Canons (then not ſo hard to be kept as known, becauſe obſcure and ſcattered) were compiled together and publiſhed, that the Clergy might know what they were bound to obſerve.

Being afterwards ſole Biſhop, he was diligent in continuall preaching, and beating down of Hereticks eſpecially the Manicheans, in whoſe Fence-ſchool he was formerly brought up, and therefore knew beſt how to hit them, and guard himſelf; alſo the Pelagians, the duelliſts againſt Grace, and for Freewill, which till S. Auguſtines time was never throughly ſifted, points in Divinity being but ſlenderly fenced till they are aſſaulted by Hereticks. He was alſo the hammer of the Donatiſts, Hereticks who did ſcatter more then they did devoure, and their Schiſme was more dangerous then their * Doctrine.

* *See their Tenets at large in our fifth book.*

He went not ſo willingly to a feaſt as to a conference, to reduce any erroneous perſons : once he diſputed with Paſcentius the Arian, who requeſted that what paſſed betwixt them might not be written, and afterwards gave out his * bragges that he had worſted Auguſtine in the diſpute, which report was believed of all who deſired it.

* *Auguſt. Tom. 2. Ep. 174.*

In other battels, if the conquered ſide ſhould be ſo impudent as to boaſt of the victory, it will ere long be confuted by the number of their men ſlain, enſignes and wagons taken, with their flight out of the field. It is not thus in the tongue-combats of diſputes, wherein no viſible wounds are given, and wherein bold men (though inwardly convinced with force of reaſon) count not themſelves conquered till they confeſſe it ; ſo that in effect none can be overcome except they will themſelves : For ſome are ſo ſhameleſſe that they count not their cauſe *wrackt* as long as any thing alive comes to the Land, ſo long as they have breath to talk though not to anſwer, and employ their hands not to untie their Adverſaries arguments, but onely obſtinately to lay hold on their own opinions ; yea after the conference ended they cry *victoria* in all companies wherein they come, whileſt their Auditours, generally as engaged as the Diſputants, will ſuccour their Champion with partiall relations, as the Arians did in this caſe of Paſcentius.

But their falſe cavills have done the Church this

true courteſie, that ever after S. Auguſtine ſet down his diſputations in writing, that ſo the eye of the Reader might more ſteddily behold his arguments preſented fixed in black and white, then when they were onely *in fluxu*, as paſsing in his words.

His clothes were neither* brave, nor baſe, but comely: As for the black Cowl of the Auguſtinians, which they pretend from his practice, it ſeemeth rather (if ſo ancient) to be cut with the ſheeres, or by the pattern, of Auguſtine the Monk. He would not receive gifts to the Church from thoſe who had poore kinred of their own: Divinitie ſaith, that mercy is better then ſacrifice; and the Law provides, that debts are to be paid before legacies.

* Veſtis nec nitida nimium, nec abjecta plurimùm, *Poſſidon. cap.* 22.

In caſe of great want he would ſell the very Ornaments of the Church, and beſtow the money on the poore, contrary to the * opinion of many (the thorn of Superſtition began very ſoon to prick) who would not have ſuch things in any caſe to be alienated. Sure a Communion-table will not catch cold with wanting a rich carpet, nor ſtumble for lack of the candles thereon in ſilver candleſticks. Beſides, the Church might afterwards be ſeaſonably repleniſhed with new furniture, whereas if the poore were once ſterved, they could not be revived again. But let not Sacriledge in the diſguize of Charity make advantage hereof, & Covetouſneſſe, which is ever hungry till it ſurfets, make a conſtant ordinary on Church-bread, becauſe David in neceſsity fed one meal thereon. His diet was very cleanly and ſparing, yet hoſpitable in the entertaining of others, and had this diſtich wrote on his table,

*De vaſis Dominicis, propter captivos quamplurimos indigentes, frangi & conflari jubebat, & indigentibus diſpenſari: quod non commemoraſſem, niſi contra carnalem ſenſum quorundam fieri pervideream, *Poſſidon. in vit. Auguſt. cap.* 24.

Quiſquis amat dictis abſentum rodere famam,
Hanc menſam indignam noverit eſſe ſibi.
He that doth love on abſent friends to jeere
May hence depart, no room is for him here.

His family was excellently well ordered, and ten of thoſe Scholars which were brought up under him came afterwards to be Biſhops. To

** Methodius Martyr & Paul. Diacon.*

To come to his death. It happened that the Northern countreys, called by * some *Vagina gentium, the Sheath of people* (though more properly they may be termed, *Ensis dei, the Sword of God*) sent forth the Vandalls, Albans, and Gothes, into the Southern parts, God punishing the pride of the Roman Empire to be confounded by Barbarous enemies. Out of Spain they came into Africa, and massacred all before them. The neighbouring villages like little children did flie to Hippo the mother-City for succour : thirteen moneths was Hippo besieged by the Gothes, and S. Augustine being therein prayed to God either to remove the siege, or to give the Christians therein patience to suffer, or to take him out of this miserable world, which he obtained, and dyed in the third moneth of the siege.

Falling very sick(besides the disease of age and grief) he lay languishing a pretty time, and took order that none should come to him save when his meat was brought, or Physicians visited him, that so he might have elbow-room the more freely to put off the clothes of his mortality.

The motion of Piety in him (by custome now made naturall) was *velocior in fine*, daily breathing out most pious Ejaculations. He died intestate, not for lack of time to make a will, but means to bestow, having formerly passed his soul to God, whilest his body of course bequeathed it self to the earth. As for the books of his own making, a treasure beyond estimation, he carefully consigned them to severall Libraries. He dyed in the seventy sixth yeare of his age, having lived a Bishop almost fourty years. Thus a Saint of God, like an oke, may be cut down in a moment ; but how many years was he a growing ! Not long after his death the City of Hippo was sack'd by the Gothes, it being no wonder if Troy was taken, when the Palladium was first fetch'd away from it.

CHAP. II.

NICHOLAS RIDLEY Biſhop *of* LONDON. *He died a constant Martyr for the Truth, and was burnt at Oxford the 16th of Octob: 1555.* *W. Marſhall ſculp:*

Chap. II.

The life of Biſhop Ridley.

NIcholas Ridley born in the Biſhoprick of Dureſme, but deſcended from the ancient and worſhipfull familie of the Ridleys of Willimotes-wike in Northumberland. He was brought up in Pembroke-hall in Cambridge, where he ſo profited in generall Learning, that he was choſen Fellow of the Colledge, and *Anno* 1533 was Proctour of the Univerſity.

At which time two Oxford men, George Throgmorton, and John Aſhwell, came to Cambridge, and in the publick Schools challenged any to dipſute with them on theſe queſtions,

An { *Jus civile ſit medicina præſtantius?* / *Mulier condemnata, bis ruptis laqueis, ſit tertio ſuſpendenda?*

It ſeems they were men of more brow then brain, being ſo ambitious to be known, that they had rather be hiſſ'd down then not come upon the ſtage. Sure Oxford afforded as many more able diſputants, as Civill Law yielded more profound and needfull queſtions. Throgmorton had the fortune of daring men, to be worſted, being ſo preſſed by John Redman and Nicholas * Ridley the opponents, that his ſecond refuſed at all to diſpute.

* *Caius de Antiquit. Cant. Acad. p. 19. 20.*

Indeed an Univerſity is an onely fit match for an Univerſity; and any private man who in this Nature undertakes a whole body, being of neceſsity put to the worſt, deſerves not Phaetons Epitaph, *magnis*, but *ſtultis tamen excidit auſis*. And though * one objects, *Neminem Cantabrigienſium conſtat Oxonienſes unquam ad certamen provocaſſe*; yet leſſe learning cannot be inferred from more modeſtie. The beſt is, the two Siſters ſo well agree together that they onely contend to ſurpaſſe each other in mutuall kindneſſe, and forbidding all duells betwixt their children, make up their joint forces againſt the common foe of them and true Religion.

* *Brian Twine pag. 336.*

He was after choſen Maſter of Penbroke Hall, and kept the ſame whileſt Biſhop of Rocheſter and London, till outed in the firſt of Queen Marie. Not that he was covetous to hold his place in the Colledge, but the Colledge ambitious to hold him; as who would willingly part with a jewell. He was in good eſteem with Henrie the eighth, and in better with pious King Edward the ſixth, and was generally beloved of all the Court, being one of an handſome perſon, comelie preſence, affable ſpeech, and courteous behaviour.

But before I go further, Reader, pardon a digreſsion,

and yet is it none, for 'tis neceſſary. I have within the narrow ſcantling of my experimentall remembrance obſerved ſtrange alteration in the worlds valuing of thoſe learned men which lived in that age; and take it plainly without welt or gard, for he that ſmarts for ſpeaking truth hath a playſter in his own conſcience.

When I was a child I was poſſeſſed with a reverend eſteem of them, as moſt holy and pious men, dying Martyrs in the dayes of Queen Marie for profeſsion of the truth; which opinion having from my Parents taken quiet poſſeſsion of my ſoul, they muſt be very forcible reaſons which eject it.

Since that time they have been much cried down in the mouthes of many, who making a *Coroners enqueſt* upon their death, have found them little better then *Felons de ſe*, dying in their own bloud, for a mere formality, *de modo*, of the manner of the Preſence, and a Sacrifice in the Sacrament, who might eaſily with one ſmall diſtinction have knockt off their fetters, & ſaved their lives. By ſuch the Coronet of Martyrdome is pluckt off from their memories; and others more moderate equally part their death betwixt their enemies cruelty, and their own over-forwardneſſe.

Since that, one might have expected that theſe worthy men ſhould have been re-eſtated in their former honour, whereas the contrary hath come to paſſe. For ſome who have an excellent facultie in uncharitable Synecdoches, to condemne a life for an action, & taking advantage of ſome faults in them do much condemne them. And * one lately hath traduced them with ſuch language, as neither beſeemed his parts (whoſoever he was) that ſpake it, nor their piety of whom it was ſpoken. If pious Latimer, whoſe bluntneſſe was incapable of flattery, had his ſimplicity abuſed with falſe informations, he is called *another Doctour Shaw, to divulge in his Sermon forged accuſations.* Cranmer and Ridley for ſome failings ſtyled, *the common ſtales to countenance*

* *Authour of the book lately printed of Cauſes hindring Reformation in England, lib. 1. pag. 10.*

with their prostituted gravities every politick fetch which was then on foot, as oft as the potent Statists pleased to employ them. And, as it follows not farre after, *Bishop Cranmer, one of King Henries Executours, and the other Bishops, none refusing (lest they should resist the Duke of Northumberland) could find in their consciences to set their hands to the disenabling and defeating of the Princesse Marie, &c.* Where Christian ingenuity might have prompted unto him to have made an intimation, that Cranmer (with pious Justice Hales in Kent) was last and least guilty, much refusing to subscribe; and his long resisting deserved as well to be mentioned, as his yielding at last. Yea, that very Verse, which Doctour Smith at the burning of Ridley used against him, is by the foresaid Authour (though not with so full a blow, with a slenting stroke) applyed to those Martyrs, *A man may give his body to be burnt, and yet have not charity.*

Pag. 11.

Thus the prices of Martyrs ashes rise and fall in Smithfield market. However their reall worth flotes not with peoples phancies, no more then a rock in the sea rises and falls with the tide: S. Paul is still S. Paul, though the Lycaonians now would sacrifice to him, and presently after would sacrifice him: These Bishops, Ministers, and Lay-people, which were put to death in Queen Maries dayes, were worthy Saints of God, holy and godly men, but had their faults, failings, and imperfections. Had they not been men they had not burn't; yea had they not been more then men (by Gods assistance) they had not burn't. Every true Christian should, but none but strong Christians will, die at the stake.

But to return to Ridley: One of the greatest things objected against him, was his counsell to King Edward (which the good Prince wash'd away with his tears) about tolerating the Masse for Princesse Mary, at the intercession of Charles the fifth Emperour, which how great it was, let the indifferent party give

judgement,

judgement, when the * Historian hath given his evidence, *The Bishops*, of Canterbury, London, Rochester, *gave their opinion, that to give licence to sinne, was sinne, but to connive at sinne, might be allowed, in case it were neither too long, nor without hope of reformation.*

* *Haywards Edward sixth pag.* 291.

Another fault, wherewith he was charged, was that wofull and unhappy discord betwixt him and reverend Bishop Hooper, about the wearing of some Episcopall garments at his consecration (then in use) which Ridley press'd, and Hooper refused with equall violence, as being too many, rather loading then gracing him; and so affectedly grave, that they were light again. All we will say is this, that when worthy men fall out, onely one of them may be faulty at the first, but if such strifes continue long, commonly both become guilty: But thus Gods diamonds often cut one another, and good men cause afflictions to good men.

It was the policy of the * Lacedemonians alwayes to send two Embassadours together, which disagreed amongst themselves, that so mutually they might have an eye on the actions each of other: Sure I am that in those Embassadours, the Ministers, which God sendeth to men, God suffereth great discords betwixt them, (Paul with Barnabas, Jerome with Ruffin, and Augustine, and the like) perchance because each may be more cautious and wary of his behaviour in the view of the other. We may well behold mens weaknesse in such dissentions, but better admire Gods strength and wisdome in ordering them to his glory, and his childrens good. Sure it is, Ridley and Hooper were afterwards cordially reconciled; and let not their discords pierce farther then their reconciliation: The worst is, mens eyes are never made sound with the clearnesse, but often are made sore with the bleernesse of other mens eyes in their company. The virtues of Saints are not so attractive of our imitation, as their vices and infirmities are prone to infect.

* *Arist. polit. lib.* 2. *cap.* 7.

Hayward Edward 6. p. 407. & sequent.

* Ridley was very gracious with King Edward the ſixth, and by a Sermon he preach'd before him ſo wrought upon his pious diſpoſition, whoſe Princely charity rather wanted a directour then a perſwader, that the King at his motion gave to the city of London,

1 Greyfriers, now called Chriſt-Church, for impotent, fatherleſſe, decrepid people by age or nature to be educated or maintained.

2 S. Bartholomews near Smithfield, for poore by faculty, as wounded ſouldiers, diſeaſ'd and ſick perſons to be cur'd and relieved.

3 Bridewell, the ancient Manſion of the Engliſh Kings, for the poore by idleneſſe or unthriftyneſſe, as riotous ſpenders, vagabonds, loyterers, ſtrumpets to be corrected and reduc'd to good order.

Fr. Quarles Enchirid. pag. 1.

I like that Embleme of Charity which * one hath expreſſed *in a naked child, giving honey to a Bee without wings*; onely I would have one thing added, namely holding *a whip in the other hand to drive away the drones*: So that King Edwards bounty was herein perfect and complete.

To return to Ridley: His whole life was a letter written full of learning and religion, whereof his death was the ſeal. Brought he was with Cranmer and Latimer to Oxford to diſpute in the dayes of Queen Mary, though before a Syllogiſme was form'd, their deaths were concluded on, and as afterwards came to paſſe, being burnt the ſixteenth of October *Anno* 1555. in the ditch over againſt Balioll Colledge.

Fox. Acts Mon: An: 1555. Octob.

He came to the * ſtake in a fair black gown furr'd and fac'd with foins, a Tippet of velvet, furr'd likewiſe, about his neck, a velvet night-cap upon his head, and a corner'd cap upon the ſame.

Doctour Smith preacht a Sermon at their burning; a Sermon which had nothing good in it but the text (though miſapplyed) and the ſhortneſſe, being not above

above a quarter of an houre long. Old Hugh Latimer was Ridleys partner at the ſtake, ſometimes Biſhop of Worceſter, who crauled thither after him, one who had loſt more learning then many ever had, who flout at his plain Sermons, though his down-right ſtyle was as neceſſary in that ignorant age, as it would be ridiculous in ours. Indeed he condeſcended to peoples capacity; and many men unjuſtly count thoſe low in learning, who indeed do but ſtoop to their Auditours. Let me ſee any of our ſharp Wits do that with the edge, which his bluntneſſe did with the back of the knife, and perſwade ſo many to reſtitution of ill-gotten goods. Though he came after Ridley to the ſtake, he got before him to heaven: his body, made tinder by age, was no ſooner touch'd by the fire, but inſtantly this old Simeon had his *Nunc dimittis*, and brought the news to heaven that his brother was following after.

But Ridley ſuffered with farre more pain, the fire about him being not well made: And yet one would think that age ſhould be skilfull in making ſuch bonefires, as being much practiſed in them. The Gunpowder that was given him did him little ſervice, and his Brother-in-law, out of deſire to rid him out of pain, encreaſed it, (great grief will not give men leave to be wiſe with it) heaping fewell upon him to no purpoſe; ſo that neither the fagots which his enemies anger, nor his Brothers good will caſt upon him, made the fire to burn kindly.

In like manner, not much before, his dear friend Maſter * Hooper ſuffered with great torment; the wind (which too often is the bellows of great fires) blowing it away from him once, or twice. Of all the Martyrs in thoſe dayes, theſe two endured moſt pain, it being true that each of them,

Quærebat in ignibus ignes:
And ſtill he did deſire,
For fire in midd'ſt of fire.

* *See Mr Fox Acts and Mon. on Hoopers death.*

Both

Both desiring to burn, and yet both their upper parts were but Confessours, when their lower parts were Martyrs, and burnt to ashes: Thus God, where he hath given the stronger faith, he layeth on the stronger pain. And so we leave them going up to Heaven, like Eliah, in a chariot of fire.

CHAP. 12.

The true Nobleman.

HE is a Gentleman in a Text Letter, because bred, and living in an higher and larger way. Conceive him when young brought up at School, *in ludo literario*, where he did not take *ludus* to himself, and leave *literarius* to others, but seriously applyed himself to learning, and afterwards coming to his estate, thus behaves himself.

Maxime 1 *Goodnesse sanctifies his Greatnesse, and Greatnesse supports his Goodnesse.* He improves the upper ground whereon he stands, thereby to do God the more glory.

2 *He counts not care for his Countreys good to be beneath his state.* Because he is a great pillar, shall he therefore bear the lesse weight? never meddling with matters of Justice. Can this be counted too low for a Lord, which is high enough for a King? our Nobleman freely serves his Countrey, counting his very work a sufficient reward. (As by our * Laws no Duke, Earl, Baron, or Baronet, though Justices of Peace, may take any wages at the Sessions.) Yea he detesteth all gainfull wayes, which have the least blush of dishonour: For the Merchant Nobility of Florence and Venice (how highly soever valued by themselves) passe in other countreys with losse and abatement of repute; as if the scarlet robes of their honour had a stain of the stamell die in them.

* *Statute* 14. *of Ric.* 2.*c.* 11.

3 *He is carefull in the thrifty managing of his estate.* Gold, though the most solid and heavy of metalls, yet may be

be beaten out ſo thin, as to be the lighteſt and ſlighteſt of all things. Thus Nobility, though in it ſelf moſt honourable, may be ſo attenuated through the ſmalneſſe of means as thereby to grow neglected. Which makes our Nobleman to practice Solomons precept, * *Be diligent to know the ſtate of thy flocks, and look well to thine herds; for the Crown doth not endure to every generation.* If not the *Crown* much leſſe the *Coronet*; and good husbandry may as well ſtand with great honour, as breadth may conſiſt with height.

* *Prov.* 27. 23.

4 *If a weak eſtate be left him by his Anceſters, he ſeeks to repair it,* by wayes thrifty, yet noble : as by travelling, ſparing abroad, till his ſtate at home may outgrow debts and penſions : Hereby he gains experience, and ſaves expence, ſometimes living private, ſometimes ſhewing himſelf at an half light, and ſometimes appearing like himſelf as occaſion requires; or elſe by betaking himſelf to the warres : Warre cannot but in thankfulneſſe grace him with an Office, which graceth her with his perſon; or elſe by warlike ſea-adventures wiſely undertaken, and providently managed : otherwiſe, this courſe hath emptied more full, then filled empty purſes, and many thereby have brought a Galeon to a Gally ; or laſtly by match with wealthy Heirs, wherein he is never ſo attentive to his profit, but he liſtens alſo to his honour.

5 *In proportion to his means, he keeps a liberall houſe.* This much takes the affections of countrey people, whoſe love is much warmed in a good kitchin, and turneth much on the hinges of a buttery-doore often open. Francis Ruſſell, ſecond Earl of Bedford of that ſirname, was ſo bountifull to the poore, that Queen Elizabeth would merrily complain of him, that he made all the beggers : ſure 'tis more honourable for Noblemen to make beggers by their liberality, then by their oppreſſion. But our Nobleman is eſpecially carefull to ſee all things diſcharged which he taketh up. When the corps

of Thomas Howard ſecond Duke of Norfolk were carried to be interred in the Abbey of Thetford, *Anno* 1524. no perſon could demand of him one * groat for debt, or reſtitution for any injury done by him.

* *Weavers fun. Mon. p.* 839.

6 *His ſervants are beſt known by the coat and cognizance of their civill behaviour.* He will not entertain ſuch ruffian-like men, who know ſo well who is their Maſter, that they know not who they are themſelves, and think their Lords reference is their innocence, to bear them out in all unlawfull actions. But our Lords houſe is the Colledge wherein the children of the neighbouring Gentry and Yeomanry are bred, and there taught by ſerving of him to rule themſelves.

7 *He hateth all oppreſſion of his tenants and neighbours*; diſdaining to cruſh a mean Gentleman for a meaner offenſe; and counts it no conqueſt but an execution from him, who on his ſide hath the oddes of height of place, ſtrength of arme, and length of weapon. But as the Proverb ſaith, *No graſſe grows where the grand Seignieurs horſe ſets his feet*; ſo too often nothing but graſſe grows where ſome Great men ſet their footing, no towns or tillage, for all muſt be turn'd into depopulating paſtures, and commons into encloſures. Nigh the city of Lunenberg in Germany flowed a plentifull ſalt ſpring, till ſuch time as the rich men, engroſſing all the profit to themſelves, would not ſuffer the poore to make any ſalt thereof; whereupon God and Nature being offended at their covetouſneſſe, the ſpring * ceaſed and ran no more for a time. Thus hath Gods puniſhment overtaken many great men, and ſtopp'd his bleſſing towards them, which formerly flowed plentifully unto them, for that they have wronged poore people of their commonage, which of right belonged unto them.

* *Moriſons Travells, chap.* 1. *Part.* 1. *pag.* 5. *Yet afterward upon readmiſſion of the poore to it it ran again.*

8 *In his own pleaſures he is carefull of his neighbours profit.* Though his horſes cannot have wings like his hawks to ſpoil no graſſe or grain as he paſſeth, yet he is very

carefull to make as little waſte as poſsible may be : his horſes ſhall not trample on loaves of bread as he hunteth, ſo that whileſt he ſeeks to gather a twig for himſelf he breaks the ſtaff of the commonwealth.

9 *All the countrey are his Retainers in love and obſervance.* When they come to wait on him, they leave not their hearts at home behind them, but come willingly to tender their reſpects. The holding up of his hand is as good as the diſplaying of a banner ; thouſands will flock to him, but it muſt be for the Kings and Countreys ſervice. For he knows that he who is more then a Lord, if his cauſe be loyall, is leſſe then a private man, if it be otherwiſe: with S. * Paul, *he can do nothing againſt the truth, but for the truth.* Thus Queen Elizabeth Chriſtned the youngeſt daughter of Gilbert Talbot Earl of Shrewsbury (now Counteſſe of Arundell) *Aletheia, Truth,* out of true * conſideration and judgement that the houſe of the Talbots was ever loyall to the Crown.

* 2. Cor. 13.8.

*Vincents diſcov. of Brooks Errours, p. 470.

10 *Some priviledges of Noblemen he endeavours to deſerve:* namely ſuch priviledges as are completely Noble, that ſo his merits as well as the Law ſhould allow them unto him. He conceives this word, *On mine Honour,* wraps up a great deal in it ; which unfolded and then meaſured, will be found to be a large atteſtation, and no leſſe then an eclipticall oath, calling God to witneſſe, who hath beſtowed that Honour upon him. And ſeeing the State is ſo tender of him, that he ſhall not be forced to ſwear in matters of moment in Courts of Juſtice, he is carefull not to ſwear of his own accord in his ſports and pleaſures. Other priviledges of Noblemen he labours not to have need of, namely ſuch as preſuppoſe a fault, are but honourable penalties, and excuſe from ſhamefull puniſhments. Thus he is not to be *bound to the * peace.* And what needs he ; who hath the peace alwayes bound to him, being of his own accord alwayes carefull to preſerve it, and of ſo noble a diſpoſition, he will never be engaged in any braules or contentions.

*Lamb. Juſtice of peace pag. 83.

To give an inſtance of ſuch a Nobleman ſeems to be needleſſe, hoping that at this time in one city of this Realm, and in one room of that city, many ſuch Noblemen are to be found together.

CHAP. 13.

The Court-Lady.

TO deſcribe an Holy State without a virtuous Lady therein, were to paint out a yeare without a Spring : we come therefore to her Character.

Maxime 1 *She ſets not her face ſo often by her glaſſe, as ſhe compoſeth her ſoul by Gods word.* Which hath all the excellent qualities of a glaſſe indeed.

1 It is clear : in all points neceſſary to Salvation, except to ſuch whoſe eyes are blinded.

2 It is true : not like thoſe falſe glaſſes ſome Ladyes dreſſe themſelves by. And how common is flattery at Court, when even glaſſes have learnt to be paraſites ?

3 It is large ; preſenting all ſpots Cap-a-pe, behind and before, within and without.

4 It is durable : though in one ſenſe it is broken too often (when Gods Laws are neglected) yet it will laſt to break them that break it, and *one tittle thereof ſhall not fall to the ground.*

5 This glaſſe hath power to ſmooth the wrinkles, cleanſe the ſpots, and mend the faults it diſcovers.

2 *She walks humbly before God in all religious duties.* Humbly : For ſhe well knows that the ſtrongeſt Chriſtian is like the city of Rome, which was never beſieged but it was taken, and the beſt Saint without Gods aſsiſtance would be as often foyled as tempted. She is moſt conſtant and diligent at her houres of private prayer. Queen Katharine Dowager never kneeld on a cuſhion

* cushion when she was at her devotions : This matters not at all ; our Lady is more carefull of her heart then of her knees, that her soul be settled aright.

* Sanders. de Schism. Anglic. lib. 1. pag. 5.

She is carefull and most tender of her credit and reputation. There is a tree in * Mexicana which is so exceedingly tender, that a man cannot touch any of his branches but it withers presently. A Ladyes credit is of equall nicenesse, a small touch may wound and kill it; which makes her very cautious what company she keeps. The Latine tongue seems somewhat injurious to the feminine sex ; for whereas therein *Amicus* is a friend, *Amica* alwayes signifies a Sweetheart, as if their sex in reference to men were not capable of any other kind of familiar friendship but in way to marriage, which makes our Lady avoid all privacie with suspicious company. 3

* Doctour Heylens Microcos. pag. 783.

Yet is she not more carefull of her own credit then of Gods glory ; and stands up valiantly in the defence thereof. She hath read how at the Coronation of King Richard the second, Dame * Margaret Dimock, wife to Sr John Dimock, came into the Court and claimed the place to be the Kings Champion, by the virtue of the tenure of her Mannour of Scrinelby in Lincolnshire, to challenge and defie all such as opposed the Kings right to the Crown. But if our Lady heares any speaking disgracefully of God or Religion, she counts her self bound by her tenure (whereby she holds possession of grace here, and reversion of glory hereafter.) to assert and vindicate the honour of the King of Heaven, whose Champion she professeth to be. One may be a lambe in private wrongs, but in hearing generall affronts to goodnesse, they are asses which are not lions. 4

* She claimed the place, but her husband performed the office, Lelands Colle. Tit. 1. pag. 299.

She is pitifull and bountifull to people in distresse. We reade how a daughter of the Duke of Exeter invented a brake or cruel rack to torment people withall, to which purpose it was long reserved and often used in the 5

Tower of London, and commonly called (was it not fit so pretty a babe should bear her mothers name?) 'The * Duke of Exeters' daughter. Me thinks the finding out of a salve to ease poore people in pain had born better proportion to her Ladiship then to have been the inventer of instruments of cruelty.

* *Vid. Stowes Chron. in the reig e of King Edward the fourth.*

6 *She is a good scholar, and well learned in usefull Authours.* Indeed as in purchases an house is valued at nothing, because it returneth no profit, and requires great charges to maintain it; so for the same reasons, Learning in a woman is but little to be prized. But as for great Ladyes, who ought to be a confluence of all rarities and perfections, some Learning in them is not onely usefull but necessary.

7 *In discourse her words are rather fit then fine, very choice and yet not chosen.* Though her language be not gaudy, yet the plainnesse thereof pleaseth, it is so proper, and handsomly put on. Some having *a set of fine phrases* will hazard an impertinency to use them all, as thinking they give full satisfaction for dragging in the matter by head and shoulders, if they dresse it in queint expressions. Others often repeat the same things: the Platonick yeare of their discourses being not above three dayes long, in which term all the same matter returns over again, threadbare talk ill suiting with the variety of their clothes.

8 *She affects not the vanity of foolish fashions*; but is decently apparelled according to her state and condition. He that should have guessed the bignesse of Alexanders souldiers by their shields left in India, would much overproportion their true greatnesse. But what a vast overgrown creature would some guesse a woman to be, taking his aim by the multitude and variety of clothes and ornaments, which some of them use: insomuch as the ancient Latines called a womans wardrope *Mundus, a World*, wherein notwithstanding was much *terra incognita* then undiscovered, but since found

found out by the curioſity of modern Faſhion-mongers. We find a mappe of this world drawn by Gods Spirit, Iſaiah the third, wherein one and twenty womens ornaments (all ſuperfluous) are reckoned up, which at this day are much encreaſed. *The * moons,* there mentioned, which they wore on their heads, may ſeem ſince grown to the full in the luxury of after-ages.

* *Iſaiah.*3.18.

She is contented with that beauty which God hath given her. 9
If very handſome, no whit the more proud, but farre the more thankfull: If unhandſome, ſhe labours to better it in the virtues of her mind, that what is but plain cloth without may be rich pluſh within. Indeed ſuch naturall defects as hinder her comfortable ſerving of God in her calling may be amended by art; and any member of the body being defective, may thereby be lawfully ſupplied. Thus glaſſe-eyes may be uſed, though not for ſeeing, for ſightlineſſe. But our Lady deteſteth all adulterate complexions, finding no preſident thereof in the Bible ſave one, and her ſo bad, that Ladyes would bluſh through their paint to make her the pattern of their imitation. Yet are there many that think the groſſeſt fault in painting is to paint groſſely (making their faces with thick daubing not onely new pictures, but new ſtatues) and that the greateſt ſinne therein, is to be diſcover'd.

In her marriage ſhe principally reſpects virtue and religion, 10
and next that, other accomodatious, as we have* formerly diſcourſ'd of. And ſhe is carefull in match not to beſtow her ſelf unworthily beneath her own degree to an ignoble perſon, except in caſe of neceſsity. Thus the Gentlewomen in * Champaigne in France ſome three hundred years ſince were enforced to marry Yeomen and Farmers, becauſe all the Nobility in that countrey were ſlain in the warres in the two voyages of King Lewis to Paleſtine: and thereupon ever ſince by cuſtome and priviledge the Gentlewomen of Champaigne

* *Vid.* 3. *Book chap. of Marriage.*

* *Andr. Favin in his Theater of Honour,* 1. *Book, chap. the* 6.

Champaigne and Brye ennoble their husbands and give them honour in marrying them, how mean ſoever before.

11 *Though pleaſantly affected ſhe is not tranſported with Court-delights* : as in their ſtatelie Maſques and Pageants. Seeing Princes cares are deeper then the cares of private men, it is fit their recreations alſo ſhould be greater, that ſo their mirth may reach the bottome of their ſadneſſe : yea God allows to Princes a greater latitude of pleaſure. He is no friend to the tree, that ſtrips it of the bark ; neither do they mean well to Majeſty, which would deprive it of outward ſhews, and State-ſolemnities, which the ſervants of Princes may in loyalty and reſpect preſent to their Sovereigne ; however, our Lady by degrees is brought from delighting in ſuch Maſques, onely to be contented to ſee them, and at laſt (perchance) could deſire to be excuſed from that alſo.

12 *Yet in her reduced thoughts ſhe makes all the ſport ſhe hath ſeen earnest to her ſelf* : It muſt be a dry flower indeed out of which this bee ſucks no honey : they are the beſt Origens who do allegoriſe all earthly vanities into heavenly truths. When ſhe remembreth how ſuddenly the Scene in the Maſque was altered (almoſt before moment it ſelf could take notice of it) ſhe conſidereth, how quickly mutable all things are in this world, God *ringing the changes* on all accidents, and making them tunable to his glorie : The lively repreſenting of things ſo curiouſly, that Nature her ſelf might grow jealous of Art, in outdoing her, minds our Lady to make ſure work with her own ſoul, ſeeing hypocriſie may be ſo like to ſincerity. But O what a wealthy exchequer of beauties did ſhe there behold, ſeverall faces moſt different, moſt excellent, (ſo great is the variety even in beſts) what a rich mine of jewells above ground, all ſo brave, ſo coſtly ! To give Court-maſques their due, of all the bubbles in this world they have the greateſt variety

riety of fine colours. But all is quickly ended : this is the ſpight of the world, if ever ſhe affordeth fine ware, ſhe alwayes pincheth it in the meaſure, and it laſts not long : But oh, thinks our Lady, how glorious a place is Heaven, *where there are joyes for evermore.* If an herd of kine ſhould meet together to phancy and define happineſſe, they would place it to conſiſt in fine paſtures, ſweet graſſe, clear water, ſhadowie groves, conſtant ſummer, but if any winter, then warm ſhelter and dainty hay, with company after their kind, counting theſe low things the higheſt happineſſe, becauſe their conceit can reach no higher. Little better do the Heathen Poets deſcribe Heaven, paving it with pearl, and roofing it with ſtarres, filling it with Gods and Goddeſſes, and allowing them to drink (as if without it no Poets Paradiſe) Nectar and Ambroſia ; Heaven indeed being *Poetarum dedecus*, the ſhame of Poets, and the diſgrace of all their Hyperboles, falling as farre ſhort of truth herein, as they go beyond it in other Fables. However the ſight of ſuch glorious earthly ſpectacles advantageth our Ladyes conceit by infinite multiplication thereof to conſider of Heaven.

She reades conſtant lectures to her ſelf of her own mortality. 13
To ſmell to a turf of freſh earth is wholſome for the body ; no leſſe are thoughts of mortality cordiall to the ſoul. *Earth thou art, to earth thou ſhalt return* : The ſight of death when it cometh will neither be ſo terrible to her, nor ſo ſtrange, who hath formerly often beheld it in her ſerious meditations. With * Job ſhe ſaith to the worm, *Thou art my ſiſter* : If fair Ladyes ſcorn to own the worms their kinred in this life, their kinred will be bold to challenge them when dead in their graves : for when the ſoul (the beſt perfume of the body) is departed from it, it becomes ſo noyſome a carcaſſe, that ſhould I make a deſcription of the lothſomneſſe thereof, ſome dainty dames would hold their noſes in reading it.

* *Job.* 17. 14.

To conclude: We reade how Henry a Germain Prince was admoniſhed by revelation to ſearch for a writing in an old wall, which ſhould nearly concern him, wherein he found onely theſe two words written, * POST SEX, AFTER SIX. Whereupon Henry conceived that his death was foretold, which after ſix dayes ſhould enſue, which made him paſſe thoſe dayes in conſtant preparation for the ſame. But finding the ſix dayes paſt without the effect he expected, he ſucceſsively perſevered in his godly reſolutions ſix weeks, ſix moneths, ſix years, and on the firſt day of the ſeventh yeare the Prophecie was fulfill'd, though otherwiſe then he interpreted it; for thereupon he was choſen Emperour of Germany, having before gotten ſuch an habit of piety that he perſiſted in his religious courſe for ever after. Thus our Lady hath ſo inur'd her ſelf *all the dayes of her appointed time to wait till her change cometh*, that expecting it every houre, ſhe is alwayes provided for that, then which nothing is more certain or uncertain.

* *Surius in vita Sancti Henr. July* 14. & *Baronius in Anno* 1007.

CHAP. 14.

JANE GRAY *proclaimed* Queen *of* England *wife to the* Lord GILFORD DUDLEY. *She was beheaded on Tower-hill* in London *Februarie* ye 12. 1553. *at* 18 *yeares of Age*. W.M. *sculp*

Chap. 14.

The life of Ladie Jane Grey.

JAne Grey, eldeſt daughter of Henry Grey Marqueſſe of Dorſet, and Duke of Suffolk, by Francis Brandon eldeſt daughter of Charles Brandon Duke of Suffolk, and Mary his wife youngeſt daughter to King Henry the ſeventh, was by her parents bred according to her high birth in Religion and Learning. They were no whit indulgent to her in her childhood, but extremely ſevere, more then needed to ſo ſweet a temper; for what need iron instruments to bow wax?

But as the sharpest winters (correcting the ranknesse of the earth) cause the more healthfull and fruitfull summers; so the harshnesse of her breeding compacted her soul to the greater patience and pietie, so that afterwards she proved the miroir of her age, and attained to be an excellent Scholar through the teaching of M[r] Elmer her Master.

Once M[r] Roger Ascham, coming to wait on her at Broad-gates in Leicestershire, found her in her chamber reading * Phœdon-Platonis in Greek, with as much delight as some Gentleman would have read a merry tale in Bocchace, *Whilest the Duke her father with the Dutchesse and all their houshold were hunting in the Park*: He askt of her, how she could lose such pastime? who smiling answered, *I wisse all the sport in the Park is but the shadow of what pleasure I find in this book*, adding moreover, that one of the greatest blessings God ever gave her, was in sending her sharp parents, and a gentle Schoolmaster, which made her take delight in nothing so much as in her studies.

* *Ascham's Schoolmaster, lib. 1. fol. 10.*

About this time John Dudley Duke of Northumberland projected for the English Crown: But being too low to reach it in his own person, having no advantage of royall birth, a match was made betwixt Guilford his fourth sonne, and this Lady Jane; the Duke hoping so to reigne in his daughter-in-law, on whom King Edward the sixth by will, passing by his own sisters, had entayled the Crown: And not long after that godly King, who had some defects, but few faults (and those rather in his age then person) came to his grave: it being uncertain whether he went, or was sent thither. If the latter be true, *the crying of this Saint under the Altar*, beneath which he was buried in King Henries Chappell (without any other monument, then that of his own virtues) hath been heard long since for avenging his bloud.

Presently

1553

Presently after Lady Jane was proclaimed Queen of England. She lifted not up her least finger to put the Diadem on her self,but was onely contented to sit still, whilest others endeavoured to Crown her; or rather was so farre from biting at the bait of Sovereignty, that unwillingly she opened her mouth to receive it.

Then was the Duke of Northumberland made Generall of an Army, and sent into Suffolk to suppresse the Lady Marie, who there gathered men to claim the Crown. This Duke was appointed out of the policie of his friend-seeming enemies for that employment: For those who before could not endure the scorching heat of his displeasure at the Counsell-table, durst afterwards oppose him, having gotten the skreen of London-walls betwixt him and them. They also stinted his journeys every day (thereby appointing the steps by which he was to go down to his own grave) that he should march on very slowly, which caused his confusion. For lingring doth tire out treacherous designes, which are to be done all on a sudden, and gives breath to loyalty to recover it self.

His army like a sheep left part of his fleece on every bush it came by, at every stage and corner some conveying themselves from him, till his Souldiers were wash'd away before any storm of warre fell upon them. Onely some few, who were chain'd to the Duke by their particular engagements, and some great Persons hopelesse to conceal themselves, as being too bigge for a cover, stuck fast unto him. Thus those enterprises need a strong hand which are thrown against the bias of peoples hearts and consciences. And not long after the Norfolk and Suffolk Protestant Gentry (Loyalty alwayes lodgeth in the same breast with true Religion) proclaimed and set up Queen Marie, who got the Crown by *Our Father*, and held it by *Pater noster*.

Then was the late Queen, now Lady Jane Grey, brought from a Queen to a priſoner, and committed to the Tower. She made miſery it ſelf amiable by her pious and patient behaviour: Adverſity, her night-clothes, becoming her as well as her day-dreſsing, by reaſon of her pious deportment.

During her impriſonment many moved her to alter her religion, and eſpecially M[r] Fecnam ſent unto her by Queen Mary: but how wiſely and religiouſly ſhe anſwer'd him, I referre the Reader to M[r] Fox,* where it is largely recorded.

* *Acts & Monum. pag.* 1419 *& deinceps.*

And becauſe I have mentioned that Book, wherein this Ladyes virtues are ſo highly commended, I am not ignorant that of late great diſgrace hath been thrown on that Authour, and his worthy Work, as being guilty of much falſehood: chiefly becauſe ſometimes he makes Popiſh Doctours, well known to be rich in learning, to reaſon very poorely, and the beſt Fencers of their Schools worſted and put out of their play by ſome countrey poore Proteſtants. But let the cavillers hereat know, that it is a great matter to have the oddes of the weapon, Gods word on their ſide; not to ſay any thing of ſupernaturall aſsiſtance given them. Sure for the main, his Book is a worthy work (wherein the Reader may rather leave then lack) and ſeems to me, like Ætna, alwayes burning, whileſt the ſmoke hath almoſt put out the eyes of the adverſe party, and theſe *Foxes firebrands* have brought much annoyance to the *Romiſh Philiſtines*. But it were a miracle if in ſo voluminous a work there were nothing to be juſtly reproved; ſo great a Pomgranate not having any rotten kernell muſt onely grow in paradiſe. And though perchance he held the beam at the beſt advantage for the Proteſtant party to weigh down, yet generally he is a true Writer, and never wilfully deceiveth, though he may ſometimes be unwillingly deceived.

To

To return to the Lady Jane: Though Queen Marie of her own diſpoſition was inclined finally to pardon her, yet neceſſity of State was ſuch, as ſhe muſt be put to death. Some report her to have been with child when ſhe was beheaded (cruelty to cut down the tree with bloſſomes on it) and that that which hath ſaved the life of many women haſtned her death; but God onely knows the truth hereof. On Tower-hill ſhe moſt patiently, Chriſtianly, and conſtantly yielded to God her ſoul, which by a bad way went to the beſt end. On whom the foreſaid Authour (whence the reſt of her life may be ſupplied) beſtows theſe verſes, 1553. *Feb.* 12.

Neſcio tu quibus es, Lector lecturus ocellis:
Hoc ſcio, quod ſiccis ſcribere non potui.

What eyes thou readſt with, Reader, know I not:
Mine were not dry, when I this ſtory wrote.

She had the innocency of childhood, the beauty of youth, the ſolidity of middle, the gravity of old age, and all at eighteen: the birth of a Princeſſe, the learning of a Clerk, the life of a Saint, yet the death of a Malefactour, for her parents offenſes. I confeſſe, I never read of any canonized Saint of her name, a thing whereof ſome Papiſts are ſo ſcrupulous, that they count it an unclean and unhallowed thing to be of a name whereof never any Saint was: which made that great Jeſuit Arthur Faunt (as his * kinſman tell's us) change his Chriſtian name to Laurence. But let this worthy Lady paſſe for a Saint; and let all great Ladyes, which bear her name, imitate her virtues, to whom I wiſh her inward holineſſe, but farre more outward happineſſe.

*Burton of Leiceſterſhire pag. 105.

Yet leſt Goodneſſe ſhould be diſcouraged by this Ladyes infelicity, we will produce another example, which ſhall be of a fortunate virtue.

ELIZABETH Queen *of* England, *She dyed at* Richmond *the* 24th *of March* 1602 *in the* 44th *yeare of Her Raign and* 70th *of Her Life* .

W Marshall sculp:

CHAP. 15.

The life of Queen ELISABETH.

WE intermeddle not with her deſcription as ſhe was a Sovereigne Prince, too high for our pen, and performed by others already, though not by any done ſo fully, but that ſtill room is left for the endeavours of Poſterity to adde thereunto. We conſider her onely as ſhe was a worthy Lady, her private virtues rendring her to the imitation, and her publick to the admiration of all.

Her royall birth by her Fathers ſide doth comparatively make her Mother-deſcent ſeem low, which otherwiſe conſidered in it ſelf was very noble and honourable. As for the bundle of ſcandalous aſperſions by ſome caſt on her birth, they are beſt to be buried without once * opening of them. For as the baſeſt raſcall will preſume to miſcall the beſt Lord, when farre enough out of his hearing; ſo ſlanderous tongues think they may run riot in railing on any, when once got out of the diſtance of time, and reach of confutation.

** See theſe ſlanders plainly confuted in* **Anti-Sander.** *Dialog.* 2. *pag.* 125. *& deinceps.*

But Majeſty which dyeth not will not ſuffer it ſelf to be ſo abuſed, ſeeing the beſt aſſurance which living Princes have, that their memories ſhall be honourably continued, is founded (next to their own deſerts) in the maintaining of the unſtained reputation of their Predeceſſours. Yea divine Juſtice ſeems herein to be a compurgatour of the parents of Queen Elizabeth, in that Nicholas Sanders, a Popiſh Prieſt, the firſt raiſer of theſe wicked reports, was accidentally famiſhed as he roved up and down in Ireland; either becauſe it was juſt he ſhould be ſterved that formerly ſurfeted with lying, or becauſe that Iland out of a naturall antipathy againſt poyſonous creatures would not lend life to ſo venemous a ſlanderer.

Under the reigne of her Father, and Brother King Edward the ſixth, (who commonly called her his Siſter Temperance) ſhe lived in a Princely faſhion. But the caſe was altered with her when her Siſter Mary came to the Crown, who ever look'd upon her with a jealous eye and frowning face: chiefly, becauſe of the difference betwixt them in religion. For though Queen Mary is ſaid of her ſelf not ſo much as to have bark'd, yet ſhe had under her thoſe who did more then bite; and rather her religion then diſpoſition was guilty in countenancing their cruelty by her authority.

This antipathy againſt her Siſter Elizabeth was encreaſed with the remembrance how Katharine Dowager, Queen Maries Mother, was juſtled out of the bed of Henry the eighth by Anna Bullen, Mother to Queen Elizabeth : ſo that theſe two Siſters were born, as I may ſay, not onely in ſeverall but oppoſite horizons, ſo that the elevation and bright appearing of the one inferr'd the neceſſary obſcurity and depreſsion of the other; & ſtill Qu. Mary was troubled with this *fit of the Mother*, which incenſed her againſt this her half Siſter.

To which two grand cauſes of oppoſition, this third may alſo be added, becauſe not ſo generally known, though in it ſelf of leſſer conſequence. Queen Mary had releaſed Edward Courtney Earl of Devonſhire out of the Tower, where long he had been detained priſoner, a Gentleman of a beautifull body, ſweet nature, and royall deſcent, intending him, as it was generally conceived, to be an husband for her ſelf. For when the ſaid Earl petitioned the Queen for leave to travel ſhe adviſed him rather to marry, enſuring him that no Lady in the land, how high ſoever, would refuſe him for an husband ; and urging him to make his choyce where he pleaſed, ſhe pointed her ſelf out unto him as plainly as might ſtand with the modeſty of a maid, and Majeſty of a Queen. Hereupon the young Earl (whether becauſe that his long durance had ſome influence on his brain, or that naturally his face was better then his head, or out of ſome private phancie and affection to the Lady Elizabeth, or out of loyall baſhfulneſſe, not preſuming to climbe higher, but expecting to be call'd up) is ſaid to have requeſted the Queen for leave to marry her Siſter the Lady Elizabeth, unhappy that his choyce either went ſo high or no higher : For who could have ſpoken worſe Treaſon againſt Mary (though not againſt the Queen) then to preferre her Siſter before her? and ſhe, innocent Lady, did afterwards dearly pay the ſcore of this Earls indiſcretion.

For these reasons Lady Elizabeth was closely kept and narrowly sifted all her Sisters reigne, S[r] Bedenifield her keeper using more severity towards her then his place required, yea more then a good man should, or a wiseman would have done. No doubt the least tripping of her foot should have cost her the losing of her head, if they could have caught her to be privy to any conspiracies.

This Lady as well deserved the title of Elizabeth *the Confessour* as ever Edward her ancient predecessour did. M[r] Ascham was a good Schoolmaster to her, but affliction was a better, so that it is hard to say whether she was more happy in having a Crown so soon, or in having it no sooner, till affliction had first laid in her a low (and therefore sure) foundation of humility, for highnesse to be afterwards built thereupon.

We bring her now from the Crosse to the Crown; and come we now to describe the rare endowments of her mind, when behold her virtues almost stifle my pen, they crowd in so fast upon it.

She was an excellent Scholar, understanding the Greek, and perfectly speaking the Latine: witnesse her extempore speech in answer to the Polish Embassadour, and another at Cambridge, *Et si fœminilis iste meus pudor* (for so it began) elegantly making the word * *Fœminilis*: and well might she mint one new word, who did * refine so much new gold and silver. Good skill she had in the French, and Italian, using Interpreters not for need but state. She was a good Poet in English, and fluently made verses. In her time of persecution, when a Popish Priest pressed her very hardly to declare her opinion concerning the presence of Christ in the Sacrament, she truly and warily presented her judgement in these verses,

Twas God the word that spake it,
He took the bread and brake it;
And what the word did make it,
That I believe and take it.

* *See her oration at large in Holinshead, p. 1026.*

* Moneta ad suum valorem reducta *is part of the Epitaph on her Tombe.*

And though perchance ſome may ſay this was but the beſt of ſhifts, and the worſt of anſwers, becauſe the diſtinct manner of the Preſence muſt be believed; yet none can deny it to have been a wiſe return to an adverſary who lay at wait for all advantages. Nor was her Poetick vein leſſe happy in Latine. When a little before the Spaniſh Invaſion in eighty eight, the Spaniſh Embaſſadour (after a larger repreſentation of his Maſters demands) had ſummed up the effect thereof in a Tetraſtich, ſhe inſtantly in one verſe rejoined her anſwer. We will preſume to Engliſh both, though confeſsing the Latine loſeth luſtre by the Tranſlation.

Te veto ne pergas bello defendere Belgas:
Quæ Dracus eripuit nunc reſtituentur oportet:
Quas Pater evertit jubeo te condere cellas:
Relligio Papæ fac reſtituetur ad unguem.
These to you are our commands,
Send no help to th' Netherlands:
Of the treaſure took by Drake,
Reſtitution you muſt make:
And thoſe Abbies build anew,
Which your Father overthrew:
If for any peace you hope,
In all points reſtore the Pope.

The Queens extempore return,

Ad Græcas, bone Rex, fient mandata calendas.
Worthy King, know this your will
At latter lammas wee'l fulfill.

Her piety to God was exemplary, none more conſtant or devout in private prayers; very attentive alſo at Sermons, wherein ſhe was better affected with ſoundneſſe of matter, then queintneſſe of expreſsion: She could not well digeſt the affected over-elegancy of ſuch as prayed for her by the title of *defendreſſe of the faith* and not the *Defender*, it being no falſe conſtruction to apply a maſculine word to ſo heroick a ſpirit.

She was very devout in returning thanks to God for her

her constant and continuall preservations ; for one traitours stabbe was scarce put by, before another took aim at her: But as if the poysons of treason by custome were turn'd naturall unto her, by Gods protection they did her no harm. In any designe of consequence she loved to be long, and well advised ; but where her resolutions once seis'd, she would never let go her hold, according to her motto, *Semper eadem*.

By her Temperance she improved that stock of health which Nature bestowed on her, using little wine, and lesse Physick. Her Continence from pleasures was admirable, and she the Paragon of spotlesse chastity, what ever some Popish Priests (who count all virginity hid under a Nunnes veil) have feigned to the contrary. The best is, their words are no slander, whose words are all slander, so given to railing, that they must be dumbe if they do not blaspheme Magistrates. * One Jesuit made this false Anagram on her name,

Elizabeth.

* *Jezabel.*

false both in matter and manner. For allow it the abatement of H, (as all Anagrams must sue in Chancery for moderate favour) yet was it both unequall and ominous that T, a solid letter, should be omitted, the presage of the gallows whereon this Anagrammatist was afterwards justly executed.

* *Edmond Campian.*

* *Our English Bibles call her Jezabel.*

Yea let the testimony of Pope * Sixtus Quintus himself be believed, who professed that amongst all the Princes in Christendome he found but two which were worthy to bear command, had they not been stained with heresie, namely Henry the fourth, King of France, and Elizabeth Queen of England. And we may presume that the Pope, if commending his enemy, is therein infallible.

* *Thuan. Hist. lib.* 82.

We come to her death, the discourse whereof was more welcome to her from the mouth of her private Confessour, then from a publick Preacher ; and she loved rather to tell her ſelf, then to be told of her mortality, becauſe the open mention thereof made (as ſhe conceived) her ſubjects divide their loyalty betwixt the preſent and the future Prince. We need look into no other cauſe of her ſickneſſe then old age, being ſeventy years old (Davids age) to which no King of England ſince the Conqueſt did attain. Her weakneſſe was encreaſed by her removall from London to Richmond in a cold winter day, ſharp enough to pierce thorow thoſe who were arm'd with health and youth. Alſo melancholy (the worſt naturall Paraſite, whoſoever feeds him ſhall never be rid of his company) much afflicted her, being given over to ſadneſſe and ſilence.

Then prepared ſhe her ſelf for another world, being more conſtant in prayer, and pious exerciſes then ever before: yet ſpake ſhe very little to any, ſighing out more then ſhe ſaid, and making ſtill muſick to God in her heart. And as the red roſe, though outwardly not ſo fragrant, is inwardly farre more cordiall then the damask, being more thrifty of its ſweetneſſe, and reſerving it in it ſelf; ſo the religion of this dying Queen was moſt turn'd inward in ſoliloquies betwixt God and her own ſoul, though ſhe wanted not outward expreſsions thereof. When her ſpeech fail'd her, ſhe ſpake with her heart, tears, eyes, hands, and other ſignes, ſo commending herſelf to God the beſt interpreter, who underſtands what his Saints deſire to ſay. Thus dyed Queen Elizabeth, whileſt living, the firſt maid on earth, and when dead, the ſecond in heaven.

Surely the kingdome had dyed with their Queen, had not the fainting ſpirits thereof been refreſh'd by the coming in of gratious King James.

She was of perſon, tall; of hair and complexion, fair, well-favoured, but high-noſed; of limbes and feature, neat; of a ſtately and majeſtick deportment.

She

She had a piercing eye wherewith ſhe uſed to touch what metall ſtrangers were made of, which came into her preſence. But as ſhe counted it a pleaſant. conqueſt with her Majeſtick look to daſh ſtrangers out of countenance, ſo ſhe was mercifull in purſuing thoſe whom ſhe overcame, and afterwards would cheriſh and comfort them with her ſmiles, if perceiving towardlineſſe, and an ingenuous modeſty in them. She much affected rich and coſtly apparell; and if ever jewells had juſt cauſe to be proud, it was with her wearing them.

Chap. 16.

The Embaſſadour.

HE is one that repreſents his King in a forrein countrey (as a Deputy doth in his own Dominions) under the aſſurance of the publick faith, authorized by the Law of Nations. He is either Extraordinary for ſome one affair with time limited, or Ordinary for generall matters during his Princes pleaſure, commonly called a Legier.

He is born, made, or at leaſtwiſe qualified honourably, both for the honour of the ſender, and him to whom he is ſent; eſpecially if the ſolemnity of the action wherein he is employed conſiſteth in ceremony and magnificence. Lewis the eleventh King of France is ſufficiently condemn'd by Poſterity for ſending Oliver his Barber in an Embaſſage to a Princeſſe, who ſo trimly diſpatch'd his buſineſſe, that he left it in the ſuddes, and had been well waſh'd in the river * at Gant for his pains, if his feet had not been the more nimble. *Maxime* 1

* *Comin. lib.* 5. *cap.* 14.

2 *He is of a proper, at leaſt paſſable perſon.* Otherwiſe if he be of a contemptible preſence, he is abſent whileſt he is preſent; eſpecially if employed in love-buſineſſes to advance a marriage. Ladyes will diſlike the body for a deformed ſhadow. The jeſt is well known: When the

* *Some say they sent three, and one of them a fool, and that Cato should say they sent an Embassy without head, heart, or feet. See Plutarchs Lives.*

the State of Rome sent* two Embassadours, the one having scarres on his head, the other lame in his feet, *Mittit populus Romanus legationem quæ nec caput habet, nec pedes*, The people of Rome send an Embassy without head or feet.

3 *He hath a competent estate whereby to maintain his port*: for a great poverty is ever suspected; and he that hath a breach in his estate lies open to be assaulted with bribes. Wherefore his means ought at least to be sufficient both to defray set and constant charges, as also to make sallies and excursions of expenses on extraordinary occasions, which we may call Supererogations of State. Otherwise if he be indigent and succeed a bountifull Predecessour, he will seem a fallow field after a plentifull crop.

4 *He is a passable scholar, well travell'd in Countreys and Histories*; well studyed in the Pleas of the Crown, I mean not such as are at home, betwixt his Sovereigne and his subjects, but abroad betwixt his and forrein Princes; to this end he is well skill'd in the Emperiall Laws. Common Law it self is outlawed beyond the seas; which though a most true, is too short a measure of right, and reacheth not forrein kingdomes.

5 *He well understandeth the language of that countrey to which he is sent*; and yet he desires rather to seem ignorant of it (if such a simulation which stands neuter betwixt a Truth and a Lie be lawfull) and that for these reasons: first, because though he can speak it never so exactly, his eloquence therein will be but stammering, compar'd to the ordinary talk of the Natives: secondly, hereby he shall in a manner stand invisible, and view others; and as Josephs deafnesse heard all the dialogues betwixt his brethren, so his not owning to understand the language, shall expose their talk the more open unto him: thirdly, he shall have the more advantage to speak and negotiate in his own language, at the least wise, if he cannot make them come over to him, he may

may meet them in the midway, in the Latine, a ſpeech common to all learned Nations.

6 *He gets his Commiſſion and inſtructions well ratified and confirm'd before he ſets forth.* Otherwiſe it is the worſt priſon to be commiſſion-bound. And ſeeing he muſt not jet out the leaſt penthouſe beyond his foundation, he had beſt well ſurvey the extent of his authority.

7 *He furniſheth himſelf with fit Officers in his family.* Eſpecially he is carefull in chooſing

1 A Secretary, honeſt and able, carefull to conceal counſels, and not ſuch a one as will let drop out of his mouth whatſoever is poured in at his eare: Yea the head of every Embaſſadour ſleeps on the breaſt of his Secretary.

2 A Steward, wiſe and provident, ſuch as can temper magnificence with moderation, judiciouſly faſhioning his ordinary expences with his Maſters eſtate, reſerving a ſpare for all events and accidentall occaſions, and making all things to paſſe with decency, without any rudeneſſe, noiſe, or diſorder.

8 *He ſeaſonably preſents his Embaſſage, and demands audience.* Such is the freſh nature of ſome Embaſſages, if not ſpent preſently, they ſent ill. Thus it is ridiculous to condole griefs almoſt forgotten, for (beſides that with a cruell courteſie it makes their ſorrows bleed afreſh) it fooliſhly ſeems to teach one to take that, which he hath formerly digeſted. When ſome Trojane Embaſſadours came to comfort Tiberius Ceſar for the loſſe of his ſonne, dead well nigh a twelvemoneth before; *And I* (ſaid the Emperour) *am very ſorry for your grief for the death of your Hector, ſlain by Achilles a thouſand years ſince.* *Suetonius in Tiberio.*

9 *Coming to have audience, he applyeth himſelf onely to the Prince to whom he is ſent.* When Chancellour Morvill, Embaſſadour from the French King, delivering his meſſage to Philip Duke of Burgundy was interrupted

* Comin. lib. 1.

by Charles the Dukes * ſonne, *I am ſent* (ſaid he) *not to treat with you, but with your father.* And our M[r] Wade is highly commended that being ſent by Queen Elizabeth to Philip King of Spain, he would not be turned * over to the Spaniſh Privy Counſel (whoſe greateſt Grandees were dwarfs in honour to his Queen) but would either have audience from the King himſelf, or would return without it. And yet afterwards our Embaſſadour knows (if deſirous that his buſineſſe ſhould take effect) how, and when to make his ſecret and underhand addreſſes to ſuch potent Favourites as ſtrike the ſtroke in the State; it often hapning in Commonwealths, that the Maſters mate ſteers the ſhip thereof, more then the Maſter himſelf.

* Cambd. Eliz. in Anno 1584. pag. 380.

10 *In delivering his meſſage he complies with the garb and guiſe of the countrey*; either longer, briefer, more plain, or more flouriſhing, as it is moſt acceptable to ſuch to whom he directs his ſpeech. The Italians (whoſe countrey is called *the countrey of good words*) love the circuits of courteſie, that an Embaſſadour ſhould not as a ſparrow-hawk flie outright to his prey, and meddle preſently with the matter in hand, but with the noble falcon mount in language, ſoar high, fetch compaſſes of complement, and then in due time ſtoop to game, and ſeiſe on the buſineſſe propounded. Clean contrary the Switzers (who ſent word to the King of France, not to ſend them an Embaſſadour with ſtore of words, but a Treaſurer with plenty of money) count all words quite out, which are not ſtraight on, have an antipathy againſt eloquent language; the flowers of Rhetorick being as offenſive to them, as ſweet perfumes to ſuch as are troubled with the Mother. Yea generally great ſouldiers have their ſtomachs ſharp ſet to feed on the matter, lothing long ſpeeches, as wherein they conceive themſelves to loſe time, in which they could conquer half a countrey, and, counting bluntneſſe their beſt eloquence, love to be accoſted in their own kind.

He

He commands himself not to admire any thing presented unto him. He looks, but not gazeth, on forrein magnificence (as countrey clowns on a city) beholding them with a familiar eye, as challenging old acquaintance having known them long before. If he be surprised with a sudden wonder, he so orders it, that though his soul within feels an admiration, none can perceive it without in his countenance. For 11

1 It is inconsistent with the steddinesse of his gravity to be startled with a wonder.

2 Admiration is the daughter of ignorance: whereas he ought to be so read in the world as to be posed with no rarity.

3 It is a tacit confession (if he wonders at State, Strength, or Wealth) that herein his own Masters kingdome is farre surpass'd. And yet he will not slight and neglect such worthy sights as he beholds, which would savour to much of sullennesse and self-addiction, things ill beseeming his noble spirit.

He is zealous of the least puntillo's of his Masters honour. Herein 'tis most true, the Law of honour *servanda in apicibus* : Yea a toy may be reall, and a point may be essentiall to the sense of some sentences, and worse to be spared then some whole letter. Great Kings wrestle together by the strength and nimblenesse of their Embassadours; wherefore Embassadours are carefull to afford no advantages to the adverse party: and mutually no more hold is given, then what is gotten, lest the fault of the Embassadour be drawn into president to the prejudice of his Master. He that abroad will lose an hair of his Kings honour deserves to lose his own head when he comes home. 12

He appears not violent in desiring any thing he would effect; but with a seeming carelesnesse most carefully advanceth his Masters businesse. If employed to conclude a Peace, he represents his Master as indifferent therein 13

 for

for his own part, but that desiring to spare Christian bloud, preponderates him for Peace, whose conscience, not purse or arms are weary of the warre: He entreats not, but treats for an accord, for their mutuall good. But if the Embassadour declareth himself zealous for it, perchance he may be forced to buy those conditions, which otherwise would be given him.

14 *He is constantly and certainly inform'd of all passages in his own Countrey.* What a shame is it for him to be a stranger to his native affairs? Besides, if gulls and rumours from his Countrey be raised on purpose to amuse our Embassadour, he rather smiles then starts at these false vizards, who by private instructions from home knows the true face of his Countrey-estate. And lest his Masters Secretary should fail him herein, he counts it thrift to cast away some pounds yearly to some private friend in the Court to send him true information of all home-remarkables.

15 *He carefully returns good intelligence to his Master that employeth him.*

1. Speedy. Not being such a sluggard as to write for news at noon, That the Sunne is risen.
2. True; so farre forth as may be: else he stamps it with a mark of uncertainty or suspicion.
3. Full: not filling the paper, but informing those to whom it is written.
4. Materiall: not grinding his advises too small, to frivolous particulars of love-toyes, and private brawls, as * one layeth it to the charge of Francis Guicciardines Historie, *Minutissima quæque narrat, parum ex lege aut dignitate Historiæ.* And yet such particulars which are too mean to be served up to the Counsel-Table, may make a feast for Ladies, or other his friends; and therefore to such our Embassadour relates them by his private letters.

* *Lipsius in the end of his Politicks, in his censure of Historians.*

5. Methodi-

5. Methodicall: not running on all in a continued ſtrain, but ſtopping at the ſtages of different buſineſſes to breath himſelf and the Reader, and to take and begin a new ſentence.

6. Well-penned, clear and plain, not hunting after language, but teaching words their diſtance to wait on his matter, intermingling ſententious ſpeeches ſparingly, leſt ſeeming affected. And if conſtrained twice to write the ſame matter, ſtill he varieth his words, leſt he may ſeem to write like Notaries by preſidents.

He will not have his houſe ſerve as a retreating-place for people ſuſpected and odious, in that State wherein he is employed. Much leſſe ſhall his houſe be a Sanctuary for Offenders, ſeeing the very horns of Gods Altar did puſh away from them ſuch notorious Malefactours as did flie unto them for protection. 16

He is cautious not to practice any treacherous act againſt the Prince under whom he lives: leſt the Shield of his Embaſſy prove too ſmall to defend him from the Sword of Juſtice, ſeeing that for ſuch an offenſe an Embaſſadour is reſolved into a private man, and may worthily be puniſhed, as in the caſes of Bernardinus Mendoza and the Biſhop of * Roſſe. Yea he will not ſo much as break forth publickly into any diſcourſe which he knows will be diſtaſtfull in that Countrey wherein he is employed. Learned Bodin, who ſome ſeventy years ſince waited on Monſieur into England, was here, though highly admired for his learning, condemned much for his indiſcretion, if his *corrivals pen may be credited. For being feaſted at an Engliſh Lords table, he fell into the odious diſcourſe, That a Princeſſe, meaning Mary Queen of Scots, was after Queen Elizabeth the preſumptive Inheritrix of the Engliſh Crown, notwithſtanding an Engliſh Law ſeemed to exclude thoſe which are born out of the land; *And yet*, ſaid he, *I know not where this Law is, for all* 17

* *See his caſe largely diſcuſſed in Cambd. Elizab. by the beſt Civilians, Anno* 1571.

* *Franciſc. Hottoman in his Treatiſe of an Embaſſ. fol.*42.

the diligence that I have used to find it out: To whom it was suddenly replyed by the Lord that entertain'd him, *You shall find it written on the backside of your Salick Law*: a judicious and biting rebound.

18 *He is carefull of suspicious complying with that Prince to whom he is sent*: as to receive from him any extraordinary gifts, much lesse pensions, which carry with them more then an appearance of evil. Sr * Amias Paulet was so scrupulous herein, that being Embassadour in France in the dayes of Queen Elizabeth he would not at his departure receive from the French King the chain of gold (wich is given of course) till he was half a league out of the city of Paris.

* *Idem. fol.* 23, 24.

19 *If he hath any* libera mandata, *unlimited instructions, herein his discretion is most admirable.*

But what go I about to do? hereof enough already, if not too much: it better complying with my profession to practice S. Pauls precept to mine own parishioners, * *Now then we are Embassadours for Christ, as though God did beseech you by us, we pray you in Christs stead, be reconciled to God.*

* 2. *Cor.* 5. 20.

Chap. 17.

The good Generall.

THe Souldier, whom we formerly described, hath since by the stairs of his own deserts climb'd up to be a Generall, and now we come, to character him.

Maxime 1 *He is pious in the ordering of his own life.* Some falsely conceive that Religion spoyleth the spirit of a Generall, as bad as a rainy day doth his plume of feathers, making it droop, and hang down; whereas indeed Piety onely begets true Prowesse.

2 *He acknowledgeth God the Generalissimo of all armies*; who in all battels, though the number be never so unequall,

quall, reſerves the caſting voice for himſelf. Yet can I ſcarce believe what * one tells us, how Walter Pletemberg, Maſter of the Teutonick order, with a ſmall number ſlew in a battel an hundred thouſand Muſcovite enemies with the loſſe of but one man on his ſide.

* *Tilman Bredenbach de bello Livon. & Fitz Herbert of Policy & Religion, part.* 1. *cap.* 14.

He hath gained skill in his place by long experience : not beginning to lead others before himſelf ever knew to follow, having never before (except in Cock-matches) beheld any battels. Surely they leap beſt in their providence forward, who fetch their riſe fartheſt backward in their experience. 3

He either is, or is preſumed valiant. Indeed courage in him is neceſſary, though ſome think that a Generall is above valour, who may command others to be ſo. As if it were all one whether courage were his naturally, or by adoption, who can make the valiant deeds of others ſeem his own ; and his reputation for perſonall manhood once raiſ'd, will bear it ſelf up; like a round body, ſome force is required to ſet it, but a touch will keep it agoing. Indeed it is extreme indiſcretion (except in extremities) for him to be prodigall of his perſon. 4

He is cheerfull and willing in undergoing of labour. Admirable are the miracles of an induſtrious armie, witneſſe the mighty ditch in Cambridge-ſhire made by the Eaſt-Angles, commonly call'd *Devils-ditch*, as if the Pioners thereof came from hell. Thus the effeminateneſſe of our age, defaming what it ſhould imitate, falſely traduces the monuments of their Anceſtours endeavours. 5

He loves, and is beloved of his ſouldiers. Whoſe good will he attaineth, 6

1. By giving them good words in his ſpeeches unto them. When wages have ſometimes accidentally fallen ſhort, ſouldiers have accepted the payment in the fair language and promiſes of their Generall.

2. By

2. By partaking with his ſouldiers in their painfull employments. When the Engliſh, at the Spaniſh Fleets approch in eightie eight, drew their ſhips out of Plimouth haven, the Lord Admirall Howard himſelf* towed a cable, the leaſt joynt of whoſe exemplarie hand drew more then twentie men beſides.

* *Cambden. Elizab. Anno* 1588.

3. By ſharing with them in their wants. When victuals have grown ſcant, ſome Generalls have pinched themſelves to the ſame fare with their ſouldiers, who could not complain that their meſſe was bad, whileſt their Generall was Fellow-commoner with them.

4. By taking notice, and rewarding of their deſerts; never disinheriting a worthy ſouldier of his birthright, of the next Office due unto him. For a worthy man is wounded more deeply by his own Generalls neglect, then by his enemies ſword: The latter may kill him, but the former deads his courage, or, which is worſe, mads it into diſcontent; Who had rather others ſhould make a ladder of his dead corps to ſcale a city by it, then a bridge of him whileſt alive for his punies to give him the *Goe-by*, and paſſe over him to preferment. For this reaſon chiefly (beſide ſome others) a great and valiant Engliſh Generall in the daies of Queen Elizabeth was hated of his ſouldiers, becauſe he diſpoſed Offices by his own abſolute will, without reſpect of orderly advancing ſuch as deſerved it, which made a Great man once ſalute him with this letter: *S^r, if you will be pleaſed to beſtow a Captains place on the bearer hereof, being a worthy Gentleman, he ſhall do that for you which never as yet any ſouldier did, namely pray to God for your health and happineſſe.*

7 *He is fortunate in what he undertakes.* Such a one was Julius Ceſar, who in * Brittain, a countrey undiſcovered,

* *Ceſar. Comment. lib.* 4.

vered, peopled with a valiant Nation, began a warre in Autumne, without apparent advantage, not having any intelligence there, being to passe over the sea into a colder climate (an enterprise, saith * one, well worthy the invincible courage of Cesar, but not of his accustomed prudence) and yet returned victorious. Indeed God is the sole disposer of successe: Other gifts he also scattereth amongst men, yet so that they themselves scramble to gather them up; whereas successe God gives immediately into their hands, on whom he pleaseth to bestow it.

The Duke of Rohan in the complete Captain, pag. 19.

He tryeth the forces of a new enemy before he encounters him. Sampson is half conquered, when it is known where his strength lies; and skirmishes are scouts for the discovery of the strength of an army, before battel be given. 8

He makes his flying enemy a bridge of gold, and disarms them of their best weapon, which is necessity to fight whether they will or no. Men forced to a battel against their intention often conquer beyond their expectation: stop a flying coward, and he will turn his legges into arms, and lay about him manfully; whereas open him a passage to escape, and he will quickly shut up his courage. 9

But I dare dwell no longer on this subject. When the Pope earnestly wrote to King Richard the first, not to detain in prison *his dear sonne*, the Martiall Bishop of Beavois, the King sent the Pope back the armour wherein the Bishop was taken, with the words of Jacobs sonnes to their Father, *See whether or no this be the coat of thy sonne.* Surely a corslet is no canonicall coat for me, nor suits it with my Clergy-profession to proceed any further in this warlike description; onely we come to give an example thereof.

GUSTAVUS Adolphus *the pious and Valiant* King *of* Sweden. *He was slaine in the Battell at* Lutzen *the 16 of November 1632. Aged 38 yeares*

W.M. sculp:

CHAP. 18.

The life of GUSTAVUS ADOLPHUS *King of Sweden.*

GUstavus Adolphus King of Sweden, born *Anno Domini* 1594 had princely education both for Arts and Armes. In Italie he learnt the Mathematicks, and in other places abroad, the French, Italian, and Germane tongues, and after he was King, he travelled under the name of Mr *G. A. R. S. being the foure initiall letters of his name, and title.

* *Gustævus Adolph. Rex Suecorum Dr. Wats in charact. ad finem 3. part. p.183.*

He

He was but ſeventeen years old at his Fathers death, being left not onely a young King, but alſo in a young kingdome; for his title to the Crown of Sweden was but five years old, to wit ſince the beginning of his Fathers reigne. All his bordering Princes (on the North nothing but the North bounded on him) were his enemies; the Duke-Emperour of Muſcovy on the Eaſt, the King of Denmark on the Weſt, and of Poland on the South: The former two laid claim to parcels, the latter, to all his kingdome. Yet was he too great for them in his minority, both defending his own, and gaining on them. *Wo be to the kingdome whoſe King is a child*, yet bleſſed is that kingdome whoſe King, though a child in age, is a man in worth.

Theſe his firſt actions had much of glory, and yet ſomewhat of poſsibility and credit in them. But Chronicle and belief muſt ſtrain hard to make his Germane Conqueſt probable with poſterity; coming in with eleven thouſand men, having no certain confederates, but ſome of his alliance, whom the Emperour had outed of all their eſtates: And yet in two years and foure moneths he left the Emperour in as bad a caſe almoſt, as he found thoſe Princes in.

Gods Providence herein is chiefly to be admired, who to open him a free entrance into Germany, diverted the Imperiall and Spaniſh forces into Italy, there to ſcramble againſt the French for the Dukedome of Mantua. For heaven onely knows how much Proteſtant fleſh the Imperialiſts had devoured, if that bone had not ſtuck in their teeth.

If we look on ſecond cauſes, we may aſcribe his victories to this Kings piety, wiſedome, valour, and other virtues. His piety to God was exemplary, being more addicted to prayer then to fight, as if he would rather conquer Heaven then Earth. He was himſelf exceeding temperate, ſave onely too much given to anger, but afterwards he would correct himſelf, and be cholerick with his choler, ſhewing himſelf a man in the one, and a Saint in the other.

He was a ſtrict obſerver of Martiall diſcipline, the life of Warre, without which an Army is but a crowd (not to ſay herd) of people. He would march all day in complete armour, which was by cuſtome no more burthen to him then his armes, and to carry his helmet, no more trouble then his head; whileſt his example made the ſame eaſie to all his ſouldiers. He was a ſtrict puniſher of miſdemeanours and wanton intemperance in his camp: And yet let me relate this ſtory from one preſent therein.

When firſt he entred Germany, he perceived how that many women followed his ſouldiers, ſome being their wives, and ſome wanting nothing to make them ſo but marriage, yet moſt paſsing for their landreſſes, though commonly defiling more then they waſh. The King coming to a great river, after his men and the wagons were paſſed over, cauſed the bridge to be broken down, hoping ſo to be rid of theſe feminine impediments; but they one a ſudden lift up a panick ſchrick which pierced the skies, and the ſouldiers hearts on the other ſide of the river, who inſtantly vowed not to ſtirre a foot farther, except with baggage, and that the women might be fetch'd over, which was done accordingly. For the King finding this ill humour ſo generally diſperſ'd in his men, that it was dangerous to purge it all at once, ſmiled out his anger for the preſent, and permitted what he could not amend: yet this abuſe was afterwards reformed by degrees.

He was very mercifull to any that would ſubmit. And as the iron gate miraculouſly opened to S. Peter of its own accord, ſo his mercy wrought miracles, making many city-gates open to him of themſelves, before he ever knock'd at them to demand entrance, the inhabitants deſiring to ſhroud themſelves under his protection. Yea he was mercifull to thoſe places which he took by assault, ever detesting the bloudinesse of Tilly at Magdenburg, under the ashes whereof he buried his honour, coming valiant thither, and departing cruell thence. In such cases he was mercifull to women (not like those Generalls who know the differences of Sex in their lust, but not in their anger) yea the very Jesuites themselves tasted of his courtesie, though merrily he laid to their charge, that they would neither *Preach faith* to, nor *keep faith* with others.

He had the true art (almost lost) of Encamping, where he would lie in his Trenches in despight of all enemies, keeping the clock of his own time, and would fight for no mans pleasure but his own. No seeming flight or disorder of his enemies should cousen him into a battel, nor their daring bravado's anger him into it, nor any violence force him to fight, till he thought fitting himself, counting it good manners in Warre to take all, but give no advantages.

It was said of his Armies, that they used to rise when the swallows went to bed, when winter began, his forces most consisting of Northern Nations, and *a Swede fights best when he can see his own breath.* He alwayes kept a long vacation in the dog-dayes, being onely a saver in the summer, and a gainer all the yeare besides. His best harvest was in the snow; and his souldiers had most life in the dead of winter.

He made but a short cut in taking of cities, many of whose fortifications were a wonder to behold; but what were they then to assault and conquer? at scaling of walls he was excellent for contriving, as his souldiers in executing: it seeming a wonder that their bodies should be made of aire, so light to climbe, whose armes were of iron, so heavy to strike. Such cities as would not presently open unto him, he shut them up, and having businesse of more importance then to imprison himself about one strength, he would consigne the besieging thereof to some other Captain. And indeed he wanted not his Joabs, who when they had reduced cities to terms of yielding knew (with as much wisdome as loyalty) to entitle their David to the whole honour of the action.

He was highly beloved of his souldiers, of whose deserts he kept a faithfull Chronicle in his heart, and advanced them accordingly. All valiant men were Swedes to him; and he differenced men in his esteem by their merits not their countrey.

To come to his death, wherein his reputation suffers in the judgements of some, for too much hazarding of his own person in the battel. But surely some conceived necessity thereof urged him thereunto. For this his third grand set battel in Germany, was the third and last asking of his banes to the Imperiall Crown; and had they not been forbidden by his death, his marriage in all probability had instantly followed. Besides, * *Never Prince hath founded great Empire, but by making warre in person, nor hath lost any, but when he made warre by his lieutenants*: which made this King the more adventurous.

* *Duke of Rohan, in his compleate Captain cap. 22.*

His death is still left in uncertainty, whether the valour of open enemies, or treachery of false friends caused it. His side *won the day*, and yet *lost the sunne* that made it; and as one saith,

Upon this place the great Gustavus dy'd,
Whilest victory lay bleeding by his side.

Thus the readiest way to lose a jewell is to overprise it: for indeed many men so doted on this worthy Prince, and his victories (without any default of his, who gave God the glory) that his death in some sort seemed necessary to vindicate Gods honour, who usually maketh that prop of flesh to break whereon men lay too great weight of their expectation.

After his death, how did men struggle to keep him alive in their reports? partly out of good will, which made

made them kindle new hopes of his life at every ſpark of probability, partly out of infidelity that his death could be true. First they thought ſo valiant a Prince could not live on earth; and when they ſaw his life, then they thought ſo valiant a Prince could never die, but that his death was rather a concealment for a time, dayly expecting when the politickly dead ſhould have a Reſurrection in ſome noble exploit.

I find a moſt * learned pen applying theſe Latine verſes to this noble Prince, and it is honour enough for us to tranſlate them:

In Templo plus quam Sacerdos.
In Republica plus quam Rex.
In ſententia dicenda plus quam Senator.
In Judicio plus quam Juriſconſultus.
In Exercitu plus quam Imperator.
In Acie plus quam Miles.
In adverſis perferendis injuriiſque condonandis plus quam vir.
In publica libertate tuenda plus quam Civis.
In Amicitia colenda plus quam Amicus.
In convictu plus quam familiaris.
In venatione feriſque domandis plus quam Leo.
In tota reliqua vita plus quam Philoſophus.

More then a Prieſt he in the Church might paſſe.
More then a Prince in Commonwealth he was.
More then a Counſeller in points of State.
More then a Lawyer matters to debate.
More then a Generall to command outright.
More then a Souldier to perform a fight.
More then a man to bear affliction ſtrong.
More then a man good to forgive a wrong.
More then a Patriot countrey to defend.
True friendſhip to maintain, more then a Friend.
More then familiar ſweetly to converſe.
And though in ſports more then a Lion fierce,
To hunt and kill the game; yet he expreſt
More then Philoſopher in all the reſt.

* Dr. *Hakewill in his Apologie for divine Providence, lib. 4. cap. 11. p. 546.*

The

*Descript. Bell. Suecici, per Aut. Anonymum, pag. 186.

The Jesuites made him to be the* Antichrist, and allowed him three years and an half of reigne and conquest: But had he lived that full term out, the true Antichrist might have heard further from him, and Romes Tragedy might have had an end, whose fift and last Act is still behind. Yet one* Jesuite, more ingenuous then the rest, gives him this testimony, that, *save the badnesse of his cause and religion, he had nothing defective in him which belonged to an excellent King, and a good Captain.*

* Silvester Petra Sancta in his book against Du Moulin.

Thus let this our poore description of this King serve like a flat grave-stone or plain pavement for the present; till the richer pen of some Grotius or Heinsius shall provide to erect some statelyer Monument unto his Memory.

Chap. 19.

The Prince or Heir apparent to the Crown.

HE is the best pawn of the future felicity of a kingdome. His Fathers Subjects conceive they take a further estate of happinesse in the hopes of his Succession.

Maxime 1

In his infancy he gives presages of his future worth. Some first-fruits are dispatch'd before, to bring news to the world of the harvest of virtues which are ripening in him: his own Royall spirit prompts him to some speeches and actions wherein the standers by will scarce believe their own eares and eyes, that such things can proceed from him: And yet no wonder if they have light the soonest, who live nearest the East, seeing Princes have the advantage of the best birth and breeding. The Gregorian account goes ten dayes before the computation of the English calendar: but the capacity of Princes goes as many years before private mens of the same age.

Antevenit ſortem meritis, virtutibus, annos.
His worth above his wealth appears,
And virtues go beyond his years.

He is neither kept too long from the knowledge, nor brought too ſoon to the acquaintance with his own Greatneſſe. To be kept too long in diſtance from himſelf, would breed in him a ſoul too narrow for his place: On the other ſide, he needs not to be taught his Greatneſſe too ſoon, who will meet with it everywhere. The beſt of all is when his Governours open him to himſelf by degrees, that his ſoul may ſpread according to his age. 2

He playeth himſelf into Learning before he is aware of it. Herein much is to be aſcribed to the wiſdome of his Teachers, who alwayes preſent Learning unto him (as Angels are painted) ſmiling, and candy over his soureſt ſtudies with pleaſure and delight, obſerving ſeaſonable time, and fit method. Not like many countrey Schoolmaſters, who in their inſtructions ſpill more then they fill, by their overhaſty pouring of it in. 3

He ſympathizeth with him that by a Proxie is corrected for his offenſe: yea ſometimes goeth further, and (above his age) conſidereth, that it is but an Embleme, how hereafter his people may be puniſhed for his own fault. He hath read how the Iſraelites, the ſecond of Sam. 24. 17. were plagued for Davids numbring of them. And yet withall he remembreth how in the firſt verſe of the ſame chapter, *The wrath of the Lord was kindled againſt Iſrael, and he* (by permitting of Satan the inſtrument 1. Chron. 21. 1.) *moved David to number them.* And as the ſtomach and vitall parts of a man are often corroded with a rheume falling from the head, yet ſo that the diſaffection of the ſtomach firſt cauſed the breeding of the ſame offenſive diſtillation; ſo our young Prince takes notice of a reciprocation of faults and puniſhments betwixt King and Kingdome (both making up the ſame body) yea that ſometimes the 4

King is corrected for the peoples offenses, and so *è contra*: Indeed in Relatives neither can be well, if both be not.

5 *He is most carefull in reading, and attentive in hearing Gods word.* King Edward the sixth (who, though a Soveraigne, might still in age passe for a Prince) accurately noted the dayes, Texts, and names of Ministers, that preached before him. Next to Gods word, our Prince studies *Basilicon Doron*, that Royall gift, which onely King James was able to give, and onely King James his sonne worthy to receive.

6 *He is carefull in chusing and using his recreations*, refusing such which in their very posture and situation are too low for a Prince. In all his exercises he affects comlinesse, or rather a kind of carelesnesse in shew, to make his activities seem the more naturall, & avoids a toyling and laborious industry, especially seeing each drop of a Princes sweat is a pearl, and not to be thrown away for no cause. And Princes are not to reach, but to trample on recreations, making them their footstool to heighten their souls for seriousnesse, taking them in passage thereunto.

7 *His clothes are such as may beseem his Greatnesse*: especially when he solemnly appears, or presents himself to forrein Embassadours. Yet he disdains not to be plain at ordinary times. The late *Henrie, Prince of Wales, being tax'd by some for his too long wearing of a plain sute of Welch frize; *Would* (said he) *my countrey cloth would last for ever.*

* *S*[r]. *Fr. Netherſol, in the fun. orat. of him, pag.* 16.

8 *He begins to study his own countrey, and the people therein*: what places are, what may be fortified; which can withstand a long siege, and which onely can make head against a present insurrection. If his land accosteth the sea, he considereth what Havens therein are barr'd, whose dangerous chanells fence themselves, and their rocks are their blockhouses; what Keys are rusty with sands and shelves, and what are

ſcoured with a free and open tide, with what ſerviceable ſhips belong thereunto. He takes notice alſo of the men in the land, and diſdains his ſoul ſhould be blurred with unjuſt prejudices, but fairly therein writes every one in order, as they are ranked by their own deſerts.

Hence he looks abroad to ſee how his countrey ſtands in relation 9
to forrein Kingdomes; how it is friended with Confederates, how oppoſ'd with Enemies. His little eyes can caſt a ſoure glance on the ſuſpicious greatneſſe of any near borderer; for he conceives others weakned by their own diſtance. He conſiders forrein Kingdomes, and States, whether they ſtand on their own ſtrength, or lean on the favour of friends, or onely hang by a Politicall Geometry, equally poyſing themſelves betwixt their neighbours, like Lucca and Geneva, the multitude of enemies mouthes keeping them from being ſwallowed up. He quickly perceives that Kings, how nearly ſoever allied, are moſt of kinne to their own intereſt; and though the ſame Religion be the beſt bond of forrein affection, yet even this breaks too often: and States when wonded, will cure themſelves with a plaiſter made of the heart-blood of their beſt friends.

He tunes his ſoul in conſort to the diſpoſition of his King-fa- 10
ther. Whatſoever his deſire be, the leaſt word, countenance, or ſigne given, of his fathers diſallowance makes him inſtantly deſiſt from further purſuit thereof with ſatisfaction, in regard he underſtands it diſagreeing to his Majeſties pleaſure, and with a reſolution not to have the leaſt ſemblance of being diſcontented: He hath read how ſuch Princes which were undutifull to their Parents either had no children, or children worſe then none, which repai'd their diſobedience. He is alſo kind to his Brothers, and Siſters, whoſe love and affection he counteth the bulwarks and redouts for his own ſafety and ſecurity.

11 *When grown to keep a Court by himſelf, he is carefull in well ordering it.* The foreſaid Prince Henries Court conſiſted of few leſſe then five hundred perſons, and yet his grave and Princely aſpect gave temper to them all, ſo that in ſo numerous a familie, not ſo much as any * blows were given.

** Sr. William Cornwallis in the life of Prince Henry.*

12 *With a frowning countenance he bruſheth off from his ſoul all Court-mothes of flattery*: eſpecially he is deaf to ſuch as would adviſe him, without any, or any juſt grounds, when he comes to the Crown, to runne counter to the practice of his Father; and who knowing that muddy water makes the ſtrongeſt beere, may conceive the troubling and embroyling of the State will be moſt advantagious for their active ſpirits. Indeed ſeldome two ſucceſsive Kings tread in the ſame path: if the former be Martiall, though the warre be juſt, honourable, and profitable, yet ſome will quarrell with the time preſent, not becauſe *it is bad*, but becauſe *it is*, and put a Prince forward to an alteration. If the former King were peaceable, yet happineſſe it ſelf is unhappy in being too common, and many will deſire warre (conceited ſweet to every palate which never taſted it) and urge a Prince thereunto. But our Prince knows to eſtimate things by their true worth and value, and will not take them upon the credit, whereon others preſent them unto him.

'Ἀεὶ τὸ παρὸν βαρύ.

13 *He conceives they will be moſt loving to the branch, which were moſt loyall to the root*, and moſt honour'd his father. We reade how Henry the fifth (as yet Prince of Wales) intending to bear out one of his ſervants for a miſdemeanour, reviled S[r] William Gaſcoine Lord chief Juſtice of the Kings Bench to his face in open court. The aged Judge conſidered how this his action would beget an immortall example, and the echo of his words (if unpuniſhed) would be reſounded for ever to the diſgrace of Majeſty, which is never more on its throne, then when either in perſon, or in his ſubſtitutes, ſitting

on the bench of Juſtice; and thereupon commanded the Prince to the priſon, till he had given ſatisfaction to his father for the affront offered. Inſtantly down fell the heart of great Prince Henry, which (though as hard as rock) the breath of Juſtice did eaſily ſhake, being firſt undermin'd with an apprehenſion of his own guiltineſſe: And King Henry the fourth his father is reported greatly to rejoyce, that he had a Judge who knew how to command by, and a Sonne who knew how to ſubmit to his Laws. And afterward this Prince when King (firſt conquering himſelf, and afterwards the French) reduced his Court from being a forreſt of wild trees, to be an orchard of ſweet fruit, baniſhing away his bad companions, and appointing and countenancing thoſe to keep the key of his honour, who had lock'd up his fathers moſt faithfully.

He ſhews himſelf to the people on fit occaſions. It is hard to ſay whether he ſees or is ſeen with more love and delight. Every one that brings an eye to gaze on him, brings alſo an heart to pray for him. But his ſubjects in reverſion moſt rejoyce to ſee him in his military exerciſes, wiſhing him as much skill to know them, as little need to uſe them, ſeeing peace is as farre to be preferred before victory it ſelf, as the end is better then the means. 14

He values his future ſovereignty, not by impunity in doing evil, but by power to do good. What now his deſire is, then his ability ſhall be; and he more joyes, that he is a member of the true Church, then the ſecond in the land. Onely he fears to have a Crown too quickly, and therefore lengthens out his fathers dayes with his prayers for him, and obedience to him. And thus we leave Solomon to delight in David, David in Solomon, their people in both. 15

EDWARD Prince *of* Wales, *commonly called the black*-Prince. *He dyed at* Canturbury *June the* 8th. 1326. *Aged* 46 *yeares*.

W *Marshall sculp*:

CHAP. 20.

The life of EDVVARD *the Black Prince.*

EDward the Black Prince (so called from his dreaded acts and not from his * complexion) was the eldest sonne to Edward the third by Philippa his Queen. He was born *Anno* 1329, on the fifteenth of June, being friday, at Woodstock in Oxfordshire. His Parents perceiving in him more then ordinary naturall perfections, were carefull to bestow on him such education in Piety, and Learning, agreeable to his high birth.

* *For King Ed. his father called him his* Fair Sonne, *Speed p.* 579.

birth. The Prince met their care with his towardlinesse, being apt to take fire, and blaze at the least spark of instruction put into him.

We find him to be the first Prince of Wales, whose * Charter at this day is extant, with the particular rites of investiture, which were the Crownet, and Ring of gold, with a rod of silver, worthily bestowed upon him, who may passe for a miroir of Princes whether we behold him in Peace or in Warre. He in the whole course of his life manifested a singular observance to his Parents, to comply with their will and desire; nor lesse was the tendernesse of his affection to his Brothers and Sisters, whereof he had many.

** See the copy thereof in Mr. Seldens titles of Honour, pag. 595.*

But as for the Martiall performances of this Prince, they are so many and so great that they would fill whole volumes: we will onely insist on three of his most memorable atchievements, remitting the Reader for the rest to our English Historians. The first shall be his behaviour in the battel of * Cressy, against the French, wherein Prince Edward, not fully eighteen years old, led the fore front of the English.

** 1346 in the twenty yeare of Ed. the third.*

There was a causlesse report (the beginning of a rumour is sometimes all the ground thereof) spread through the French army, that the English were fled: whereupon the French posted after them, not so much to overcome (this they counted done) but to overtake them, preparing themselves rather to pursue then to fight. But coming to the town of Cressy, they found the English fortified in a wooddy place, and attending in good array to give battel. Whereat the French falling from their hopes were extremely vext (a fools paradise is a wisemans hell) finding their enemies faces to stand where they look'd for their backs. And now both armies prepared to fight, whilest behold flocks of ravens and vulturs in the aire flew thither; bold guests to come without an invitation: But these smell-feast birds when they saw the cloth laid (the tents of two armies

armies pitch'd) knew there would be good cheere, and came to feed on their carcases.

The English divided themselves into three parts : The formost consisting most of Archers, led by the Black Prince ; the second, by the Earl of Northampton ; the third, commanded by King Edward in person. The French were treble in number to the English, and had in their army the three Kings, of France, Bohemia, and Majorca : Charles Duke of Alenson, with John the Bohemian King, led the vanguard; the French King Philip, the main battel ; whilest Amie Duke of Savoy brought up the rere.

The Genoan Archers in the French forefront, wearied with marching, were accus'd for their slothfulnesse, and could neither get their wages nor good words, which made many of them cast down their bows, and refuse to fight ; the rest had their bowstrings made uselesse, being wetted with a sudden showre which fell on their side : But Heavens smiling offended more then her weeping, the sunne suddenly shining out in the face of the French, gave them so much light that they could not see.

However Duke Charles, breaking through the Genoans, furiously charged the fronts of the English, and joyned at hand-strokes with the Princes battel, who though fighting most couragiously was in great danger : Therefore King Edward was sent unto (who hitherto hovered on a hillock, judiciously beholding the fight) to come and rescue his sonne. The King apprehending his case dangerous but not desperate, and him rather in need then extremity, told the messenger, *Is my sonne alive, let him die or conquer, that he may have the honour of the day.*

The English were vext, not at his deniall, but their own request ; that they should seem to suspect their Kings fatherly affection, or Martiall skill, as needing a remembrancer to tell him his time. To make amends, they

they laid about them manfully, the rather becauſe they knew that the King looked on, to teſtifie their valour, who alſo had the beſt cards in his own hand, though he kept them for a revie.

The victory began to incline to the Engliſh, when, rather to ſettle then get the conqueſt, the King (hitherto a ſpectatour) came in to act the Epilogue. Many Engliſh with ſhort knifes for the nonce ſtabb'd the bellies of their enemies, cut the throats of more, letting out their ſouls whereſoever they could come at their bodies: and to all ſuch as lay languiſhing, they gave a ſhort acquittance, that they had paid their debt to nature. This makes French Writers complain of the Engliſh cruelty, and that it had been more honour to the Generall, and profit to the ſouldiers to have drawn leſſe bloud, and more money in ranſoming captives, eſpecially ſeeing many French Noblemen, who fought like lions, were kill'd like calves. Others plead that in Warre all wayes and weapons are lawfull, where it is the greateſt miſtake not to take all advantages.

Night came on, and the King commanded no purſuit ſhould be made for preventing of confuſion; for ſouldiers ſcarce follow any order, when they follow their flying enemy; and it was ſo late, that it might have proved too ſoon to make a purſuit.

The night proved exceeding dark (as mourning for the bloud ſhed) nor was the next morning comforted with the riſing of the ſun, but remained ſad and gloomy, ſo that in the miſt many French men loſt their way, and then their lives, falling into the hands of the Engliſh: ſo that next dayes gleanings for the number, though not for the quality of the perſons ſlain, exceeded the harveſt of the day before. And thus this victory, next to Gods Providence, was juſtly aſcribed to the Black Princes valour, who there wonne and wore away the Eſtridge feathers, then the Arms of John King of Bohemia, there conquer'd and kill'd, and therefore since made the* hereditary Emblemes of honour to the Princes of Wales.

* *Vid. Cambd. Remains pag.* 344.

The battel of Poictiers followed ten years after, which was fought betwixt the foresaid Black Prince, and John King of * France. Before the battel began the English were reduced to great straits, their enemies being six to one. The French conceived the victory, though not in hand, yet within reach, and their arm must be put out not to get but take it. All articles with the English they accounted alms, it being great charity but no policy to compound with them. But what shall we say? warre is a game wherein very often that side loseth which layeth the oddes. In probability they might have famished the English without fighting with them, had not they counted it a lean conquest so to bring their enemies to misery, without any honour to themselves.

* *September* 19. 1356.

The conclusion was, that the French would have the English lose their honour to save their lives, tendring them unworthy conditions, which being refused, the battel was begun. The French King made choice of three hundred prime horsmen to make the first assault on the English; the election of which three hundred made more then a thousand * heartburnings in his army: every one counted his loyalty or manhood suspected, who was not chosen into this number; and this took off the edge of their spirits against their enemies, and turned it into envy and disdain against their friends.

* *Paulus Æmil. in the life of King John, pag.* 286.

The French horse charged them very furiously, whom the English entertain'd with a feast of arrows, first, second, third course, all alike. Their horses were galled with the bearded piles, being unused to feel spurres in their breasts and buttocks. The best horses were worst wounded, for their mettall made one wound many; and that arrow which at first did but pierce, by their struggling did tear and rend. Then would

would they know no riders, and the riders could know no ranks; and in ſuch a confuſion, an army fights againſt it ſelf. One rank fell foul with another, and the rere was ready to meet with the front: and the valiant Lord Audley, charging them before they could repair themſelves, overcame all the Horſe, *Qua parte belli* (ſaith my Authour) *invicti Galli habebantur*. The Horſe being put to flight, the Infantry conſiſting moſt of poore people (whereof many came into the field with conquered hearts, grinded with oppreſsion of their Gentry) counted it neither wit nor manners for them to ſtay, when their betters did flie, and made poſt haſt after them. Six thouſand common ſouldiers were ſlain, fifty two Lords, and ſeventeen hundred Knights and Eſquires; one hundred Enſignes taken, with John the French King, and two thouſand priſoners of note.

The French had a great advantage of an after-game, if they had returned again, and made head, but they had more mind to make heels, and run away. Prince Edward, whoſe proweſſe herein was conſpicuous, overcame his own valour, both in his piety, devoutly giving to God the whole glory of the conqueſt, and in his courteſie, with ſtately humility entertaining the French Priſoner-King, whom he bountifully feaſted that night, though the other could not be merry albeit he was ſupped with great cheere, and knew himſelf to be very welcome.

The third performance of this valiant Prince, wherein we will inſtance, was acted in Spain, on this occaſion. Peter King of Caſtile was driven out of his kingdome by Henry his baſe Brother, and the aſsiſtance of ſome French forces. Prince Edward on this Peters petition, and by his own Fathers permiſsion, went with an army into Spain, to re-eſtate him in his kingdome: For though this Peter was a notorious Tyrant, (if Authours in painting his deeds do not overſhadow them, to make them blacker then they were) yet our Prince, not looking into his vices but his right, thought he was bound to aſsiſt him : For all Sovereignes are like the ſtrings of a Baſevioll equally tuned to the ſame height, ſo that by ſympathy, he that toucheth the one moves the other. Beſides, he thought it juſt enough to reſtore him, becauſe the French helpt to caſt him out ; and though Spain was farre off, yet our Prince never counted himſelf out of his own countrey, whileſt in any part of the world ; valour naturalizing a brave ſpirit through the Univerſe.

With much adoe he effected the buſineſſe through many difficulties, occaſioned partly by the treachery of King Peter, who performed none of the conditions promiſed, and partly through the barrenneſſe of the countrey, ſo that the Prince was forced to ſell all his own plate (Spain more needing meat then diſhes) to make proviſion for his ſouldiers; but eſpecially through the diſtemper of the climate, the aire (or fire ſhall I ſay) thereof being extreme hot, ſo that it is conceived to have cauſed this Princes death, which happened ſoon after his return. What Engliſh heart can hold from inveighing againſt Spaniſh aire which deprived us of ſuch a jewell ? were it not that it may ſeem ſince to have made us ſome amends, when lately the *breath of our noſtrills* breathed in that climate, and yet by Gods providence was kept there, and returned thence in health and ſafety.

Well may this Prince be taken for a Paragon of his age, and place, having the feweſt vices, with ſo many virtues. Indeed he was ſomewhat given to women, our Chronicles fathering two baſe children on him ; ſo hard it is to find a Sampſon without a Dalila. And ſeeing never King or Kings eldeſt ſonne ſince the conqueſt before his time married a ſubject, I muſt confeſſe his Match was much beneath himſelf, taking the double reverſion of a ſubjects bed, marrying Joan Counteſſe of Salisbury, which had been twice a widow. But her ſurpaſsing beauty pleads for him herein, and yet her beauty was the meaneſt thing about her, being ſurpaſſ'd by her virtues. And what a worthy woman muſt ſhe needs be her ſelf, whoſe very *garter* hath given ſo much honour to Kings and Princes?

He dyed at Canterbury, June the eighth 1376 in the fourty ſixth yeare of his age: it being wittily * obſerved of the ſhort lives of many worthy men, *fatuos a morte defendit ipſa inſulſitas; ſi cui plus cæteris aliquantulum ſalis inſit (quod miremini) ſtatim putreſcit.*

* Sr Francis Netherſole in his fun. orat. on Prince Henry, pag. 16.

CHAP. 21.

The King.

HE is a mortall God. This world at the firſt had no other Charter for its being, then Gods *Fiat*: Kings have the ſame in the Preſent tenſe, *I have ſaid ye are Gods.* We will deſcribe him, firſt as a good man (ſo was Henry the third) then as a good King (ſo was Richard the third) both which meeting together make a King complete. For he that is not a *good man*, or *but a good man*, can never be a good Sovereigne.

Maxime 1

He is temperate in the ordering of his own life. O the Mandate of a Kings example is able to do much! eſpecially he is,

1 Temperate in his diet. When Æſchines commended Philip King of Macedon, for a joviall man that would drink freely, * Demoſthenes anſwered, *that this was a good quality in a ſpunge, but not in a King.*

* Plutarch in the life of Demoſthenes.

2 Continent in his pleaſures. Yea Princes lawfull children are farre eaſier provided for then the *rabida fames* of a ſpurious offſpring can be ſatisfied, whileſt their Paramors and Concubines (count-

ing it their beſt manners to carve for themſelves all they can come by) prove intolerably expenſive to a State. Beſides, many rebellions have riſen out of the marriage-bed defiled.

2 *He holds his Crown immediately from the God of Heaven.* * *The most high ruleth in the kingdomes of men, and giveth them to whomſoever he will. Cujus juſſu naſcuntur homines, ejus juſſu conſtituuntur Principes,* ſaith a * Father : *Inde illis poteſtas unde ſpiritus,* ſaith * another. And whoſoever ſhall remount to the firſt originall of Kings, ſhall loſe his eyes in diſcovering the top thereof, as paſt ken, and touching the heavens. We reade of a place in Mount Olivet (wherein the laſt footſteps, they ſay, of our Saviour before he aſcended into heaven are to be ſeen) that it will ever lie open to the skies, and will not admit of any cloſe or * covering to be made over it how coſtly ſoever. Farre more true is this of the condition of abſolute Kings, who in this reſpect are ever *ſub dio*, ſo that no ſuperiour power can be interpoſed betwixt them and heaven. Yea the Character of loyalty to Kings ſo deeply impreſſ'd in Subjects hearts ſhews that onely Gods finger wrote it there. Hence it is if one chance to conceive ill of his Sovereigne, though within the cabinet of his ſoul, preſently his own heart grows jealous of his own heart, and he could wiſh the tongue cut out of his tell-tale thoughts, leſt they ſhould accuſe themſelves. And though ſometimes Rebels (Atheiſts againſt the Gods on earth) may labour to obliterate loyalty in them, yet even then their conſcience, the Kings Aturney, frames Articles againſt them, and they ſtand in daily fear leſt Darius Longimanus (ſuch a one is every King) ſhould reach them, and revenge himſelf.

* *Dan.* 4. 17.

* *Irenæus l.* 5.

* *Tertull. Apol. pag.* 6. 5.

* Nullo modo contegi aut concamerari poteſt, ſed tranſitus ejus à terra ad cœlum uſque patet apertum, *Adricom. de terra Sancta ex Hieron. & aliis Autoribus.*

3 *He claimeth to be ſupreme Head on earth over the Church in his Dominions.* Which his power over all perſons and cauſes Eccleſiaſticall

1. Is given him by God, who alone hath the originall propriety thereof.

2 Is

2. Is derived unto him by a prescription time out of mind in the Law of Nature, declared more especially in the Word of God.
3. Is cleared and averred by the private Laws and Statutes of that State wherein he lives. For since the Pope (starting up from being the Emperours Chaplain to be his Patron) hath invaded the rights of many earthly Princes, many wholsome Laws have been made in severall Kingdomes to assert and notifie their Kings just power *in Spiritualibus*.

Well therefore may our King look with a frowning face on such, whose tails meet in this firebrand (which way soever the prospect of their faces be) to deny Princes power in Church-matters. Two * Jesuites give this farre-fetch'd reason, why * Samuel at the Feast caused the shoulder of the Sacrifice to be *reserved and kept on purpose* for Saul to feed on; *because*, say they, *Kings of all men have most need of strong shoulders patiently to endure those many troubles and molestations they shall meet with*, especially, I may well adde, if all their Subjects were as troublesome and disloyall as the Jesuites. The best is, as God hath given Kings shoulders to bear, he hath also given them armes to strike such as deprive them of their lawfull Authority in Ecclesiasticall affairs.

* *Zanchez & Velasquez in their Comments on the Text.*
* 1. *Sam.* 9 14.

4

He improves his power to defend true Religion. Sacerdotall Offices though he will not doe, he will cause them to be done. He will not offer to burn incense with Uzziah, yet he will burn Idolaters bones with Josiah, I mean advance Piety by punishing Profanenesse. God* saith to his Church, *Kings shall be thy Nursing-fathers, and their Queens thy Nursing-mothers.* And oh let not Princes out of State refuse to be so themselves, and onely hire others, it belonging to Subjects to suck, but to Princes to suckle Religion by their authority. They ought to command Gods Word to be read and practised, wherein the blessed Memory of King James shall never

* *Isaiah.* 49. 23.

ver be forgotten. His Predeceſſour in England reſtored the Scripture to her Subjects, but he in a manner, reſtored theScripture to it ſelf in cauſing the *New Tranſlation* thereof, whereby the meaneſt that can reade Engliſh, in effect underſtands the Greek and Hebrew. A Princely act, which ſhall laſt even when the leaſe of Time ſhall be expired: Verily I ſay unto you, whereſoever this Tranſlation ſhall be read in the whole realm, there ſhall alſo this that this King hath done be told in memoriall of him.

5 *He uſeth Mercy and Juſtice in his proceedings againſt Offenders.* Solomon * ſaith, *The throne is eſtabliſhed by Juſtice*: and Solomon * ſaith,*The throne is upholden by Mercy*. Which two Proverbs ſpeak no more contradiction, then he that ſaith that the two oppoſite ſide-walls of an houſe hold up the ſame roof. Yea as ſome Aſtronomers (though erroneouſly) conceived the Cryſtalline Sphere to be made of water,and therefore to be ſet next the *Primum mobile* to allay the heat thereof, which otherwiſe by the ſwiftneſſe of his motion would ſet all the world on fire; ſo Mercy muſt ever be ſet near Juſtice for the cooling and tempering thereof. In his mercy our King deſires to reſemble the God of heaven, who meaſureth his judgements by the ordinary cubit, but his kindneſſes by the cubit of the Sanctuary, twice as big; yea all the world had been a hell without Gods mercy.

* Prov. 16. 12.
* Prov. 20. 28.

6 *He is rich in having a plentifull exchequer of his peoples hearts. Allow me*, ſaid Archimedes, *to ſtand in the aire, and I will move the earth*. But our King having a firm footing in his Subjects affections, what may he do, yea what may he not do? making the coward valiant, the miſer liberall; for love, the key of hearts, will open the cloſeſt coffers. Mean time how poore is that Prince amidſt all his wealth, whoſe Subjects are onely kept by a ſlaviſh fear, the jaylour of the ſoul. An iron arm faſtned with ſcrues may be ſtronger, but never ſo uſefull,

because

becauſe not ſo naturall, as an arm of fleſh,joined with muſcles & ſinews.Loving Subjects are moſt ſerviceable, as being more kindly united to their Sovereigne then thoſe which are onely knock'd on with fear and forcing. Beſides,where Subjects are envaſſaled with fear, Prince and People mutually watch their own advantages, which being once offered them, 'tis wonderfull if they do not, and woſull if they do, make uſe thereof.

He willingly orders his actions by the Laws of his realm. Indeed ſome maintain that Princes are too high to come under the roof of any Laws, except they voluntarily of their goodneſſe be pleaſed to bow themſelves thereunto, and that it is Corban, a gift and courteſy, in them to ſubmit themſelves to their Laws. But whatſoever the Theories of abſolute Monarchy be, our King loves to be legall in all his practices, and thinks that his power is more ſafely lock'd up for him in his Laws then kept in his own will; becauſe God alone makes things lawfull by willing them, whileſt the moſt calmeſt Princes have ſometimes guſts of Paſsion, which meeting with an unlimited Authority in them may prove dangerous to them and theirs. Yea our King is ſo ſuſpicious of an unbounded power in himſelf, that though the wideneſſe of his ſtrides could make all the hedge ſtiles, yet he will not go over,but where he may. He alſo hearkneth to the adviſe of good Counſellers, remembring the ſpeech of Antoninus the Emperour, *Aequius eſt ut ego tot taliumque. amicorum conſilium ſequar, quam tot taleſque amici meam unius voluntatem.* And yet withall our King is carefull to maintain his juſt Prerogative, that as it be not outſtretched, ſo it may not be overſhortned.

Such a gratious Sovereigne God hath vouchſafed to this Land. How pious is he towards his God! attentive in hearing the Word, preaching Religion with his ſilence, as the Miniſter doth with his ſpeech! How loving to his Spouſe, tender to his Children, faithfull to his ſervants whileſt they are faithfull to their own innocence ; otherwiſe leaving them to Juſtice under marks of his diſpleaſure. How doth he with David walk in the *midſt of his houſe* without partiality to any! How juſt is he in puniſhing wilfull murder! ſo that it is as eaſie to reſtore the murthered to life, as to keep the murtherer from death. How mercifull is he to ſuch who not out of leigier malice, but ſudden paſsion may chance to ſhed bloud! to whom his pardon hath allowed leiſure to drop out their own ſouls in tears by conſtant repentance all the dayes of their lives. How many wholſome Laws hath he enacted for the good of his Subjects! How great is his humilitie in ſo great height! which maketh his own praiſes painfull for himſelf to heare, though pleaſant for others to report. His Royall virtues are too great to be told, and too great to be conceal'd. All cannot, ſome muſt break forth from the full hearts of ſuch as be his thankfull Subjects.

But I muſt either ſtay or fall. My ſight fails me dazell'd with the luſtre of Majeſtie : all I can do is pray.

Give the King thy judgements, O Lord, and thy righteouſneſſe to the Kings Sonne : ſmite through the loins of thoſe that riſe up againſt his Majeſtie, but upon him and his let the Crown flouriſh : Oh cauſe his Subjects to meet his Princely care for their good, with a proportionable cheerfulneſſe and alacrity in his ſervice, that ſo thereby the happineſſe of Church and State may be continued. Grant this, O Lord, for Chriſt Jeſus his ſake our onely Mediatour and Advocate. Amen.

The

THE
PROFANE
STATE.

BY

THOMAS FULLER, *B. D.*
and Prebendarie of
Sarum.

ISAIAH 32. 5.

The vile person shall be no more called liberall, nor the churl said to be bountifull.

EZEK. 44. 23.

And they shall teach my people the difference betwixt the Holy and the Profane.

CAMBRIDGE:
¶ Printed by ROGER DANIEL for
John Williams, and are to be sold at the signe
of the Crown in S. Pauls
Churchyard. 1642.

Zz 2

The Profane State.

THE FIFTH BOOK.

Chap. I.
The Harlot

IS one that her ſelf is both merchant and merchandiſe, which ſhe ſelleth for profit, and hath pleaſure given her into the bargain, and yet remains a great loſer. To deſcribe her is very difficult; it being hard to draw thoſe to the life, who never ſit ſtill: ſhe is ſo various in her humours, and mutable, 'tis almoſt impoſsible to character her in a fixed poſture; yea indeed ſome cunning Harlots are not diſcernable from honeſt women. Solomon ſaith, *ſhe wipeth her mouth*; and who can diſtinguiſh betwixt that which was never foul, and that which is cleanly wiped.

Her love is a blank, wherein ſhe writeth the next man that tendreth his affection. Impudently the Harlot lied (Prov. 7.15.) *Therefore came I forth to meet thee, diligently to ſeek thy face, and I have found thee:* elſe underſtand her that ſhe came forth to meet him, not *qua talis*, but *qua primus*, becauſe he came firſt; for any other youngſter in his place would have ſerv'd her turn: yet ſee how ſhe makes his chance her courteſie, ſhe affecting him as Maxime 1

 much

much above others, as the common road loves the next paſſenger beſt

2 *As ſhe ſees, ſo her ſelf is ſeen by her own eyes.* Sometimes ſhe ſtares on men with full fixed eyes; otherwhiles ſhe ſquints forth glances, and contracts the beams in her burning glaſſes, to make them the hotter to inflame her objects; ſometimes ſhe dejects her eyes in a ſeeming civility, and many miſtake in her a cunning for a modeſt look. But as thoſe bullets which graze on the ground do moſt miſchief to an army; ſo ſhe hurts moſt with thoſe glances which are ſhot from a down-caſt eye.

3 *She writes characters of wantonneſſe with her feet as ſhe walks*: And what Potiphars wife ſaid with her tongue, ſhe ſaith unto the paſſengers with her geſture and gate, *Come lie with me*; and nothing angrieth her ſo much, as when modeſt men affect a deafneſſe and will not heare, or a dulneſſe and will not underſtand the language of her behaviour. She counts her houſe a priſon, and is never well till gadding abroad: ſure 'tis true of women what is obſerved of elm, if lying within doores dry, no timber will laſt ſound longer, but if without doores expoſ'd to weather, no wood ſooner rots and corrupts.

4 *Yet ſome Harlots continue a kind of ſtrange coyneſſe even to the very laſt*: which coyneſſe differs from modeſty as much as hemlock from parſely. They will deny common favours, becauſe they are too ſmall to be granted: They will part with all or none, refuſe to be courteous, and reſerve themſelves to be diſhoneſt; whereas women truly modeſt will willingly go to the bounds of free and harmleſſe mirth, but will not be dragg'd any farther.

5 *She is commonly known by her whoriſh attire*: As criſping and curling, (making her hair as winding and intricate as her heart) painting, wearing naked breaſts. The face indeed ought to be bare, and the haſt ſhould lie

out of the sheath ; but where the back and edge of the knife are shown, 'tis to be feared they mean to cut the fingers of others. I must confesse some honest women may go thus, but no whit the honester for going thus. The ship may have Castor and Pollux for the badge, and notwithstanding have S. Paul for the lading : yet the modesty and discretion of honest Matrons were more to be commended, if they kept greater distance from the attire of Harlots.

Sometimes she ties her self in marriage to one, that she may the more freely stray to many : and cares not though her husband comes not within her bed, so be it he goeth not out beyond the Foure-seas. She useth her husband as an hood, whom she casts off in the fair weather of prosperity, but puts him on for a cover in adversity, if it chance she prove with child. 6

Yet commonly she is as barren as lustfull. Yea who can expect that malt should grow to bring new increase. Besides, by many wicked devices she seeks on purpose to make her self barren (a retrograde act to set Nature back) making many issues, that she may have no issue, and an hundred more damnable devices, 7

Which wicked projects first from hell did flow,
And thither let the same in silence go,
Best known of them who did them never know.

And yet for all her cunning, God sometimes meets with her (who varieth his wayes of dealing with wantons, that they may be at a losse in tracing him) and sometimes against her will she proves with child, which though unable to speak, yet tells at the birth a plain story to the mothers shame.

At last when her deeds grow most shamefull she grows most shamelesse. So impudent, that she her self sometimes proves both the poyson and the antidote, the temptation and the preservative ; young men distasting and abhorring her boldnesse. And those wantons, who perchance would willingly have gathered the fruit from fruit from the tree, will not feed on ſuch fallings.

9 *Generally ſhe dies very poore.* The wealth ſhe gets is like the houſes ſome build in Gothland, made of * ſnow, no laſting fabrick ; the rather, becauſe ſhe who took money of thoſe who taſted the top of her wantonneſſe, is fain to give it to ſuch who will drink out the dregs of her luſt.

**Olaus magnus de Rit. Gent. ſept. lib. 1. c. 23.*

10 *She dieth commonly of a lothſome diſeaſe.* I mean that diſeaſe, unknown to Antiquity, created within ſome hundreds of years, which took the name from Naples. When hell invented new degrees in ſinnes, it was time for heaven to invent new puniſhments. Yet is this new diſeaſe now grown ſo common and ordinary, as if they meant to put divine Juſtice to a ſecond task to find out a newer. And now it is high time for our Harlot, being grown lothſome to her ſelf, to runne out of her ſelf by repentance.

Some conceive that when King Henry the eighth deſtroyed the publick Stews in this Land (which till his time ſtood on the banks ſide on Southwark next the Bear-garden, beaſts and beaſtly women being very fit neighbours) he rather ſcattered then quenched the fire of luſt in this kingdome, and by turning the flame out of the chimney where it had a vent, more endangered the burning of the Commonwealth. But they are deceived : for whileſt the Laws of the Land tolerated open uncleanneſſe, God might juſtly have made the whole State do penance for whoredome; whereas now that ſinne though committed, yet not permitted, and though (God knows) it be too generall, it is ſtill but perſonall.

CHAP. 2.

JOAN the first of that Name Queen of Naples, which for her Incontinency and other wicked Practises was put to Death. Anno 1381

Page 360. W M sculp:

Chap. 2.

The life of Joan *Queen of Naples.*

JOan, grandchild to Robert King of Naples by Charles his ſonne, ſucceeded her grandfather in the Kingdome of Naples and Sicily, *Anno* 1343. a woman of a beautifull body and rare endowments of nature, had not the heat of her luſt ſoured all the reſt of her perfections, whoſe wicked life * and wofull death we now come to relate: And I hope none can juſtly lay it to my charge, if the foulneſſe of her actions ſtain through the cleaneſt language I can wrap them in.

* *Taken out of Brovius An. Eccle.an.*1344. *Petrarch.lib.*5. *Epiſt. & Summontius Hiſt. Neopol. lib.* 3.

She was firſt married unto her coſen Andrew, a Prince of royall extraction, and of a ſweet and loving diſpoſition. But he being not able to ſatisfie her wantonneſſe, ſhe kept company with lewd perſons, at firſt privately, but afterwards ſhe preſented her badneſſe viſible to every eye, ſo that none need look through the chinks where the doores were open.

Now Elizabeth Queen of Hungary, her husband Andrews mother, was much offended at the badneſſe of her daughter-in-law, whoſe deeds were ſo foul ſhe could not look on them, and ſo common ſhe could not look beſides them; wherefore in a matronly way ſhe fairly adviſed her to reform her courſes. For the lives of Princes are more read then their Laws, and generally more practiſed: Yea their example paſſeth as current as their coin, and what they do they ſeem to command to be done. Cracks in glaſſe though paſt mending are no great matter; but the leaſt flaw in a diamond is conſiderable: Yea her perſonall fault was a nationall injury, which might derive and put the Sceptre into a wrong hand.

Theſe her mild inſtructions ſhe ſharpned with ſevere threatnings: But no razor will cut a ſtony heart. Queen Joan imputed it to ages envy, old people perſwading

ſwading youth to leave thoſe pleaſures, which have left themſelves. Beſides, a Mother-in-laws Sermon ſeldome takes well with an audience of Daughter-in-laws. Wherefore the old Queen finding the other paſt grace (that is never likely to come to it) reſolved no longer to puniſh anothers ſinne on her ſelf, and vex her own righteous ſoul, but leaving Naples return'd into Hungary.

After her departure Queen Joan grew weary of her husband Andrew, complaining of his inſufficiency, though thoſe who have *caninum appetitum* are not competent judges what is ſufficient food : And ſhe cauſed her husband in the city of Averſa to be hung upon a beam and ſtrangled in the night time, and then threw out his corps into a garden, where it lay ſome dayes unburied.

There goes a * ſtory that this Andrew on a day coming into the Queens chamber, and finding her twiſting a thick ſtring of ſilk and ſilver, demanded of her for what purpoſe ſhe made it : She anſwered, *To hang you in it*, which he then little believed, the rather becauſe thoſe who intend ſuch miſchief never ſpeak of it before. But ſuch blows in jeſt-earneſt are moſt dangerous, which one can neither receive in love, nor refuſe in anger.

* *Collenuſius, l. 5. Regn. Neop.*

Indeed ſhe ſought in vain to colour the buſineſſe, and to divert the ſuſpicion of the murther from her ſelf, becauſe all the world ſaw that ſhe inflicted no puniſhment on the actours of it which were in her power. And in ſuch a caſe, when a murther is generally known, the ſword of the Magiſtrate cannot ſtand neuter, but doth juſtify what it doth not puniſh.

Beſides, his corps was not cold before ſhe was hot in a new love, and married Lewis Prince of Tarentum, one of the beautifulleſt men in the world. But it was hard for her to pleaſe her love and her luſt in the ſame perſon. This Prince waſted the ſtate of his body to pay her the conjugall debt, which ſhe extorted beyond all modeſty or reaſon, ſo unquenchable was the wild-fire of her wantonneſſe.

After his death (ſhe hating widowhood as much as Nature doth *vacuum*) maried James King of Majorca, and commonly ſtyled Prince of Calabria. Some ſay he dyed of a naturall death: Others, that ſhe beheaded him for lying with another woman (who would ſuffer none to be dishoneſt but her ſelf) Others, that he was unjuſtly put to death, and forced to change worlds, that ſhe might change husbands.

Her fourth husband was Otho of Brunſwick, who came a Commander out of Germany, with a company of ſouldiers, and performed excellent ſervice in Italy. A good ſouldier he was, and it was not the leaſt part of his valour to adventure on ſo skittiſh a beaſt: But he hoped to feaſt his hungry fortune on this reverſion. By all foure husbands ſhe had no children; either becauſe the drougth of her wantonneſſe parched the fruit of her wombe; or elſe becauſe provident Nature prevented a generation of Monſters from her.

By this time her ſinnes were almoſt hoarſe with crying to heaven for revenge. They miſtake who think divine Juſtice ſleepeth when it winks for a while at Offenders. Hitherto ſhe had kept herſelf in a whole skin by the rents which were in the Church of Rome. For there being a long time a Schiſme betwixt two Popes, Urban, and Clement, ſhe ſo poyſed herſelf between them both, that ſhe eſcaped unpuniſhed. This is that Queen Joan that gave Avignon in France (yet under a pretence of ſale) to Pope Urban and his Succeſſours: the ſtomach of his Holineſſe not being ſo ſqueamiſh, but that he would take a good almes from dirty hands. It may make the chaſtity of Rome ſuſpicious with the world that ſhe hath had ſo good fortune to be a gainer by Harlots.

But see now how Charles Prince of Dyrachium, being next of kin to Prince Andrew that was murdered, comes out of Hungary with an army into Naples to revenge his uncles bloud. He was received without resistance of any, his very name being a Petrard to make all the city-gates fly open where he came. Out issues Otho the Queens husband with an army of men out of Naples, and most stoutly bids him battel, but is overthrown; yet was he suffered fairly to depart the kingdome, dismiss'd with this commendation, That never a more valiant Knight fought in defence of a more vitious Lady.

Queen Joan finding it now in vain to bend her fist, fell to bowing of her knees, and having an excellent command of all her passions save her lust, fell down flat before Charles the Conquerour, and submitted her self: *Hitherto*, said she, *I have esteemed thee in place of a sonne, but seeing God will have it so, hereafter I shall acknowledge thee for my Lord.* Charles knew well that Necessity, her Secretary, endited her speech for her, which came little from her heart; yet, to shew that he had as plentifull an Exchequer of good language, promis'd her fairly for the present: But mercy it self would be asham'd to pity so notorious a malefactour. After some moneths imprisonment she was carried to the place where her husband was murder'd, and there accordingly hang'd, and cast out of the window into the garden, whose corps at last was buried in the Nunnery of S. Clare.

CHAP. 3.

The Witch.

BEfore we come to deſcribe her, we muſt premiſe and prove certain propoſitions, whoſe truth may otherwiſe be doubted of.

1 *Formerly there were Witches.* Otherwiſe Gods * Law had fought againſt a ſhadow, *Thou ſhalt not ſuffer a Witch to live*: yea we reade how King Saul, who had formerly ſcoured Witches out of all Iſrael, afterwards drank a draught of that puddle himſelf.

* *Exod.* 18.21.

2 *There are Witches for the preſent, though thoſe Night-birds flie not ſo frequently in flocks ſince the light of the Goſpel.* Some ancient arts and myſteries are ſaid to be loſt; but ſure the devil will not wholly let down any of his gainfull trades. There be many Witches at this day in Lapland, who ſell winds to Mariners for money (and muſt they not needs go whom the devil drives?) though we are not bound to believe the old ſtory of Ericus King of Swedeland, who had a * cap, and as he turned it the wind he wiſh'd for would blow on that ſide.

* *Therefore called,* Ventoſus pileus, *Olaus mag. de Gent. ſeptent. lib.* 3. *cap.* 14.

3 *It is very hard to prove a Witch.* Infernall contracts are made without witneſſes. She that in preſence of others will compact with the devil deſerves to be hang'd for her folly as well as impiety.

4 *Many are unjuſtly accuſed for Witches.* Sometimes out of ignorance of naturall, & miſapplying of ſupernaturall cauſes; ſometimes out of their neighbours mere malice, and the ſuſpicion is increaſ'd, if the party accuſed be notoriouſly ill-favoured; whereas deformity alone is no more argument to make her a Witch, then handſomneſſe had been evidence

to prove her an Harlot; ſometimes out of their own cauſleſſe confeſsion. Being brought before a Magiſtrate they acknowledge themſelves to be Witches, being themſelves rather bewitch'd with fear, or deluded with phancy. But the ſelf-accuſing of ſome is as little to be credited, as the ſelf-praiſing of others, if alone without other evidence.

5 *Witches are commonly of the feminine ſex.* Ever ſince Satan tempted our grandmother Eve, he knows that that ſex is moſt licoriſh to taſt, and moſt careleſſe to ſwallow his baits. * *Neſcio quid habet muliebre nomen ſemper cum ſacris*: if they light well, they are inferiour to few men in piety, if ill, ſuperiour to all in ſuperſtition.

* *Fulgentius in Sermon.*

6 *They are commonly diſtinguiſhed into white and black Witches.* White, I dare not ſay good Witches (*for woe be to him that calleth evil good*) heal thoſe that are hurt, and help them to loſt goods. But better it is to lap ones pottage like a dog, then to eat it mannerly with a ſpoon of the devils giving: Black Witches hurt, and do miſchief. But in deeds of darkneſſe there is no difference of colours: The white and the black are both guilty alike in compounding with the devil. And now we come to ſee by vvhat degrees people arrive at this height of profaneneſſe.

Maxime 1

At the firſt ſhe is onely ignorant, and very malicious. She hath uſually a bad face, and a worſe tongue, given to railing and curſing, as if conſtantly bred on mount Ebal, yet ſpeaking perchance worſe then ſhe means, though meaning worſe then ſhe ſhould. And as the harmleſſe wapping of a curſ'd curre may ſtir up a fierce maſtiffe to the vvorrying of ſheep; ſo on her curſing the devil may take occaſion by Gods permiſsion to do miſchief, vvithout her knovvledge, and perchance againſt her will.

*Multi dum vitare ſtudent quæ vitanda non ſunt, fugâ vanâ ſuperſtitionis ſuperſtitioſi fiunt, *Cardan. de Subtil. p.924. lib. 8.*

2

*Some have been made * Witches by endeavouring to defend themſelves*

themselves against witchcraft: for fearing some suspected Witch should hurt them, they fence themselves with the devils shield against the devils sword, put on his *whole armour*, beginning to use spells and charms to safeguard themselves. The art is quickly learnt to which nothing but credulity and practice is required; and they often fall from defending themselves to offending of others, especially the devil not being dainty of his company where he finds welcome; and being invited once he haunts ever after.

She begins at first with doing tricks rather strange then hurtfull: yea some of them are pretty and pleasing. But it is dangerous to gather floures that grow on the banks of the pit of hell, for fear of falling in; yea they which play with the devils rattles, will be brought by degrees to wield his sword, and from making of sport they come to doing of mischief. 3

At last she indents downright with the devil. He is to find her some toies for a time, and to have her soul in exchange. At the first (to give the devil his due) he observes the agreement to keep up his credit, else none would trade with him; though at last he either deceives her with an equivocation, or at some other small hole this Serpent winds out himself, and breaks the covenants. And where shall she poore wretch sue the forfeited band? in heaven she neither can nor dare appear; on earth she is hang'd if the contract be proved; in hell her adversary is judge, and it is wofull to appeal from the devil to the devil. But for a while let us behold her in her supposed felicity. 4

She taketh her free progresse from one place to another. Sometimes the devil doth locally transport her: but he will not be her constant hackney, to carry such luggage about, but oftentimes to save portage deludes her brains in her sleep, so that they brag of long journeys, whose heads never travell'd from their bolsters. These vvith Drake sail about the vvorld, but it is on an ocean of 5 of their own phancies, and in a ship of the same: They boast of brave banquets they have been at, but they would be very lean should they eat no other meat: Others will perswade, if any list to believe, that by a Witch-bridle they can make a fair of horses of an acre of besome-weed. Oh silly souls! Oh subtle Satan that deceived them.

6 *With strange figures and words she summons the devils to attend her*: using a language which God never made at the confusion of Tongues; and an interpreter must be fetch'd from hell to expound it. With these, or Scripture abused, the devil is ready at her service. Who would suppose that roaring lion could so finely act the spaniel? one would think he were too old *to suck*, and yet he will do that also for advantage.

7 *Sometimes she enjoyns him to do more for her then he is able*; as to wound those whom Gods providence doth arm, or to break through the tents of blessed Angels, to hurt one of Gods Saints. Here Satan is put to his shifts, and his wit must help him where his power fails; he either excuseth it, or seemingly performs it, lengthning his own arm by the dimnesse of her eye, and presenting the seeming bark of that tree which he cannot bring.

8 *She lives commonly but very poore.* Methinks she should bewitch to her self a golden mine, at least good meat, and whole clothes: But 'tis as rare to see one of her profession as an hangman in an whole suit. Is the possession of the devils favour here no better? Lord, what is the reversion of it hereafter?

9 *When arraigned for her life the devil leaves her to the Law to shift for her self.* He hath worn out all his shoes in her former service, and will not now go barefoot to help her; and the circle of the halter is found to be too strong for all her Spirits. Yea * Zoroastes himself, the first inventer of Magick (though he laught at his birth) led a miserable life, and dyed a wofull death in banishment

* *Plinius, lib.* 3. *cap.* 1.

ment. We will give a double example of a Witch : first of a reall one, out of the Scripture, because it shall be above all exception ; and then of one deeply suspected, out of our own Chronicles.

Chap. 4.

The Witch of Endor.*

* 1. Sam. 28.

HEr proper name we neither find, nor need curiously enquire : without it she is describ'd enough for our knowledge, too much for her shame.

King Saul had banish'd all Witches and Sorcerers out of Israel ; but no besom can sweep so clean as to leave no crumme of dust behind it: This Witch of Endor still keeps her self safe in the land. God hath *his remnant* where Saints are cruelly persecuted ; Satan also his remnant, where offenders are severely prosecuted, and(if there were no more)the whole *species* of Witches is preserved in this *individuum*, till more be provided.

It happened now that King Saul, being ready to fight with the Philistines, was in great distresse, because God answered him not concerning the successe of the battel. With the silent, he will be silent : Saul gave no reall answer in his obedience to Gods commands, God will give no vocall answer to Sauls requests.

Mens minds are naturally ambitious to know things to come : Saul is restlesse to know the issue of the fight. Alas, what needed he to set his teeth on edge with the sourenesse of that bad tidings, who soon after was to have his belly full thereof.

He said to his servants, *Seek me out* (no wonder she was such a jewell to be sought for) *one with a familiar Spirit* : vvhich vvas accordingly perform'd, and Saul came to her in a disguise. Formerly Samuel told him

 that

that his *disobedience was as witchcraft* ; now Saul falls from the like to the same, and tradeth with Witches indeed (the receiver is as bad as the thief) and at his request she raiseth up Samuel to come unto him.

What, true Samuel ? It is above Satans power to degrade a Saint from glory, though for a moment ; since his own fall thence, he could fetch none from heaven. Or was it onely the true body of Samuel ? no ; the pretious ashes of the Saints (the pawn for the return of their souls) are lock'd up safe in the cabinet of their graves, and the devil hath no key unto it. Or lastly was it his seeming body ? he that could not counterfeit the least and worst of * worms, could he dissemble the shape of one of the best and greatest of men ?

* *Exod.* 8. 18.

Yet this is most probable, seeing Satan could change himself into an Angel of light, and God gives him more power at some times then at other. However, we will not be too peremptory herein, and build standing structures of bold assertions on so uncertain a foundation : rather with the Rechabites we will live in tents of conjectures, which on better reason we may easily alter and remove.

The devils speech looks backward and forward, relates and foretells : the Historicall part thereof is easie, recounting Gods speciall favours to Saul, and his ingratitude to God, and the matter thereof very pious. *Not every one that saith Lord, Lord* (whether to him or of him) *shall enter into the kingdome of heaven:* for Satan here useth the Lords name six times in foure verses. The Propheticall part of his speech is harder, how he could foretell *to morrow shalt thou and thy sonnes be with me*: what, with me true Samuel in heaven ? that was too good a place (will some say) for Saul : or with me true Satan in hell ? that was too bad a place for Jonathan. What then ? with me pretended Samuel in ᾅδῃ, in the state of the dead.

But

But how came the Witch or Satan by this knowledge? surely that uggly monster never look'd his face in that beautifull glasse of the Trinity, which (as some will have it) represents things to the blessed Angels. No doubt then he gathered it by experimentall collection, who, having kept an exact Ephemerides of all actions for more then five thousand years together, can thereby make a more then probable guesse of future contingents; the rather because accidents in this world are not so much new as renewed. Besides, he saw it in the naturall causes, in the strength of the Philistines, and weaknesse of the Israelitish army, and in Davids ripenesse to succeed Saul in the Throne. Perchance as vulturs are said to smell the earthlinesse of a dying corps; so this bird of prey resented a worse then earthly savour in the soul of Saul, an evidence of his death at hand. Or else we may say the devil knew it by particular revelation; for God to use the devil for his own turn might impart it unto him, to advance wicked mens repute of Satans power, that they who would be deceived should be deceived to believe that Satan knows more then he does.

The dismall news so frighted Saul, that he fell along on the earth, and yet at last is perswaded to arise and eat meat, she killing and dresing a fat calf for him.

Witches generally are so poore they can scarce feed themselves: see here one able to feast a King. *That which goeth into the mouth defileth not:* better eat meat of her dresing, then take counsell of her giving; and her hands might be clean, whose soul meddled with unclean spirits. Saul must eat somewhat, that he might be strengthned to live to be kill'd, as afterwards it came to passe. And here the mention of this Witch in Scripture vanisheth away, & we will follow her no farther. If afterward she escaped the justice of man, Gods judgement, without her repentance, hath long since overtaken her.

Chap. 5.

The life of Joan of Arc.

Joan of Arc was born in a village called Domrenny upon the Marches of Bar, near to Vaucoleurs. Her parents, James of Arc and Isabell, were very poore people, and brought her up to keep sheep: where for a while we will leave her, and come to behold the miserable estate of the kingdome of France wherein she lived.

In her time Charles the seventh was the distressed French King, having onely two entire Provinces left him, Gascoigne and Languedoc, and his enemies were about them, and in all the rest, which were possessed by the English, under their young King Henrie the sixth, and his aged Generalls the Duke of Bedford, and the Earls of Salisbury and Suffolk. Besides they had besieged the city of Orleance, and brought it to that passe that the highest hopes of those therein was to yield on good terms.

Matters standing in this wofull case, three French * Noblemen projected with themselves to make a cordiall for the consumption of the spirits of their King and Countreymen; but this seemed a great difficulty to perform, the French people being so much dejected: and when mens hearts are once down, it is hard to fasten any pullies to them to draw them up. However they resolved to pitch upon some project out of the ordinary road of accidents, to elevate the peoples phancies thereby, knowing that mens phancies easily slip off from smooth and common things, but are quickly catch'd & longest kept in such plots as have odde angles, and strange unusuall corners in them.

Gyrard Seigneur du Haillizan in Charles the seventh.

Hereupon they concluded to set up the foresaid Joan of Arc, to make her pretend that she had a revelation

JOAN *of* Arc *the Victorious* Leader *of the* French *Armyes*, *She was condemned by the* English *for a* Witch, *& burnt at* Rohan *July the* 6th 1461. *being about* 22. *yeares of Age*.

Page 373. W: Marshall *sculp*:

lation from heaven, to be the leader of an army, to drive all the Engliſh out of France: and ſhe being an handſome, witty, and bold maid (about twentie years of age) was both apprehenſive of the plot, and very active to proſecute it. But other Authours will not admit of any ſuch complotting, but make her moved thereunto either of her own, or by ſome Spirits inſtigation.

By the mediation of a Lord ſhe is brought to the preſence of King Charles, whom ſhe inſtantly knew, though never ſeen before, and at that time of ſet purpoſe much diſguiſed. This very thing ſome heighten to a miracle, though others make it fall much beneath a wonder, as being no more then a Scholars ready ſaying of that leſſon, which he hath formerly learned without book. To the King ſhe boldly delivers her meſſage, how that this was the time wherein the ſinnes of the Engliſh, and the ſufferings of the French, were come to the height, and ſhe appointed by the God of heaven to be the French leader to conquer the Engliſh. If this opportunity were let ſlip, let them thank heavens bounty for the tender, and their own folly for the refuſall; and who would pity their eternall ſlavery, who thruſt their own liberty from themſelves.

He muſt be deaf indeed who heares not that ſpoken which he deſires. Charles triumphs at this news: Both his armes were to few too embrace the motion. The Fame of her flies through France, and all talk of her, whom the Divines eſteem as Deborah, the Souldiers as Semiramis. People found out a neſt of miracles in her education, that ſo lyon-like a ſpirit ſhould be bred amongſt ſheep like David.

Ever after ſhe went in mans clothes, being armed cap-a-pe, and mounted on a brave Steed: and which was a wonder, when ſhe was on horſeback, none was more bold and daring; when* alighted, none more tame and meek; ſo that one could ſcarce ſee her for

* *Gerſon. lib. de mirab. victoria cujuſdam puellæ, paulò poſt initium.*

for her ſelf, ſhe was ſo chang'd and alter'd as if her ſpirits diſmounted with her body. No ſword would pleaſe her, but one taken out of the * Church of S. Katharin in Fierebois in Tourain. Her firſt ſervice was in twice victualling of Orleance, whileſt the Engliſh made no reſiſtance, as if they had eyes onely to gaze, and no arms to fight.

* Polidor. Virg. in Hen. ſixth, pag. 471.

Hence ſhe ſent a menacing * letter to the Earl of Suffolk, the Engliſh Generall, commanding him in Gods and her own name to yield up the keyes of all good cities to her, the Virgin ſent by God to reſtore them to the French. The letter was received with ſcorn; and the trumpeter that brought it commanded to be burnt, againſt the Law of Nations, ſaith a French * Authour, but erroneouſly: for his coming was not warranted by the authority of any lawfull Prince, but from a private maid, how highly ſoever ſelf-pretended, who had neither eſtate to keep, nor commiſsion to ſend a trumpeter.

* See the copy thereof in Speeds King Hen. ſixth, pag. 654.

* Du Serres in his French Hiſt. tranſlat. by Grimſton, p. 326.

Now the minds of the French were all afloat with this the conceit of their new Generall, which miraculouſly raiſed their Spirits. Phancie is the caſtle commanding the city; and if once mens heads be poſſeſt with ſtrange imaginations, the whole body will follow, and be infinitely tranſported therewithall. Under her conduct they firſt drive away the Engliſh from Orleance: nor was ſhe a whit daunted, when ſhot through her arm with an arrow; but taking the arrow in one hand, and her ſword in another, *This is a * favour*, ſaid ſhe; *let us go on, they cannot eſcape the hand of God*: and ſhe never left off, till ſhe had beaten the Engliſh from the city. And hence this virago (call her now John or Joan) marched on into other countreys, which inſtantly revolted to the French crown. The example of the firſt place was the reaſon of all the reſt to ſubmit. The Engliſh in many skirmiſhes were worſted and defeated with few numbers. But what ſhall we ſay? when

* Idem. p. 317.

when God intends a Nation ſhall be beaten, he ties their hands behind them.

The French followed their blow, loſing no time, leſt the height of their Spirits ſhould be remitted: (mens Imaginations when once on foot muſt ever be kept going, like thoſe that go on ſtilts in fenny countreys, leſt ſtanding ſtill they be in danger of falling) and ſo keeping the conceit of their ſouldiers at the height; in one twelvemoneth they recovered the greateſt part of that the Engliſh did poſſeſſe.

But ſucceſſe did afterwards fail this She-Generall: for ſeeking to ſurpriſe S. Honories ditch near the city of S. Denis, ſhe was not onely wounded her ſelf, but alſo loſt a Troup of her beſt and moſt reſolute ſouldiers; and not long after, nigh the city of Compeigne, being too farre engaged in fight, was taken priſoner by the baſtard of Vendoſme, who ſold her to the Duke of Bedford, and by him ſhe was kept a priſoner a twelvemoneth in Rohan.

It was much diſputed amongſt the Statiſts what ſhould be done with her: Some held that no puniſhment was to be inflicted on her, becauſe

Nullum memorabile nomen
Fœminea in pœna.
Cruelty to a woman,
Brings honour unto no man.

Beſides, putting her to death would render all Engliſh men guilty which ſhould hereafter be taken priſoners by the French. Her former valour deſerved praiſe, her preſent miſery deſerved pity; captivity being no ill action but ill ſucceſſe: let them rather allow her an honourable penſion, and ſo make her valiant deeds their own by rewarding them. However, ſhe ought not to be put to death: for if the Engliſh would puniſh her, they could not more diſgrace her then with life, to let her live though in a poore mean way, and then ſhe would be the beſt confutation of her own glorious

glorious prophesies; let them make her the Laundresse to the English, who was the Leader to the French army.

Against these arguments necessity of State was urged, a reason above all reason; it being in vain to dispute whether that may be done which must be done. For the French superstition of her could not be reformed except the idole was destroyed; and it would spoil the French puppet-playes in this nature for ever after, by making her an example. Besides she was no prisoner of warre, but a prisoner of Justice, deserving death for her witchcraft and whoredomes; whereupon she was burnt at Rohan the sixth of July 1461, not without the aspersion of * cruelty on our Nation.

* Sententia post homines natos durissima, *Pol.Vir. pag.* 477.

Learned * men are in a great doubt what to think of her. Some make her a Saint, and inspired by Gods Spirit, whereby she discovered strange secrets and foretold things to come. She had ever an old * woman which went with her, and tutoured her; and 'tis suspicious, seeing this clock could not go without that rusty wheel, that these things might be done by confederacie, though some more uncharitable conceive them to be done by Satan himself.

* *Gerson in the book which he wrote of her, after long discussing the point leaves it uncertain, but is rather charitably inclined.*

**Serres, pag.* 325.

Two customes she had which can by no way be defended. One was her constant going in mans clothes, flatly against Scripture: yea mark all the miracles in Gods Word, wherein though mens estates be often chang'd (poore to rich, bond to free, sick to sound, yea dead to living) yet we reade of no old Æson made young, no woman Iphis turn'd to a man, or man Tiresias to a woman; but as for their age or sex, where nature places them, there they stand, and miracle it self will not remove them. Utterly unlawfull therefore was this Joans behaviour, as an occasion to lust; and our English Writers say that when she was to be condemned she confess'd her self to be with * child to prolong her life; but being reprived seven moneths for the triall

Pol. Virgil. ut prius.

triall thereof, it was found falſe. But grant her honeſt: though ſhe did not burn herſelf, yet ſhe might kindle others, and provoke them to wantonneſſe.

Beſides, ſhe ſhaved her hair in the faſhion of a * Frier, againſt Gods expreſſe word, it being alſo a Solecisme in nature, all women being born votaries, and the veil of their long hair minds them of their obedience they naturally owe to man: yea, without this comely ornament of hair, their moſt glorious beauty appears as deformed, as the ſunne would be prodigious without beams. Herein ſhe had a ſmack of Monkery, which makes all the reſt the more ſuſpicious, as being ſent to maintain as well the Friers as the French Crown. And if we ſurvey all the pretended miracles of that age, we ſhall find what tune ſoever they ſung, ſtill they had ſomething in the cloſe in the favour of Friers, though brought in as by the by, yet perchance chiefly intended, ſo that the whole ſentence was made for the parentheſis.

* Gerſon.

We will cloſe the different opinions which ſeverall Authours have of her with this Epitaph,

Here lies Joan of Arc, the which
Some count ſaint, and ſome count Witch;
Some count man, and ſomething more;
Some count maid, and ſome a Whore:
Her life's in queſtion, wrong, or right;
Her death's in doubt, by laws, or might.
Oh innocence take heed of it,
How thou too near to guilt doſt ſit.
(Mean time France a Wonder ſaw,
A Woman rule 'gainſt Salique Law.)
But, Reader, be content to ſtay
Thy cenſure, till the Judgement-day:
Then ſhalt thou know, and not before,
Whether Saint, Witch, Man, Maid, or Whore.

Some conceive that the Engliſh conqueſts, being come to the verticall point, would have decayed of

 themſelves,

themselves, had this woman never been set up, which now reaps the honour hereof as her action: Though thus a very child may seem to turn the waves of the sea with his breath, if casually blowing on them at that very instant when the tide is to turn of it self. Sure after her death the French went on victoriously, and wonne all from the English, partly by their valour, but more by our dissensions; for then began the cruell warres betwixt the Houses of York and Lancaster, till the Red rose might become White, by losing so much bloud, and the White rose Red by shedding it.

Chap. 6.

The Atheist.

THe word *Atheist* is of a very large extent: every Polytheist is in effect an Atheist, for he that multiplies a Deitie, annihilates it; and he that divides it, destroyes it.

But amongst the heathen we may observe that whosoever sought to withdraw people from their idolatry, was presently indited and arraign'd of Atheisme. If any Philosopher saw God through their Gods, this dust was cast in his eyes, for being more quick-sighted then others, that presently he was condemn'd for an Atheist; and thus Socrates the Pagan Martyr was put to death * ὡς Ἄθεος. At this day three sorts of Atheists are extant in the world:

* *Justin. Martyr secund. Apolog. pro Christian. pag. 56.*

1 In life and conversation. Psal. 10. 4. *God is not in all his thoughts*; not that he thinks there is no God, but thinks not there is a God, never minding or heeding him in the whole course of his life and actions.

2 In will and desire. Such could wish there were no God, or devil, as thieves would have no judge nor jaylour; *Quod metuunt periisse expetunt.*

In

3 In judgement and opinion. Of the former two ſorts of Atheiſts, there are more in the world then are generally thought; of this latter, more are thought to be, then there are, a contemplative Atheiſt being very rare, ſuch as were * Diagoras, Protagoras, Lucian, and Theodorus, who though carrying God in his name was an Atheiſt in his opinion. Come we to ſee by what degrees a man may climbe up to this height of Profaneneſſe. And we will ſuppoſe him to be one living in wealth and proſperity, which more diſpoſeth men to Atheiſme then adverſity: For affliction mindeth men of a Deity, as thoſe which are pinched will cry, *O Lord*: but much outward happineſſe abuſed occaſioneth men, as wiſe Agur obſerveth, *to deny God, and ſay, who is the Lord.*

* *Auguſt. tom. 7. lib. 3. contra Petilianum, c. 1. David cùm dicit,* Stultus dixit in corde, *&c. videtur Diagoram prædixiſſe.*

First he quarrels at the diverſities of religions in the world: complaining how great Clerks diſſent in their judgements, which makes him ſcepticall in all opinions: Whereas ſuch differences ſhould not make men careleſſe to have any, but carefull to have the beſt religion. *Maxime* 1

He loveth to maintain Paradoxes, and to ſhut his eyes againſt the beams of a known truth; not onely for diſcourſe, which might be permitted: for as no cloth can be woven except the woof and the warp be caſt croſſe one to another, ſo diſcourſe will not be maintained without ſome oppoſition for the time. But our enclining-atheiſt goes further, engaging his affections in diſputes, even in ſuch matters where the ſuppoſing them wounds piety, but the poſitive maintaining them ſtabs it to the heart. 2

He ſcoffs and makes ſport at ſacred things. This by degrees abates the reverence of religion, and ulcers mens hearts with profaneneſſe. The Popiſh Proverb well underſtood hath a truth in it, *Never dog bark'd againſt the Crucifix, but he ran mad.* 3

4 *Hence he proceeds to take exception at Gods Word.* He keeps a regiſter of many difficult places of Scripture, not that he deſires ſatisfaction therein, but delights to puzzle Divines therewith, and counts it a great conqueſt when he hath poſed them. Unneceſſary queſtions out of the Bible are his moſt neceſſary ſtudy; & he is more curious to know where Lazarus his ſoul was the foure dayes he lay in the grave, then carefull to provide for his own ſoul when he ſhall be dead. Thus is it juſt with God that they who will not feed on the plain meat of his Word, ſhould be choked with the bones thereof. But his principall delight is to ſound the alarum, and to ſet ſeverall places of Scripture to fight one againſt another, betwixt which there is a ſeeming, and he would make a reall, contradiction.

5 *Afterwards he grows ſo impudent as to deny the Scripture it ſelf.* As Sampſon being faſtned by a web to a pin, carried away both web and pin; ſo if any urge our Atheiſt with arguments from Scripture, and tie him to the Authority of Gods Word, he denies both reaſon and Gods Word, to which the reaſon is faſtened.

6 *Hence he proceeds to deny God himſelf.* Firſt in his Adminiſtration; then in his Eſſence. What elſe could be expected but that he ſhould bite at laſt, who had ſnarl'd ſo long? Firſt he denies Gods ordering of ſublunarie matters; *Tuſh doth the Lord ſee, or is there knowledge in the moſt Higheſt?* making him a maimed Deity, without an eye of Providence or an arm of Power, and at moſt reſtraining him onely to matters above the clouds. But he that dares to confine the King of heaven, will ſoon after endeavour to depoſe him, and fall at laſt flatly to deny him.

7 *He furniſheth himſelf with an armoury of arguments to fight againſt his own conſcience*: Some taken from

1. The impunity and outward happineſſe of wicked men: as the heathen * Poet, whoſe verſes for me ſhall paſſe unengliſhed.

Eſſe

Esse Deos credamne? fidem jurata fefellit,
Et facies illi, quæ fuit ante, manet. * *Ovid.lib.3. Amor. Eleg.3.*

And no wonder if an Atheist breaks his neck thereat, whereat the foot of David himself did almost * slip, when he saw the prosperity of the wicked; whom God onely reprives for punishment hereafter. * *Psal.73. 2,3.*

2. From the afflictions of the godly, whilest indeed God onely tries their faith and patience. As Absalom complain'd of his Father Davids government, that none were deputed to redresse peoples grievances; so he objects that none righteth the wrongs of Gods people, and thinks (proud dust) the world would be better steered if he were the Pilot thereof.

3. From the delaying of the day of Judgement, with those mockers 2. Peter 3. Whose objections the Apostle fully answereth. And in regard of his own particular the Atheist hath as little cause to rejoyce at the deferring of the day of Judgement, as the Thief hath reason to be glad, that the Assizes be put off, who is to be tryed, and may be executed before, at the Quarter-sessions: So death may take our Atheist off before the day of Judgement come.

With these and other arguments he struggles with his own conscience, and long in vain seeks to conquer it, even fearing that Deity he flouts at, and dreading that God whom he denies. And as that famous Athenian souldier * Cynegirus catching hold of one of the enemies ships held it first with his right hand, and when that was cut off, with his left, and when both were cut off, yet still kept it with his teeth; so the conscience of our Atheist, though he bruise it, and beat it, and maim it never so much, still keeps him by the teeth, still feeding and gnawing upon him, torturing and tormenting him with thoughts of a Deity, which the other desires to suppresse. * *Justin. lib.2.*

8 *At last he himself is utterly overthrown by conquering his own conscience.* God in justice takes from him the light which he thrust from himself, and delivers him up to a seared conscience, and a reprobate mind, whereby hell takes possession of him. The Apostle saith, Acts 17. 27. That a man may feel God in his works: But now our Atheist hath a dead palsey, is past all sense, and cannot perceive God who is everywhere presented unto him. It is most strange, yet most true, which is reported, that the armes of the Duke of Rohan in France, which are *fusills* or *lozenges*, are to be seen in the wood or stones throughout all his countrey, so that break a stone in the middle, or lop a bough of a tree, and one shall behold the grain thereof (by some secret cause in Nature) * diamonded or streaked in the fashion of a lozenge: yea the very same in effect is observed in England: for the resemblances of starres, the armes of the worshipfull family of the Shugburies in Warwickshire, are found in the * stones within their own mannour of Shugbury. But what shall we say? The armes of the God of heaven, namely Power, Wisdome, and Goodnesse, are to be seen in every creature in the world, even from worms to men, and yet our Atheist will not acknowledge them, but ascribes them either to Chance (but could a blind painter limme such curious pictures) or else to Nature, which is a mere slight of the devil to conceal God from men, by calling him after another name; for what is *natura naturans* but God himself?

** Because of these naturall forms in wood and stone, it seems that from thence the Dukes assum'd their armes.*

** Cambd. Brit. in Warwickshire.*

9 *His death commonly is most miserable*: either burnt, as Diagoras, or eaten up with lice, as * Pherecydes, or devoured by dogs as Lucian, or thunder-shot and turn'd to ashes, as Olimpius. However descending impenitent into hell, there he is Atheist no longer, but hath as much religion as the devil, *to confesse God and tremble*:

** Paul. Diacon. lib. 15.*

Nullus in inferno est Atheos, ante fuit.
On earth were Atheists many,
In hell there is not any.

All

All ſpeak truth, when they are on the rack; but it is a wofull thing to be hells Convert. And there we leave the Atheiſt, having dwelt the longer on his Character, becauſe that ſpeech of worthy Mr. * Greenham deſerves to be heeded, *That Atheiſme in England is more to be feared then Popery.*

* *In his grave Counſell*, p. 3.

To give an inſtance of a ſpeculative Atheiſt, is both hard and dangerous: hard; for we cannot ſee mens ſpeculations otherwiſe then as they cloth themſelves viſible in their actions, ſome Atheiſticall ſpeeches being not ſufficient evidence to convict the ſpeaker an Atheiſt. Dangerous; for what ſatisfaction can I make to their memories, if I challenge any of ſo foul a crime wrongfully? We may more ſafely inſiſt on an Atheiſt in life and converſation; and ſuch a one was he whom we come to deſcribe.

CHAP. 7.

The life of CESAR BORGIA.

CEſar Borgia was baſe-ſon to Rhoderick Borgia, otherwiſe called Pope Alexander the ſixth. This Alexander was the * firſt of the Popes who openly owned his baſtards; & whereas his Predeceſſours (counting fig-leaves better then nothing to cover their nakedneſſe) diſguiſed them under the names of Nephews and God-ſonnes, he was ſuch a ſavage in his luſt as nakedly to acknowledge his baſe children, and eſpecially this Ceſar Borgia, being like his Father in the ſwarthineſſe of the complexion of his ſoul.

* *Guicciard. Hiſtory of Italy lib.* 1. *pag.* 10.

His Father firſt made him a Cardinall, that thereby his ſhoulders might be enabled to bear as much Church preferment as he could load upon him. But Borgia's active ſpirit diſliked the profeſſion, and was *aſhamed of the Goſpel*, which had more cauſe to be aſhamed of him; wherefore he quickly got a diſpenſation to uncardinall himſelf.

The

The next hindrance that troubled his high deſignes was, that his elder brother, the Duke of Candia, ſtood betwixt him and preferment. It is reported alſo that theſe two brothers juſtled together in their * inceſt with their own ſiſter Lucretia, one as famous for her whoredomes, as her nameſake had * formerly been for her chaſtity. The throne and the bed cannot ſeverally abide partners, much leſſe both meeting together as here they did. Wherefore Ceſar Borgia took order that his brother was kill'd one night as he rode alone in the city of Rome, and his body caſt into Tyber; and now he himſelf ſtood without competitour in his fathers and ſiſters affection.

* *Idem lib.* 3. *pag.* 179.

* *Liv. lib.* 1.

His father was infinitely ambitious to advance him, as intending not onely to create him a Duke, but alſo to create a Dukedome for him, which ſeemed very difficult if not impoſsible; for he could neither lengthen the land, nor leſſen the ſea in Italie, and petty Princes therein were already crouded ſo thick, there was not any room for any more. However the Pope by fomenting the diſcords betwixt the French and Spaniſh about the kingdome of Naples, and by embroyling all the Italian States in civill diſſenſions, out of their breaches pick'd forth a large Principality for his ſonne, managed in this manner.

There is a fair and fruitfull Province in Italie, called Romania, parcelled into ſeverall States, all holding as feodaries from the Pope, but by ſmall penſions, and thoſe ſeldome paid. They were bound alſo not to ſerve in armes againſt the Church, which old tie they little regarded, and leſſe obſerved, as conceiving time had fretted it aſunder; ſouldiers generally more weighing his gold that entertaineth them, then the cauſe or enemy againſt whom they fight. Pope Alexander ſet his ſonne Borgia to reduce that countrey to the Churches juriſdiction, but indeed to ſubject it to his own abſolute hereditary Dominion. This in ſhort time he * effected, partly by the asſiſtance of the French King, whoſe penſioner he was (and by a French title made Duke Ualentinois) and partly by the effectuall aid of the Urſines, a potent Family in Italie.

* *Guicciard. lib. 4. pag. 237.*

But afterward the Urſines too late were ſenſible of their errour herein, and grew ſuſpicious of his greatneſſe. For they in helping him to conquer ſo many petty States, gathered the ſeverall twigs, bound them into a rod, and put it into his hands to beat them therewith. Whereupon they began by degrees to withdraw their help, which Borgia perceived, and having by flattery and fair promiſes got the principall of their Family into his hands, he put them* all to the ſword. For he was perfect in the deviliſh art of dealing an ill turn, doing it ſo ſuddenly his enemies ſhould not heare of him before, and ſo ſoundly, that he ſhould never heare of them afterwards, either ſtriking alwayes ſurely, or not at all.

* *Machiavill in his Prince, cap. 7.*

And now he thought to caſt away his crutches, and ſtand on his own legs, rendring himſelf abſolute, without being beholden to the French King or any other: Having wholly conquer'd Romania, he caſt his eyes on Hetruria, and therein either wan to ſubmiſſion or compliance moſt of the cities, an earneſt of his future finall conqueſt, had not the unexpected death of his father Pope Alexander prevented him.

This Alexander with his ſonne Ceſar Borgia intended to poyſon ſome rich Cardinalls, to which purpoſe a flagon of poyſoned wine was prepared: But through the * errour of a ſervant, not privy to the project, the Pope himſelf and Borgia his ſonne drank thereof, which coſt the former his life, and the other a long languiſhing ſickneſſe.

* *Guicciard. l. 6. pag. 307.*

This Ceſar Borgia once bragg'd to Machiavill, that he had ſo cunningly contrived his plots, as to warrant himſelf againſt all events. If his father ſhould die firſt, he had made himſelf maſter of ſuch a way, that by the ſtrength of his party in the city of Rome, and conclave of Cardinalls, he could chuſe what Pope he pleaſed, ſo from him to get aſſurance of this province of Romania to make it hereditary to himſelf. And if (which was improbable) Nature ſhould croſſe her hands, ſo that he ſhould die before his father, yet even then he had chalked out ſuch a courſe as would enſure his conqueſt to his poſterity : ſo that with this politick dilemma he thought himſelf able to diſpute againſt heaven it ſelf.

But (what he afterwards complained of) he never expected that at the ſame time, wherein his father ſhould die, he himſelf ſhould alſo lie deſperately ſick, diſenabled to proſecute his deſignes, till one unexpected counterblaſt of Fortune ruffled yea blew away all his projects ſo curiouſly plaited. Thus three aces chance often not to rub ; and Politicians think themſelves to have ſtopp'd every ſmall cranny, when they have left a whole doore open for divine providence to undo all which they have done.

The Cardinalls proceed to the choice of a new Pope, whileſt Borgia lay ſick abed, much bemoaning himſelf ; for all others (had they the command of all April ſhowrs) could not beſtow on drop of pity upon him. Pius the third was firſt choſen Pope, anſwering his name, being a devout man (ſuch black ſwans ſeldome ſwim in Tyber) but the chair of Peſtilence choked him within twenty ſix dayes, and in his room Julius was choſen, or rather his greatneſſe choſe himſelf, a ſworn enemy to Ceſar Borgia, who ſtill lay under the Phyſicians hands, and had no power to oppoſe the election, or to ſtrengthen his new-got Dukedome of Romania : the ſtate of his body was to be preferred before the body of his ſtate, and he lay ſtriving to keep life, not to make a Pope. Yea the operation of this poyſon made him vomit up the Dukedome of Romania which he had ſwallowed before, and whileſt

whilest he lay sick the States and cities therein recovered their own liberties formerly enjoyed.

Indeed this disease made Borgia lose his nails, that he could never after scratch to do any mischief; and being banished Italie, he fled into Navarre, where he was obscurely kill'd in a tumultuous insurrection.

He was a man master in the art of dissembling, never looking the same way he rowed; extremely lustfull, never sparing to tread hen and chickens. At the taking of Capua, where he assisted the French, he reserved * fourty of the fairest Ladies to be abused by his own wantonnesse. And the prodigality of his lust had long before his death made him bankrupt of all the moysture in his body, if his Physicians had not dayly repaired the decayes therein. He exactly knew the operations of all hot and cold poysons, which would surprise nature on a sudden, and which would weary it out with a long siege. He could contract a hundred toads into one drop, and cunningly infuse the same into any pleasant liquour, as the Italians have poysoning at their fingers ends. By a fig (*which restored Hezekiahs * life*) he took away the lives of many. In a word, if he was not a practicall Atheist, I know not who was.

* *Idem, lib. 5. pag. 250.*

* *2. Kings 20. 7.*

If any desire to know more of his badnesse, let them reade Machiavills Prince, where Borgia is brought in as an * instance of all vilany. And though he deserves to be hiss'd out of Christendome, who will open his mouth in the defence of Machiavills precepts, yet some have dared to defend his person; so that he in his Book shews not what Princes should be, but what then they were, intending that work, not for a glasse for future Kings to dresse themselves by, but onely therein to present the monstrous face of the Politicians of that Age. Sure he who is a devil in this book, is a Saint * in all the rest; and those that knew him, * witnesse him to be of honest life and manners: so that

* Nunquam verebor in exemplum Valentinum subjicere, *Machiavel Prince, cap. 13. pag. 73.*

* *His notes on Livy, but especially his Florentine History savours of Religion.*

* *Boissardus part. 3. Iconum virorum illustrium.*

that which hath sharpned the pens of many against him, is his giving so many cleanly wipes to the foul noses of the Pope and Italian Prelacy.

Chap. 8.

The Hypocrite.

BY *Hypocrite* we understand such a one as doth (Isaiah 32. 6.) *practise hypocrisie*, make a trade or work of dissembling: For otherwise, * *Hypocriseorum macula carere, aut paucorum est aut nullorum.* The best of Gods children have a smack of hypocrisie.

* *Hieronym. lib. 2. contra Pelag. & August in eadem verba, Serm. 59. de Tempore*

Maxime 1. *An Hypocrite is himself both the archer and the mark, in all actions shooting at his own praise or profit.* And therefore he doth all things that they may be seen: What with others is held a principall point in Law, is his main Maxime in Divinity, To have good witnesse. Even fasting it self is meat and drink to him, whilest others behold it.

2 *In the outside of religion he out-shines a sincere Christian.* Guilt cups glitter more then those of massie gold, which are seldome burnish'd. Yea, well may the Hypocrite afford gaudy facing, who cares not for any lining; brave it in the shop, that hath nothing in the ware-house. Nor is it a wonder if in outward service he out-strips Gods servants, who out-doeth Gods command by will-worship, giving God more then he requires, though not what most he requires, I mean, his heart.

3 *His vizard is commonly pluckt off in this world.* Sincerity is an entire thing in it self: Hypocrisie consists of severall pieces cunningy closed together; and sometimes the Hypocrite is smote (as Ahab with an arrow, 1. Kings 22. 34.) betwixt the joynts of his armour, and so is mortally wounded in his reputation. Now by these shrewd signes a dissembler is often discovered: First, heavie

heavie censuring of others for light faults: secondly, boasting of his own goodnesse: thirdly, the unequall beating of his pulse in matters of pietie, hard, strong and quick, in publick actions; weak, soft and dull, in private matters: fourthly, shrinking in persecution; for painted faces cannot abide to come nigh the fire.

4 *Yet sometimes he goes to the grave neither detected nor suspected.* If Masters in their art, and living in peaceable times wherein pietie and prosperity do not fall out, but agree well together. Maud, mother to King Henry the second, being besieged in * Winchester castle, counterfeited herself to be dead, and so was carried out in a coffin whereby she escaped. Another time being besieged at * Oxford in a cold winter, with wearing white apparell she got away in the snow undiscovered. Thus some Hypocrites by dissembling mortification that they are dead to the world, and by professing a snow-like purity in their conversations, escape all their life time undiscerned by mortall eyes.

* *Cambd. Brit. in Hantshire.*

* *Matth. Paris in Anno Dom.* 1141.

5 *By long dissembling piety he deceives himself at last*: Yea, he may grow so infatuated as to conceive himself no dissembler but a sincere Saint. A scholar was so possessed with his lively personating of King Richard the third, in a Colledge-Comedy, that ever after he was transported with a royall humour in his large expences, which brought him to beggery, though he had great preferment. Thus the Hypocrite by long acting the part of piety, at last believes himself really to be such an one, whom at first he did but counterfeit.

6 *God here knows, and hereafter will make Hypocrites known to the whole world.* Ottocar King of Bohemia refused to do homage to Rodulphus the first, Emperour, till at last, chastised with warre, he was content to do him homage privately in a tent; which tent was so contrived by the * Emperours servants, that by drawing one cord, it was all taken away, and so Ottocar presented on his knees doing his homage, to the view of three Armies

* *Pantaleon in vita Rodulph. Imperat lib. de Illustrib. Germ. part. 2.* 285.

in presence. Thus God at last shall uncase the closest dissembler to the sight of men angels and devils, having removed all veils and pretences of piety: no goat in a sheepskin shall steal on his right hand at the last day of judgement.

Chap. 9.

The life of Jehu.

JEhu the sonne of Jehosaphat, the sonne of Nimshi, was one of an active spirit, and therefore employed to confound the house of Ahab; for God, when he means to shave clear, chooses a razour with a sharp edge, and never sendeth a slug on a message that requireth haste.

A sonne of the Prophets sent by Elisha privately anointed him King at Ramoth Gilead, whereupon he was proclaimed King by the consent of the army. Surely God sent also an invisible messenger to the souls of his fellow-captains, and anointed their hearts with the oyl of Subjection, as he did Jehu's head with the oyl of Sovereignty.

Secrecie and celerity are the two wheels of great actions. Jehu had both: he marched to Jezreel faster then Fame could flie, whose wings he had clipt by stopping all intelligence, that so at once he might be seen and felt of his enemies. In the way meeting with Jehoram and Ahaziah, he conjoyned them in their deaths who consorted together in idolatrie. The corps of Jehoram he orders to be cast into Nabaoths vineyard, a garden of herbs royally dung'd, and watered with bloud.

Next he revengeth Gods Prophets on cruell Jezabell, whose wicked carcase was devoured by dogs to a small reversion, as if a head that plotted, & hands that practis'd so much mischief, & feet so swift to shed bloud were not meat good enough for dogs to eat. Then by a letter he commands

mands the heads of Ahabs ſeventy ſonnes (their Guardians turning their executioners) whoſe heads being laid on two heaps at the gate of Jezreel ſerved for two ſoft pillows for Jehu to ſleep ſweetly upon, having all thoſe corrivalls to the Crown taken away.

The Prieſts of Baal follow after. With a pretty wile he fetches them all into the temple of their Idole, where having ended their ſacrifice, they themſelves were ſacrificed. However I dare not acquit Jehu herein. In Holy Fraud I like the Chriſtian but not the ſirname thereof, and wonder how any can marry theſe two together in the ſame action, ſeeing ſurely the parties were never agreed. This I dare ſay, Be it unjuſt in Jehu, it was juſt with God, that the worſhippers of a falſe God ſhould be deceived with a feigned worſhip.

Hitherto I like Jehu as well as Joſiah; his zeal blazed as much: But having now got the Crown, he diſcovers himſelf a diſſembling Hypocrite. It was an ill ſigne when he ſaid to Jonadab the ſonne of Rechab, *Come with me, and ſee my zeal for the Lord.* Bad inviting gueſts to feed their eyes on our goodneſſe. But Hypocrites rather then they will loſe a drop of praiſe will lick it up with their own tongue.

Before, he had diſſembled with Baal, now he counterfeits with God. *He took no heed to walk in the way of the Lord God of Iſrael with all his heart*: formerly his ſword had two edges, one cut for Gods glory, the other for his own preferment. He that before drove ſo furiouſly, whileſt his private ends whipt on his horſes, now will not go a footpace in Gods commandments, *He departed not from the golden calves in Dan and Bethel.*

I know what Fleſh will object, that this State-ſinne Jehu muſt commit to maintain his kingdome: for the lions of gold did ſupport the throne of Solomon, but the calves of gold the throne of Jeroboam and his Succeſſours. Should he ſuffer his Subjects to go up to Jeruſalem

*Exod. 34.23. salem *thrice a yeare* (as the Law * of Moses commanded)this would un-King him in effect,as leaving him no able Subjects to command. And as one in the heathen Poet complains,

Tres sumus imbelles numero, sine viribus uxor,
Laertesque senex, Telemachusque puer.

Three weaklings we, a wife for warre too mild,
Laertes old, Telemachus a child.

So thrice a yeare should Jehu onely be King over such an impotent company of old men, women, and children. Besides, it was to be feared that the ten Tribes going to Jerusalem to worship, where they fetch'd their God, would also have their King.

But Faith will answer, that God that built Jehu's throne without hands, could support it without buttresses, or being beholden to idolatry : And therefore herein Jehu, who would needs piece out Gods providence with his own carnall policie, was like a foolish greedy gamester, who having all the game in his own hand steals a needlesse card to assure himself of winning the stake, and thereby loses all. For this deep diver was drown'd in his own policie, and Hazael King of Syria was raised up by God to trouble and molest them. Yet God rewarded him with a lease of the Kingdome of foure successive lives, who had he been sincere would have assured him of a Crown here and hereafter.

CHAP. 10.

Chap. 10.

The Heretick.

IT is very difficult accurately to define him. Amongst the Heathen *Atheist* was, and amongst Christians *Heretick* is the disgracefull word of course, alwayes cast upon those who dissent from the predominant current of the time. Thus those who in matters of opinion varied from the * Popes copie the least hair-stroke, are condemned for Hereticks. Yea, Virgilius Bishop of Saltzburg was branded with that censure for maintaining that there were * Antipodes opposite to the then known world. It may be, as Alexander, hearing the Philosophers dispute of more worlds, wept that he had conquered no part of them; so it grieved the Pope that these Antipodes were not subject to his jurisdiction, which much incensed his Holinesse against that strange opinion. We will branch the description of an Heretick into these three parts.

* Hìc videtur quòd omnis qui non obedit statutis Romanæ sedis sit Hæreticus, *Glossa in c. nulli dist.* 19. *in verbo* Prostratus.

* *Joh. Avent. lib.* 3. *Annal. Boior*

First, he is one that formerly hath been of the true Church: * *They went out from us, but they were not of us.* These afterwards prove more offensive to the Church then very Pagans; as the English-Irish, descended anciently of English Parentage (be it spoken with the more shame to them, and sorrow to us) turning wild become worse enemies to our Nation then the Native Irish themselves.

* 1. John 2. 19.

2. Maintaining a Fundamentall errour. Every scratch in the hand is not a stab to the heart; nor doth every false opinion make a Heretick.

3. With obstinacy. Which is the dead flesh, making the green wound of an errour fester into the old soare of an Heresie.

It matters not much what manner of person he hath. If beautifull, perchance the more attractive of feminine fol- *Maxime* 1.

lowers: If deformed, so that his body is as odde as his opinions, he is the more properly entitled to the reputation of *crooked Saint*.

2 *His naturall parts are quick and able.* Yet he that shall ride on a winged horse to tell him thereof, shall but come too late to bring him stale news of what he knew too well before.

3 *Learning is necessary in him if he trades in a criticall errour*: but if he onely broches dregs, and deals in some dull sottish opinion, a trovell will serve as well as a pencill to daub on such thick course colours. Yea in some Heresies deep studying is so uselesse, that the first thing they learn, is to inveigh against all learning.

4 *However some smattering in the originall tongues will do well.* On occasion he will let flie whole vollies of Greek and Hebrew words, whereby he not onely amazeth his ignorant Auditours, but also in conferences daunteth many of his opposers, who (though in all other learning farre his superiours) may perchance be conscious of want of skill in those languages, whilest the Heretick hereby gains credit to his cause and person.

5 *His behaviour is seemingly very pious and devout.* How foul soever the postern and backdoore be, the gate opening to the street is swept and garnished, and his outside adorned with pretended austerity.

6 *He is extremely proud and discontented with the times*, quarrelling that many beneath him in piety are above him in place. This pride hath caused many men which otherwise might have been *shining lights* prove smoaking firebrands in the Church.

7 *Having first hammered the heresie in himself, he then falls to seducing of others*: so hard it is for one to have the itch and not to scratch. Yea Babylon her self will alledge, that *for Sions sake she will not hold her peace*. The necessity of propogating the truth is errours plea to divulge her falshoods. Men, as naturally they desire to know, so they desire what they know should be known.

If

If challenged to a private diſpute, his impudence bears him out. He counts it the onely errour to confeſſe he hath erred. His face is of braſſe, which may be ſaid either ever or never to bluſh. In diſputing his *Modus* is *ſine modo* ; and as if all figures (even in Logick) were magicall, he neglects all forms of reaſoning, counting that the onely Syllogiſme which is his concluſion. 8

He ſlights any Synod if condemning his opinions ; eſteeming the deciſions thereof no more then the forfeits in a barbers ſhop, where a Gentlemans pleaſure is all the obligation to pay, and none are bound except they will bind themſelves. 9

Sometimes he comes to be put to death for his obſtinacy. Indeed ſome charitable Divines have counted it inconſiſtent with the lenity of the Goſpel, which is to expect and endeavour the amendment of all, to put any to death for their falſe opinions ; and we reade of S. Paul (though the Papiſts paint him alwayes with a ſword) that he onely came *with a rod*. However the * mildeſt Authours allow that the Magiſtrate may inflict capitall puniſhment on Hereticks, in caſes of 10

1. Sedition againſt the State wherein he lives. And indeed ſuch is the ſympathy betwixt Church and Commonwealth that there are few Hereſies, except they be purely ſpeculative (and ſo I may ſay have heads without hands or any practicall influence) but in time the violent maintainers of them may make a dangerous impreſſion in the State.
2. Blaſphemy againſt God , and thoſe points of religion which are awfully to be believed.

For either of theſe our Heretick ſometimes willingly undergoes death, and then in the Calendar of his own conceit he canonizeth himſelf for a Saint, yea a Martyr.

*Gerards Common places de Magiſtrat. Polit. p. 1047.

Chap. II.

The rigid Donatists.

Anno Domini 331.

THe Donatists were so called from a double Donatus, whereof the one planted the sect, the other water'd it, & the devil by Gods permission gave the increase. The elder Donatus being one of tolerable parts, and intolerable pride, rais'd a Schisme in Carthage against good Cecilian the Bishop there, whom he loaded unjustly with many crimes, which he was not able to prove; and vexed with this disgrace he thought to right his credit by wronging religion, and so began the * heresie of Donatists.

His most dominative tenet was, that the Church was perished from the face of the earth, the reliques thereof onely remaining in his party. I instance the rather on this Heresie, because the reviving thereof is the new disease of our times. One * Vibius in Rome was so like unto Pompey, *ut permutato statu Pompeius in illo, & ille in Pompeio salutari possit*: Thus the Anabaptists of our dayes, and such as are Anabaptistically inclin'd, in all particulars resemble the old Donatists, abating onely that difference which is necessarily required to make them alike.

The epithet of *rigid* I therefore do adde, to seperate the Donatists from themselves, who seperated themselves from all other Christians. For there were two principall sides of them: first, the Rogatists, from Rogatus their teacher, to whom S. Augustine beareth witnesse that *they had zeal but not according to knowledge.* These were pious people for their lives, hating bloudy practices, though erroneous in their doctrine. The learned * Fathers of that age count them part of the true Church, and their brethren, though they themselves disclaim'd any such brotherhood with other Christians.

* *Augustin. ad Quod vult Deum.*

* *Valer. Max. lib. 9. cap. 15.*

* Ipsum Fraternitatis nomen utcunque Donatistis fastidiosum, est tamen orthodoxis erga ipsos Donatistas necessarium, *Optat. lib. 3. init.*

Christians. Oh the sacred violence of such worthy mens charity in plucking those to them which thrust themselves away! But there was another sort of Jesuited Donatists, as I may say, whom they called *Circumcellions*, though as little reason can be given of their * name as of their opinions, whom we principally intend at this time.

Their number in short time grew not onely to be considerable but terrible: their tenet was plausible and winning; and that Faith is easily wrought which teacheth men to believe well of themselves. From Numidia, where they began, they overspread Africa, Spain, France, Italie and Rome it self. We find not any in Brittain, where * Pelagianisme mightily reigned: either because God in his goodnesse would not have one countrey at the same time visited with a double plague, or else because this infection was to come to this Iland in after-ages, furbished up under a new name.

Their greatest increase was under Julian the Emperour. This Apostate next to no religion loved the worst religion best, and was a professed friend to all foes of goodnesse. The Donatists, being punished under former Christian Emperours, repaired to him for succour, not caring whether it was an Olive or a Bramble they fled to, so be it afforded them shelter. They extoll'd him for such a godly man (flattery and false doctrine go ever together) *with whom alone * justice did remain*, and he restored them their good Churches again, & armed them with many priviledges against Christians. Hereupon they raised a cruell persecution, killing many men in the very Churches, murthering women and infants, defiling virgins, or ravishing them rather, for consent onely defiles. God keep us from standing in the way where blind zeal is to passe, for it will trample down all before it, and mercy shall as soon be found at the hands of prevailing cowards. What the

* *S. August. in Psal.* 132. quia circum cel as vagantur, *count them so called; which is rather his Allusion then the true Etymologie.*

* *Sr H. Spelman Councells, pag.* 416.

* *Quòd apud eum solum justitia locum haberet*, Aug. contra literas Petil. lib. 2. cap. 97.

Anabaptists did in Germany, we know; what they would do here, had they power, God knows. The best security we have they will do no harm is because they cannot.

We come to set down some of their principall opinions: I say, Principall; for at last they did enterfere with all Hereticks, Arians, Macedonians, &c. ignorant zeal is too blind to go right, and too active to stand still: yea all errours are of kinne, at the farthest but cousens once removed; and when men have once left the truth, their onely quiet home, they will take up their lodging under any opinion which hath the least shadow of probability. We will also set down some of their reasons, and how they torture Scripture with violent interpretations to wrest from it a confession on their side, yet all in vain.

First Position.

That the true Church was perished from the face of the earth, the remnants thereof being onely *in parte Donati*, in that * part of Africa where Donatus and his followers were. The Anabaptists in like manner stifle Gods Church by crowding it into their corner, confining the monarchy of Christ in the Gospel unto their own toparchy, and having a quarrell to the words in the Creed, *Catholique Church.*

* *August. lib 2. contra Crescon. cap. 37.*

The Donatists Reasons.

It is said, Canticles. 1. 7. *Tell me, O thou whom my soul loveth, where thou feedest, where thou makest thy flocks to rest in the South.* By this the Donatists are meant: Africa wherein they lived was in the South.

Confutation.

An argument drawn from an * allegorie is weak, except all the obscurities therein be first explained. Besides, Africa Cesariensis (where the Donatists were) was much more West then South from Judea. But Gods Church cannot be contracted to the Chapell of Donatus, to which God himself (the truest surveyour) alloweth

* Quis non impudentissimè nitatur aliquid in allegoria positum pro se interpretari, nisi habeat & manifesta testimonia quorum lumine illustrentur obscura, *Aug. Tom. 2. Epist. 48. ad Vincent.*

alloweth larger bounds, Psalm. 2. 8. *Ask of me, and I will give thee the Heathen for thine inheritance, and the uttermost parts of the earth for thy possession.* Now the restrainers of the Church to a small place (as much as in them lies) falsifie Gods promise and shorten Christs portion. Many other * places speak the large extent of the Gospel, Gen. 22. 17. Gen. 28. 14. Psal. 72. 8. &c.

*Optat. Milev. lib. 2. & Aug. contra liter. Petil. cap. 6, 7, 8.

Second Position.

That their Church consisted of an holy company, pure and undefiled indeed. Thus also the Anabaptists brag of their holinesse, as if nothing else were required to make men pure but a conceit that they are so. Sure had they no other fault but want of charity, their hands could not be clean who throw so much dirt on other mens faces.

Reasons.

It is said, Ephes. 5. 27. *That Christ might present to himself a glorious Church, without spot, or wrinkle, or any such thing, but that it should be holy and without blemish*: which the Donatists appropriate to themselves.

Confutation.

This glorious presentation of the Church is * performed in the world to come. Here it consisteth of sinners (who had rather confesse their wrinkles then paint them) and had need to pray dayly, *And forgive us our trespasses.*

*Aug. ut prius ad Vincentium, & epist. 50. ad Bonifac.

Third Position.

That mixt Communions were infectious, and the pious promiscuously receiving with the profane are polluted thereby. Heare the Anabaptizing sing the same note, *By * profane and ignorant persons coming to the Lords table, others also that communicate with them are guilty of the same profanation.*

*Protestation protested, p. 14.

Reasons.

Because severall places of Scripture commend, yea command, a separation from them. Jerem. 15. 19. *Take forth the pretious from the vile.* 2. Cor. 6. 17. *Be ye separate,*

parate and touch no unclean thing. 2. Theſſ. 3. 6. *Withdraw your ſelves from every brother that walketh diſorderly.* 1. Cor. 5. 7. *Purge out therefore the old leven, &c.*

Confutation.

In theſe and the like places two things are enjoyned: firſt, a ſeparation from intimate familiarity with profane perſons; ſecondly, a ſeparation from their vices and wickedneſſe, by deteſting and diſclaiming them: but neither civill State-ſociety, nor publick Church-communion is hereby prohibited. By *purging out the old leven*, Church-cenſures are meant, to excommunicate the openly profane. But that mixt Communions pollute not, appears, becauſe S. Paul ſaith, 1. Cor. 11. 28. *But let a man examine himſelf, and ſo let him eat of that bread*, &c. but enjoyns not men to examine others; which was neceſſary if bad Communicants did defile. It neither makes the cheere or welcome the worſe to ſit next to him at Gods table who wants a wedding-garment, for he that touches his perſon, but diſclaims his practices, is as farre from him, as the Eaſt from the Weſt, yea as heaven from hell. In bodily diſeaſes one may be infected without his knowledge, againſt his will: not ſo in ſpirituall contagions, where * *acceditur ad vitium corruptionis vitio conſenſionis*, and none can be infected againſt their conſent.

Auguſt. contr. Don. poſt Coll. Lib.

Fourth Poſition.

That the godly were bound to ſever from the ſociety of the wicked, and not to keep any communion with them. Thus the moſt rigid of modern Factours for the Independent congregations would draw their files out of the army of our Nationall Church, and ſet up a congregation wherein Chriſt ſhall reigne in Beautie and Puritie. But they may flie ſo far from myſticall Babylon as to run to literall Babel, I mean bring all to confuſion, and founder the Commonwealth: For they that ſtride ſo wide at once will go farre with few paces.

Reaſon.

Reason.

Becauſe it is written, 2 Cor. 6. 14. *What * communion hath light with darkneſſe ?* and in other places, to the ſame effect.

* *Aug. lib. 2. contra Petill. cap. 39.*

Confutation.

The anſwer is the ſame with the former : But the tares ſhall grow with the corn. And in the viſible militant Church and kingdome of grace, that wicked men ſhall be unſeparablie mingled with the godly, beſides our Saviours teſtimonie, Matt. 13. 30. theſe reaſons do approve : firſt, becauſe Hypocrites can never be ſevered, but by him that can ſearch the heart ; ſecondly, becauſe if men ſhould make the ſeparation, weak Chriſtians would be counted no Chriſtians, and thoſe who have a grain of grace under a load of imperfections would be counted reprobates ; thirdly, becauſe Gods veſſells of honour from all eternitie, not as yet appearing, but wallowing in ſinne, would be made caſtawayes ; fourthly, becauſe God by the mixture of the wicked with the godly will try the watchfulneſſe and patience of his ſervants ; fifthly, becauſe thereby he will beſtow many favours on the wicked, to clear his juſtice, and render them the more inexcuſable : laſtly, becauſe the mixture of the wicked, grieving the godly, will make them the more heartily pray for the day of judgement. The deſire of future glory makes the godly to cry, *Come Lord Jeſus* ; but the feeling of preſent pain (whereof they are moſt ſenſible) cauſeth the ingemination, *Come Lord Jeſus, come quickly.* In a word as it is wholſome for a flock of ſheep for ſome goats to feed amongſt them, their bad ſent being good Phiſick for the ſheep to keep them from the *Shakings* ; ſo much profit redounds to the godly by the neceſſary mixture of the wicked amongſt them, making the pious to ſtick the faſter to God and goodneſſe.

Fifth Poſition.

That * the efficacie of the Sacrament depends on the

* *Aug. lib. 1. contra liter. Petil. cap. 1.*

 piety

piety of the Minister; so that in effect his piety washeth the water in baptisme, and sanctifieth it, whereas the profanenesse of a bad man administring it doth unsacrament baptisme it self, making a nullity thereof. Herein the Anabaptists joyn hands with them, as 'tis generally known by their re-baptizing: Yea * some tending that way have maintained, that Sacraments received from ignorant and unpreaching Ministers are of no validity.

* *J. Penry p. 46. and 49.*

Reason.

It is written, Matth. 7. 18. *A good tree cannot bring forth evil fruit, neither can a corrupt tree bring forth good fruit.*

Confutation.

This is true of mens personall, but not of their ministeriall acts: that Minister that can adde the word * of institution to the element, makes a sufficient Sacrament: And Sacraments, like to shelmeats, may be eaten after fowl hands, without any harm. *Cum * obsint indigne tractantibus, prosint tamen digne sumentibus.* Yet God make all Ministers pious, painfull, and able: we, if beholding the present age, may justly bemoan their want, who remembring the former age, must as justly admire their plenty.

* *Aug. tract. 80. in Johan.*

* *Idem contra Parmen. lib. 2. cap. 10.*

Sixth Position.

That all learning and * eloquence was to be condemn'd. Late Sectarists go farther: Greenwood and Barrow * moved Queen Elizabeth to abolish both Universities,

Which we believe and wish may then be done,
When all blear eyes have quite put out the sunne.

* *Idem. lib. 1. contra Cresco. cap. 30.*

* *Dr Soame writing against them, lib. 2. pag. 4.*

Reason.

Because learning hath been the cause of many Heresies, and discords in the Church.

Confutation.

Not learning but the conceit thereof in those that wanted it, and the abuse thereof in such as had it, caused Hereticks.

Seventh

Seventh Position.

That Magistrates have no power to compell people to serve God by outward punishment: which is also the distill'd position of our Anabaptists, thus blinding the Ministers, and binding the Magistrate, what work do they make?

Reason.

Because it is a breach of the * liberty of the creature: The King of heaven gave not men freewill, for the Kings of the earth to take it away from them.

* *August lib. 3. cont. Crescon. cap. 51.*

Confutation.

God gave men freewill to use it well; if they abuse it, God gave Magistrates power to punish them, else they *bear the sword in vain.* They may command people to serve God, who herein have no cause to complain; better *to be compell'd to a feast*, Luke 14. 23. then to runne to a fray. But these men who would not have Magistrates compell them, *quære* whether if they had power they would not compell Magistrates.

The Donatists also did mightily boast of miracles and visions: they made nothing to step into the third heaven, and have familiar * dialogues with God himself: they used also to cite their revelations as arguments for their opinions; we will trust the coppy of such their visions to be true, when we see the originall produc'd: herein the Anabaptists come not behind them. Strange was the Donatists ambition of Martyrdome; they used to force such as they met to wound them mortally, or violently to stab and kill them; and on purpose to fall down from * steep mountains, which one day may wish the mountains to fall on them. For Martyrs are to die willingly but not wilfully; and though to die be a debt due to nature, yet he that payes it before the time, may be called upon for repayment to die the second death.

* Donatus oravit, respondet ei Deus de cœlo, *Aug. in Johann. tract. 3. prope finem.*

* *Theodoretus in fabulis Hæret.*

Once many Donatists met a noble * Gentleman, and gave him a sword into his hand, commanding him

* *Centuriator. cent. 4 c. 5 p. 211. ex Theodoreto.*

to kill them, or threatning to kill him. Yet he refus'd to do it, unlesse first they would suffer him to bind them all; for fear, said he, that when I have kill'd one or two of you, the rest alter their minds and fall upon me. Having fast bound them all, he soundly whipt them, and so let them alone. Herein he shewed more wit then they wanted, and more charity then wit, denying them their desires, and giving them their deserts, seeking to make true Saints by marring of false Martyrs.

These Donatists were opposed by the learned writings of private Fathers, Optatus Milevitanus, and S. Augustine (no Heresie could bud out, but presently his pruning-hook was at it) and by whole Councells, one at Carthage, another at Arles. But the Donatists, whilest blessing themselves, cared not for the Churches Anathema's, being so farre from fearing her excommunications, that they prevented them in first excommunicating themselves by separation; and they count it a kindnesse to be shut out, who would willingly be gone. Besides, they called at * Carthage an Anti-councell of their own faction, consisting of two hundred seventy Bishops, to confirm their opinions. Let Truth never challenge Errour at the weapon of number alone, without other arguments; for some Orthodox Councells have had fewer suffrages in them, then this Donatisticall conventicle; and we may see small Pocket-Bibles, and a great Folio-Alchoran.

** Aug. Epist. ad Vincentium.*

But that which put the period to this Heresie (for after the six hundredth yeare of Christ the Donatist appears not, *I looked after his place and he was not to be found*) was partly their own dissensions, for they * crumbled into severall divisions amongst themselves: Besides the honest Rogatists (of whom before) they had severall sects, some more, some lesse strict, called from their severall masters, Cresconians, * Petilians, Ticonians, Parmenians, Maximians, &c. which much differed amongst

** In minutula frustula, Idem.*
** Petilian went not so farre as the rest, Aug. lib. 3. de correct. Donati c. 17. 19. Vid Aug. de schism. Maxim. brevi. collat. 3 diei.*

amongſt themſelves. Thus is it given to all Hereſies to break out into under-factions, ſtill going further in their tenets; and ſuch as take themſelves to be twice-refined will count all others to be but droſſe, till there be as many Hereſies as Hereticks, like the Ammonites, ſo ſcattered by Saul, 1. Sam. 11. 11. *that there remained not two of them which were together.*

But chiefly they were ſuppreſſed by the civill Magiſtrate (Moſes will do more with a frown then Aaron with a blow, I mean with Church-cenſures) for * Honorius the godly Emperour (with his arm above a thouſand miles long) eaſily reach'd them in Europe, Aſia, and Africa, and by puniſhments mixt with the Churches inſtructions converted and reclaimed very many.

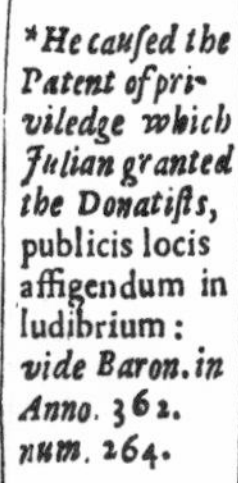
* *He cauſed the Patent of priviledge which Julian granted the Donatiſts,* publicis locis affigendum in ludibrium: *vide Baron. in Anno. 362. num. 264.*

In ſuch a caſe teaching without puniſhment had done little good, and puniſhment without teaching would have done much harm; both mingled together, by Gods bleſsing, cauſed the converſion of many, and finall ſuppreſsion of that Hereſie.

The ſame God of his goodneſſe grant that by the ſame means ſuch as revive this Hereſie nowadayes may have their eyes opened and their mouthes ſtopp'd, their pride leſſe and their knowledge more, that thoſe may be ſtayed which are going, and thoſe brought back which are gone into their dangerous opinions. For if the angels in heaven rejoyce at the converſion of a ſinner, none but devils and men deviliſhly minded will be ſorrowfull thereat.

CHAP. 12.

The Lyer

IS one that makes a trade to tell falshoods with intent to deceive. He is either open or secret. A secret Lyer or Equivocatour is such a one as by mentall reservations and other tricks deceives him to whom he speaks, being lawfully called to deliver all the truth. And sure speech being but a coppy of the heart, it cannot be avouched for a true coppy, that hath lesse in it then the originall. Hence it often comes to passe,

When Jesuites unto us answer Nay,
They do not English speak, t'is Greek they say.

Such an Equivocatour we leave, more needing a Book then Character to describe him. The open Lyer is first, either Mischievous, condemn'd by all; secondly, Officious, unlawfull also, because doing ill for good to come of it; thirdly, Jesting, when in sport and merriment. And though some count a Jesting lie to be like the dirt of oysters, which (they say) never stains, yet is it a sinne in earnest. What Policie is it for one to wound himself to tickle others, and to stab his own soul to make the standers by sport? We come to describe the Lyer.

Maxime 1. *At first he telles a lie with some shame and reluctancy.* For then if he cuts off but a lap of Truths garment his heart smites him; but in processe of time he conquers his Conscience, and from quenching it there ariseth a smoak which soots and fouls his soul, so that afterwards he lyes without a ny regret.

2 *Having made one lye he is fain to make more to maintain it.* For an untruth wanting a firm foundation needs many buttresses. The honour and happinesse of the

* *Deut.* 7. 14. * Israelites is the misery and mischief of lyes, *Not one amongst them shall be barren,* but miraculously procreative to beget others.

He

He hath a good memory which he badly abuseth. Memory in a Lyer is no more then needs. For first lies are hard to be remembred, because many, whereas truth is but one: secondly, because a lie cursorily told takes little footing and settled fastnesse in the tellers memory, but prints it self deeper in the hearers, who take the greater notice because of the improbability and deformity thereof; and one will remember the sight of a monster longer then the sight of an handsome body. Hence comes it to passe that when the Lyer hath forgotten himself, his Auditours put him in mind of the lye, and take him therein. 3

Sometimes though his memory cannot help him from being arrested for lying, his wit rescues him: which needs a long reach to bring all ends presently and probably together, gluing the splinters of his tales so cunningly that the cracks cannot be perceived. Thus a relique-monger bragg'd he could shew a feather of the dove at Christs baptisme; but being to shew it to the people, a wag had stollen away the feather and put a coal in the room of it. *Well*, quoth he to the Spectatours, *I cannot be so good as my word for the present; but here is one of the coals*that broil'd S. Laurence, and that's worth the seeing.* 4

* *Chamnitius in exam. conc. Trident. part.* 4. *p.* 12.

Being challenged for telling a lye no man is more furiously angry. Then he draws his sword and threatens, because he thinks that an offer of revenge, to shew himself moved at the accusation, doth in some sort discharge him of the imputation; as if the condemning of the sinne in appearance acquitted him in effect: or else because he that is call'd a Lyer to his face, is also call'd a Coward in the same breath if he swallows it; and the party charged doth conceive that if he vindicates his valour, his truth will be given him into the bargain. 5

At last he believes his own lies to be true. He hath told them over and over so often, that prescription makes 6

a

a right, and he verily believes that at the firſt he gathered the ſtory out of ſome authenticall Authour, which onely grew in his own brain.

7 *No man elſe believes him when he ſpeaks the truth.* How much gold ſoever he hath in his cheſt, his word is but braſſe, and paſſeth for nothing: yea he is dumb in effect, for it is all one whether one cannot ſpeak, or cannot be believed.

To conclude: Some of the weſt Indians to expiate their ſinne of lying uſe to let themſelves bloud in their tongues, and to offer the bloud to their idols: A good cure for the ſquinancie, but no ſatisfaction for lying. Gods word hath taught us better, *What profit is there in my bloud?* The true repentance of the party waſh'd in the bloud of Chriſt can onely obtain pardon for this ſinne.

Chap. 13.

The common Barreter.

A Barreter is an horſeleach that onely ſucks the corrupted bloud of the Law. He trades onely in tricks and quirks: His highway is in by-paths, and he loveth a cavill better then an argument, an evaſion then an anſwer. There be two kinds of them: either ſuch as fight themſelves, or are trumpeters in a battel to ſet on others. The former is a profeſt dueller in the Law that will challenge any, and in all ſuite-combats be either principall or ſecond.

Maxime 1 *References & compoſitions he hates as bad as an hangman hates a pardon.* Had he been a Scholar, he would have maintained all paradoxes; if a Chirurgion, he would never have cured a wound but alwayes kept it raw; if a Souldier, he would have been excellent at a ſiege, nothing but *ejectio firma* would out him.

2 *He is half ſtarv'd in the lent of a long vacation for want of imployment;*

imployment; ſave onely that then he brews work to broach in Term-time. I find one ſo much delighted in Law-ſport, that when*Lewis the King of France offered to eaſe him of a number of ſuits, he earneſtly beſought his Highneſſe to leave him ſome twenty or thirty behind, wherewith he might merrily paſſe away the time.

* Stephens Apol. for Herodotus.

3 *He hath this property of an honeſt man, that his word is as good as his band*; for he will pick the lock of the ſtrongeſt conveiance, or creep out at the lattice of a word. Wherefore he counts to enter common with others as good as his own ſeverall; for he will ſo vex his partners, that they had rather forgoe their right, then undergoe a ſuit with him. As for the trumpeter Barretour,

4 *He falls in with all his neighbours that fall out, and ſpurres them on to go to law*. A Gentleman, who in a duell was rather ſcratcht then wounded, ſent for a Chirurgion, who having opened the wound, charged his man with all ſpeed to fetch ſuch a ſalve from ſuch a place in his ſtudy. *Why* (ſaid the Gentleman) *is the hurt ſo dangerous? Oh yes* (anſwered the Chirurgion) *if he returns not in poſt-haſt the wound will cure it ſelf, and ſo I ſhall loſe my fee*. Thus the Barretour poſts to the houſes of his neighbours, leſt the ſparks of their ſmall diſcords ſhould go out before he brings them fuell, and ſo he be broken by their making up. Surely he loves not to have the bells rung in a peal, but he likes it rather when they are jangled backward, himſelf having kindled the fire of diſſenſion amongſt his neighbours.

5 *He lives till his clothes have as many rents as himſelf hath made diſſenſions*. I wonder any ſhould be of this trade, when none ever thrived on't, paying dear rates for their counſells: for bringing many crack'd titles, they are fain to fill up their gaping chinks with the more gold.

But I have done with this wrangling companion, half afraid to meddle with him any longer leſt he ſhould commence a ſuit againſt me for deſcribing him.

The Reader may eaſily perceive how this Book of the Profane State would ſwell to a great proportion, ſhould we therein character all the kinds of vicious perſons which ſtand in oppoſition to thoſe which are good. But this pains may well be ſpared, ſeeing that *rectum eſt index ſui & obliqui*; and the luſtre of the good formerly deſcribed will ſufficiently diſcover the enormity of thoſe which are otherwiſe. We will therefore inſtance in three principall offenders, and ſo conclude.

Chap. 14.

The Degenerous Gentleman.

SOme will chalenge this title of incongruity, as if thoſe two words were ſo diſſonant, that a whole ſentence cannot hold them; for ſure where the Gentleman is the root, Degenerous cannot be the fruit. But if any quarrell with my words, Valerius Maximus ſhall be my champion, who ſtyleth ſuch, * *Nobilia Portenta*. By *Gentleman* we underſtand one whom the Heralds (except they will deny their beſt Records) muſt allow of ancient parentage. Such a one, when a child, being kept the devils Nazarite, that no razor of correction muſt come upon his head in his fathers family, ſee what he proves in the proceſſe of time, brought to extreme poverty. Herein we intend no invective glance on thoſe pious Gentlemen, whoſe ſtates are conſumed through Gods ſecret judgement, and none of the owners viſible default; onely we meddle with ſuch as by careleſneſſe and riot cauſe their own ruine.

* *Valer. Max. lib. 3 cap. 5.*

Maxime 1. *He goes to ſchool to learn in jeſt and play in earneſt.* Now this Gentleman, now that Gentlewoman begges him a playday, and now the book muſt be thrown away, that he may ſee the buck hunted. He comes to ſchool late,

late, departs ſoon, and the whole yeare with him (like the fortnight when Chriſtmas day falls on a tueſday) is all Holidayes and half-Holidayes. And as the Poets feigne of Thetis, that ſhe drench'd Achilles her ſonne in the Stygian waters, that he might not be wounded with any weapon ; ſo cockering mothers inchant their ſonnes to make them rod-free, which they do by making ſome golden circles in the hand of the Schoolmaſter : thus theſe two conjoyning together make the indentures to bind the youth to eternall ignorance ; yet perchance he may get ſome almes of learning, here a ſnap, there a piece of knowledge, but nothing to purpoſe.

His fathers Servingmen (which he counts no mean preferment) admit him into their ſociety. Going to a drinking match they carry him with them to enter him, and applaud his hopefulneſſe, finding him vicious beyond his age. The Butler makes him free (having firſt pai'd his fees accuſtomed) of his own fathers cellar, and gueſſeth the profoundneſſe of his young maſters capacity by the depth of the whole-ones he fetcheth off. 2

Coming to the Univerſity, his chief ſtudy is to ſtudy nothing. What is Learning but a cloakbag of books, cumberſome for a Gentleman to carry ? and the Muſes fit to make wives for Farmers ſonnes : perchance his own Tutour, for the promiſe of the next living (which notwithſtanding his promiſe he afterwards ſells to another) contributes to his undoing, letting him live as he liſt : yea, perhaps his own mother (whileſt his father diets him for his health with a moderate allowance) makes him ſurfet underhand by ſending him money. Thus whileſt ſome complain that the Univerſity infected him, he infected the Univerſitie, from which he ſuck'd no milk but poyſoned her nipples. 3

At the Innes of Court under pretence to learn Law, he learns to be lawleſſe ; not knowing by his ſtudy ſo much as what an Execution means, till he learns it by his own 4 dear experience. Here he grows acquainted with the *Roaring Boyes*, I am afraid ſo called by a wofull Prolepſis, Here, for Hereafter. What formerly was counted the chief credit of an Oratour, theſe eſteem the honour of a Swearer, *Pronunciation*, to mouth an oath with a graceleſſe grace. Theſe (as David ſaith) *cloath themſelves with curſes as with a garment*, and therefore deſire to be in the lateſt faſhion both in their cloaths and curſes : Theſe infuſe all their skill into their young novice, who ſhortly proves ſuch a proficient, that he exceeds his Maſters in all kinds of vicious courſes.

5 *Through the mediation of a Scrivener he grows acquainted with ſome great Uſurer.* Nor is this youngſter ſo ravenous, as the other is ready to feed him with money, ſometimes with a courteous violence forcing on him more then he deſires, provided the ſecurity be good, except the Uſurer be ſo valiant as to hazard the loſing of a ſmall hook to catch a great fiſh, and will adventure to truſt him, if his eſtate in hope be overmeaſure, though he himſelf be under age. Now the greater part of the money he takes up is not for his own ſpending, but to pay the ſhot of other mens riot.

6 *After his fathers death he flies out more then ever before.* Formerly he took care for means for his ſpending, now he takes care for ſpending for his means. His wealth is ſo deep a gulf, no riot can ever ſound the bottome of it. To make his gueſts drunk is the onely ſeal of their welcome. His very meaneſt ſervant may be maſter of the cellar, and thoſe who deſerve no beere may command the beſt wine : ſuch dancing by day, ſuch masking by night, ſuch roaring, ſuch revelling, able to awake the ſleeping aſhes of his Great-great-grandfather, and to fright all bleſſing from his houſe.

7 *Mean time the old ſoare of his London-debts corrupts and feſters.* He is careleſſe to take out the dead fleſh, or to diſcharge either principall or intereſt. Such ſmall leaks are not worth the ſtopping or ſearching for till they be greater ;

greater; he ſhould undervalue himſelf to pay a ſumme before it grew conſiderable for a man of his eſtate. Nor can he be more careleſſe to pay, then the Uſurer is willing to continue the debt, knowing that his bands, like infants, battle beſt with ſleeping.

8 *Vacation is his vocation, and he ſcorns to follow any profeſsion;* and will not be confin'd to any laudable employment. But they who count a calling a priſon, ſhall at laſt make a priſon their calling. He inſtills alſo his lazie principles into his children, being of the ſame opinion with the Neapolitane Gentry, who ſtand ſo on the * puntoes of their honour, that they preferre robbery before induſtry, and will rather ſuffer their daughter to make merchandiſe of her chaſtity, then marry the richeſt merchant.

* Sr William Segar in his Honours milit. and civill.

9 *Drinking is one of the principall Liberall Sciences he profeſſeth.* A moſt ungentile quality, fit to be baniſhed to rogues and rags. It was anciently counted a Dutch vice, and ſwarmed moſt in that countrey. I remember a ſad accident which hapned to Fliolmus King of Gothland, who whileſt a Lord of miſrule ruled in his Court, and both he and his ſervants were drunk, in mere merriment, meaning no harm, they took the King and put him in * jeſt into a great veſſel of beere, and drowned him in earneſt. But * one tells us that this ancient and habited vice is amongſt the Dutch of late years much decreaſed: which if it be not, would it were. Sure our Mariners obſerve that as the ſea grows dayly ſhallower and ſhallower on the ſhoars of Holland and Zeland, ſo the channell of late waxeth deeper on the coaſts of Kent and Eſſex. I pray God if drunkenneſſe ebbes in Dutchland, it doth not flow in England, and gain not in the Iland what it loſeth in the Continent. Yea ſome plead, when overwhelm'd with liquour, that their thirſt is but quenched: as well may they ſay, that in Noahs floud the duſt was but ſufficiently allayed.

* Olaus mag. Hiſt. ſeptent. p. 531.
* Verſteg. reſtitut. of decaid intellig. p. 53.

10 *Gaming is another art he studies much* : an enticing witch, that hath caused the ruine of many. * Hannibal said of Marcellus, that *nec bonam nec malam fortunam ferre potest*, he could be quiet neither conquerour nor conquered ; thus such is the itch of play, that Gamesters neither winning nor losing can rest contented. One propounded this question, Whether men in ships on sea were to be accounted among the living or the dead, because there were but few inches betwixt them and drowning. The same scruple may be made of great Gamesters, though their estates be never so great, whether they are to be esteemed poore or rich, there being but a few casts at dice betwixt a Gentleman (in great game) and a begger. Our Gallant games deeply, and makes no doubt in conscience to adventure Advousands, Patronages, and Church-livings in gaming. He might call to mind Sr Miles Pateridge, who (as the Souldiers cast lots for Christ his coat) plaid at dice for * Jesus bells with King Henry the eighth, & wonne them of him. Thus he brought the bells to ring in his pocket, but the ropes afterwards catch'd about his neck, and for some offenses he was hang'd in the dayes of King Edward the sixth.

* *Liv. lib. 27.*

* *These were foure bells the greatest in London hanging in a fair Tower in Pauls Churchyard, Stowes Survey of London, pag. 357.*

11 *Then first he sells the outworks of his state, some stragling mannour*. Nor is he sensible of this sale, which makes his means more entire, as counting the gathering of such scattering rents rather burdensome then profitable. This he sells at half the value, so that the feathers will buy the goose, and the wood will pay for the ground : with this money if he stops the hole to one Creditour, by his prodigality he presently opens a wider gappe to another.

12 *By this time the long dormant Usurer ramps for the payment of his money*. The Principall, the grandmother, and the Use, the daughter, and the Use upon use, the grandchild, and perchance a generation farther, hath swell'd the debt to an incredible summe, for the satisfying whereof

whereof our Gallant ſells the moity of his eſtate.

Having ſold half his land he abates nothing of his expenſes: 13
but thinks five hundred pounds a yeare will be enough to maintain that for which a thouſand pound was too little. He will not ſtoop till he falls, nor leſſen his kennell of dogs, till with Acteon he be eaten up with his own hounds.

Being about to ſink he catcheth at every ruſh to ſave himſelf. 14
Perchance ſometimes he ſnatcheth at the thiſtle of a project, which firſt pricks his hands, and then breaks. Herein it may be he adventured on a matter wherein he had no skill himſelf (hoping by letting the Commonwealth bloud to fill up his own veins again) and therefore trades with his partners brains, as his partner with his purſe, till both miſcarry together: or elſe it may be he catcheth hold on the heel of another man, who is in as dangerous a caſe as himſelf, and they embracing each other in mutuall bands haſten their drowning together. His laſt mannour he ſells twice, to a countrey-Gentleman, and a London-uſurer, though the laſt, as having the firſt title, prevails to poſſeſſe it: Uſurers herein being like unto Foxes; they ſeldome take pains to digge any holes themſelves, but earth in that which the fooliſh Badger made for them, and dwell in the mannours and fair houſes which others have built and provided.

Having loſt his own legs, he relyes on the ſtaff of his kinred; 15
firſt viſiting them as an intermitting ague, but afterwards turns a quotidian, wearing their threſholds as bare as his own coat. At laſt he is as welcome as a ſtorm; he that is abroad ſhelters himſelf from it, and he that is at home ſhuts the doore. If he intrudes himſelf, yet ſome with their jeering tongues give him many a gird, but his brazen impudence feels nothing; and let him be arm'd on free-coſt with the pot and the pipe, he will give them leave to ſhoot their flouts at him till they be weary. Sometimes he ſadly paceth over the ground

he

he ſold, and is on fire with anger with himſelf for his folly, but preſently quencheth it at the next ale-houſe.

16 *Having undone himſelf, he ſets up the trade to undoe others.* If he can but ſcrue himſelf into the acquaintance of a rich heir, he rejoyceth as much at the prize as the Hollanders when they had intercepted the Plate-Fleet. He tutours this young Gameſter in vice, leading him a more compendious way to his ruine then poſsibly he could find out of himſelf. And doth not the guide deſerve good wages for his direction?

17 *Perhaps he behaves himſelf ſo baſely that he is degraded*; the ſad and ſolemn Ceremonies whereof we may meet with in old Preſidents: but of them all, in my apprehenſion, none ſhould make deeper impreſsion in an ingenuous ſoul then this one, That at the ſolemn degradation of a Knight for high miſdemeanour, the *King and twelve Knights more did put on mourning garments, as an embleme of ſorrow for this injury to honour, that a man Gentile by birth and bloud, or honoured by a Princes favour, ſhould ſo farre forget not onely himſelf but his Order, as to deſerve ſo ſevere puniſhment.

*Markams Decads of Honour, pag. 76.

18 *His death is as miſerable, as his life hath been vicious.* An Hoſpitall is the height he hopes to be advanced to: But commonly he dies not in ſo charitable a priſon, but ſings his laſt note in a cage. Nor is it impoſsible, but that wanting land of his own he may incroch on the Kings high-way, and there, taking himſelf to be Lord of the ſoyl, ſeiſe on Travellers as Strayes due unto him, and ſo the hangman give him a wreath more then he had in his Armes before. If he dyes at liberty in his pilgrimage betwixt the houſes of his acquaintance, perhaps ſome well-diſpoſed Gentleman may pay for his buriall, and truly mourn at the funerall of an ancient Family. His children, if any, muſt ſeek their fortunes the farther off, becauſe their father found his too ſoon,

before he had wiſdome to manage them. Within two generations his name is quite forgotten that ever any ſuch was in the place, except ſome Herald in his viſitation paſſe by, and chance to ſpell his broken Arms in a Church-window. And then how weak a thing is Gentry, then which (if it wants virtue) brittle glaſſe is the more laſting monument?

We forbear to give an inſtance of a degenerous Gentleman; would to God the world gave no examples of them. If any pleaſe to look into the forenamed * Valerius Maximus, he ſhall there find the baſe ſon of Scipio Africanus, the conquerour of Hanniball and Africk, ſo ill imitating his father, that for his viciouſnes he received many diſgracefull repulſes from the people of Rome, the fragrant ſmell of his Fathers memory making him to ſtink the more in their noſtrils; yea they forced him to pluck off from his finger a ſignet-ring, whereon the face of his Father was engraven, as counting him unworthy to wear his picture who would not reſemble his virtue.

* *Loco prius citato.*

Chap. 15.

The Traytour.

A Traitour * works by fraud as a Rebell does by force, and in this respect is more dangerous, because there's lesse stock required to set him up: Rebellion must be managed with many swords, Treason to his Princes person may be with one knife. Generally their successe is as bad as their cause, being either detected before, defeated in, or punished after their part acted; detected before, either by wilfulnesse or weaknesse of those which are privie to it.

* *He is either against the Sovereigne Person alone, or against the State wherein he lives. We deal onely in describing the former, because to character the other, exact skil in the Municipal Laws of that State is required, wherein he is charged of treason.*

Maxime 1. *A plotter of Treason puts his head into the halter, and the halter into his hand to whom he first imparts it.* He oftentimes reveals it, and by making a foot-stool of his friends head, climbs up the higher into the Princes favour.

2 *Some mens souls are not strong enough, but that a weighty secret will work a hole through them.* These rather out of folly then falseneſse, unawares let fall words, which are taken up by the judicious eares of such who can spell Treason by putting together distracted syllables, and by piecing of broken sentences. Others have their hearts swoln so great with hope of what they shall get, that their bodyes are too little to hold them, and so betray themselves by threatnings and blustring language. Others have cut their throats with their own hands, their own writings, the best records, being produced against them. And here we must know, That

3 *Strong presumptions sometimes serve for proofs in point of Treason*: For it being a deed of darknesse, it is madnesse to look that the Sunne should shine at midnight, and to expect evident proof. Should

Princes

Princes delay till they did plainly ſee Treaſon, they might chance to feel it firſt. If this *ſemiplena probatio* lights on a party ſuſpected before, the partie himſelf is the other part of the proof, and makes it complete. And here the Rack, though Fame-like it be

Tam ficti pravique tenax, quam nuncia veri,

is often uſed; and the wooden horſe hath told ſtrange ſecrets. But grant it paſſe undiſcovered in the plotting, it is commonly prevented in the practiſing,

By the Majeſtie, Innocency, or Valour of the Prince, or his attendants. Some have been dazeled with the divine beams ſhining in a Princes face, ſo that coming to command his life, they could not be maſters of their own ſenſes. Innocency hath protected others, and made their enemies relent; and pitie (though a ſtranger to him for many years before) hath viſited a Traitours heart in that very inſtant. If theſe fail, a Kings valour hath defended him; it being moſt true of a King, what Plinie reports of a * lion, in hunting if he be wounded and not killed, he will be ſure to eye and kill him that wounded him. 4

* *Nat. hiſt. lib.* 8. *cap.* 16.

Some by flouriſhing aforehand, have never ſtricken a blow: but by warning have armed thoſe to whom they threatned. Thus madde Somervile, coming to kill Queen Elizabeth, by the way (belike to trie whether his ſword would cut) quarrelled with and wounded one or two, and therefore was apprehended before he came to the Court. 5

The palſie of guiltineſſe hath made the ſtouteſt Traitours hands to ſhake, ſometimes to miſſe their mark. Their conſcience ſleeping before, is then awakened with this crying ſinne. The way ſeems but ſhort to a Traveller when he views it from the top of an hill, who finds it very long when he comes into the 6 plain: so Treason surveyed in the heat of bloud, and from the height of passion, seems easie to be effected; which reviewed in cold bloud on even terms, is full of dangers and difficulties. If it speed in the acting, generally it's revenged afterwards: For,

7 *A King though killed is not killed, so long as he hath sonne or subject surviving.* Many who have thought they have discharged the debt, have been broken afterwards with the arrearages. As for journey-men-Traytours who work for others, their wages are ever paid them with an halter; and where one gaineth a garland of bayes, hundreds have had a wreath of hemp.

Chap. 16.

Chap. 16.

The Pazzians conſpiracie.

Anno 1478. April 26.

The ſumme hereof is taken out of Machiavels Florent. Hiſt lib. 8. pag. 407. & ſequent.

IN the city of * Florence, being then a Popular State, the honourable familie de-Medices managed all chief affairs, ſo beloved of the people for their bounty, that the honour they had was not extorted by their greatneſſe, but ſeemed due to their goodneſſe. Theſe Mediceans depreſſed the Pazzians, another familie in that State, as big ſet, though not ſo high grown, as the Medicei themſelves, loading them with injuries, and debarring them not onely from Offices in the city, but their own right. The Pazzians, though highly wrong'd, counterfeited much patience, and, which was a wonder, though malice boyled hot in their hearts, yet no ſcumme ran over in their mouthes.

At laſt, meeting together, they concluded, that ſeeing the Legall way was ſtopp'd with violence, the violent way was become Legall, whereby they muſt right themſelves; and they determined to invite Julian and Laurence Medices, the Governours of the State, to dinner, with Cardinall Raphael Riarius, and there to murther them. The matter was counted eaſie, becauſe theſe two brethren were but one in effect, their heads in a manner ſtanding on the ſame ſhoulders, becauſe they alwayes went together, and were never aſunder. Fifty were privy to this plot; each had his office aſsigned him. Baptiſta Monteſeccius was to kill Laurence, Francis Pazzius and Bernardus Bandinius were to ſet on Julian, whileſt the Archbiſhop of Piſa, one of their allies, was with a band of men to ſeiſe on the Senate-houſe. Cardinall Raphaels company rather then aſsiſtance was required, being neither to hunt, nor kill, but onely to ſtart the game, and by his preſence to bring the two brothers to the dinner All appointed the next morning to meet at Maſſe, in the chief Church of S. Reparata.

Here meeting together, all the deſigne was daſh'd: for here they remembred that Julian de Medices never uſed to * dine. This they knew before, but conſidered not till now, as if formerly the vapours ariſing out of their ambitious hearts had clouded their underſtanding. Some adviſed to referre it to another time, which others thought dangerous, conceiving they had ſprung ſo many leaks of ſuſpition, it was impoſsible to ſtop them, and feared, there being ſo many privie to the plot, that if they ſuffered them to conſult with their pillows, their pillows would adviſe them to make much of their heads; wherefore not daring to ſtay the ſeaſonable ripening of their deſigne, they were forced in heat of paſsion to parch it up preſently, and they reſolved to take the matter at the firſt bound, and to commit the murther (they intended at dinner) here in the Church, taking it for granted, the two Mediceans would come to Maſſe, according to their dayly cuſtome.

* *Machiav. diſput. de Repub. lib. 3. cap. 6. pag. 397.*

But changing their ſtage, they were fain alſo to alter their Actours. Monteſeccius would not be employed in the buſineſſe, to ſtain a ſacred place with bloud; and the breaking of this ſtring put their plot quite out of tune. And though Anthony Volateran and Stephen a Prieſt were ſubſtituted in his room, yet theſe two made not one fit perſon; ſo great is the difference betwixt a choice and a ſhift. When the Hoſt was elevated, they were to aſſault them; and the Sacrament

ment was a ſigne to them, not of Chriſts death paſt, but of a murther they were to commit.

But here again they were at a loſſe. Treaſon, like Pope Adrian, may be choak'd with a flie, and marr'd with the leaſt unexpected caſualtie. Though Laurence was at Church, Julian was abſent. And yet by beating about, they recover'd this again: for Francis Pazzius and Bernard Bandinius going home to his houſe, with complements and courteous diſcourſe brought him to the Church. Then Bandinius with a dagger ſtabb'd him to the heart, ſo that he fell down dead, and Francis Pazzius inſulting over his corps (now no object of valour but cruelty) gave it many wounds, till blinded with revenge, he ſtrook a deep gaſh into his own thigh.

But what was over-meaſure in them, in over-acting their parts, was wanting in Anthony and Stephen, who were to kill Laurence in the Quire. *You * Traitour,* ſaid Anthony; and with that Laurence ſtarting back avoided the ſtrength of the blow, and was wounded onely to honour, not danger, and ſo recovered a ſtrong chapell. Thus Malice, which vents it ſelf in threatning, warns men to ſhun it, and like hollow ſinging bullets, flies but halfway to the mark. With as bad ſucceſſe did the Archbiſhop of Piſa ſeiſe on the Senate-houſe, being conquered by the Lords therein aſſembled, and, with many of his Complices, hung out of a window.

* *Machiav. diſp. de Repub. lib. 3. cap. 6. pag. 399.*

The Pazzians now betake themſelves to their laſt refuge which their deſperate courſes had left them. James the chief of their family with one hundred more repair to the market-place, and there crie, *Liberty, Liberty.* A few followed them at firſt, but the ſnow-ball by rolling did rather melt then gather, and thoſe, who before had ſeen the foul face of their treaſon naked, would not be allured to love it now masked with the pretences of the publick good ; and at laſt, the whole ſtrength of the State ſubdued them.

Every tree about the city bare the fruit of mens heads, and limbes : many were put to death with torment, more with ſhame, and onely one Renatus Pazzius with pity, who loved his conſcience better then his kinred, that he would not be active in the conſpiracy ; and yet his kinred better then his conſcience, that he would not reveal it ; Treaſon being like ſome kind of ſtrong poyſon, which though never taken inwardly by cordiall conſenting unto it, yet kill's by being held in ones hand, and concealing it.

Chap. 17.

Chap. 17.

The Tyrant.

A Tyrant * is one whoſe liſt is his law, making his ſubjects his ſlaves. Yet that is but a tottering Kingdome which is founded on trembling people, which fear and hate their Sovereigne.

* He is twofold, 1. *In Titulo,* (properly an Uſurper. 2. *In Exercitio,* whom we onely deſcribe.

Maxime 1. *He gets all places of advantage into his own hands:* yea he would diſarm his ſubjects of all ſythes and pruning hooks, but for fear of a generall rebellion of weeds and thiſtles in the land.

2 *He takes the Laws at the firſt, rather by undermining then aſſault:* And therefore to do unjuſtly with the more juſtice, he counterfeits a legalitie in all his proceedings, and will not butcher a man without a Statute for it.

3 *Afterwards he rageth freely in innocent bloud.* Is any man vertuous? then he is a Traytour, and let him die for it, who durſt preſume to be good when his Prince is bad. Is he beloved? he is a rebell, hath proclaimed himſelf King, and reignes already in peoples affections, it muſt coſt him his life. Is he of kinne to the Crown, though ſo farre off that his alliance is ſcarce to be derived? all the veins of his body muſt be dreined, and emptyed to find there and fetch thence that dangerous drop of royall bloud. And thus having taken the prime men away, the reſt are eaſily ſubdued. In all theſe particulars Machiavell is his onely Confeſſour, who in his Prince ſeems to him to reſolve all theſe caſes of conſcience to be very lawfull.

4 *Worſt men are his greateſt favourites.* He keeps a conſtant kennel of bloud-hounds to accuſe whom he pleaſeth. Theſe will depoſe more then any can ſuppoſe, not ſticking to ſwear that they heard fiſhes ſpeak,

ſpeak, and ſaw through a mil-ſtone at mid-night: theſe fear not to forſwear, but fear they ſhall not forſwear enough, to cleave the pinne and do the deed. The leſſe credit they have, the more they are believed, and their very accuſation is held a proof.

5 *He leaves nothing that his poore ſubjects can call their own but their miſeries.* And as in the Weſt-Indies thouſands of kine are killed for their tallow alone, and their fleſh caſt away: ſo many men are murdered merely for their wealth, that other men may make mummey of the fat of their eſtates.

6 *He counts men in miſerie the moſt melodious inſtruments:* Eſpecially if they be well tuned and play'd upon by cunning Muſicians, who are artificiall in tormenting them, the more the merrier, and if he hath a ſet, and full conſort of ſuch tortur'd miſerable ſouls, he danceth moſt cheerfully at the pleaſant dittie of their dying grones. He loves not to be prodigall of mens lives, but thriftily improves the objects of his cruelty, ſpending them by degrees, and epicurizing on their pain: So that as Philoxenus wiſhed a cranes throat, he could deſire aſſes eares, the longer to entertain their hydeous and miſerable roaring. Thus Nature had not racks enough for men (the Colick, Gout, Stone, &c.) but Art muſt adde to them, and devils in fleſh antedate hell here in inventing torments; which when inflicted on malefactours, extort pitie fom mercifull beholders, (and make them give what is not due) but when uſed by Tyrants on innocent people, ſuch tender hearts as ſtand by ſuffer what they ſee, and by the proxie of ſympathy feel what they behold.

7 *He ſeeks to ſuppreſſe all memorialls and writings of his actions:* And as wicked Tereus after he had raviſhed Philomela cut out her tongue; ſo when Tyrants have

have wronged and abused the times they live in, they endeavour to make them speechlesse to tell no tales to posterity. Herein their folly is more to be admired then their malice, for learning can never be dreined dry: though it may be dambd up for one Age, yet it will break over; and Historians pens, being long kept fasting, will afterwards feed more greedily on the memories of Tyrants, and describe them to the full. Yea, I believe their ink hath made some Tyrants blacker then they were in their true complexion.

At last he is haunted with the terrours of his own conscience. If any two do but whisper together (whatsoever the Propositions be) he conceives their discourse concludes against him. Company and solitarinesse are equally dreadfull unto him, being never safe; and he wants a Guard to guard him from his Guard, and so proceeds *in infinitum.* * The Scouts of Charles Duke of Burgundy brought him news that the French army was hard by, being nothing else but a field full of high thistles, whose tops they mistook for so many spears: On lesser ground this Tyrant conceives greater fears. Thus in vain doth he seek to fence himself from without, whose foe is within him. 7

* *Comineus Comment. lib.* 1. *juxta finem*

He is glad to patch up a bad nights sleep, out of pieces of slumber. They seldome sleep soundly, who have bloud for their bolster. His phansie presents him with strange masques, wherein onely Fiends and Furies are actours. The fright awakes him, and he is no sooner glad that it was a dream, but fears it is propheticall. 8

In vain he courts the friendship of forrein Princes. They defie his amity, and will not joyn their clean hands with his bloudy ones. Sometimes to ingratiate himself he doth some good acts, but virtue becomes him worse then vice, for all know he counter- 9 counterfeits it for his own ends.

10 *Having lived in other mens bloud, he dies commonly in his own.* He had his will all his life, but ſeldome makes his Teſtament at his death, being ſuddenly taken away either by a private hand, or a publick inſurrection. It is obſerved of the camell that it lies quietly down till it hath its full load, and then riſeth up. But this *Vulgus* is a kind of beaſt, which riſeth up ſooneſt when it is overladen; immoderate cruelty cauſing it to rebell. Yet *Fero* is a fitter motto then *Ferio* for Chriſtians in their carriage towards lawfull Authoritie, though unlawfully uſed.

We will give a double example of a Tyrant: the one an abſolute Sovereigne, the other a Subſtitute or Vice-roy under an abſolute Prince.

Chap. 18.

Chap. 18.

The life of Andronicus.

Andronicus Comnenus, * descended of the Grecian Emperiall bloud, was a Prince most vicious in his life, and perfidious in his dealing, and for his severall offenses, after long banishment, was at length by Emmanuel the Grecian Emperour, his kinsman, confined to a private city in Paphlagonia.

* *The summe of this chapter is taken out of Nicetas Choniates his Analls lib. 1. & 2. of Andronic. Comnenus.*

Here Andronicus hugg'd himself in his privacie, though all that time he did but levell, and take aim, intending at last to shoot at the Empire, though for a while he lay very still, and with the Hedgehog seemingly dead, he rounded himself up in his own prickles without any motion.

Leave we him there, and come to behold the face of the Grecian Empire, which presents us with all the Symptomes of a dying State. Emmanuell being dead Alexius his sonne succeeds him, a Minor of twelve years of age, wanting wit to guide himself, and his friends care to govern him. Xena the Mother-Empresse wholly given to her pleasures, with her minion Alexius Protosebastus, who ruled all in the State. The Nobility factious, snatching what they could get, and counting violent possession the best and onely title. The people of Constantinople valiant onely to make mutinies on every occasion, in confused multitudes, without any Martiall discipline; as who could expect that a rolling snow-ball should have any curious fashion?

Andronicus, hearing of these misdemeanours, found that opportunity courted him to procure the Empire for himself. Wherefore he remonstrates to the whole world the great grief he conceived at these disorders: For though patience had made him past feeling of any private injuries offered to himself, yet he must be stark dead indeed, if he were not moved with these generall miseries of the Empire. He being a Prince of the bloud could not without grief behold how Xena the Empresse, and Protosebastus had conspired to abuse the tender age of young Alexius, so to draw all dominion to themselves; and who kowing that their strength consisted in the young Emperours weaknesse, intended so to breed him, that in point of judgement he should never be of age, and onely *able in pleasures.* Whereupon Andronicus resolved to free his young kinsman, and the Empire from this thraldome. Treason is so uggly in her self, that every one that sees it will cast stones at it, which makes her seldome appear but with a borrowed face, for the good of the Commonwealth; but especially when ambition hath caught hold on pretended religion, how fast will it climbe?

Andronicus with an army of Paphlagonians marched to Constantinople, in which city he had a great party on his side, Maria Cesarissa, half sister to the Emperour, with her husband, and many other good Patriots, which bemoaned the distempers in the State, applying themselves to Andronicus for help, counting a bad physician better then none at all. Besides, there were in the city many turbulent spirits, desirous of alterations, as profitable unto them, counting themselves the petty-Landlords of the times, to whom rich fines and herriots would accrue upon every exchange, and all those took part with Andronicus.

Many more did Andronicus winne to his party by his cunning behaviour, for he could speak both eloquently and religiously. He would ordinarily talk Scripture-language (often fouly misapplyed) as if his memory were a Concordance of the whole Bible, but especially of S. Pauls Epistles, which he had by heart. Besides, no man had better command of rain and sunshine

ſunſhine in his face, to ſmile and weep at pleaſure: his tears flowed at will, which caught the affections of many, though others, better acquainted with his tricks, no more pitied his weeping, then they bemoaned the moiſt dropping of ſtone walls againſt rainy weather.

Small reſiſtance was made againſt him, onely ſome ſeemed to fight againſt him in complement, ſo that with eaſe he made himſelf maſter of Conſtantinople, and not long after he cauſed Xena the Empreſſe to be choked, the eyes of whoſe Favourite Protoſebaſtus he had formerly bored out.

The next care of Andronicus was to cut off all thoſe ſteps by which he had aſcended to this height, leſt leaving thoſe ſtairs ſtill ſtanding, others alſo might climbe up the ſame way. All thoſe friends who had aſsiſted him in this his deſigne, he rewarded with death: yea though at firſt his cruelty might ſeem to ſhoot at a mark,in taking of ſome prime men, for whoſe death ſome reaſon might be rendred, his malice afterwards ſhot at rovers, as if he had a quarrell at mankind, killing all he came near. When any party accuſed recriminated the accuſer, the ſword of Andronicus cut on both ſides; the accuſer and accuſed were ſent the ſame way, and what cup one began, the other was made to pledge. Thoſe Sycophants which ingratiated themſelves with him, eſcaped no better then others, it being equally dangerous to pleaſe and diſpleaſe him. Men met every where with his cruelty, but no where with the reaſons thereof. But who can expect other reaſons of Tyrants actions, but that they are Tyrants actions?

But his dealing with young Alexius the Emperour (whoſe death was methodically contrived with ſome politick pauſes) deſerves obſervation. At firſt entrance into the city, Andronicus obſerved his awfull diſtance towards the Emperour, teaching others that the minority of Princes ought not to lessen their Subjects reverence unto them. Afterwards, he emboldned himself to make his nearer approches, chalenging in young Alexius that interest which carefull tutours claim in those whose protection they tender. Hence he proceeded to set a guard about him, not to defend but watch him, and to guard him from his friends; who, though allowed to follow his sports in hunting, was indeed made sport of himself, and the hunter kept in a net. Then Andronicus was forced by his friends importunity (whom he himself had secretly importun'd) to be elected joynt-Emperour with Alexius, and with much unwillingnesse this great dissembler (who could have taught Tiberius craft, and Nero cruelty) was driven up the Emperiall throne. Next day in all publick Edicts the name of Andronicus was set before Alexius, it seeming preposterous that a child should be preferred before so sage and grave a man.

Hitherto the life of Alexius was profitable to Andronicus, but now his death would be more behooffull. Wherefore Andronicus counting it cumbersome now any longer to wear a cloke in the sunshine and heat of his happinesse, abandoned all uselesse dissembling, and appear'd like himself. The next news we heare of Alexius, is that his neck is broken with a
1181 bowstring by command from Andronicus; his body was spurn'd and abus'd, a hole bored in his ear with a spit, his head cut off, and shamefully dealt with, his body cast into the sea, with many more cruell outrages, as much against policie as piety, and not onely needlesse, but scandalous to Andronicus. Thus Tyrants, having once given the rains to their cruelty, are not able to stop themselves.

But this innocent bloud cryed to God for revenge, and obtained it. Next yeare Isaacius Angelus was chosen Emperour by the people, and Andronicus chased

chaſed out of the city and purſued after. Andronicus got into a ſhip, and had conveyed himſelf away, had not the winds and the waves (as if knowing him though diſguiſ'd) refuſed to be acceſſary to his eſcape, and beaten him back again, till he was taken by his purſuers. Being carried into the preſence of Iſaacius the new Emperour, he there was beaten, ſpurn'd, kick'd on, and had an arm cut off, and an eye bored out. But all this was mercy, in reſpect of what he next day ſuffered by the raſcall multitude, being carried on a ſcabb'd Camell thorow Conſtantinople, happy he that could do moſt unhappineſſe unto him : all ſorts of people ſought to miſchief him, throwing that upon him, in compariſon whereof that which runneth in the channell may be counted roſewater. Thus orphanes thought to revenge the death of their fathers, widows of their husbands : one ran him thorow with a ſpit, another threw ſcalding water in his face. At laſt he could hardly die, being hang'd up by the feet betwixt two pillars after a thouſand abuſes offer'd unto him.

It may ſeem miraculous how his body could make room for all their blows, or that he ſo old a man could find ſo many lives for their cruelty, were it not that paſsing with ſome ſpeed thorow the city, few had their full blows at him ; and they were ſomewhat mannerly in their revenge, in that they would not take all to themſelves, but leave ſome to others. And indeed after long throwing of dirt upon him, their darts became his ſhield, being ſo covered over with the filth, that the mire kept him from the mire.

All which time he brake not out into any impatience, but ſtill cryed, *Lord have mercy upon me*, and, *Why break you a bruiſed reed* ? and bore all with an invincible quietneſſe of mind. Surely God meaſured unto him a time of repentance by a large houreglaſſe ; and haply (it were tyranny to think otherwiſe of the worſt Tyrant) the tempeſt of the peoples fury might drive his ſoul to the beſt * ſhelter, the mercy of the God of heaven. It is a good ſigne when one hath his hell in this world, and true repentance is never too late. As for thoſe that hold repentance on the death-bed unprofitable, by this their tenet they would make heaven very empty, and yet never a whit the more room therein for the maintainers of ſo uncharitable an opinion.

* *See how charitably Drexelius is opinion'd of him in his book de Æternitate, Conſider. 5. Sect. 3.*

Andronicus reigned two years, having a beautifull aſpect, and majeſtick ſtature, almoſt ten foot high, of a ſtrong conſtitution, advantaged by the temperateneſſe of his diet. In all his life time he took but one antidote, and never purged but once, and then the Phyſick found no obnoxious humour to work upon, ſo healthfull was his temper. His death happened *Anno Dom.* 1183.

FERDINAND *Alvarez de Toledo* Duke *of* Alva, *Viceroy of the* Netherlands *under* Philip *the 2d. He dyed in* Portugall *Anno* Dm 1582. *in the 75. yeare of his Age.* W.M. *ſculp:*

CHAP. 19.

The life of Duke D'ALVA.

FErdinand Alvarez de Toledo, Duke of Alva, one bred abroad in the world in ſeverall warres (whom Charles the fifth more employed, then affect-ed, uſing his churliſh nature to hew knotty ſervice) was by Philip the ſecond, King of Spain, appointed Gover-nour of the Netherlands.

At his firſt arrivall there, the loyalty of the Nether-landers to the King of Spain was rather out of joint,

then

then broken off, as not being weary of his government but their own grievances. The wound was rather painfull then deadly, onely the skirts of their lungs were tainted, ſending out diſcontented not rebellious breath, much regretting that their Priviledges, Civil and Eccleſiaſticall, were infringed, and they grinded with exactions againſt their Laws and Liberties.

But now Duke D'Alva coming amongſt them, he intended to cancell all their charters with his ſword, and to reduce them to abſolute obedience. And whereas every city was fenced not onely with ſeverall walls, but different locall liberties, and municipall immunities, he meant to lay all their priviledges levell, and caſting them into a flat to ſtretch a line of abſolute command over them. He accounted them a Nation rather ſtubborn then valiant, and that not from ſtoutneſſe of nature, but want of correction, through the long indulgence of their late Governours. He ſecretly accuſed Margaret Dutcheſſe of Parma, the laſt Governeſſe, for too much gentleneſſe towards them, as if ſhe meant to cure a gangren'd arm with a lenitive plaiſter, & affirmed that a Ladies hands were too ſoft to pluck up ſuch thiſtles by the root. Wherefore the ſaid Dutcheſſe, ſoon after D'Alva's arrivall (counting it leſſe ſhame to ſet, then to be outſhin'd) petitioned to reſigne her regencie, and return'd into Italie.

Ann.Dom. 1568.

* *Famianus Stra. de Bello Belgico, p.*430.

To welcome the Duke at his entrance, he was entertain'd with prodigies and monſtrous * births, which hapned in ſundry places; as if Nature on ſet purpoſe miſtook her mark, and made her hand to ſwerve, that ſhe might ſhoot a warning-piece to theſe countreys, and give them a watch-word of the future calamities they were to expect. The Duke, nothing moved hereat, proceeds to effect his project, and firſt ſets up the *Counſell of troubles*, conſiſting of twelve, the Duke being the Preſident. And this Counſell was to order all things in an arbitrary way, without any appeal from

from them. Of theſe twelve ſome were ſtrangers, ſuch as ſhould not ſympathize with the miſeries of the countrey; others were upſtarts, men of no bloud, and therefore moſt bloudy; who being themſelves grown up in a day, cared not how many they cut down in an houre. And now rather to give ſome colour, then any virtue to this new compoſition of counſellours, foure Dutch Lords were mingled with them, that the native Nobility might not ſeem wholly neglected. Caſtles were built in every city to bridle the inhabitants, and Gariſons put into them. New Biſhops Seas erected in ſeverall cities, and the Inquiſition brought into the countrey. This Inquiſition, firſt invented againſt the Moores, as a trappe to catch vermine, was afterwards uſed as a ſnare to catch ſheep, yea they made it hereſie for to be rich. And though all theſe proceedings were contrary to the ſolemn oath King Philip had taken, yet the Pope (who onely keeps an *Oath-office*, and takes power to diſpence with mens conſciences) granted him a faculty to ſet him free from his promiſe.

Sure as ſome adventurous Phyſicians, when they are poſed with a mungrell diſeaſe, drive it on ſet purpoſe into a fever, that ſo knowing the kind of the maladie they may the better apply the cure: So Duke D'Alva was minded by his cruell uſage to force their diſcontents into open rebellion, hoping the better to come to quench the fire when it blazed out, then when it ſmok'd and ſmother'd.

And now to frighten the reſt, with a ſubtle train he ſeiſeth on the Earls of Egmond and Horn. Theſe counted themſelves armed with innocencie and deſert, having performed moſt excellent ſervice for the King of Spain. But when ſubjects deſerts are above their Princes requitall, oftentimes they ſtudy not ſo much to pay their debts, as to make away their creditours. All theſe victories could not excuſe them, nor the laurel wreaths on their heads keep their necks from the ax, and the rather, becauſe their eyes muſt firſt be closed up, which would never have patiently beheld the enslaving of their countrey. The French Embassadour was at their execution, and wrote to his Master Charles the ninth, King of France, concerning the Earl of Egmond, * *That he saw that head struck off in the Market-place of Brussels, whose valour had twice made France to shake.*

* *Fam. Strad. de bell. Belgico, pag.* 449.

This Counsell of troubles having once tasted Noble bloud, drank their belly-fulls afterwards. Then descending to inferiour persons by apprehensions, executions, confiscations, and banishments, they raged on mens lives and states. Such as upon the vain hope of pardon returned to their houses, were apprehended, and executed by fire, water, gibbets, and the sword, and other kinds of deaths and torments: yea the bodyes of the dead (on whom the earth as their common mother bestowed a grave for a childs portion) were cast out of their * tombes by the Dukes command, whose cruelty outstunk the noysomnesse of their carcases.

* *Grimst. Hist. of the Netherlands, pag.* 413.

And lest the maintaining of Garisons might be burdensome to the King his Master, he laid heavy impositions on the people: the Duke affirming that these countreys were fat enough to be stewed in their own liquour, & that the Souldiers here might be maintained by the profits arising hence; yea he boasted that he had found the mines of Peru in the Low-countreys, though the digging of them out never quitted the cost. He demanded the hundredth peny of all their moveable and immoveable goods, and besides that, the tenth peny of their moveable goods that should be bought and sold, with the twentieth peny of their immoveable goods; without any mention of any time, how long those taxes and exactions should continue.

The States protested against the injustice hereof, alledging that all trading would be press'd to death under the weight of this taxation: weaving of stuffs (their staple trade) would soon decay, and their shuttles would be very ſlow, having ſo heavy a clog hanging on them; yea hereby the ſame commodity muſt pay a new tole at every paſſage into a new trade. This would diſhearten all induſtry, and make lazineſſe and painfulneſſe both of a rate, when beggery was the reward of both, by reaſon of this heavy impoſition, which made men pay dear for the ſweat of their own brows. And yet the weight did not grieve them ſo much, as the hand which laid it on, being impoſ'd by a forein power againſt their ancient priviledge. Hereupon many Netherlanders, finding their own countrey too hot, becauſe of intolerable taxes, ſought out a more temperate climate, and fled over into England.

As for ſuch as ſtayed behind, their hearts being brimfull before with diſcontents, now ran over. 'Tis plain theſe warres had their originall, not out of the Church, but the State-houſe. Liberty was true doctrine to Papiſt and Proteſtant, Jew and Chriſtian. It is probable that in Noahs Ark the wolf agreed with the lambe, and that all creatures drowned their antipathy, whileſt all were in danger of drowning. Thus all ſeverall religions made up one Commonwealth to oppoſe the Spaniard: and they thought it high time for the Cow to find her horns, when others not content to milk her, went about to cut off her bag.

It was a rare happineſſe that ſo many ſhould meet in one chief, William of Naſſaw, Prince of Orange, whom they choſe their Governour. Yea he met their affections more then half way in his loving behaviour; ſo that Alva's cruelty did not drive more from him, then Naſſaw's courteſie invited to him. His popular nature was of ſuch receipt, that he had room to lodge all comers. In peoples eyes his light ſhined bright, yet dazled none, all having free acceſſe unto him: every one was as well pleaſed as if he had been Prince himſelf, becauſe he might be ſo familiar with the Prince. He was wont to content thoſe, who reproved his too much humanity, with this ſaying,* *That man is cheap bought, who coſts but a ſalutation.*

*Barcl. Icon. Anim. cap. 5

I report the Reader to the Belgian Hiſtories, where he may ſee the changes of warre betwixt theſe two ſides. We will onely obſerve that Duke D'Alva's covetouſneſſe was above his policy in fencing the rich inland and neglecting the barren maritime places. He onely look'd on the broad gates of the countrey whereby it openeth to the continent of Germany and France, whileſt in the mean time almoſt half the Netherlands ran out at the poſtern doore towards the ſea. Naſſaw's ſide then wounded Achilles in the heel indeed, and touch'd the Spaniard to the quick, when on Palm-ſunday (as if the day promiſed victory) at Brill they took the firſt livery and ſeaſin of the land, and got ſoon after moſt cities towards the ſea. Had Alva herein prevented him, probably he had made thoſe Provinces as low in ſubjection as ſituation.

Now at laſt he began to be ſenſible of his errour, and grew weary of his command, deſiring to hold that ſtaff no longer, which he perceived he had taken by the wrong end. He ſaw that going about to bridle the Netherlanders with building of caſtles in many places, they had gotten the bit into their own teeth : He ſaw that warre was not quickly to be hunted out of that countrey, where it had taken covert in a wood of cities : He ſaw the coſt of ſome one cities ſiege would pave the ſtreets thereof with ſilver, each city, fort, and ſconce being a Gordian knot, which would make Alexanders ſword turn edge before he could cut thorow it, ſo that this warre and the world were likely to end together, theſe Netherlands being like the headblock in the chimney, where the fire of warre is alwayes kept in (though out every where elſe) never quite quench'd though rak'd up ſometimes in the aſhes of a truce. Beſides, he ſaw that the ſubdued part of the Netherlands obeyed more for fear then love, and

their

their loyalty did rather lie in the Spaniſh Gariſons, then their own hearts, and that in their ſighes they breathed many a proſperous gale to Naſſaw's party: Laſtly, he ſaw that forrein Princes, having the Spaniards greatneſſe in ſuſpicion, deſired he might long be digeſting this break-faſt, leſt he ſhould make his dinner on them, both France and England counting the Low-countreys their outworks to defend their walls: wherefore he petitioned the King of Spain his Maſter to call him home from this unprofitable ſervice.

Then was he called home, and lived ſome years after in Spain, being well reſpected of the King, and employed by him in conquering Portugall, contrary to the expectation of moſt, who look'd that the Kings diſpleaſure would fall heavy on him, for cauſing by his cruelty the defection of ſo many countreys; yet the King favourably reflected on him, perchance to fruſtrate on purpoſe the hopes of many, and to ſhew that Kings affections will not tread in the beaten path of vulgar expectation: or ſeeing that the Dukes life and ſtate could amount to poore ſatisfaction for his own loſſes, he thought it more Princely to remit the whole, then to be revenged but in part: or laſtly, becauſe he would not meaſure his ſervants loyalty by the ſucceſſe, and lay the unexpected rubs in the allie to the bowlers fault, who took good aim though miſsing the mark. This led many to believe that Alva onely acted the Kings will, and not willed his acts, following the inſtructions he received, and rather going beyond then againſt his Commiſsion.

However moſt barbarous was his cruelty. He bragg'd as he ſate at dinner (and was it not a good grace after meat) that he had cauſed eighteen thouſand to be executed by the ordinary miniſter of juſtice within the ſpace of ſix years, beſides an infinite more murthered by other tyrannous means. Yea ſome men he killed many times, giving order to the executioners to pronounce each ſyllable of torment long upon them, that the thred of their life might not be cut off but unravell'd, as counting it no pain for men to die, except they dyed with pain; witneſſe Anthony Utenhow, whom he cauſed to be tied to a ſtake with a chain in *Bruſſells, compaſsing him about with a great fire, but not touching him, turning him round about like a poore beaſt, who was forced to live in that great torment and extremity, roaſting before the fire ſo long, untill the Halberdiers themſelves, having compaſsion on him, thruſt him through, contrary to the will both of the Duke and the Spaniſh Prieſts.

Grimſt. Hiſt. of the Netherlands, pag. 411.

When the city of Harlem ſurrendred themſelves unto him on condition to have their lives, he ſuffered ſome of the Souldiers and Burgers thereof to be ſtarved to death, ſaying that *though he promiſed to give them their lives, he did not promiſe to find them meat.* The Netherlanders uſed to fright their children with telling them, Duke D'Alva was coming; and no wonder if children were ſcared with him, of whom their fathers were afraid.

He was one of a lean body and viſage, as if his eager ſoul, biting for anger at the clog of his body, deſired to fret a paſſage through it. He had this humour, that he neglected the good counſel of others, eſpecially if given him before he ask'd it, and had rather ſtumble then beware of a block of another mans telling.

But as his life was a miroir of cruelty, ſo was his death of Gods patience. It was admirable, that his tragicall acts ſhould have a comicall end; that he that ſent ſo many to the grave, ſhould go to his own, & die in peace. But Gods juſtice on offenders goes not alwayes in the ſame path, nor the ſame pace: And he is not pardoned for the fault, who is for a while reprived from the puniſhment; yea ſometimes the gueſt in the inne goes quietly to bed, before the reckoning for his ſupper is brought to him to diſcharge.

FINIS.